e157

SOCIAL AND CULTURAL CHANGE
IN CONTEMPORARY WALES

SOCIAL AND CULTURAL CHANGE IN CONTEMPORARY WALES

Edited by
GLYN WILLIAMS

ROUTLEDGE DIRECT EDITIONS

ROUTLEDGE & KEGAN PAUL
London, Henley and Boston

First published in 1978
by Routledge & Kegan Paul Ltd
39 Store Street,
London WC1E 7DD,
Broadway House,
Newtown Road,
Henley-on-Thames,
Oxon RG9 1EN and
9 Park Street,
Boston, Mass. 02108, USA
Printed in Great Britain by
Thomson Litho Ltd
East Kilbride, Scotland

British Library Cataloguing in Publication Data

Social and cultural change in contemporary Wales
1. Wales - Social conditions
I. Williams, Glyn
301.29'429   HN398.W26   78-40389

ISBN 0 7100 8864 7

CONTENTS

vi   Contents

CONTRIBUTORS

CHRIS BOLLOM: Department of Social Theory and Institutions, University College of North Wales, Bangor.
HAROLD CARTER: Department of Geography, University College of Wales, Aberystwyth.
PAT CLAYTON: Department of Social Work, Liverpool Polytechnic.
ANTHONY COXON: Department of Sociology, University College, Cardiff.
GRAHAM DAY: Department of Sociology and Social Anthropology, University College of Wales, Aberystwyth.
ISOBEL EMMETT: Department of Sociology, Manchester University.
MARTIN FITTON: Countryside Commission, Cheltenham.
COLIN FLETCHER: Sutton-in-Ashfield Project, Department of Adult Education, Nottingham University.
HOWARD GILES: Department of Psychology, Bristol University.
GORDON GRANT: Department of Social Services, Gwynedd County Council, Caernarfon, Gwynedd.
GODFREY HARRISON: Department of Psychology, University College, Cardiff.
RUSSELL ISAAC: Department of Social Theory and Institutions, University College of North Wales, Bangor.
BUD KHLEIF: Department of Sociology and Social Anthropology, University of New Hampshire, Durham, New Hampshire, U.S.A.
PETER MADGWICK: Department of Political Science, University College of North Wales, Bangor.
ROY NASH: Department of Education, University College of North Wales, Bangor.
ELLIS ROBERTS: Department of Social Theory and Institutions, University College of North Wales, Bangor.
DONALD M. TAYLOR: Department of Psychology, McGill University, Toronto, Canada.
COLIN THOMAS: Department of Geography, University College, Swansea.
G. CLARE WENGER: Department of Economics, University College of Wales, Aberystwyth.
COLIN WILLIAMS: Department of Geography, North Staffordshire Polytechnic, Stafford.
GLYN WILLIAMS: Department of Social Theory and Institutions, University College of North Wales, Bangor.

STEPHEN WILLIAMS: Department of Geography, University College of
Wales, Aberystwyth.
MARTYN WINROW: Department of Geography, Hereford College of
Education.

ACKNOWLEDGMENTS

Many people have contributed to the preparation and publication of these papers. The conference from which they derive was supported by the Social Science Research Council to whom thanks are due for their efforts to stimulate interest in researching Welsh problems. At the conference several people were asked to comment on the various papers; I am sure that all of the authors would agree that their comments were invaluable. They were: Bleddyn Davies, John Gumperz, Chris Harris, Cyril Parry, Emrys Peters and Alan Thomas. Finally I am also indebted to Peter Hopkins for his guidance and encouragement in bringing the contributions together.

Chapter 1

INTRODUCTION

Glyn Williams

Throughout the period of rapid growth of the social sciences in British institutions of higher education, which began during the 1950s Wales remained a neglected area of study. While this may derive partly from the relative lack of specialization within some of the relevant disciplines one suspects that it also stems from the tendency to neglect the concept of culture as a relevant tool of analysis and to regard Wales as merely a region within a homogeneous Britain, or, alternatively, as a rapidly disappearing linguistic minority worthy of neither a theoretical consideration nor a research focus. Thus, for example, in sociological courses which encompass what is grandly referred to as 'The Social Structure of Modern Britain' Wales receives little or no attention. In the standard texts which service such courses reference to Wales, if it appears at all, is restricted to a footnote, the occasional sentence, or now and again a paragraph.(1) Not even the shift of attention to the policy orientated field of 'Race and Ethnic Relations' has yielded any increase in the study of specifically Welsh cultural and social phenomena, but has tended almost exclusively to focus upon the problem of assimilating immigrants to the larger industrial and urban centres of England. Thus, at a recent conference sponsored by the Royal Anthropological Institute on the theme 'Ethnic and Racial Relationships in Britain' not a single paper was devoted to any aspect of Celtic ethnicity.(2) While we applaud the focus of attention upon the condition of various minorities in Britain one does wonder about the puzzling blind-spot with reference to Wales. The centralist ethnocentricity may be one explanation but the absence of a long-standing social science tradition within the centres of higher education in Wales itself must also bear part of the blame. As several participants in the conference from which this volume derives commented, even when the social sciences were eventually firmly established the tendency within most departments was either to ignore Wales altogether as an area of study or to study Welsh society, quite justifiable in some cases, with no reference to the fact that it was Welsh rather than English society that was being studied. Yet there are few who would deny that Wales is a nation with a unique history which produced a distinct social organization. This

is clear from the work of those researchers who stand as a contradiction to the above claim that Welsh society and culture has
remained an unstudied phenomenon.

On the whole it is very difficult to provide a comprehensive
reading list on the social structure of Wales. Despite this claim
there are numerous contributions that can be grouped around certain
traditions, themes and issues.

Probably the most notable of these contributions were those
undertaken by members of the University College of Wales, Aberystwyth, in the early 1950s.(3)   Stemming from the initiative of
Professor Daryl Forde, who was eager to extend the methods of
social anthropology, they established a community studies tradition
that has shaped many subsequent analyses and studies of communities
in Britain. Although the studies have been criticized for their
historical and descriptive emphasis they do contain important
analytical contributions and suggestions for further research.
Perhaps the best known of the work is the study of Llanfihangel yng
Ngwynfa by Alwyn D. Rees (1950), which preceded similar studies
undertaken by Frankenberg (1957), Emmett (1964), Jenkins (1974),
Owen and others. Jenkins's (1960) analysis of social stratification and mobility in Cardiganshire in terms of 'bucheddau' has
sparked off the present debate about the nature of stratification
in rural Wales.(4)   Trefor Owen (1960) in his study of Glanllyn
shows the social functions of familism and kinship in sustaining
the potency and strength of Nonconformity.

By the end of the 1950s the social sciences placed less
emphasis upon community studies as such and concentrated far more
upon general issues such as stratification and education; the
authors of the Aberystwyth contributions also turned to other
issues. Trefor Owen (1966), himself a contributor to the Aberystwyth school, suggested, in a lecture to the Graduates Guild of
the University of Wales in 1965, a list of alternative themes for
study.

The Aberystwyth school appears to have been the only academic
tradition in Wales with an institutional and unified basis for
social scientific studies specifically on aspects of the social
structure of Wales. The other contributions, equally valuable and
valid, cannot be seen in quite the same light.

Although Government reports and investigations have an institutional backing in the form of the Government itself, such studies
combine action and policy with the process of careful description
and analysis itself. Despite this, they very often provide
valuable data and statistics upon key issues and topics that affect
Wales, such as depopulation, local government, social services,
communication, the constitution, the economy and industry.(5)
Local government has also done much in this respect, numerous
reports and statistical evidence are available for the social
scientist. Both central and local Government have in this respect
commissioned social scientists to undertake such work; economists
figure largely in these reports.(6)

Several important contributions were made by members of the
University College of Wales, Swansea, on a wide range of subjects
that were not always related to the social structure of Wales. Of
those relating specifically to Wales the one that explored aspects

of social change, in south-west Wales related to the 'community study' emphasis of the social sciences in the 1950s (Brennan et al., 1954). A later study by Rosser and Harris (1964) provides an analysis of family and kinship in a period of social change.

The other contributions cover a wide range of topics that fall largely into those that reflect a particular individual subject or problem interest, historical studies that so often provide the basis for social scientific work, and educational studies, which also provide a focus for other disciplines.

Education has received a great deal of attention in Wales since the so called 'Treachery of the Blue Books' in 1846. Since that report education has been the subject of many Government reports and publications. In 1968 the Welsh Committee of the Schools Council published a well-documented and referenced pamphlet on the state and direction of educational research in Wales. Educational research has also in many instances been interconnected with various issues such as the Welsh language, the technical and the industrial needs of Wales.[7]

Although references and works on political issues and nationalism abound in Wales, the quality of the commentary is often erratic; very often it is difficult to differentiate between the propagandist and objective elements. Commentary upon nationalism range from those that give emphasis to cultural heritage and history to those that assert that contemporary nationalism is a product of the alienative influences of modern industrial phenomena such as bureaucracy and automation.[8] Other studies have emphasized the regional autonomy of Wales, a product, it is claimed, of a deliberate policy of an out-of-touch centralist executive.[9]

Several historical studies exist on the development of various industries throughout Wales, but predominantly in the south-Wales coalfield. Although these refer to social conditions, labour history and industrial relations, the main emphasis is upon the technical and productive aspects of the development of the industry concerned.[10]

Again like the central and local Government reports and publications these historical works provide and have provided essential material upon which many studies have and will be grounded.

Valuable though these contributions may be they are limited in number and in perspective. The net consequences of the general neglect are the absence of descriptive and analytical studies of contemporary Wales and a dearth of data upon which to base relevant socio-cultural policy action. Workers in local and regional administration frequently express a frustration with the lack of such data and indeed the creation of the new administrative units has resulted in an increased awareness of the need for research, even if only in order to expand the data upon which reasonable policy statements can be made.

The problem is accentuated by virtue of the fact that those researchers working in this field of study tend to remain isolated from one another, so that 'findings' are rarely co-ordinated, or even related to Welsh society as a whole. The professional bodies which exist do not resolve the situation for they tend to be organized on an ostensibly British basis which means, in effect, being based in England and dominated by the issues and concerns of English social scientists. There are signs that the expansion in the social sciences is at least beginning to yield fruit in the form of research relevant to Wales but this involves researchers working in isolation from one another and bereft of any formal framework for contact and discussion. In order to try to stimulate further research and to generate a forum where those currently undertaking research could discuss their efforts and formulate more coherent research objectives the Social Science Research Council was approached with the view of sponsoring a conference which would focus on the theme of 'Social and Cultural Change in Contemporary Wales'. The committees for social anthropology, sociology and social administration responded generously and the conference was held at Gregynog Hall in September of 1976.

Given that this was an initial venture involving such wide objectives it is not surprising that the papers offered at the conference are drawn from such diverse disciplinary interests. Most of the papers reflect the concerns of the committees which funded the conference, i.e. sociology, social anthropology and social administration. The other papers derive from geographers who in many respects share an affinity with one or other of the above disciplines, social psychology and political science. Not only did this variety of perspectives contribute to a healthy basis for discussion but it also brought contrasting insights to focus on the broad topics under discussion. What is surprising is the limited number of such topics that were discussed, for many they were too limited and there are many topics relevant to Wales which were not discussed. However, we do not claim that this volume serves to resolve very much, we are beginners in the field. Rather it should be seen as an initial contribution in an enterprise to be continued.

At the conference the papers were organized along the following themes: language, ethnicity, social problems and social organiz- ation. However, as I shall indicate below these themes and the papers in general can be discussed around the themes of class and ethnicity as alternative principles of inequality. It is not the perspective which all of the contributors necessarily agree with.

Earlier studies of ethnicity regarded it as a primordial quality in which ethnic identity was treated as a given. The limitations of such an approach was obvious when it was recognized that cultural attributes are of no intrinsic interest from a dynamic structural perspective. Thus the acculturation perspective, which dealt with ethnicity in cultural terms, with the strength of ethnicity being determined by the position of cultural groups on a continuum of cultural traits involving those of distinct cultural groups at either end, was soon dispensed with. Its limitations involved its failure to adequately deal with contact while also focusing attention upon cultural features rather than social process. The alternative approach treated ethnicity as a variable rather than as a given and attempted to discuss ethnic salience with reference to social context within an interactional framework. The tour de force of this approach was the seminal work of Fredrik Barth (1969) and his associates who conceived of ethnic groups in terms of the social boundaries which existed between

such groups. While this was an important step forward more recent
work has not only recognized that it failed to account for interaction across the boundary but also tended to ignore the institutional aspects of ethnicity.

Recent years have seen an upsurge of interest in ethnicity and
an associated attempt to account for the pronounced ethnic salience
that has become so apparent in many parts of the world. Some have
gone as far as to claim that it represents a new social phenomenon
(Glazer and Moynihan, 1975:2), as significant as social class in
its importance. Such a view stems from the recognition that
ethnicity can serve as the basis for the mobilization of a population in order to promote a redress of the inequalities that derive
from ethnically based inequality (Shibutani and Kwan, 1965). Thus
it is claimed that ethnic identities are ranked, that is, rooted,
in the institutionalization of inequality. Placed in such terms
the key concept in the understanding of ethnic stratification is
power and the struggle for it. Prejudice and discrimination arise
in the competition for the scarce resources of society such as
power, wealth and prestige. Within such a situation one group
defines the rules by which the other group must act and the
meaningful political, economic and social power to maintain the
subservient/dominant relationship is vested in the majority group.

This is the standpoint taken by Khleif in his paper. Drawing
upon the work of Hechter (1975) and others he refers to the internal
colonial nature of the relationship between the English core and
the Welsh periphery and the associated tendency for cultural
assimilation. He suggests that an ethnically aware emergent middle
class has consciously striven to achieve socio-economic reform with
the language movement being a symbol of such aspirations.

Such an argument is not unlike the one that is often projected
with reference to class and it is useful to turn to Weber (1958)
for a distinction between class and ethnicity.(11) For Weber the
ethnic group was a form of status group, action based upon status
being undertaken as a member of a community which could be an
ethnic group, the individual sharing a 'style of life' with other
members of the community in terms of ethnic style. In contrast,
action based upon class he viewed as individualistic since a
person's class position was dependent only upon his position in the
market place. Thus the status group serves as a basis for group
formation and a consequent stratification which is analytically
independent of the means of production. Classes and ethnic groups
are therefore viewed as complementary bases of group formation.
This clearly begs the question of what determines the respective
strength of these different principles of group formation and
stratification and under what circumstances. In some contexts
they can be seen as competing types of identification while in
others they may well be complementary.

One rather obvious hypothesis is that ethnicity can serve as
the basis for collective upward mobility as opposed to the
individual mobility implicit in class action. This would appear
to assume that under certain circumstances inequality becomes more
apparent in regional or ethnic rather than class terms. Such a
situation might pertain when regional aid is seen in zero-sum
terms which engenders regional competition for scarce resources

even on a sectorial basis, while embourgeoisement serves to
diminish the power of corporate class-consciousness. Dahrendorf
(1969) in claiming that inequality derives from differential
success in achieving social norms implies that different groups
have different norms and that the unsuccessful group has a greater
chance of changing the system if it behaves with the cohesiveness
of a group. Thus ethnicity becomes more salient because it
combines an interest with an affective tie whereas class has ceased
to be an ideology and has become an interest. Certainly there has
been a shift in power and values in which ethnic identification
has an affective quality. Presumably the change is to a condition
in which economic and non-economic decisions which had once been
left either to the market or to privately negotiated bargains now
come under the purview of political entities and everyone is aware
of who is making such decisions. In effect the market has become
vague. Therefore, in addition to regional aid one can talk about
economic sectors involving, e.g. coal and steel, bringing branches
of the sectors which are located in different regions into competition for scarce resources and even for survival. In a sense
the centralized political entity cannot win. By defining a region
as deserving of aid they are acknowledging a relative deprivation
so that it becomes recognized, defined and labelled internally and
externally, thereby inviting a region, especially if it is
coterminus with a national boundary, to act in concert. This
allows the focusing of emotional aggression against an outside
neighbour, an aggression which may be superimposed upon a
resentment against social and cultural dominance. Such a process
ties in with an anxiety about the bases of one's identity and a
related quest for liberation.

Three of the papers deal with the relationship between macro-
economic process and social organization in a manner that throws
some light on the preceding argument. Whilst the social indicator
approach has its limitations, Winrow uses it to good effect to
demonstrate the distribution of what are regarded as measures of
deprivation over space and time by using aggregate data. His work
not only serves to demonstrate the distribution of such deprivation
and the nature of deprivation emanating from the raw data but also
indicates that the situation appears to have deteriorated for Wales
as a whole between 1961 and 1971.

Fletcher on the other hand tackles the response to such
deprivation resulting from economic decline in his discussion of
the impact of regional aid in the industrial area of south-west
Wales. He suggests that rather than being of overall general
assistance to the area in many respects it is detrimental. Not
only does it fail to generate local economic growth but it also
promotes an antagonism towards, and a failure to integrate, the
new 'gentry' which entered the area with the introduction of
regional aid. Perhaps his main criticism is aimed at the failure
of the new industries to utilize the traditional skills of the
labour force, a tendency which has been identified elsewhere in
Wales, and which has been claimed to deprive the workforce of
pride in its skills and communal work environment.

The separation between the local labour force and an alien
management and ownership discussed by Fletcher has been referred

to by Thomas (1966) in his discussion of industrialization in
mid-Wales and is implicit in the work of Lovering and Tomkins
(1973) who indicate that only 38 per cent of the industries
employing more than 24 workers in Wales are Welsh owned. Hechter
(1975) argues that every heterogeneous social formation demonstrates a cultural division of labour and suggests that it is the
existence of such a division of labour which partly accounts for
the saliency of ethnicity. This does not imply that there is
anything conspiratorial in such a development but that it is part
of the centralization of economic control.

An awareness of the structural inequality that is implicit in
the papers which discuss the economic perspective does not derive
directly from an understanding of economic principles but rather
from an awareness of more obvious symptoms of economic decline.
Within rural Wales the depopulation which has been associated with
such economic decline has produced its own problems for the
residual population. Among the more controversial of these
'problems' is that of the second home syndrome associated with
the leisure boom of the 1960s. The entry of an affluent non-Welsh
population into the area has aroused much resentment at different
levels and it is reasonable to assume that this resentment relates
partly to the differences between the local and intrusive groups,
a condition which, according to the above argument, would be
conducive to an increase in ethnic salience. Bollom set out to
investigate the extent and nature of whatever antagonism towards
the phenomenon and the associated actors existed. He discovered
evidence of both antagonism and acceptance but unfortunately as a
result of his research brief, he was unable to investigate
internal structural differences in attitudes from one settlement
to the other. The most reasonable explanation of the apparent
contradiction in attitudes which he discovered is that while the
local residents are antagonistic to the abstract phenomenon of
second homes and the resultant polarization of groups it is quite
another thing to translate such antagonism on a personal level.

Another phenomenon which derives from the pronounced rural
depopulation is that of school closure, which Nash implies is
perceived by the population involved as symptomatic of the threat
to the entire structure of local communities and even to Welsh
rural society however it may be perceived. Such attitudes are
based partly upon an awareness that many young people are reluctant to continue to reside in communities whose schools are
threatened with closure. As a result the existing demographic
imbalance resulting from selective out-migration of young people
and the in-migration of retired English people becomes more visible
and the cause is partly seen in terms of official policy. In his
paper Nash discusses the contrasting perceptions among the representatives of the different groups involved in the decision about
closure. In so doing he begins to bring out the internal variation
of attitudes associated with the struggle for status and power
which to some is equated with survival. His discussion of the role
of schoolteachers in the struggle for survival is supported by
Khleif's (1976) study of their importance in this respect.

This inequality, both in intra- and inter-regional terms could
be ameliorated by the compensatory provision of social services.

However, the difficulty of implementing desired policy in rural
areas manifests against such a facile solution as is clear from
Grant's paper.   One of the problems which he focuses upon is the
inadequacy of social work training, with its urban bias, to
prepare social workers for work in rural areas.   This has prompted
some observers to proclaim that it is perhaps a blessing that as
many as 75 per cent of the social workers in some Welsh counties
are not professionally qualified.   Grant outlines some of the
alternatives being experimented with within Gwynedd in order to
maximise effectiveness with reference to the client.   Perhaps the
most interesting suggestion in this respect is the use of the
local social organization as a support structure, a role which
many claim already exists outside the boundaries of the centralized
bureaucracy.   .
    Whatever the value of the argument presented above as a basis
for a heuristic statement it does not predetermine a discussion of
identity formation.   Bell (1975) distinguishes between identity
which he considers to be the psychological basis of individual
motivation, and 'belonging' which he sees as the consequence of
group membership.   Thus ethnic identity involves the self-
definition by the individual and ultimately by the out-group.
What is clear is that such self-evaluation is partly related to
a sense of belonging to a group and a distinctive identity is
rooted in a distinctive sense of history which will often focus
upon the group.   Thus, if we accept that identities tend to
crystalize around symbols it is conceivable that the relevant
symbols involve an evaluation in historical terms.   While the
symbols employed to differentiate group from group may be of
widely divergent character at different levels of identity an
overarching identity might be indicated by language for example.
It is therefore no coincidence that ethnicity and the sociology
of language have simultaneously become something of vogue topics
in the social sciences; they are inherently inter-related.   Where
cultural identity is closely tied with language and where language
erosion is seen to occur as a result of the dominance of the
majority ethnic group then it becomes clear that part of the
identity formation focuses on the emotional aggression against the
dominant neighbour as a resentment against cultural and social
dominance.   The situation in Britain where the peripheral nations
of Wales, Scotland and Ireland all demonstrate a certain dissatisfaction, weak though it may be, is a dissatisfaction with the
dominance of England within a Union which was conceived as being
based upon equal national status for each of the four nations.
The confusion of political sovereignty with primary or secondary
identification is hardly relevant to England where there is a
general tendency to equate Britain with being English.   However,
in the peripheral nations each group can emphasize its own
uniqueness, be it based on language, religion, territoriality or
a sense of historical separateness, as being of intrinsic value
and can assert a pride in the aggressive declaration of one's own
ethnicity.   In this sense the salience of ethnicity can be viewed
as a response to the breakup of older and historically fused
social and cultural, political and economic dominance structures
and represents an effort by these groups to use a cultural mode

for economic and political advancement.   It would be interesting
to see someone study English ethnicity and latent nationalism in
these terms.

Given that language can serve as a symbol of ethnic identity
around which the ethnic group can be mobilized and that this is so
clear from the strength of language as a dividing force; if
people from two groups can not communicate then the language
division is as real as that of colour and the hostility to learning
a language is analogous to hostility to blackness.   If, as has
been suggested above, language erosion can be seen as a form of
positive discrimination on the part of the majority ethnic group
then it brings institutionalized differences in power and privilege
between the majority and minority into focus and gives a new
salience to minority group membership while also intensifying
hostility and rivalry.   In the long run this means that the
individual, in order to make his claims, will have to determine
to which group he belongs.   This becomes particularly true if
language becomes the marker of mobilizing the group with that
group tending to define its ethnicity largely in terms of language.

The link between history, language and ethnicity is referred to
in several of the papers which refer to the tendency until recently
for the ideological stress to be placed upon individual social
mobility via the vehicle of assimilation into the majority ethnic
group whose norms set the terms for such mobility.   One could not
achieve access to status positions by emphasizing one's Welshness
but rather it was a case of 'If you want to get ahead you must get
an English head', with an associated downgrading of Welsh culture
and identity.   Until recently the status that accrued from
succeeding in British terms contributed to one's status within
Wales.   The recent reorientation of ethnicity within Wales means
a member of the older generation who takes pride in the status
that derives from the wider frame of reference may be regarded as
a 'Dic Sion Dafydd' (Uncle Tom) by many of the younger generation.
Being Welsh is no longer as simple as being born in Wales or being
able to speak the Welsh language.

Giles and Taylor investigate the dimensions of Welsh identity
and relate it to the Welsh language.   They indicate that for the
bilingual the Welsh language is the most important dimension but
that for those who do not speak the Welsh language there is a
feeling of separation from what they accord considerable importance
to in terms of national identity - the Welsh language.   Interesting
as these findings are they derive from a sample that is based
with reference to class, age and geographical locality.   Furthermore the multidimensional nature of the identity may pertain to
dimensions not considered in this particular study.   The positive
evaluation given to the Welsh language in this part of Wales is
referred to in the paper by Williams, Roberts and Isaac.   The
language resurgence which they encountered is accounted for by
the tendency for language to be employed as the basis for inter-
generational mobility aspirations within a very restricted labour
market in an area of industrial decline.   An unpublished study
(C. Davies's personal communications) has indicated that such
language converts appear to develop an associated political
reorientation involving heightened ethnicity.

The optimism of the above papers with reference to language retention is not echoed in the other papers which refer to language, the emphasis being upon a continued language erosion. What this suggests is that as has been suggested in the discussion of ethnic salience attitude towards language and in particular language loyalty varies by structural position and geographic location. This is one of the phenomena which requires a focused attention. Giles and Taylor refer to ethnic variation and context and Wenger similarly discusses the strategic use of ethnicity in different contexts. While emphasizing that the salience of ethnicity varies according to social context she appears to treat ethnicity as primordial and we are not told why the salience varies in the way that it does. This facet should be the focus of future studies. My own feeling is that in an area such as north-east Wales where there is a relatively low proportion of language speakers and where the area is dominated in an economic and administrative sense by a central place outside of Wales there is insufficient institutional support to generate vitality. Harrison's paper discusses the difficulties involved in language maintenance in such areas, among families where only one parent is Welsh-speaking. Furthermore such outside centres also set the trends which determine group status. This is particularly relevant in the consideration of age and class as major variables in the structuring of identity and group orientation. While Wenger does refer to youth it is unfortunate that she does not introduce more discussion of variation in terms of structure, although her methodological approach involving participant observation would be ideal for assessing such a relationship. We are given the impression that the Welsh language is limited to certain contexts and that overall it is given an inferior status, especially among the youth of the community. This does not of course mean that such an orientation is permanent and it may well refer to a specific age set. Thus the predominance of the trend-setting out-group in the domains which are of importance to the young determines the status they accord to the respective languages that represent the in- and out-groups. This is apparent in Emmett's paper which refers to the dominance of non-Welsh centres on 'trendiness' among the young while also suggesting that of late there has been an increase in self-pride in being Welsh which, together with a lessening of traditional family and community authoritarianism, has allowed such innovative tendencies to be given a Welsh expression. The low self-esteem which derives from the in-group is substantiated among those whose class position is low and the combination of perceived low socio-economic status and low ethnic status leads to a repudiation of the in-group and a tendency to use the relevant class position in the out-group as the reference group, this being sufficient to increase self esteem. In brief the actor will assimilate to the out-group by insuring that class and ethnicity complement one another. Of course, as Wenger suggests, while this process may predominate there is a leeway for drawing upon the minority group identity when the social context demands it and as the individual's activities shift to different domains there may well develop a readoption of the in-group as the reference group. Historically the forces which

have promoted this type of assimilation have been particularly
powerful in Wales.

Part of this argument is presented in Clayton's paper which
discusses language erosion and maintenance in terms of domains of
activity within a community in north Wales. She suggests that
although there has been a recent heightening of ethnic salience
there remains a tendency for language erosion to proceed in association with certain domains. These domains are those which are
associated with the English-dominated economic activities and where
the opportunity for the use of the Welsh language is limited.
This theme is taken up by Carter and Williams who, by using
aggregate data, are able to indicate that erosion is at least
partly to be accounted for by the introduction of such intrusive
elements. This is done by identifying spatial foci of language
erosion and maintenance and assessing the nature of non-linguistic
changes in such areas. What is implied is that the nature of
economic development which is not in Welsh hands, is disadvantageous
to the Welsh language.

This in turn appears to suggest that given the existing balance
of economic power there must be a choice between language maintenance and economic development. Alternatively a language
planning policy could attempt to monitor economic development and
restrict it to the type of development which will not be detrimental to the language. As is suggested in the paper by Williams,
Roberts and Isaac the economic variable is crucial in that people
will tend to maximize their social and economic status and minimize
their survival risks, with the association of language with
economic viability being sufficient induction to facilitate
language loyalty and even conversion. In any case some policy of
economic development is essential since its absence will only
further the process of depopulation within which the young, Welsh
speaker appears to be the most geographically mobile.

Illuminating as the work of Carter and Williams may be, as they
acknowledge, it is only a prelude to further work since the interference of process from macro-spatial analysis is problematic.
Thus Thomas and Williams attempt to take the issue further by
focusing on a micro-scale of analysis involving a sampling procedure based at least in part upon the spatial variables indicated
as of potential relevance in the work of Carter and Williams.
Operating from the assumption that the early gains of Plaid Cymru
were in the areas of high percentage of Welsh-language speakers
and that securing legal rights for the language was one of the
early objectives of the party they investigate the relationship
between ethnic politics and language loyalty. Their findings offer
some interesting insights. They indicate that attitude to the
language is highly related to the vitality generated by demographic
support and that an ethnically based political orientation relates
to language ability. Here again there is an obvious need to extend
the range of the sampling. The methodological approach of this
study, which focused upon sixth-form students, shows an obvious
age and class bias which should be remedied in future work. There
is also a need to focus upon negative correlations and to account
for example for the fact that there are more Welsh-language
speakers who do not support Plaid Cymru than there are supporters,

while the strength and multi-dimensionality of the Welsh identity seems in many cases to be independent of language, and, as Wenger claims in her paper, there are many who explicitly expose the tenets of ethnic politics but feel that the requisite party allegiance lacks credibility.

Ultimately as has been mentioned above the language issue boils down to a conflict over scarce resources. The conflict perspective is clear in the paper by Madgwick who seeks to consider methods of accommodating such conflict by comparing similar contexts in other countries. Of course there are those who would claim that such accommodative suggestions merely serve to preserve the status quo which, so far as one of the language groups is concerned, implies subservience and continued erosion. To them the only accommodative posture is one which reverses the power situation.

It should be clear that it is insufficient to conduct future research with correlative hypotheses which do not accommodate alternative explanations. This should be one of the objectives of any future research. A second objective should be to extend some of the issues discussed in these papers by accommodating a wider range of structural variables which would allow for a more refined evaluation of social phenomena.

The emphasis upon language and ethnicity is probably a reflection of the concern expressed by many Welsh people about their distinctive identity with the researchers bringing their own subjectivity to bear by their choice of research topic. It is also of course a reflection of current trends in the social sciences and of the emerging relevance of ethnicity in political terms. Yet salience does not mean predominance and as has been previously stated class remains, albeit in a latent form.

The final two papers address themselves to a discussion of the economic basis of inequality. Williams considers the relationship between the economic, power and status dimensions of inequality within a small community by referring to alternative aspects of social ranking. Such a perspective allows a more refined basis of social differentiation to emerge than that pertaining to an analysis in terms of class. While identifying a general tendency towards status consistency across the different dimensions it is also clear that aspects of esteem can contradict the expected consistency that might be expected by commencing from the economic ranking. Furthermore, much of the associational patterns within the community are to be explained by factors other than those which pertain to economic rank.

Finally, Day and Fitton give a preliminary account of their research into religion and community in mid-Wales. This research project seeks to establish the relationship between the geographical mobility and associated rural depopulation on the one hand and the communitarian religious organization on the other. In this paper they seek to identify the relationship between social structure and secularization. They conclude that secularization is selective with reference to age, class, language and sex with the young, non-Welsh speaking, working-class male being most prone to disassociate themselves from formal religion. Given the preceding discussion it would have been interesting to have the data re-analysed with reference to the consideration of language groups as status groups while also learning of the possible use of religious organization as a means of access to status positions by newcomers.

It is hoped that the papers in this volume go some way towards redressing some of the deficiencies outlined at the beginning of the introduction. If the recent attempts to stimulate further work in the social sciences which focuses attention upon Wales yields any result there is little doubt that much of the work reported upon here will be quickly superseded. However, the questions that they generate serve as the basis for such work while the omissions indicate the need for an expansion of focus.

NOTES

1 See for example, Urry and Wakeford (1973), Butterworth and Weir (1975), and Marsh (1965).
2 RAIN, no.16, October 1976, p.1.
3 Some of these studies can be found in Rees (1950), and Davies and Rees (1960).
4 See Plowman, Minchinton and Stacey (1962), and Day and Fitton (1975).
5 Among such reports are the following: HMSO (1964, 1967), and The Council for Wales and Monmouthshire (1963).
6 See for example Nevin (1957), and Tomkins and Lovering (1973).
7 The most useful of these reports are Sharp et al. (1973), Central Advisory Council for Education (Wales) (1967, 1953, 1960 and 1961), and Welsh Joint Education Committee (1961).
8 Both Osmond (1974) and Mayo (1974) assume this position.
9 See Hechter (1975).
10 Among the best of these studies are John (1950), Lewis (1959) and Minchinton (1969).
11 For an extension of this argument see Hechter (1976).

REFERENCES

BELL, D. (1960), 'The End of Ideology', Free Press, Chicago.
BELL, D. (1975), Ethnicity and social change, in N. Glazer and D.P. Moynihan (eds), 'Ethnicity: Theory and Experience', Harvard University Press, Cambridge, Mass.
BARTH, F. (1969) (ed.), 'Ethnic Groups and Boundaries', Little, Brown, Boston.
BRENNAN, T., COONEY, E.W. and POLINS, H. (1954), 'Social Change in South West Wales', Watts, London.
BUTTERWORTH, E. and WEIR, D. (1975), 'The Sociology of Modern Britain', Fontana, London.
CENTRAL ADVISORY COUNCIL FOR EDUCATION (WALES) (1953), 'The Place of Welsh and English in the Schools of Wales', HMSO.
CENTRAL ADVISORY COUNCIL FOR EDUCATION (WALES) (1960), 'Education in Rural Wales', HMSO.
CENTRAL ADVISORY COUNCIL FOR EDUCATION (WALES) (1961), 'Technical Education in Wales', HMSO.

CENTRAL ADVISORY COUNCIL FOR EDUCATION (WALES) (1967), 'Primary Education in Wales', HMSO.
COUNCIL FOR WALES AND MONMOUTHSHIRE (1963), 'Report on the Welsh Holiday Industry', HMSO.
DAHRENDORF, R. (1969), On the origin of inequality among men, in A. Beteille (ed.), 'Social Inequality', Penguin, Baltimore.
DAY, G. and FITTON, M. (1975), Religion and social status in rural wales: 'Buchedd' and its lessons for concepts of stratification in community studies, 'Sociological Review', vol.23, no.4, November, pp. 867-91.
EMMETT, I. (1964), 'A North Wales Village', Routledge & Kegan Paul, London.
FRANKENBERG, R. (1957), 'Village on the Border', Cohen & West.
HECHTER, M. (1975), 'Internal Colonialism: The Celtic Fringe in British National Development 1536-1966', Routledge & Kegan Paul, London.
HECHTER, M. (1976), Reply to Cohen: Max Weber on ethnicity and ethnic change, 'American Journal of Sociology', vol.81, no.5, March, pp. 1162-8.
HMSO (1964), 'Depopulation in Mid-Wales'.
HMSO (1967), 'Wales: The Way Ahead'.
JENKINS, D. (1960), Aberporth: A study of a coastal village in South Cardiganshire, in E. Davies and A. D. Rees (eds), 'Welsh Rural Communities', University of Wales Press, Cardiff, pp. 1-63.
JOHN, A.M. (1950), 'The Industrial Development of South Wales', Cardiff.
KHLEIF, B.B. (1978), Cultural regeneration and the school: an anthropological study of Welsh-medium schools in Wales, 'International Review of Education', vol.22, no.2, pp. 177-92.
LEWIS, E.D. (1959), 'The Rhondda Valleys: A Study in Industrial Development 1800 to the Present', Phoenix House.
MARSH, D.C. (1965), 'Changing Social Structure of England and Wales 1871-1961', Routledge & Kegan Paul, London.
MAYO, P.E. (1974), 'The Roots of Identity', Allen Lane, London.
MINCHINTON, W.E. (1969), 'Industrial South Wales 1750-1914: Essays in Welsh Economic History', Frank Cass, London.
NEVIN, E.T. (1957), 'The Social Accounts of the Welsh Economy 1948-1956', University of Wales Press, Cardiff.
OSMOND, John (1974), 'The Centralist Enemy', Christopher Davies, Swansea.
OWEN, Trefor M. (1960), Chapel and community in Glan-llyn, Merioneth, in E. Davies and A.D. Rees (eds), 'Welsh Rural Communities', University of Wales Press, Cardiff, pp. 185-248.
OWEN, Trefor M. (1966), Rhai Agweddau ar Astudio Cymdeithas yng Nghymru, in M.J. Jones and R.O. Roberts (eds), 'Trafodion Economaidd a Chymdeithasol', University of Wales Press, Cardiff, pp. 20-43.
PLOWMAN, D.E.G., MINCHINTON, W.E. and STACEY, M., Local social status in England and Wales, 'Sociological Review', vol.10, no.2, July.
REES, A.D. (1950), 'Life in a Welsh Countryside', University of Wales Press, Cardiff.
REES, A.D. and E. DAVIES (eds) (1960), 'Welsh Rural Communities', University of Wales Press, Cardiff.

ROSSER, C. and HARRIS, C.C. (1965), 'Family and Social Change', Routledge & Kegan Paul, London.
RAIN (Royal Anthropological Institute Newsletter) (1976), October, no.16.
SHARP, D., THOMAS, B., PRICE, E., FRANCIS, G., and DAVIES, I. (1973), 'Attitudes to Welsh and English in the Schools of Wales', Schools Council Research Studies, Macmillan - University of Wales Press.
SHIBUTANI, T. and KWAN, K.M. (1965), 'Ethnic Stratification: A Comparative Approach', Macmillan, London.
THOMAS, R. (1966), 'Industry in Rural Wales', Welsh Economic Studies No. 3, University of Wales Press, Cardiff.
TOMKINS, C. and LOVERING, J. (1973), 'Location, Size, Ownership and Control Tables for Welsh Industry', Cyngor Cymru, Cardiff.
URRY, J. and WAKEFORD, J. (1973), 'Power in Britain, Sociological Readings', Heinemann, London.
WEBER, M. (1958), 'From Max Weber: Essays in Sociology', translated and edited by H.H. Gerth and C. Wright Mills, Oxford University Press, New York.
WELSH JOINT EDUCATION COMMITTEE (1962), 'Language Survey 1961', HMSO.

Chapter 2

SOCIAL DEPRIVATION IN WALES: 1961 TO 1971

Martyn Winrow

The spatial structure of society is increasingly coming under the careful scrutiny of the social scientist. That both the city and its environs are in a constant state of flux are beyond doubt. Changes in spatial structure are closely related to the process of social change (Davidson, 1975). This paper is directed towards furthering the understanding of the complex interrelationships between structure and change. The research reported here is a development of a project on deprivation in Wales (Priestley and Winrow, 1975) which used a multivariate analysis of census and employment data.

A symposium on social indicators (Stockford, 1976) reviewed some of the basic issues facing social indicator research, and pointed out that a certain amount of confusion existed in research approach, due to the different intellectual traditions of researchers. There appears to be a needs approach, concerned with resource allocation and intervention, and second, a social areas approach. This part- icular study is developed from a research format essentially con- forming to the latter approach. The validity of analyses using multivariate procedures has been questioned (Edwards, 1975), on the grounds that they produce composite indices from highly intercorrelated variables before adequately defining deprivation or malaise. In defence of a similar procedure carried out in this research it can be argued that such analysis only aims to produce greater comprehension of the structure of society rather than seeking the causes of the problems, and second, that the many ways of manipulating the data produce a number of different ways of examining the general problem. Warman (1976) argues that this is more of an advantage than a disadvantage.

In post-war years there has emerged a broad-based research tradition aimed at identifying and, hopefully, solving the problem of poverty. It would appear that in the years after Booth (1903) and Rowntree (1899) the concern for the distribution of poverty was limited, especially in the period immediately after the Second World War (Holman, 1971, p.3). By 1970 the trend had been reversed and a wealth of information exists in studies undertaken under the auspices of several disciplines having a common interest in the structure of society. This broad-based research tradition appears to have had several consequences.

In the first instance, due to its relative infancy and the broad
extent of its subject coverage it has tended to be lacking in depth
in theoretical terms.   Second, given such wide coverage there have,
necessarily, been a number of diverse approaches to the study of
poverty in present-day society.   These different methodologies
include the Marxist standpoint of Harvey (1973), in which he argues
that social objectives must aim to alter the capitalist market
structure, and the contrasting view, typified by the statement that
'Planning, despite its avowedly social aims, has been in the main a
physical activity' (Cullingworth, 1972, p.122), and that all social
welfare requires is a separate set of social policies initiated
from within the existing political framework.

   Much of the recent research carried out by local authorities has
been of the latter category (Amos, 1969; Kegie and Thomas, 1974)
and it is only in recent years that the reaction against traditional research/planning has been evident.   In the British
Community Development programme the Southwark group have evolved
a form of advocacy planning in direct contrast to the more conservative approaches of the other Community Development Projects
(North Southwark C.D.P., 1974).

   A third consequence is that there has been a tendency not to
clearly define exactly what the selected indicators claim to
measure.   In the following research, for example, it is important
to note that social deprivation can be described in general terms,
but it is only possible to 'define (assume) deprivation in terms
of the indicators used to identify its areal concentration'
(Edwards, 1975, p.284).

   Clearly, there is no concensus on the optimum research framework
in which to study the social inequalities of society.   If we
accept that such inequalities exist it follows that certain
sections of the population suffer malaise or are in need.   Attempts
to measure social need, and more specifically, to identify areas
which require positive discrimination in policy terms, have led to
the development of social indicators.   The use of such indicators
in the United Kingdom is less well advanced than in America, where
complex indices are in use in a variety of social programmes.   The
majority of the indicators in use in the United Kingdom are
descriptive variables based on the census (for a recent review of
such indicators see Hakim, 1975).   In studies of social deprivation
indicators have mainly covered the population, housing and employment characteristics, with some researchers adding indices measuring
health and social services, education and even environmental
factors.   The indicators must normally be nationally applicable,
comparable on an area to area basis and be readily available.   (For
a review of deprivation research see Holman, 1970; Edwards, 1975;
and Williams, 1976.)

   The analyses presented here are an attempt to identify the areal
concentration of indicators associated with deprivation.   Social
deprivation is not defined in terms of the indicators used in the
analysis.   The exercise is seen as a useful method of highlighting
areas which have relative concentrations of those variables associated with malaise.   However, in the discussion the general term
social deprivation is used to describe the malaise situation.

   The concern here is with three main points; first, the changes in the dimensions of social deprivation; second, the distribution of deprivation in Wales in the period 1961 to 1971; and finally, the implications of any changes, in nature or pattern. Two general assumptions are made at this point. These are that deprivation involves a dynamic situation with the mix of input variables changing through time, and that there will be changes in the distribution of social deprivation throughout Wales in the inter-censal period.

Social deprivation is a multiple deprivation situation (Eversley, 1973). No one measurable variable can be claimed to indicate the scope of such deprivation since 'the deprived often suffer in more than one direction' (Holman, 1970, p.143-4). In addition to being multiple in nature social deprivation is also relative and dynamic. Relative deprivation indicates that such deprivation is compared on an area basis. It is not to say that there is a datum above, or below, which deprivation does or does not exist. Clearly, when using statistical techniques there is a need for cut-off points, but these should not be interpreted as base lines defining the very existence of deprivation. That deprivation is dynamic is simply to state that societal processes are not static. The elements of social change are constantly evolving and what is worst in one area at time x may well be satisfactory in (a previous) time y; equally, at time x areas A and B may well have very different concentrations of deprivation producing phenomena, but by time y conditions in these areas may have deteriorated, improved or remained static.

INTEGRAL CHANGE IN THE DIMENSIONS OF DEPRIVATION

If social deprivation is a multiple phenomenon which is both relative and dynamic, it is conceivable that the central indicators will not necessarily remain the same through time. By using a number of indicators it is hoped that it will be possible to isolate the key criteria producing deprivation at each time period.

This is not to say that such practice can isolate specific deprivation producing phenomena which account above all for the very existence of deprivation at that time, it will only provide an insight into the relative importance of each input variable in the general term social deprivation. This is to say that the concern is for a complex malaise and that it is possible that the interrelationships of its constituent parts, as determined by the input variables, will change relative to each other through time.

Such change could occur as a result of several factors, but these can be generalised under two main headings - natural features producing change, and policy orientated factors. The former would include changes in the birth and death rates and improved standards of living. The second set of factors involve the positive and negative effects of planning strategies. Positive planning should produce an improvement in conditions in specific areas. Inadequate, or a complete lack of, planning could produce deterioration in relative deprivation terms.

The indicators used in this research are listed in Tables 2.4 and 2.5. They were chosen as a result of a selection process

dependent upon several criteria. In the first instance they had
to be of use in a macro-scale study of limited resources (Priestley
and Winrow, 1975, p.10), which obviated the use of enumeration
district data. The indices had to be available for the whole of
Wales and had to have a common areal base to allow inter-variable
comparisons and intra-area change through time. The areal unit
chosen was the local authority, and the sources of most of the
indices were the readily available County Reports of the census.
They include variables usually believed to be associated with the
existence of social deprivation. While it was not possible to use
exactly the same set of variables for each time period, it is felt
that the two lists are compatible.
     Some comments regarding the lists of indices are in order.
First, it should be reiterated that the variables selected do not
specifically define deprivation. They represent those variables
in the census which are associated with malaise. Second, it was
felt that in order to determine whether the dimensions of deprivation changed through time, at least a dozen variables were
required in the analysis.

METHODOLOGY: THE ANALYTICAL TECHNIQUES

The basic problem at this stage of the research was to determine a
satisfactory method of analysing data for 168 areas measured on up
to 13 variables. Equally, the techniques chosen had to verify the
assumptions; and in addition it was hoped that the model could
possibly be used as an aid to planning strategies.
     Two multivariate statistical techniques are used, namely,
Principal Components Analysis (PCA) and Cluster Analysis (CA):
     Principal Components Analysis PCA is performed on both the
1961 and 1971 data sets. The procedure utilises a basic data
matrix which is normalised. The normalised data are then used to
calculate a Pearson Product Moment correlation matrix. Eigenvectors are extracted and both areas and original variables are
related to the eigenvectors. Output is in three forms, these are
eigenvalues, component loadings and component scores. Eigenvalues measure the diagnostic power of each component. Component
loadings measure the association between the original input
variables and each component. Each area has a score on every
component, and these scores measure the strength of each component
in a particular area.
     Cluster Analysis CA uses the same input variables as PCA.
Unlike the latter technique, which is used to examine the association between variables, CA is essentially a classificatory
procedure. The stages are as follows:
   (i) The data matrix is normalised.
  (ii) The local authority areas are considered as points in
       Euclidean space, the number of spatial dimensions dependent
       upon the number of input variables.
 (iii) The procedure fuses together the two points which are
       closest, that is most similar, and the mid-point of the two
       fused points becomes the location point (centroid) of a
       group consisting of the two fused points. The procedure is
       repeated until all the points are fused into one group.

(iv) Each fusion or linking can be represented on a dendrogram
which is a linkage diagram illustrating each pair-wise
fusion, and the point at which each fusion took place (see
Figure 2.1). Listings are produced to enable the observer
to examine the characteristics of each group formed.

ANALYSIS AND RESULTS

The integral nature of social deprivation has been assumed to change
through time. It is possible to test this assumption by examining
the components derived from the PCA. The importance of each
component's contribution to the total variance (explanation) is
presented in Tables 2.1 and 2.2. In each case the first four
components account for approximately 70 per cent of the total
variance. In this paper only the first four components are discussed since the other components, with less explanatory powers,
proved difficult to interpret. There is a tendency in research
using PCA to only use the first few components. However, it should
be noted that the cut-off point depends on the amount of information
that can be interpreted and not the percentage explanation.

Table 2.1   1961 PCA: Components and their percentage explanation

Component	% explan.	Cumulative % explan.
1 'Life Cycle'	35.7	35.7
2 'Amenities'	14.4	50.1
3 'Pop. Structure'	11.9	62.0
4 'Tenure'	7.0	69.0

Table 2.2   1971 PCA: Components and their percentage explanation

Component	% explan.	Cumulative % explan.
1 'Life Cycle'	33.9	33.9
2 'Amenities'	18.3	52.2
3 'Pop. Structures'	10.4	62.6
4 'Tenure'	9.0	71.6

Table 2.3   Components as dimensions of deprivation

	Components							
	1		2		3		4	
	61	71	61	71	61	71	61	71
High negative	*	*	*		*	*	*	
High positive				*				*

The loadings for the first four components are presented in
Tables 2.4 and 2.5. Examination of these tables and of the
corresponding component scores for the local authority areas
allows a detailed interpretation of the most useful components.

Table 2.4   PCA 1961 Data: Component loadings

	Variable description	Components			
		1	2	3	4
1	% population change 1951-61	0.361	-0.744	0.038	-0.189
2	% population 0-14	0.872	-0.120	-0.324	0.149
3	% population 15-24	0.566	0.062	0.528	-0.092
4	% population 15-64	0.306	0.302	0.738	-0.421
5	% population over 65	-0.901	-0.125	-0.255	0.177
6	% population 55-64	-0.836	0.290	0.133	-0.028
7	% hhlds 1-1½ persons/room	0.677	0.219	-0.042	0.283
8	% hhlds rented furnished	-0.430	-0.456	0.409	0.260
9	% hhlds owner occupied	-0.511	0.168	0.207	0.306
10	% hhlds without 3 amenities	0.054	0.744	-0.313	0.026
11	Birth Rate / 1000 pop.	0.698	-0.328	-0.170	0.026
12	Death Rate / 1000 pop.	-0.641	0.039	-0.007	-0.021
13	Economic Activity (*1)	0.571	0.543	-0.099	0.059
14	Housing Need (*2)	0.221	0.099	0.557	0.636

*1 = Males in socio-econ. grps 7,10,11 and 15/male pop. x 1000.
*2 = No. of permanent hhlds minus no. of structurally separate
     dwellings/permanent hhlds x 100.

Table 2.5   PCS 1971 Data: Component loadings

	Variable description	Components			
		1	2	3	4
1	% population change 1961-71	0.315	0.731	-0.172	0.165
2	% population 0-14	0.835	0.032	-0.325	-0.037
3	% population 15-24	0.495	-0.197	0.670	0.198
4	% population 15-64	0.409	-0.421	0.389	0.451
5	% population over 65	-0.915	0.099	0.051	-0.143
6	% hhlds 1-1½ persons/room	0.633	-0.252	-0.288	-0.345
7	% hhlds owner occupied	-0.488	0.017	-0.362	0.747
8	% hhlds rented unfurnished	-0.437	-0.429	0.044	-0.364
9	% hhlds rented from council	0.725	0.201	0.194	-0.431
10	% hhlds without 3 amenities	-0.051	-0.916	-0.179	0.007
11	% hhlds sharing inside WC	-0.223	0.186	0.669	0.079
12	Birth Rate / 1000 pop.	0.625	0.303	-0.296	0.009
13	Death Rate / 1000 pop.	-0.696	0.059	0.080	-0.277

THE 1961 SITUATION

Component one - 'Life cycle'

The first component indexes young families in urban areas. The
high positive loadings are for the percentage of population 0-14,
population 15-24, high birth rate and overcrowding (percentage
households with 1-1½ persons per room). The highest negative
loadings occur for population over 65, population 55-64 and a high
death rate. Other positive loading is observed on the variable
measuring number of males in less-skilled occupations, while
negative loading is indicated for the percentage of owner-occupied
households.
     If the areas scoring highly on this component are mapped it is
apparent that the high positive scores occur in urban areas, the
majority of these being in the valleys of south-east Wales.

Component two - 'Amenities'

The second component is identified with those areas having older
populations and a lack of basic household amenities. This is
reflected in the high positive loadings for the percentage of
households without three amenities and the percentage of males in
the less-skilled occupations; while also having negative loadings
for the percentage of population change 1951-61 and the birth rate.
The loadings suggest that the component is indexing the older,
predominantly rural areas of Wales, an interpretation which is
confirmed if the areas with high positive scores are mapped.

Component three - 'Population structure'

Older urban areas with stable mature population structures are
indexed by the third component. High positive loadings on the
percentage of population 15-24, percentage of population 15-64 and
housing need contrasted with negative scores on the very young and
old confirm that population structure characteristics are indicated
by this component. Urban areas of varying sizes and locations
score highly on this component while most rural areas have negative
scores indicating the different population structure.

Component four - 'Tenure'

Component four is identified essentially with dwellings and tenure.
Positive loadings occur on housing need and owner occupied households plus over-crowding in households. These household characteristics tend to be associated with urban areas and this is confirmed
by the component scores with high positive values in some of the
larger south-Wales towns.

Summary: 1961 Dimensions of deprivation

The dimensions of social deprivation in Wales in 1961 are seen as
possessing four basic characteristics (components) interpreted as
young urban families, the lack of rural amenities, the older urban
areas of mature population structure and finally a measure associated with tenure. The stressful conditions associated with
deprivation are likely to occur in areas having high scores at the
'stressful' end of the scale as portrayed in Table 2.3.

THE 1971 SITUATION

A similar procedure is repeated for the 1971 data. Reference to
Table 2.5 produces the following summary interpretation. Component
one is identified as a life-cycle measure very similar in nature to
the 1961 first component. Component two, as in 1961, measures
amenity, but does so from the reverse situation (a mirror image).
The third component indexes the working age groups of the population structure with low birth rates and few owner occupied households. Finally, the fourth component is again a measure of tenure,
which like the second component is a mirror image of its 1961
counterpart.

DIMENSIONS OF INTEGRAL CHANGE 1961 TO 1971

The dimensions of social deprivation, while being complex, do not
apparently change so dramatically as was assumed. The first
components in both periods are extremely similar. Again, component
three remains relatively stable in the ten-year period. However,
components two and four are mirror images of the earlier situation
(see Table 2.3). King in his study of the urban dimensions of
Canadian cities observed a similar situation. He called the
phenomenon 'flipping over' and he stated 'that this may well be
only a mathematical consequence of the procedures and order by
which the principal components are extracted. However, it may also
be suggestive of stronger relationships among certain of the
variables and this possibility warrants further study' (King, 1966,
p.223). The final sentence of the quotation casts some doubt on
the complete rejection of the assumption that the dimensions of
deprivation change.
     The final statement apart, it would appear that using a dozen or
so indicators has not isolated any clear dimensional changes. This
would point the way to selecting fewer indicators in the next stage
of the research, along the lines argued by Edwards (1974).

PATTERNS OF DEPRIVATION

The second assumption at the beginning of this paper was that there
would be changes in the distribution of deprivation in the inter-
censal period. In order to test this assumption both the PCA and
the CA are used. The output in the PCA contained the component

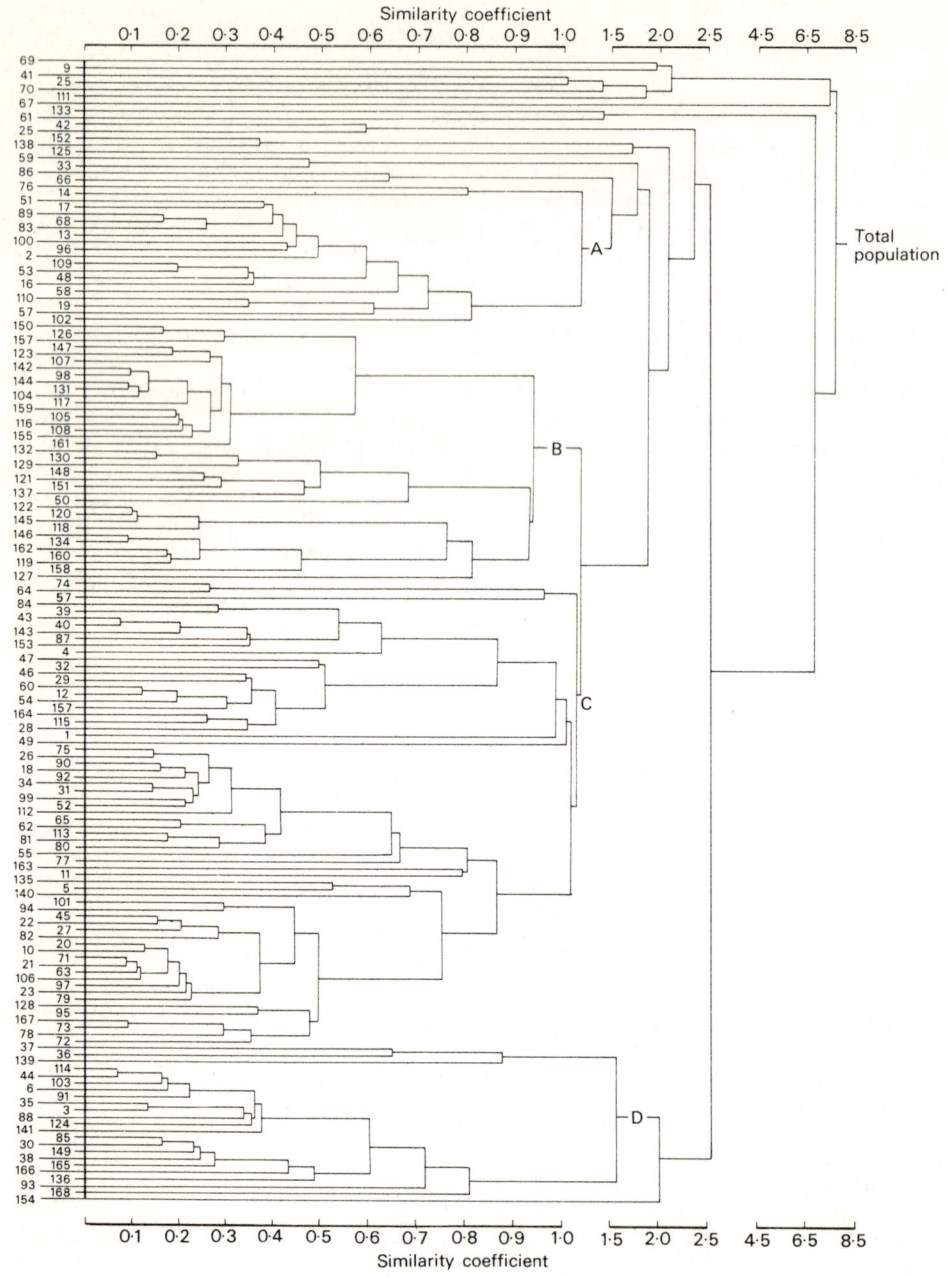

FIGURE 2.1   Example of dendrogram – 1971 data

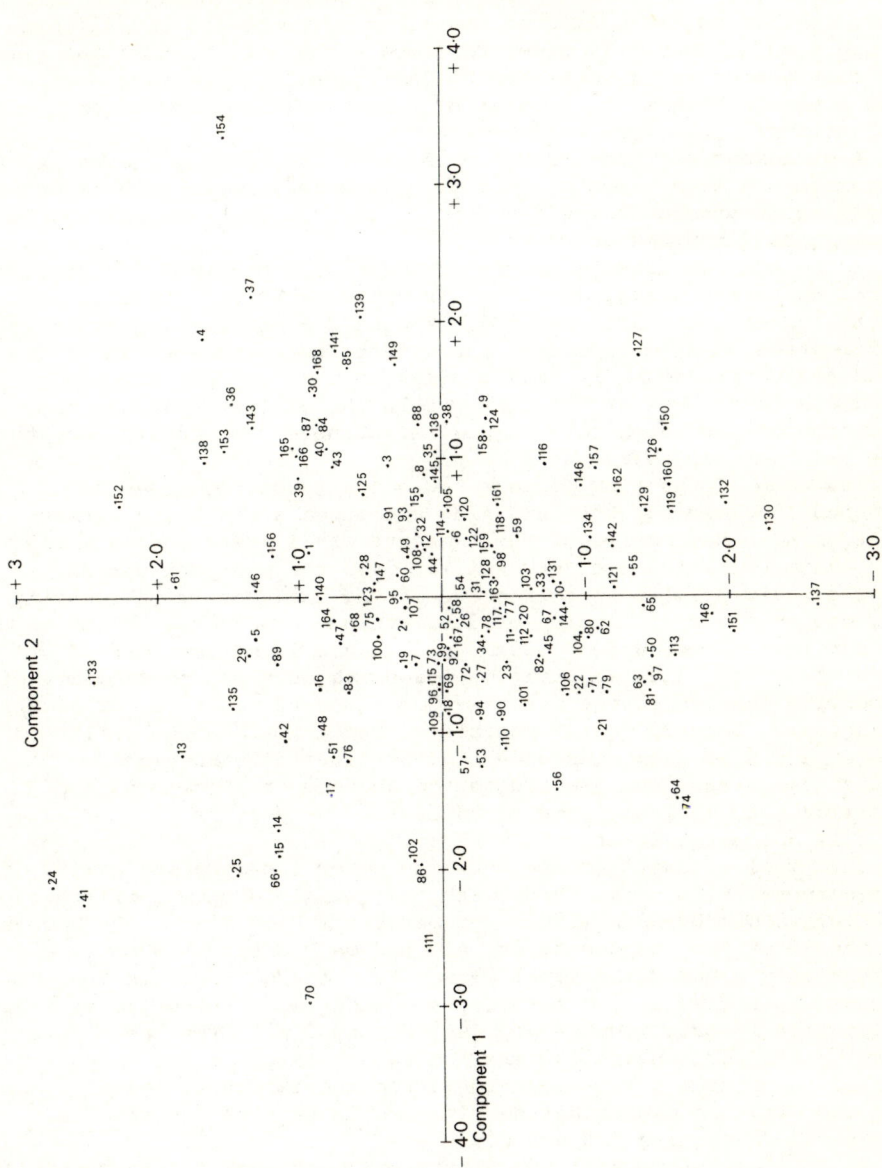

FIGURE 2.2   Two-dimensional deprivation space ‒ 1971 data

scores for all the local authority areas (referred to above in the
methodology). Using these scores it is possible to map the components, either on an individual basis, or by combining several components on one map. In order to compare the situation at the time
of each census it is necessary to individually check each of the
168 areas on each map. Such an exercise would be both arduous and
subjective.

A different solution to the problem of identifying change is
required. A model, tentatively described as a Deprivation Space
model is at present being developed. It uses both the PCA and CA
techniques described above. In addition to the component scores
from the PCA the linkage diagram (Figure 2.1) provides groupings of
local authority areas. For each group the centroid measures of
each cluster point are examined. Tables 2.6 and 2.7 contain the
information used to interpret the cluster characteristics. The
examination procedure is very similar to that of the component
loadings in the PCA except that within the cluster analysis the
measures do not refer to a composite variable (component), but to
the original variables.

For each of the time periods the majority of the areas are
grouped in clusters, the remaining ungrouped areas being termed
residuals. Examination of the two sets of clusters suggests that
the characteristics are very similar over the ten-year period.

The basic problem at this stage of the analysis is to identify
changes in the distribution of deprivation. Two forms of movement
(= spatial change) appear possible. In the first case the adoption
of a model of social deprivation space suggests the possibility of
observing changes in the relative positions of clusters (or groups
of areas). Second, it is possible to check for changes in the
member areas of each cluster - that is to examine movement of
individual areas from one cluster to another or from a residual
position into a cluster (or vice versa). The former type of movement is discussed first.

The model attempts to use both the major interpretive powers of
the components in conjunction with the clustered groups of areas.
Following work by King (1966) and Berry and Rees (1969) the scores
of the first two components are plotted on a graph in what is
essentially a two-dimensional Deprivation Space. This is done
separately for both time periods, and each local authority area has
a location in this model space (see Figure 2.2). The areas which
make up the particular clusters are then located on the graph and
linked to produce a two-dimensional representation of the cluster.
The two diagrams depicting the clusters in deprivation space are
presented in Figures 2.3 and 2.4.

It has been shown that the first two components remain virtually
unchanged in the inter-censal period and therefore any changes in
the locations of the clusters are interpreted as cluster movements
within deprivation space. If the two components constituting the
axes of the model (Figure 2.5) are re-examined it can be shown that
deprivation increases in a clockwise direction from A to B.

If Figures 2.3 and 2.4 are examined it is apparent that cluster
A has expanded towards the point of minimum deprivation. The
cluster is made up of coastal holiday resorts, but only includes
seven such areas in 1961. By 1971 this cluster has twenty areas

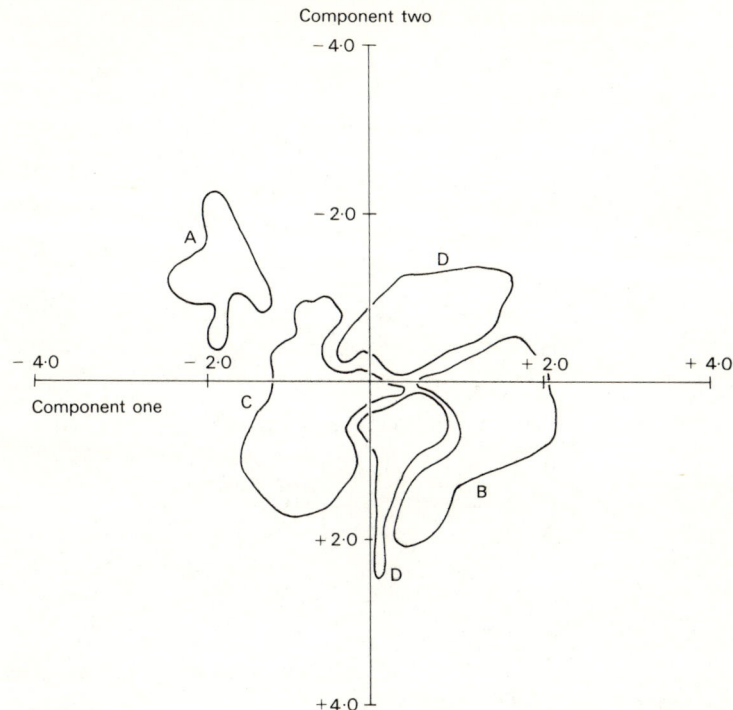

FIGURE 2.3   1961 clusters linked in 'deprivation space'

and includes the inland spa towns plus several small market towns.
Cluster B, however, has moved nearer to the position of maximum
deprivation.   In 1961 clusters C and D are not clearly defined with
D being in two sections.   By 1971 clearer definition is apparent.
Cluster C has a majority of rural districts which do not have the
major amenity problems associated with those rural areas of cluster
B.   Cluster D has contracted into the upper-right section of the
model.   In this position the amenity problems have subsided.
    The general trend would seem to be one of movement away from the
intersection of the axes.   The 'wealthy' retirement cluster appears
to be improving its position and gaining membership.   The cluster
mose likely to include areas of multiple deprivation (cluster B)
does not seem to be improving, indeed a decline is apparent.
Between these two clusters the areas are in a status quo situation
with some segregation of rural areas from Urban (C from D).
    Since it is now assumed that the dimensions of deprivation (in
this study) have not changed through the inter-censal period and
that the life-cycle and amenity components are important stable
dimensions, then direct comparisons of the two sets of clusters in
their two-dimensional deprivation space would seem feasible.   The
assumption was made (above) that changes would occur in the distribution of deprivation.   In the case of the relative positions of the
clusters change has been apparent.   Initial observation of the

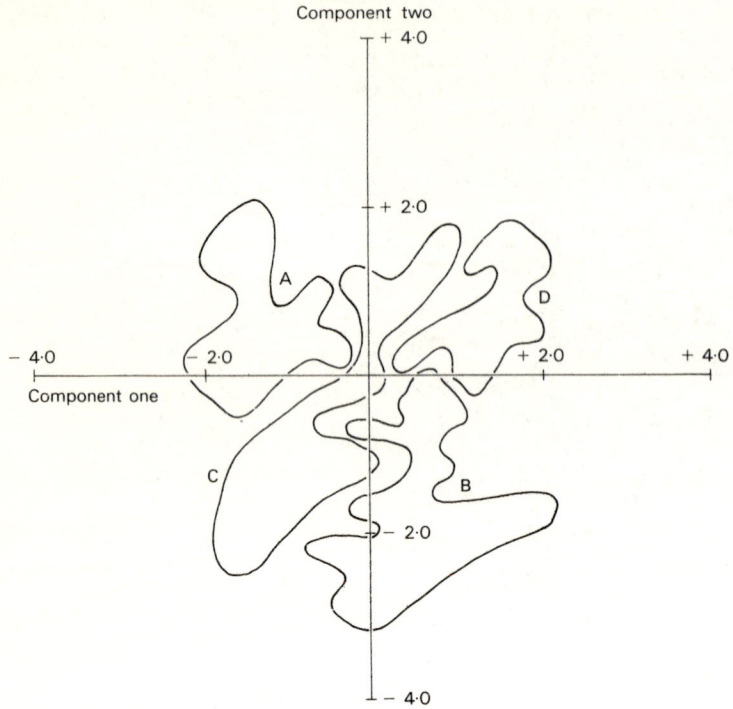

FIGURE 2.4   1971 clusters linked in 'deprivation space'

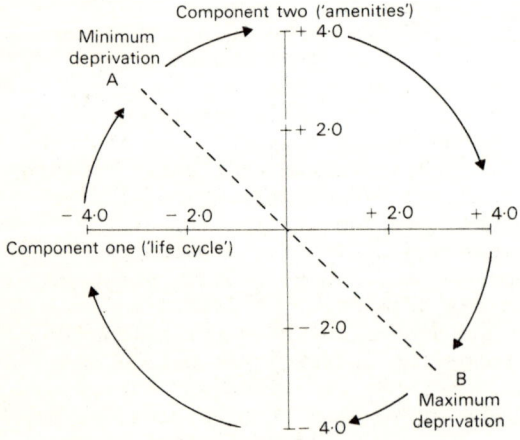

FIGURE 2.5   Social deprivation model

Table 2.6   CA 1961 data: measures on the centroids of the clusters

		Cluster/Groups			
	Variable description	A	B	C	D
1	% population change 1951-61	0.651	-0.013	-0.480	1.307
2	% population 0-14	-1.380	1.198	-0.052	0.217
3	% population 15-24	-1.325	0.576	-0.480	0.028
4	% population 15-64	-1.711	0.130	-0.775	0.780
5	% population over 65	2.368	-1.005	0.622	-0.736
6	% population 55-64	1.596	-0.704	0.093	-0.491
7	% hhlds 1-1½ persons/room	-1.142	1.391	0.002	-0.002
8	% hhlds rented furnished	1.777	-0.349	-0.237	-0.310
9	% hhlds owner occupied	1.598	-0.415	0.224	1.019
10	% hhlds without 3 amenities	-1.566	-0.057	0.760	-1.028
11	Birth Rate / 1000 pop.	-0.250	1.076	0.202	0.604
12	Death Rate / 1000 pop.	0.584	-0.530	0.510	1.886
13	Economic Activity (*1)	-0.904	1.123	-0.139	-1.654
14	Housing Need (*2)	-0.288	1.174	-0.341	-0.523

*1 = Males in socio-econ. grps 7,10,11 and 15/male pop. x 1000.
*2 = No. of permanent hhlds minus no. of structurally separate
     dwellings/permanent hhlds x 100.

Table 2.7   CA 1971 data: measures on the centroids of the clusters

		Cluster/Groups			
	Variable description	A	B	C	D
1	% population change 1961-71	-0.400	-0.494	-0.316	1.498
2	% population 0-14	-1.479	0.669	-0.283	1.294
3	% population 15-24	-1.131	0.323	-0.583	0.937
4	% population 15-64	-0.803	0.247	-0.284	0.693
5	% population over 65	1.877	-0.591	0.529	-1.619
6	% hhlds 1-1½ persons/room	-1.520	0.624	-0.289	0.219
7	% hhlds owner occupied	-0.122	-0.208	0.160	-0.170
8	% hhlds rented unfurnished	1.366	-0.172	0.637	-0.809
9	% hhlds rented from council	-0.762	0.384	-0.493	0.528
10	% hhlds with 3 amenities	0.653	-1.175	-0.471	1.036
11	% hhlds sharing inside WC	0.245	-0.108	-0.317	-0.500
12	Birth Rate / 1000 pop.	0.096	0.227	-1.291	0.990
13	Death Rate / 1000 pop.	1.906	-0.333	0.384	-1.412

cluster membership would suggest that here, too, there have been changes, however, no clear method of determining the extent of such change has been found.

Further research is currently being undertaken in an attempt to determine any changes in the distribution of social deprivation, especially with regard to deprivation levels in specific areas. Research is incomplete but the following leads are being investigated:

(a) The cluster membership is being examined. Since it has been established that cluster characteristics are stable, then if areas change their cluster it might be possible to interpret this change in terms of a potential improvement or decline in that area's deprivation situation.

(b) It is eventually hoped to use the model to measure changes in specific local authority areas. Such changes might be measured by locating both the 1961 and 1971 points (derived from the component scores) on the model, and to interpret such movement in the two-dimensional deprivation space. This approach has similarities to work done in Hull by Davidson (1975), in which he uses a regression model to analyse spatial change in the distribution of social deprivation.

(c) Given the constraints of an analysis such as this (see the introductory sections, above), it may well be that once the model has been used to make certain suggestions regarding the areal concentrations of selected variables the next step should be to undertake research at a more local level. The use of enumeration district data is possible, but equally, other techniques such as questionnaires and interviews could be used.

IMPLICATIONS AND CONCLUSIONS

Two assumptions are made at the beginning of this paper. The first, that the dimensions of deprivation are changing through time has been shown not to be true in the present study. In the context of this paper the implications are two-fold. If the integral nature of deprivation is relatively stable then solving existing planning problems, and predicting those areas likely to suffer from depriva-tion, should be possible. Second, it is pointed out that given such stability in the nature of deprivation the list of variables used in this study (and other studies using a large number of indicators) should be refined.

The second assumption, that there would be changes in the distribution of deprivation, has been validated. In assessing this change the results attributable to the analysis using the depriva-tion model would suggest that in the inter-censal period the situation had deteriorated. The model suggests a diverging situation with the 'wealthy' areas improving at the expense of the relatively 'poor' areas. This study did not attempt to identify causes of deprivation, but causality must necessarily be a recurrent theme on the conceptual side of such work. The model developed here essentially considers change; such changes are really the effects of the malaise problem. The causes of that problem require unrav-elling, and a host of research problems face those who attempt to find the solutions. This paper has attempted to clarify some of the problems associated with the dimensions of deprivation, and changes in the areal concentrations of malaise.

REFERENCES

AMOS, J. (1969), 'Social Malaise in Liverpool', Liverpool Planning Dept, Liverpool.

BERRY, B.J.L. and REES, P.H. (1969), Factorial ecology of Calcutta, 'Amer. J. of Sociology', 74, pp.445-91.

BOOTH, C. (1963), 'Life and Labour of the People of London', Macmillan, London.

CULLINGWORTH, J.B. (1973), 'Problems of an Urban Society', vol.2, 'The Social Content of Planning', Allen & Unwin, London.

DAVIDSON, R.N. (1975), Social deprivation: An analysis of inter-censal change, 'Proc.Inst.Br.Geogr.', New Series, vol.1, no.1, pp.108-17.

EDWARDS, J. (1974), 'Identification of Areas of Deprivation', unpub., Home Office.

EDWARDS, J. (1975), Social indicators, urban deprivation and positive discrimination, 'J. of Soc.Policy', vol.4, pp.275-88.

EVERSLEY, D.E.C. (1973), 'The Planner in Society', Faber, London.

HAKIM, C. (1975), 'Social Indicators from the Census', paper presented to the PTRC Meeting, held at the University of Warwick, July.

HARVEY, D. (1973), 'Social Justice and the City', Arnold, London.

HOLMAN, R. (ed.) (1970), 'Socially Deprived Families in Britain', Bedford Square Press, London.

KEGIE, J. and THOMAS, D.G. (1974), 'Monmouthshire Social Malaise Study, An Interim Report', Monmouthshire County Planning Dept, Cwmbran.

KING, L.J. (1966), Cross-sectional analysis of Canadian urban dimensions 1951-61, 'Canad.Geogr.', vol.10, pp.205-24.

NORTH SOUTHWARK C.D.P. (1974), 'The Council and The Thames-side Strategy Plan: Social Planning or Private Profit?', unpublished paper.

PRIESTLEY, M.M. and WINROW, M. (1975), 'Social and Economic Stress in Wales', unpub. paper, Dept of Geography, University College, Lampeter.

ROWNTREE, S. (1901), 'Poverty, a Study of Town Life', Macmillan, London.

STOCKFORD, D. (ed.) (1976), 'Social Indicators and Community Profiles in Rural Areas', Proceedings of a symposium (SSRC), Norwich.

WARMAN, P. (1976), quoted in Stockford, D. (ed.), 'Social Indicators and Community Profiles in Rural Areas', Proceedings of a symposium (SSRC), Norwich.

WILLIAMS, G. (1976), 'The Identification of Social Need: The Case of Greater Manchester', unpublished manuscript, Dept of Rural Planning, Manchester University.

Chapter 3

'REGIONAL COMMUNITY AND THE ERA OF REGIONAL AID'

Colin Fletcher

This paper is barely an orthodox research report. The bones of the matter lie in the details of company history in relation to local knowledge. Nevertheless, the intention is to weld a social economics by using a term from sociology, a term from industrial finance and a term from geography, namely community, industrial development grants and region. The purpose here is to inform the debate on devolution with the lessons of the recent past. The region is question, Llanelli and its villages and small towns, had been a colony of basic raw production and then in the post-war period industrial finance led to an economy which is hard to summarise. Now a rather short-term future has to be faced should devolution prove to more than promises. The paper begins, therefore, with a brief summary of what makes a community according to those who live in the town and villages. The ideas are largely expressed in sociological terms. A sketch of the region's history is given and followed by a listing of the value of grants for industry in 'development areas'. The details of post-war companies 'coming-in' do not all prove to spell disaster but they do show that money has been 'irrevocably lost'.

Finally, a conclusion is drawn that depends upon a republican regionalism that few may find acceptable. The approach may indicate, though, that local control has been so weak that there is now what some call a vacuum or a real chance for a broader power-base. The conclusion is political.

THE CRITERIA OF COMMUNITY

There are four headings under which conditions for a community may be grouped. They are a necessary condition and some sufficient, historical and emergent conditions.

First the necessary condition. The term community applies to a 'psychic sphere', a place is 'our *space*'. A community reflects upon itself to the extent that people say 'it is ours'. This demands an us and them orientation. Strictly speaking it may cast a line between us and the rest. In any event it is a subtle blend of geographical space and social sentiment; an elbow in a valley,

an estuary to the sea, or the fording of a river. In saying 'us'
and 'our place' the person indicates a common character born of
common experience since that settlement's personal fortune has been
bound up with collective fortune. 'Lived together, laughed
together and loved together' they say, 'and we've fought each
other, abused each other and then ignored each other.'

Second there are the sufficient conditions. It will be evident
that these conditions suffuse that which is necessary; they are the
loci of co-operation, collaboration and conflict. At least three
generations are to be found involved in collective constructions.
Men and women have built houses and churches and subscribed to halls
and memorials. So too, there are collective symbols, which involve
occasions when groups make music, play games and organize festivals,
carnivals and galas.

We can remember the depression, mind. We can remember no work.
The men in this village built the swimming pool entirely without
pay. They brought their own picks and shovels. The women came
with a penny for a packet of five Woodbines. When it was done
children came from all over the area to learn to swim. It was
the first - a little village like this.

In all probability a community has a simple beginning, a simple
economic beginning, that is. The setting was conducive to commerce
or work. It was a place to which those from scattered settlements
could come for trade, or it was a place which gave shelter, water-
power, and raw resources. It was not as cosy as it sounds. Men
were serfs, and then men were evicted for great tracts of land to
be enclosed. Whatever the circumstances, a rigid three-fold
hierarchy invariably was to be found; owner, manager and worker; a
lord and master, a few free men relatively well-paid, and the mass
that was free to find work. In any event the community may have
been self-sufficient; it may even have been 'run at a profit', but
it did not possess the means of accruing vast capital. More often
than not most surplus went to making homes into palaces and places
of worship and education. Consequently, the simple beginning was
developed by 'outside' capital. Either the agriculture or the
industry diversified and intensified; there was an 'infra-structure'
and tec .ological change. What may have been an island has long
since been a peninsular.

This brings us to 'emergent conditions'. A community may be
distinct, but only its name is likely to be unique. Strangers have
come in the wake of capital; 'foreign' owners, managers and workers.
What was a condition of strength for the community has become a
weakness, whoever can afford to live in it and pay its prices can
stay. Once, this rule may have driven out mediocre and brilliant
alike but it kept the community true to its simple beginnings. Now
strangers can settle and make their fortune. Such strangers are
accommodated, used and virtually incorporated. But they remain
strangers, and can be held responsible for squabbles and disputes.

In a sense to be the same 'old' community, the same people should
be in power. The pecking order is still the same. Whatever the
setting, those who are powerful patronise those less powerful who
do 'the doing'. All this suggests, of course, that the community
organizes its own life for itself; there is a marked inability to
cope with formal or legalistic procedures. In a sense a community

is anti-democratic because the 'same people' make all the decisions
in different capacities. Furthermore the community is an anti-
progressive force because of its efforts to maintain the hierarchy.
This is not to say that the *whole* community is either anti-democratic
or anti-progressive; only that part of it which represents the whole;
the 'leading families' and 'men of influence', and only then when
they wish to be.

A defensive tone is to be anticipated. Since the 'influx of
foreign capital' the community has lost whatever internal holistic
symmetry it had achieved. Now there are laws to challenge custom,
principles to ensnare practices. Perhaps naturally enough, these
very emergent conditions are part of the community itself as well
as being a reason for becoming more vociferous in its own praises.
For those who have always lived in the community it is not the
darkness of its eclipse that is frightening but the harsh glare of
having to make everything explicit. The emergent condition of all
communities is how they cope with that which exposes them; with
private capital encouraged by State aid.

CRITERIA FOR A COMMUNITY - A SUMMARY

1 Necessary conditions - a sense of identity:
     (a) distinctive name,
     (b) distinctive dialect/vocabulary,
     (c) use of landmarks as boundaries with neighbours.
2 Sufficient conditions -
     (a) more than 10 per cent of the population in three generations
         and 2 per cent in the fourth generation (great-grandparents),
     (b) established churches, chapels, clubs and institutes, also
         greens, ponds, common land; plaques, war memorials and
         squares,
     (c) established teams, festivals, fairs.
3 Historical conditions -
     (a) evidence of original economic base,
     (b) evidence of co-operation between 'classes',
     (c) evidence of infra-structure activity, e.g. market;
         brickworks, housing associations.
4 Emergent conditions -
     (a) 'strangers' incorporated in on-going activity,
     (b) resistance to changes in sense of identity items, e.g.
         through postal codes; telephone exchanges, road signs and
         demolition of 'part of the community',
     (c) a struggle to make sense of the requirements of recently
         arrived 'industries'.
The facts brought to bear here concern Llanelli, the 'Shadife'
dialect region; the industrial coastal belt of Southern Dyfed. In
many respects it will seem too neat a coincidence for the argument.
Bounded by bay and estuary to the south with mountains to the north;
capital of the tinplate industry for its formative years and home
of a rugby team which sets cycles to the lives of 15,000 active
supporters, Llanelli is regarded as the centre of its region, as
the pivot of an open fan of Welsh speaking pit villages.

BEFORE REGIONAL AID

Llanelli does not have a great and glorious history. What matters,
though, is the past that is telescoped into the present. For
example the feudal period did not end until the 1870s - about 50
years after neighbouring England. Small farmers were only recently
dispossessed and driven to the coast. They had little choice
between homelessness and hardship in mines and steelworks. The
town was controlled by men of very similar mannerisms to those who
ruled the country. In fact the incoming 'capitalists' and the
retrenched 'gentry' combined forces in the 1890s, they inter-
married their young, formed clubs on the city style, filled the
magistrates benches with each other, and close relatives, and lived
within the range of an invigorating horse ride. Industrialist and
squire; landowner and shareholder were so closely related that it
was an eccentricity to separate them. Without capital and land a
'noted family' did not withstand the First World War. By the time
of the world war a long depression had already been experienced by
the work people. International tariffs had made the goods unattrac-
tive, men had taken to the streets - the town hall square had been
filled by people who had marched up from the marshes and crossed
the railway line. The two who were shot dead died just over the
tracks. Their children came out in sympathy and initiated a
schools strike that grew to national proportions. By the time of
the First World War, that is, class lines were clearly drawn across
the townscape. The tinplate workers had tasted resistance and had
been sensible enough to put together strong union organization and
representation. The owners were wholly detached from their workforce and may have already been having second thoughts, for it
seems that the rundown from the First World War was rapid. Owners
sold assets including holdings in breweries; builders and shipping
were shed; estates changed hands through another cycle and began to
show the lack of maintenance. The phrase 'lack of maintenance'
would also apply to the industries inherited from the 1870s to the
1890s. Those with fewer than 200 employees and a lack of speciality
disappeared. There was negligible investment in new building and
machinery in the larger works (which averaged 400 workers and 35
staff). There was little point in safety or labour-saving devices,
so lifting and pulling was done by hand. Despite the availability
of cheap labour involving men and women preoccupied with making a
living rather than improving the comforts of 'conditions of work',
tinplate workers were subject to one seventh of the population
being permanently unemployed and many of the remainder working
merely to meet sporadic orders which gave them an average of
between two and three days work a week. The population had 'boomed'
between 1891 and 1901 then 'stabilized' and then began to diminish.
No schools or chapels were built. Like every town more than 150
miles from London, Llanelli had a siege mentality during the
depression.
    A depression, that is, takes the form not merely of suspended
endeavour and unchecked deterioration, but also houses a double-
edged guilt involving a choice between staying and doing nothing
and leaving and breaking social bonds. Those who did leave may
well have literally had 'more go in them' and effected a silent

criticism of those who remained. Certainly the working-class
emigrants were likely to leave permanently and on average every
family 'lost' at least one child as they came of age. The mood
was simply to be prepared to do as you were told. The old masters
still had their paternalistic ways of running a few shifts just
before Christmas and stocking the goods but it was clear that the
power had passed out of their hands. Smaller works closed in rapid
succession and were re-used as war supply storage depots. Another
slight occurs when a building ceases to be used for production and
becomes a warehouse for consumption.

Few skills are needed and work is associated with noise rather
than silence.

Conscription and essential works orders followed quickly. The
foundries of east Wales and especially the midlands were allocated
dark-eyed, dark-haired, pit-prop sized men in large numbers. 'I
was a Bevin boy. I was moved around for five years before they
let me come home', men will say.

Also important was the effect of this mixing. Ninety per cent
of the Llanelli population was Welsh-speaking in 1901. Non-Welsh
immigrants were few in number. The war drafted many nationalities
into the region, while permanently removing many local people from
the region. English-speaking conscripts could not get out of the
ordnance factories and Welsh-speaking natives could not return.

Albeit that many of the lines in this sketch deserve a pen-
portrait in their own right the tone of the end of an epoch should
be evident. Local landowners had given way to migrant capitalist
families and then both in their turn had lost ground. Without the
skill and loyalty of partially employed workers they may not have
come through the depression at all. As it was, coal, steel and
tinplate processes were a century old apart from modification and
the local resources that had made them profitable were in most
cases deleted. Meanwhile, national companies had been buying up
the better works.

Other 'buyers' were actually recouping debts. Only the banks or
the government were wealthy enough to undertake the long overdue
investments. Coal was nationalized at the end of the war and
Lloyds Bank formed the Steel Company of Wales.

Looking back from the present it would appear that British
capital in Llanelli leapfrogged from the production processes of
the 1870s to the American technology of the 1930s during the
realizations of that Second World War. In any event the size and
scope of the next generation of machinery made local ownership
simply out of the question. In that brief 55 years the protracted
experiences of the north and midlands had been compressed into a
glorious boom; depression, war, a brief ray of hope; a seemingly
endless depression and six further years of war.

From 1945 onwards the notion of a regional community is seen as
a necessarily fractured idea. The region possessed neither the
resources nor the resistance essential for the era that was to
come. As it happens this was a good thing at first since it was
the government that was to sustain the losses. With reference to
the present however any passive dependency that remains from the
past is to be regretted. In jargon terms the frozen form of
structured dependency suits personal and short-term advantages, it

is living from day-to-day. Such a frozen form does not facilitate
the reconstitution of the region from within.

WHAT IS REGIONAL AID?

Regional aid is part of the tapestry of provisions designed to
redistribute industry to areas of declining opportunity. It is
different from the Location of Offices Bureau's activity in that it
aims to encourage new developments rather than relocation away from
London. It depends on a region's status as either an intermediate
or development area, the development areas being all those whose
earliest industry was primary and extractive. Mining areas virtually
coincide with development areas in all but south-east England.
    The overt aspects of regional aid entail three kinds of
incentives. Purpose-built buildings are let on low leases and often
whole industrial estates are constructed. If these buildings are
unsuitable then up to 80 per cent of a building's cost can be paid
and all services connected. Capital grants can be made to pay up
to 80 per cent of equipment costs and low interest loans are available. Employment premiums are paid. Before the 'Equal Pay Act of
1975' premiums amounted to £8 per male employee and £5 per female
employee, assuming both to be employed on a full-time basis. The
overt incentives are immediate cash aids that virtually guarantee
an initial profitability. One area's advertisement is as follows:
 Facts about Advance Factories in the Areas
 for Expansion
  1 Two year rent-free period; option to purchase on favourable
    terms.
  2 Rents are often lower in the area than elsewhere
  3 Units available from 2,500 sq. ft. to 50,000 sq. ft.
    (230-4,650 sq. metres).
  4 Expansion potential of up to 300 per cent.
  5 Brand-new factories are available now in all areas.
    The covert aspects may be so called because they depend on
forceful negotiations with local authorities. They include key-
worker housing - that is allocated council houses at the employer's
disposal; low rateable values on the property occupied by the firm
or its senior management and a variety of services such as
searching for appropriate properties for these personnel. Further
the Inland Revenue can be generous towards capital depreciation,
director's personal accounts and other items 'allowable before
tax'. It appears that an acceptable contribution is expected.
Rarely are stringent taxation regulations applied. Considered
overall therefore, regional aid is conceived of as having the
social value of arresting depopulation and the economic value of
the taxable receipts and purchases of the employee rather than
the employer.
    Since it is the social consequences which concern us it is not
possible to effect the separations of regional aid 'outcomes' and
post-war centralization 'outcome', not possible, that is, to neatly
separate 'aid' from the other State and financial institutional
activity. These London-based movements of nationalization and
share dealing must be accounted for in their turn and I have tried

to do this elsewhere (Fletcher, forthcoming). The social consequences of economic activity are further entangled within the
significance of doing certain things, like singing 'Hen Wlad fy
Nhadau' or going cockling; or going out shooting before a rugby
match; with a town that is busy in its own praises. The consequences affect everyday life as well as the control of the region.
    What follows is a particular history and one with a sociological
flavour. I am not in a position to generalise and I do not wish to
do more than inform the term 'regional community' and draw attention
to strengths that have yet to be strained.

WHAT HAVE BEEN THE CONSEQUENCES OF REGIONAL AID?

Regional aid is most readily understood as attractive terms to
employers (industrialists) to enter an area and create jobs.
Within the study area those who did not enter responded to their
own needs, of course, but some were more welcome than others. It
is difficult in 1976 to account for 25 years of changing attitudes
but two preferences in the Llanelli region are detectable. In
principle, 'in the early days', the ideal firm was light engineering.
In practice this gave rise to assembly and packaging plants
employing many more semi-skilled women than skilled men. It seems
that such firms would bring keyworkers and most 'key' management,
occupy an 'advance factory' and employ less than 100 local
employees. They grew - rapidly or sporadically - to level off at
350 to 400 employees.
    More recently, the most prized project has been a petro-chemical
plant. Around such plants, it is believed many others mushroom and
grow. The refineries have the greatest prestige value even though
they take very few employees in relation to their cost. Instead
they are a big investment in plant equipment within the region and
so are also unlikely to move.
    In any event, the most marked consequences in the Llanelli region
has probably been the employment of women on day and part-day shifts
working at piecework rates. In sociology a story is often told that
this puts great strains on the masculinity of the husbands, that is
it weakens the 'primary role' of the mother and so weakens family
life (Harris, 1969; 111-16). Initial findings do not confirm this
belief. Rather most of the women are very glad to go out to work,
and glad of the company. They leave their homes whilst the
children are at school or to accommodate the shifts of their husbands. Thus, the husband works from 7.00 a.m. to 3 or 4.00 p.m. and
his wife turns in a valuable 5.00 p.m. to 10.00 p.m. The husbands
are generally in the higher earning jobs and so the net increase in
income has produced a real increase in wealth, with continental
holidays and good homes and cars constituting the consumptive
evidence. Employers also receive faster rates of work from part-
time women. They need to compensate for high levels of absenteeism
which can average 14 per cent. The trend of taking more days off
may well have begun with this part of the workforce but it has
spread to male colleagues in the same factories as well as to other
workers too. The acceptance by employees of this rate may partly
derive from the tendency for the employees to recruit themselves and

then each other. The social bonds of family, street, neighbourhood and village have taken a lot of strain out of transport and training arrangements. The workpeople make do themselves, attempt to incorporate co-operation in work tasks and teach each other techniques.

All employers benefit from the workpeople's arrangements on their behalf. Employers moved into new buildings which were neither damp nor cramped. The product did not appear to be as dangerous as coal and steel even though many work with unhealthy substances as a matter of course. Steelworkers attract industrialists; as do their wives who usually often work without the job chafing them. Steelworkers' families avoid contact with 'the masters' and yet maintain an interest in similar sports and pastimes. Thus the new 'employers', including manager-directors, could meet their workers at the points of co-operation - they could join the clubs.

No picture is complete without its tensions and the remarkable tension is that each new employer 'created' full employment. In reality there was a scarcity of labour which could have been influential in determining wage rates. There was certainly a tendency to 'poach' and the nationalized industries lost a steady stream of fitters, electricians, older and reliable process workers. Messages had to be transmitted about these rates and scarcities. It was no disadvantage to keep rates down and the regional premiums inflated the 'real pay' to £20 to £25 a week until the early 1970s. There was also a very real conflict over young strong men - that is, until the coal mines closed. Even now there is a need to get young strong men early enough in order to extract both loyalty *and* hard work.

As Wenger shows elsewhere in this volume there is no traditional means of incorporating English males in parts of Wales. The many clubhouses built during the 1960s did more than encourage sport, and there are clear links through clubs with the interpenetrating Independent Baptist Churches (Chapels) as they interpenetrate with the Masonic Orders.

In sum the stage was set for particular dramas. Local control was all but lost and yet it was subsequently regained. While a large part of the regional community was run from London and other capitals of the world, the concern 'within' was to incorporate or exclude newcomers. The rugby clubs' relevance was unnecessarily exaggerated by always extending an invitation to become a Vice-President and to use the private bar after the home matches. Some 'industrialists', however, decline whilst others prefer a local squire style. Incorporation always brings compromise but rarely more so when polite refusals are interpreted as a bid to increase the stakes.

In time the pre-war industrialists were forced closer to their employees; their influence contracted from being region-wide to the pull upon immediate employees. This produced a head count and those employers who had more employees were more prestigeous and yet this form of distribution of honour was challenged if the employer did not live up to it in the customary manner, that is, if they were unwilling to be patrons. No doubt the 1950s was the most confusing decade since the 1880s. Yet it is still difficult to generalise even within the region itself. What strikes the observer is the *difference* between recipients of regional aid. It

is only recently that similarities have been detectable as their
different histories have come close to convergence. Only since the
late 1960s, that is, have all the newer industries been so open to
take-over bids. Only recently has the merit of being located in
the region been so openly in question.

In order to illustrate some of the preceding points I would like
to consider the following case studies.

A musical instrument maker

Mr H. Gallowsky had begun his business in northern London and
became a director of his own company in the early 1920s. He later
moved a few miles to larger premises in the same area. His financial
support came from the Liverpool timber merchants who supplied his
materials. The articles of association seem to suggest that he had
actually begun in the footwear trade and that it's unlikely that he
ever did all the things which the Company was established to do.
Though they may be too detailed for a balance with the rest of this
essay, they are reproduced here in full to give the flavour of
small companies formed by individuals to give themselves enough
latitude to survive in business.(1)

'The Objects for which the Company is established are' -
(a) To carry on in such place or places in the United Kingdom or
    abroad as may be determined by the Directors of the Company
    the businesses of Manufacturers, Tuners, Repairers, Importers,
    Exporters, Factors, Hirers and Wholesale and Retail Dealers
    of and in Pianolas, Gramophones, Gramophone Records and
    Needles, Cuckoo, Musical, Chiming and other Clocks and Time-
    keeping Instruments, Electrical and Musical Motor and other
    Horns, Sirens, and Signals, Wireless and other Electrical
    Telegraphical, Telephonic, and Television Instruments,
    Apparatus, and Equipment, and Manufacturers, Importers,
    Exporters, and Dealers of and in Parts, whether assembled
    or partially assembled or otherwise, of the same; to carry
    on the business of Public and Private Entertainers,
    Proprietors of Concert and Musical Halls, and Dealers in all
    kinds of Real and Personal Property; and to buy, sell,
    manipulate, manufacture, and deal, both wholesale and retail
    in commodities of all kinds which can be conveniently dealt
    in or manufactured by the Company.
(b) To carry on the business or businesses as boot and shoe
    dealers, manufacturers and designers of heels, soles and
    components of all kinds, in leather, wood, rubber, plastic
    or any other materials that the Company shall consider suit-
    able for the footwear industry and footwear of all kinds
    whatsoever, leather, rubber and plastic merchants, dealers
    in manufactured woodwork of every description, leather
    dressers, tanners, curriers, dyers and dealers in hides and
    skins.
(c) To manufacture, buy, sell, win, gain, import, export, deal in,
    repair, maintain and prepare for market, boots, shoes and
    their components, footwear of every sort, kind and descrip-
    tion, lasts, boot-stretchers, boot-jacks, shapes, patterns,

portmanteaux, bags, trunks, dressing cases and other
travelling and luggage receptacles, saddlery and harness of
all descriptions; leather and other polishes, pastes, pre-
servatives and dyes, and all component parts of and
accessories to any such articles and things as aforesaid,
and all such further articles and things as can or may
conveniently be used for the manufacture of or in connection
with any such articles and things aforesaid, and generally
all commodities of household, office or personal use, orna-
ment and consumption.

What concerns the region is, of course, the occupancy of a purpose-
built brick factory on Trostre Road during August 1948. Mr Gallowsky
moved down with relatives and bought a house on the Gower, 30 miles
from Llanelli. They did not expect to become involved with the
locals. They may have had good advice in seeking a home on the
south side of Gower. However business did not 'go well' and there
were local rumours about 'going on the rocks'. There were illnesses
and deaths in the family. In less than eight years, Mr Gallowsky,
his wife and brother were all dead. A receiver took over for a
while until a buyer was found. The buyer was to be Mr A.E. Knight,
O.B.E., a director of Alfred Knight Ltd, Loughton, Essex. Alfred
Knight Limited have six associated companies as an expression of
Mr Knight's personality. In this case, however, two local men were
to run the firm and Mr Knight was to share his holdings equally
with four other directors; one American, one Canadian, one South
African and a property developer living in Kent.

From 1965 the pattern was to settle and run without disturbance.
Profits were to be a low average and taxation low. Turnover more
than doubled, and the low profit was retained, as the following
table illustrates.

Table 3.1 A musical instrument maker's profit and loss account

	1966	1968	1970	1972	1974
Turnover	237,446	370,114	504,043	475,189 (loss)	799,024
Profit	6,214	19,817	13,798	1,750 (credit)	41,952
Taxation	595	9,000	6,000	300	19,629

In 1968, a director's report was able to say:
The company's principal activity is the manufacture of piano
actions and keys. The average number of persons employed by the
company in each week in the year was 233. The aggregate remun-
eration paid in respect of those persons, excluding employers
State and other pension contributions was £169,171. Turnover
from exports in the year was £238,105.

During 1975 it was still possible for a local authority executive to say 'we don't know much about them'.

In brief the company has changed hands and is now working for
its customers with a 'British' professional chairman and two local

men in charge of day-to-day affairs. The machinery remains much as
it was and the factory supplies the valuable actions virtually at
cost. It is the low price of the actions that keeps the orders
steady. The customers take the profit of assembly and sale as well
as the advantage of cheap supply. Piano Actions Ltd is, therefore,
a 'cost-warehouse'. By 'cost-warehouse' is meant that all costs
are contained within; the same machinery, skilled employees,
suppliers and customers and that it produces at cost a commodity
which is already 'bought'. It functions as doubly profitable for
its foreign owners because they have a profit on their shares and a
better profit on the goods they sell as a result of shared ownership. The firm has not gone full cycle but rather has witnessed a
revolution involving a transition from being owned by its suppliers
to being part owned by its customers.

A fitted kitchen manufacturer

Whereas the instrument maker's firm was relocated there is no
record of the fitted kitchen firm having existing before May 1967.
Most of the private capital came from individuals - and especially
married couples living in Kent and Sussex. (Many of them living
in the same town.) From the very beginning the company affairs
are complicated because though the ordinary shares are widely
distributed the managing director holds 42,500 of them and his
brother - as financial director - held 2,250, whilst his wife was
secretary.
    Further the company was actually the selling organization of its
own manufacturing divisions which were also limited companies in
their own right:
 Kitchens Limited
 Bathrooms Limited
 Bedrooms Limited
 Home Improvements Limited
 Exporters and Importers Limited
 Gifts Limited.
    A Receiver and Manager was appointed in December 1969. The
receivership was terminated on the 20 February 1973. The Board of
Trade had made substantial loans. As itemized on the companies'
mortgage documents, they were £40,000 on the 22 September 1967;
£75,000 on the 4 February 1969; and a further £115,000 on the 22
November 1973. In addition investment grants averaged £30,000 per
year. The turnover of the firm was £2½ million a year with more
than 400 employees and an expansion to a brand new purpose-built
office block and factory. The managing director and his wife
became local celebrities whilst he became Vice-President of the
rugby club and benefactor of the works sports and social club. The
local radio regularly advertised their bargains in luxury kitchens.
The luxury became ever more luxurious; lines were continuously
changed; foreign markets were sought and the firm produced a dream
kitchen fit for an oil sheik.
    However local disbelief remained unchanged. The receivership was
a clear warning to many. Some delayed payment on their purchases
hoping to pay less. Others waited for the clearance lines of

discontinued ranges relying on inside knowledge of what price would be acceptable.   Then the firm would only take cash with orders. Delays in delivery occurred and customers discussed taking anything from the factory in lieu of payments made.   Their concern was not wholly justified as the firm was completely taken over by a case manufacturer from the Cardiff area in September 1976.

Local disbelief stands in contrast to the granting of regional aid.   The firm received £38,957 directly in 1973 and £46,282 in 1974.   On the 10 March 1975 there occurred a change of hands in London, the details of which are financially complicated.   A company called Pulverlodge Limited passed over 11,496 preference shares to Control Nominees Limited.   On the same day there was a transfer of Ordinary shares bringing their respective totals to 1,059,164 and 245,518.   Control Nominees Limited represent the interests of a major bank.   The other shareholders, those in the south east of England and the creditors with more than 1,000 shares who included major public corporations, were no longer in a position to influence policy after 1973 and they may have had little impact on discussions of directors' and employees' pay. Throughout the period the company was repaying loan capital.

The inflatable goods company

In 1891 Rubber Ltd was formed from India Rubber; it was to acquire estates for rubber supply and enter into the manufacture of goods. In November 1964 it began operations for the manufacture of Rubber Dinghies in Llanelli by which time there were at least six companies under its Head Office at Bradford-upon-Avon.   In the Llanelli region, the new branch Inflatables Ltd is to be found next to the fitted kitchen manufacturers in Dafen and at the Northdock.   The new branch took to local sense and pride.   By beginning with a small number of employees it has known complete informality and every person internalizing each other's seniority. During the period of operation there have been two very strong takeover rumours and on each occasion the managing director has felt it necessary to publish notices saying that he has heard nothing himself and that the share movements were without foundation.

The directors themselves are unaware of any individual holding more than 10 per cent of shares.   In the collection of nominees: insurance companies; individuals and companies, two of the second group are sizeable and yet together do not hold more than one part in eight of the total.   The directors are equally divided between five employees and five men with other directorees: a bank-nominee; a solicitor; a director of five companies; a director of Remploy and a director of a Waterworks.

Locally, the board are involved through their product as well as their employees.   Their employees are the wives of men at other factories and who attend their husbands' clubs.   Llanelli rugby club is patronized.   The product services the yachting community and costs a lot less than its price.   The product, being to a high quality, needs loyalty; hard work and a good company image.   For the year ending most years the Inflatables Division reported -

'Turnover increased, profit improved and exports, mostly to the US accounted for half of the turnover'.

It may be guessed that this account is concerned with criticizing the companies and this is partly true. Another part is to begin to work out the types of receivers of regional aid. R. Morley (1975; 159-82) reports that in a survey of 117 employers (employing more than 50,000 workers in the northern region), two-thirds of them would not have entertained their investment plans if there had been no regional aid at all. It is true that people have been found or 'given work'. It is also true that employers have greatly benefited already. But it is not possible to generalize from a case-study and gross comparisons can only follow turbulent details, and too little effort has been made to enable comparisons to be made. Two further companies complete my list but they do not give all the 'types', nor is it the concern of this paper to do so.

The multi-national company

Year	Company	Activity
1954	(G.B.) Limited Civil Engineering	Shaft-sinking
1958	Engineering Limited	Machine maintenance
1971	(G.B.) Limited	Glass-fibre and concrete products
1972	(G.B.) Limited	Compressed Anthracite Plant

This company has also acquired:
Plastics Ltd, which arrived in August 1973; Old Castle Tin Works and the Bury Box Works as part of its vast civil engineering activity which includes joinery and roads as well as buildings. Thyssen Ltd is so big that I expect that from most points in the company it stretches out of sight above and below.
   The company is a wholly owned subsidiary of Schachtban G.mbh. and the 'Ultimate Holding Company' is Vermuegens Verwaltunng G.mbh.
   Five other companies are direct subsidiaries including an insurance brokerage. The Investment Grants have been paid and are spent as assets and periodically credited as income over a long period. Taxation is deferred as long as possible and less is set aside that is calculably due (£724,665 was due in March 1974; at a discount of 50 per cent £362,332 should be paid and a reserve of £100,000 was actually made). Corporation tax amounted then, as previously, to between £5,500 and £7,000. Thyssen Ltd was paying 30 times this sum a year in bank interest on two loans. Meanwhile the value of the assets 'on the books' had dropped to a third of its original £3,300,000. All these figures are made the more difficult to comprehend because of their size.
   The company was felt to own at least half of Bynea and run the valuable anthracite deep mine of Cynheidre as a going concern.

They undertook to sink shafts and to process dust from the wash-
eries. People in Bynea were not enthusiastic about the dust but
their council was enthusiastic about giving maintenance contracts
to the firm as were, in fact, all three councils; the community,
district and county. Thyssen Ltd then sub-contracted relatively
small parts of the work to old-established local firms who, in
turn, assumed some of the responsibility. Most of the jobs were
therefore government contracts - be they nationalized industry or
local authority - with few serious competitors and a large margin
for expertise. In 1974, Mining Civil Engineering, Tunnelling,
Building and Electrical Contracting accounted for 72.15 per cent
of the firm's turnover. Turnover itself was 10¼ million pounds.
For those within the region being German meant that at least the
company was not English, further, the English squirearchy style
its directors preferred made understanding wishes easier. The
directors wanted to live in grand style with parkland homes and
indoor swimming pools; to be the biggest patron of favoured
events. Directors became Presidents of Bynea Rugby Club and
Cycling Club and the Kidwelly Horticultural Society. Thyssen Ltd
were reputed to pay well and may have done so. The hours they
demanded were exacting and they needed an inexhaustible supply of
fit young men.

Working alongside Councils' and Boards' employees produced a
swift and secure superiority. There were keyworkers housed in
caravan sites and provided for in departmental stores and
delicatessen. There was always a reminder of everything being
German and what can only be described as the fear of steel; the
metallic quality to speech. For Welshmen this meant bearing with
the lovelessness of hard men. Thyssen Ltd was quickly established
as *the* major private industry and some sort of homage was due.

Thyssen Ltd had sited its British Headquarters in Llanelli.
Its effect on local expenditure was almost incidental except in
magnitude. The local contracts could not be very important since
they only amounted to a small fraction of the total turnover. The
fraction of local expenditure was very much higher of course but
not enough to be more than an important customer. As so often
occurs a comparison of the turnover of the firm with that of the
District or County Council made the members of the latter feel
quite insignificant. Meanwhile Thyssen Ltd credited its development grants; deferred tax payments, exported good and profits to
the parent company and repaid British bank loans. A National Bank
held most of the mortgages on property as with every other company
discussed. The one consistent group to gain has been the major
banks whose loans have been steadfastly repaid.

DISCUSSION

By 1973 one-third of the region's employment was in post-Second
World War industries. Without the intervention of regional aid,
therefore, the region would have had approximately 9,000 fewer
jobs and would have been almost entirely under State or Council
ownership.

The implications of these observations are complicated. First,

regional aid is a set of subsidies to bring work in whilst there
are also subsidies called the employment transfer scheme which help
workers leave. Not all the effort, therefore, is directed *against*
depopulation. Second, regional aid's prime cause may have been
the closure of basic industries. Much of this change has taken
place, now the problem includes coping with the short-time and
redundancies in firms who have and are receiving aid. So many of
these firms cater for the quality, consumer market. They are
needed less than are the primary industries which they helped to
replace. Third, the emphasis upon community is altering to that
of region. The era is making it necessary to consider work and
industry rather than culture as the unifying factor. Rather than
a sense of identity being fragile there is a sense of urgency to
determine what happens from within.

Obviously I am arguing for regional development rights to be
devoted to the regions to whom they apply. However, I am also
arguing that the criteria of community, at least as detailed here,
may reach a 'saturation point'. That in addition to their defensive tone they may break when there are:

1 Too many strangers to properly incorporate.
2 Too many pieces of the past destroyed particularly by the
   State or Councils who can always resort to compulsion.
3 Too many trivial jobs for the community to have an industrial
   base.

Taking these observations in turn we find that:

1 The working class, who give their Labour MP such a huge
   majority, are now often working as husband-and-wife teams.
   The middle class is new and special; local clerks have become
   managers, local foremen have become managers and white-collar
   work is clean, salaried and respectable. What makes the
   white-collar workers special is their political activity.
   When they choose to be active they favour Welsh Nationalism in
   distinction to the Liberalism of the old and professional
   middle class, and the Labour Party affiliations of teachers.
   The tiers of new employers, of course, remain out of politics
   and remain Conservative; their links with the country rather
   than the region then become clear. A few 'old masters'
   remain. The class structure has developed though it has not
   changed. Outside class in the formal sense are the artisans;
   the self-employed tradesmen and the farmers. Farmers have
   their standing in village life and through the chapels. Artisans very rarely develop as employers, not being eligible for
   grant-aid and finding tax laws prohibitive. They have benefited from the era as the region itself has benefited, selling
   land, produce and services.
   Strangers can be incorporated in this expanded class structure.
   Incorporation still to a large extent means speaking Welsh.
   It also means acceptance of the forms of inter-class relations.
   At this point there is tension because some English people can
   be more militant and both useful and embarassing.
2 Just at a time when some determination is needed to sort out
   the relations between parts of the State apparatus there is a
   feeling running from distrust to disgust. Within the regions
   there are nationalized industries working in opposition to one

another. Coal prices force power stations to close, and the
closure of power stations is followed by the closure of the
mines that served them. Rail freight costs put goods on the
roads and compel a disproportionate expenditure on their construction across difficult terrain. To take a trivial example;
trivial to all those not directly affected that is; all the
halts on the Central Wales Railway in the Llanelli region had
their station buildings destroyed as a rate reduction exercise.
However, an equally pressing problem is the need for initiatives to process resources and sell products rather than raw
materials and energy on low tariffs. The region, like many
others, may come to depend upon capital intensive industry,
upon a high level of skill being applied to a costly material.
The contrast can be made between 16 ton sheet coils and 1
ounce watches perhaps. The important fact is that the middle
range size of products and complexity is most suitable at
present because it reintegrates craftsmen 'in industry' and
artisans who are 'self-employed'.

It may well be that realization of the responsibilities of
collective ownership are more readily recognizable at the
regional level. So, too, the change in occupational structure
may be apparent earlier. 'Basic' industries are the hub of
craft training. Development industries very rarely train in
the same proportions. They are usually 'supplied' by the basic
industries. The era may be part of a process of 'deskilling'
to put it bluntly and thereby attract fewer 'industrialists'
in any case. The 'trivialization' of the occupational structure is a cause for concern for those now in the region.

3   But what of the recently arrived industries? No one expects
further great waves of investment. The recent arrivals will
have to be lived with and perhaps new conditions will have to
be created.

From a regional point of view these industries are balanced
unfavourably towards being a cost centre. Products are made
at a profit but the profit is taken at 'the point of sale'
rather than at the factory. In some cases reinvestment is
negligible and so the advantages of their machinery depend
more on material, labour and transport costs. After a take
over or two the question can be asked 'Well why are we making
it *down there*?' by worried employers.

Regions may be caught in a cleft stick by people whom they
have hardly had enough time to get to know. There are already
culprits. Some 'industrialists' seem more concerned with their
aid payments than with production. Others have collected
their subsidies and very quickly disappeared.

My final observation, therefore, concerns regional determination.
The central priorities for subsidy have been summarized by Byatt
(1976; 75): 'The Treasury has tended to adopt ... a "demand
effect" approach.... Such as maintains an appropriate internal
pressure of demand and balance of payments.' It is this 'approach'
that enables regional aid to run alongside the transfer scheme and
not be incompatible with it (the scheme allows a worker or manager
with earnings below a limit to leave his home and family for up to
two years with grants towards lodgings, 6 weekly returns home,

removal and legal costs on moving to this place of work). It
would take another essay to outline what approach could or should
come from within a region. It may be sufficient just to say that
one would expect them to be different. To put the argument
briefly regional aid has played a large part in straining 'the
community'. It now constrains the development of a regional
identity that would change the way money is spent or allowed to
be made.

NOTE

1 This information derives from the Articles of Association as
   deposited at Company House, City Road, London.

REFERENCES

BYATT, I.C.R. (1976), A discussant's comment, in Alan Whiting (ed.),
'The Economics of Industrial Subsidies', Proceedings of a confer-
ence on the economics of industrial subsidies held at the Civil
Service College, Sunningdale, 1975, HMSO, London, pp.75-6.
FLETCHER, C. (forthcoming), 'Tinplate Town', Routledge & Kegan
Paul, London.
HARRIS, C.C. (1969), 'The Family: An Introduction', George Allen &
Unwin, London.
MORLEY, R. (1975), Unemployment, Profits, Share and Regional
Policy, in Alan Whiting (ed.), 'The Economics of Industrial
Subsidies', Proceedings of a conference on the economics of
industrial subsidies held at the Civil Service College, Sunningdale,
1975, HMSO, London, pp.159-82.

Chapter 4

ATTITUDES TOWARDS SECOND HOMES IN RURAL WALES

Chris Bollom

The past decade or so has seen a considerable upsurge of interest at many levels in the social and economic consequences of second home ownership in receiving areas. This is especially true of north Wales where fears of these consequences have been linked with a general concern over the social and economic decline which has been a feature of much of the area since the last war, and with growing fears of the state of the Welsh language and the gradual erosion of what have been called the 'Welsh Way of Life' (Tuck, 1973:2) and the 'Calvinist Sunday' (Jacobs, 1972:2). A number of County Council Planning Departments have gone into print in this respect, notably those of the old counties of Denbigh in Clwyd (Jacobs, 1972), and Merioneth (Tuck, 1973) and Caernarfon (Pyne, 1972) in Gwynedd. Their reports have primarily examined the costs and benefits of second home ownership in economic terms and their findings have been related to both central and local government policy.

It would be fair to say that when second home ownership has been examined in terms of social factors it has been concluded that rather than being the cause second homes are the symptom of social and economic decline. The commonly held view of the process involved has recognized an original out-movement of population from an area in response to a lack of employment opportunities following the decline of a traditional industry such as slate quarrying or the amalgamation of farm holdings, and the in-movement of a predominantly English-speaking population, employed elsewhere, who purchase or rent a second property primarily for leisure purposes and, in the first instances at least, at a fairly low price. Admitting an element of caricature in its description a national survey of second home ownership (Downing and Dower, 1973:30) has expressed the view that much concern over second homes comes from the natural instinct of the human group to fear and feel threatened by the incursion of aliens into that group, and that a low income, conservative farming group will react to wealthy liberal or agnostic town dwellers who are buying houses where generations of farmers have lived and are seeking to ease themselves into the community, with the feeling that local traditions may be eroded by the incomers' influence.

As the density of second homes in an area increases the cultural
shock which may accompany the social invasion may turn to hostility,
and increasingly so where examples of the inability of native
people to compete in the housing market are identified. The
Denbighshire Report (Jacobs, 1972:42) identifies a level of ownership of 12 per cent or more dwellings as the saturation point for
parishes in the county, a density above which, perhaps, social
problems will become more acute. An increasingly dissatisfying
and frustrating situation for the remaining native population may
be perpetuated, containing within itself the seeds of their wish
to leave for both economic and social reasons, and as the proportion of second homes in the local housing stock increases and the
all-year-round population declines the demise of local services
and institutions serving a declining number of people will further
reinforce the chain of events. We may now regard second homes
more as a complication of the original 'disease' of economic decline
than merely a symptom of it. Given the expected rise in real
incomes and an associated increase in leisure time, most authorities
have predicted that there will be an increase in the number of
properties used as second homes, especially in the more scenic and
environmentally pleasing areas of rural Wales.

The main concern of the present study was to ascertain whether
such variables as the density and scatter of second homes in
particular areas exert a uniform effect on the reactions of native
people to the phenomenon of second home ownership. Two quite
closely related hypotheses were formulated primarily concerning
the density of second home ownership as a percentage of the housing
stock, namely:

1 That the attitudes of native people towards second homes will
   be less favourable and that hostility between local people and
   second home owners will be greater in those areas where this
   density is greatest.
2 That polarization between local people and second home incomers
   will be greater (whether expressed in class or ethnic terms) in
   those areas where this density is greatest, and that in these
   areas too there will be a greater perception of differences and
   distinctions based on socio-economic or ethnic criteria.

The second hypothesis derives partly from the work of Raymond
Pahl (1970) in the commuter villages of south-east England. He
suggests that the middle-class people entered rural areas in search
of a meaningful community and by their very presence help to destroy
whatever community was there, and he argues that their presence
makes the native working-class people aware of national class
divisions thus polarizing local society. Bell and Newby (1975)
contend that problems arise with the stereotyped expectations of
what the village should consist of, which are held by the newcomers.
They hold an idealized view of the 'village in the mind', and their
paternalism demands a deferential response from the local native
people which is frequently withheld as they lack traditional
authority. The local people respond by excluding the immigrants
as strangers and foreigners and interaction between the two groups
is restricted to symbolic occasions. Pahl sees the changeover from
the hierarchical social structure which was functionally suited to
the village as a community to what now appears to be a polarized

two-class division as possibly the chief cause of working-class
resentment. In this context, too, in a recent paper in which they
question whether total status was indeed absent from the Aberporth
studied by David Jenkins (1960), Day and Fitton (1975) argue that
the notion of Buchedd has gained so wide a currency that the
absence of clear Bucheddau has been taken as prima facie evidence
of social change, and they quote a study of Bow Street, Cardiganshire, by Gareth Lewis (1970:157) where the author states that a
'Welsh rural community in transition is one in which the traditional
Buchedd system is being replaced by newer socio-economic values.'

In her study of a north Wales village, Isabel Emmett (1964:13)
argues that Buchedd groups have been merged as a result of the
development of a Welsh consciousness in response to the pressures
of anglicization. She says that 'The frequent presence of English
visitors ... makes Llan people very aware of their Welshness. In
the presence of the enemy, Welshness is the primary value ... old
schizms become unimportant', and argues that 'The English take the
place of the upper, upper-middle or ruling class, and nationalism
is the dress in which class antagonism is expressed' (Emmett,
1964:23).

It was hoped that we would be able to relate perceptions of
class and ethnic polarization to the density of second homes in
particular areas, whilst viewing the second home phenomenon as a
symptom if not a complication of depopulation and the associated
social malaise it is reasonable to assume that where the density
of second homes is high the vitality of the in-group will be low
and that there will be a tendency for scapegoating, with the
second home owners being blamed for the community decline, thereby
incurring the hostility of native residents.

Five villages in north Wales were investigated - Penmachno,
Cwm Penmachno, Croesor and Rhiw in Gwynedd, and Llansannan in
Clwyd. The first three are old slate-quarrying villages, the
Croesor quarries having closed in the 1930s and those in Penmachno
and Cwm somewhat more recently, whilst Rhiw and Llansannan are in
historically agricultural areas. Five localities were chosen for
purposes of comparison and in the hope that it would be possible
to apply any findings more generally to other areas of north Wales
than would have been the case if one or two areas were examined in
depth, but both financial and temporal constraints restricted the
extent to which any particular village could be investigated in
detail. It was hoped to gain in width what was lost in depth.
Hostility was approached in terms of a recognized attitude
measuring technique, the Semantic Differential (Osgood, Suci and
Tannenbaum, 1957) which consists of a number of bi-polar adjectival
rating scales through which probability samples of the over-18
population in the five villages were asked to rate a number of
concepts. The test was scored on seven, seven-point rating scales
ranging from +3 to -3, (2) and Table 4.1 presents the mean attitude
scores obtained for six selected concepts, together with the
densities of second homes as a percentage of the housing stock in
the respective villages.

The table shows that all the concepts were rated most highly
and positively in Rhiw, and that here and in Penmachno both the
concepts 'Second Homes' and 'Second Home Owners' were rated

Table 4.1 Mean scores and standard deviations for selected concepts

Village	Second homes as % of housing stock	Second homes		Second home owners		Englishness	
		Mean score on scale -3 to +3	Standard deviation	Mean score on scale -3 to +3	Standard deviation	Mean score on scale -3 to +3	Standard deviation
Llansannan	8.8	-0.170	1.005	-0.051	1.153	0.236	0.871
Penmachno	23.4	0.260	0.901	0.250	0.825	0.107	0.728
Croesor	33.3	-0.130	1.343	-0.114	1.280	0.085	1.384
Cwm Penmachno	51.8	-0.010	0.709	0.330	0.732	0.131	0.709
Rhiw	52.7	0.873	1.061	1.253	0.995	0.682	0.749

Village	Second homes as % of housing stock	Welshness		The Welsh language		Local people	
		Mean score on scale -3 to +3	Standard deviation	Mean score on scale -3 to +3	Standard deviation	Mean score on scale -3 to +3	Standard deviation
Llansannan	8.8	1.480	0.791	1.769	0.659	1.419	0.560
Penmachno	23.4	1.274	0.770	1.434	0.711	0.897	0.692
Croesor	33.3	1.314	1.117	1.485	1.150	1.493	1.200
Cwm Penmachno	51.8	0.681	0.800	1.100	1.041	0.977	0.330
Rhiw	52.7	2.063	0.362	1.936	0.438	1.713	0.635

positively. In Cwm Penmachno 'Second Home Owners' were positively
rated. 'Englishness' was positively scored in all the villages.
In view of the publicity which has been given to rural Wales and in
view of the differing densities of ownership in the five villages
it was somewhat surprising to find that, with the exception of Rhiw
where they were rated positively, these concepts were rated so
neutrally on the positive-negative scale.

The concepts 'Welshness', 'The Welsh Language' and 'Local People'
were rated as expected uniformly more positively than 'Second Homes',
'Second Home Owners' and 'Englishness'.

In looking at the attitudes of native people we were concerned
to find whether a 'Structural anti' person could be located across
the five villages,(3) and in this respect we examined mainly such
factors as socio-economic grouping, chapel attendance, and whether
or not the native residents had been invited into the homes of second
home owners or had invited members of second home families into their
homes. If it is accepted that chapel membership is an example of
in-group vitality it was interesting that membership of and frequency
of attendance at chapel bore little congruence with either a favourable or unfavourable disposition towards second homes. Equally
objective socio-economic grouping did not appear to be a factor.
In this respect it must be said that in Cwm Penmachno, Croesor and
Rhiw only small numbers of people were interviewed which made
categorization in terms both of chapel membership and objective
class position somewhat difficult. However, because in all these
villages the native population is small and members of at least one
in two households occupied by native people were contacted, combined
with the fact that the objective class positions of native people
did not vary considerably, there is cause to be fairly confident in
the results obtained. As far as the frequency of visiting households is concerned the evidence was somewhat contradictory in that,
for example, in Penmachno twice as many people who felt that second
homes had unfavourable effects had never visited a second home
compared with those who felt that the effects were favourable, while
in Cwm Penmachno these proportions were almost reversed.

A number of secondary hypothese were tested concerning the mean
attitude scores obtained for certain concepts. Statistically the
concepts 'Second Homes' and 'Second Home Owners' were rated significantly more positively in Rhiw, the village with the greatest
density of second homes as a percentage of its housing stock, than
in all the other villages, whilst 'Second Homes' were also rated
significantly more positively in Penmachno than Llansannan, and
'Second Home Owners' more positively in Cwm Penmachno than in
Llansannan. The concept 'Englishness' was scored significantly more
positively in Rhiw than in Penmachno, Cwm Penmachno and Llansannan.
Interestingly correlations of the density of second homes in the
localities with the mean scores are positive with 'Second Homes',
'Second Home Owners', 'Englishness' and 'Local People' but negative
with 'Welshness' and 'The Welsh Language', whilst this impression
of ambiguity was reinforced when the mean scores for 'Second Home
Owners' and 'Englishness' were correlated with an index of ethnic
orientation, a proxy measure of which was obtained by averaging the
mean scores for 'Welshness' and 'The Welsh Language'. These correlations are shown in Tables 4.2a and 4.2b, and all are positive.

Table 4.2(a)   Correlations of density of second homes with mean
scores for selected concepts

Concept	r	r^2
Second homes	0.549	0.301
Second home owners	0.687	0.472
Englishness	0.424	0.180
Welshness	−0.028	0.043
Welsh language	−0.208	0.001

Table 4.2(b)   Correlations of ethnic orientation with mean scores
for selected concepts

Concept	r	r^2
Second homes	0.643	0.414
Second home owners	0.511	0.261
Englishness	0.574	0.330

With this prevailing pattern in mind it is interesting that
while there was a close correlation between the percentage of second
home owners known to native residents by name and address in each of
the villages with their density of ownership, the percentages of
native people who had been invited into more than two second homes
were low (98 per cent in Llansannan, 89 per cent in Penmachno, 84
per cent in Croesor, 77 per cent in Cwm Penmachno and 69 per cent
in Rhiw had not), as were the percentages who had invited members
of more than two second home families into their own homes (98 per
cent in Llansannan, 89 per cent in Penmachno, 77 per cent in Croesor
and Cwm Penmachno and 31 per cent in Rhiw had not). This illustrates
the likelihood that people become identified with properties in that
whilst Mr and Mrs Smith may not be identified as second home owners
per se, local people will still be aware that a particular property
is no longer occupied by a native person. It also illustrates that
whilst local people may know of second home owners this does not
necessarily imply interaction with them.

Although specific data were not collected conversations with
local people and with second home owners who were contacted revealed
that second home owner membership of local voluntary organizations
was very limited. The two factors which were commented on in this
respect were that some of the organizations, in fact the majority,
only conduct their activities through the medium of the Welsh
language, and that some only do so in the winter months, when somewhat less attention in agricultural areas has to be paid to the land
and when second home owners' visits to their properties are of
shorter duration and are less frequent. In Llansannan, Penmachno,
Cwm Penmachno and Croesor Welsh is certainly the language of the
chapels, although a prominent member of the church in Penmachno

opined that 'the church itself is better off because it is the
English who form the core of the congregation'. Whether English
people do not attend some organizations because services and meetings
are held in Welsh or whether they are held in Welsh because English
people do not attend is somewhat problematic, but it is possible
that second home owners do not acknowledge a commitment to their
second home area which is sufficient to facilitate membership of
those organizations which do not conduct their activities in English,
or sufficient to facilitate the setting up of their own. Nevertheless, because selective association in voluntary organizations is
one of the most formalized and public ways in which status differentiation can be channelled and maintained, and because it is one way
which the interaction of local residents and second home owners and
the participation of the latter in the community can be fostered,
the consequences of membership and non-membership of such organizations will be important variables affecting whether they do indeed
participate in their second home areas.

     In relation to our second hypothesis we wanted to discover the
extent of local people's awareness of groups in their environment,
which were examined, especially in the light of the low level of
organizational membership among second homers, both to find out
whether a second home owner/local people divide was apparent and to
understand more fully other types of groupings within the localities
concerned. It was necessary to ascertain people's images of their
villages in terms of their perceptions of lines of social exclusion,
of social groupings and social class divisions. Although these
images will often be imprecise they can be shared by people of
similar background in particular areas. Table 4.3 indicates those
social groupings which were identified by people in more than one
area.

     Clearly the English/Welsh divide received most comment, and
somewhat more so in those areas of greater second home density, but
the major feature of the table is the high percentage of people who
were unable or unwilling to identify groups in their localities.
The main reasons given in all the villages for this absence of
social groupings were the similar and unified nature of the population and the fact that everyone mixes. This is somewhat at variance
with the previous evidence of low second home owner membership of
local voluntary organizations, and that of the low incidence of
house visiting between second home owners and native people. In
response to another question, 31 per cent in Cwm Penmachno, 23 per
cent in Croesor and Rhiw, 7 per cent in Penmachno and 6 per cent in
Llansannan identified second home owners and English incomers in
general as the type of people who are socially isolated in their
villages. Amongst those who felt this way the Welsh language was
seen as an important contributory factor to this isolation, but
these views were held by a minority of people. This feeling of the
social isolation of the incomers was somewhat greater again in those
areas of greater density second home ownership, but it is illuminating that 80 per cent in Penmachno, 70 per cent in Cwm Penmachno,
Rhiw and Llansannan, and 46 per cent in Croesor felt that there were
no types of people in their villages who did not mix.

     Table 4.4 shows local people's perceptions of social class in
their areas which were akin to the sociological sense of class. A

Table 4.3 Perceptions of social groupings

	Llansannan (8.8%)	Penmachno (23.4%)	Croesor (33.3%)	Cwm Penmachno (51.8%)	Rhiw (52.7%)
English people/ Welsh people	3.8%	14.8%	15.4%	15.4%	23.1%
Broadminded people/ traditional people	3.8%	-	15.4%	-	-
Chapel people/ pub people	1.9%	3.7%	7.7%	-	-
Young people/ old people	1.9%	7.4%	7.7%	-	-
No groups	50.8%	37.1%	30.7%	23.1%	76.9%
Don't knows	13.1%	37.1%	23.1%	61.5%	-

Table 4.4 Perceptions of social class

	Llansannan (8.8%)	Penmachno (23.4%)	Croesor (33.3%)	Cwm Penmachno (51.8%)	Rhiw (52.7%)
Middle/working	5.7%	3.7%	15.4%	-	15.4%
Professional/ordinary	1.9%	7.4%	15.4%	-	-
Richer incomers/ natives	-	3.7%	-	-	-
No classes	79.1%	55.6%	53.8%	84.6%	84.6%
Don't knows	1.9%	25.9%	7.7%	-	-

number of people found difficulty in using the vocabulary of class
(the only terms in Welsh for upper, middle, working and lower class
are literal translations from the English), but interestingly the
villages with the highest densities of second homes, Rhiw and Cwm
Penmachno, did not differ noticeably in this respect from the others,
and in fact the percentages of local people who were unable or
unwilling to identify social classes were slightly higher in these
villages. It may have been expected that in areas of high density
ownership the presence of people from 'outside', people with
experience of social class and to some extent bringing it in with
them, might have engendered more clear-cut perceptions of social
class divisions, but this does not seem to be the case. The primary
reason given by people in every village for this absence, as in the
case of social groups, was the homogeneous nature of the village
concerned. Only in Penmachno were 'richer incomers' identified as
a class apart from the 'ordinary' native people.

In general, then, where an incomer/native divide was apparent it
was couched in ethnic rather than class terms, although such a
division was identified by minorities of people. The geographical
separation of second home properties from those still occupied by
all-year-round residents has not occurred in the five villages to
the extent that it has often done between properties occupied by
incomers and native residents in some of the commuter villages of
south-east England and coupled with the fact that second home owners
so often are not conspicuously consumptive this may partly explain
the low incidence of class perception on the part of native people.
Equally there is no permanent population about which native people
can come to conclusions.

Finally in relation to people's images of their villages, it is
interesting to note that while very few people in Llansannan, Croesor
and Rhiw said that they had ever considered moving away from their
villages, majorities of those interviewed in Penmachno and Cwm
Penmachno said that they had given 'serious thought' to the possibility of leaving. While this cannot be directly related to the
previous discussion it is possible that we may see a further out-
movement of population from the former as yet lesser affected
village.

The data collected did not enable a positive acceptance of the
hypotheses with which we started. To the extent that the Semantic
Differential test successfully measured attitudes it could not be
said that hostility towards second homes and their owners was
greater in areas of greater density ownership. Equally people did
not exhibit a significantly greater tendency to talk of polarized
divisions, whether expressed in ethnic or class terms, in these
areas. It was the generally low level of hostility in all five
villages, however, which surprised us most.

In this respect it is interesting to note the responses to a
'social distance' question - where respondents were asked whether
they would have an objection to a second home being sited in a
number of areas - which can be seen in Table 4.5. The majority in
all the villages, except in Croesor where opinions were equally
split, said that they would have nothing against anyone owning a
second home in England, but over 30 per cent of respondents in all
villages except Rhiw where the figure reached 70 per cent said that

Table 4.5   Would you have an objection to a second home being
            sited in?

Area	Reply	Penmachno %	Cwm %	Croesor %	Rhiw %	Llansannan %
England	Yes	7.4		46.15	15.4	20.7
	No	92.6	100.0	46.15	76.9	79.3
	Don't know			7.7*	7.7**	
South Wales	Yes	29.6	46.1	53.9	15.4	38.0
	No	70.4	53.9	38.4	76.9	62.0
	Don't know			7.7*	7.7**	
Outside county	Yes	37.0	53.9	53.9	15.4	41.5
	No	63.0	46.1	38.4	76.9	58.5
	Don't know			7.7*	7.7**	
Outside area	Yes	37.0	53.9	61.5	15.4	43.4
	No	63.0	46.1	30.8	76.9	56.6
	Don't know			7.7*	7.7**	
In village	Yes	51.9	53.9	61.5	15.4	52.8
	No	48.1	46.1	30.8	76.9	47.2
	Don't know			7.7*	7.7**	
Next door	Yes	59.3	61.5	61.5	23.1	62.3
	No	40.7	38.5	30.8	69.2	37.7
	Don't know			7.7*	7.7**	

 * Depending on the housing shortage.
** Depending on whether it was occupied all the year round.

they would have no objection either to living next door to a property which was used as a second home. Nevertheless the most clear-
cut changes in people's opinions occur in Penmachno, Cwm Penmachno
and Llansannan during the move from England to Wales, whilst the
change during the move from England to the village is readily
apparent in all the villages except Rhiw and this indicates that
there may be a greater negative reaction towards second homes on
this level than towards second homes in the village situation per
se. It might be easier to express objection to the abstract
phenomenon than to the personal aspect of the phenomenon.
     Two considerations suggest themselves in this respect. Pahl
(1970) suggests that part of the basis of a local village community
was the sharing of the deprivations due to the isolation of country

life and the sharing of the limited world of the families within the village. To a large extent the community is based on a feeling of 'getting on' and for this to survive the need exists for people to reinforce the norms associated with it. Second homes may generate a general feeling of hostility in the abstract but when they are personalized native people may react locally in that they may be embarrassed to be openly hostile towards second home owners. Yet they may not accept them positively unless they are seen to be accepting the norms and values of the locality. Second home owners may not really be prepared to acknowledge this commitment in terms of, say, learning Welsh, but nor are they committed to values which are in direct conflict with that of 'getting on'. They are content to play a minor role, not seeking conflict. Within the locality situation, people are concerned with 'getting on' because this is what the village was and is about.

Closely related to this line of thinking is the view that a geographical approach in terms of the density and scatter of second homes in particular areas may not be a particularly rewarding one. Some macro-variables may be countered by, for example, particular instances of hardship in second home affected areas. Factors peculiar to a particular area may importantly influence the reactions of native people towards second homes and their owners, factors which, despite other similarities between areas, may not be in evidence elsewhere and they may serve to concentrate attention on particular effects of social change in particular areas.

Consequently, the present study may best serve a heuristic purpose in that hypotheses other than those with which we began are suggested, hypotheses more of a micro-nature which can best be approached in these terms. If it is considered that there is a need to delve deeper into the factors influencing hostility and conflict and the sources of their generation in second home receiving areas, and the reactions of native people to the social change brought about by second home ownership, then for this to be achieved it is likely that width will have to be sacrificed in favour of depth.

NOTES

1 The study to which this paper refers was commissioned by the Social Science Committee of the Board of Celtic Studies of the University of Wales and was co-financed by the Social Science Research Council. A more detailed report can be found in Bollom (1978).
2 The Semantic differential is a technique for the refined measurement of semantic connotations and its purpose is to evaluate the meaning of given terms or concepts to individuals or groups of individuals. When responses to concepts have been repeatedly factor-analysed three predominant factors, the evaluative factor, the activity factor and the potency factor, have been extracted. Of these the evaluative factor, which essentially measures like and dislike, has been found to be dominant. In the present study the Semantic Differential test was compiled using seven, seven-point scales selected as having high evaluative loadings from lists presented by Osgood et al. (1957).

3 It may seem rather naive to have omitted such factors as, say, age, sex, education, interests, but in view of our expressed preoccupation with examining attitudes in relation to the densities of second home ownership in the villages, this was something of a secondary concern.
4 Chapel here refers to non-conformist churches, whilst church refers to the Church of England in Wales.

REFERENCES

BELL, C. and NEWBY, H. (1975), The Sources of Variation in Agricultural Workers' Images of Society, in Bulmer, M. (ed.), 'Working Class Images of Society', Routledge & Kegan Paul, London, pp.83-98.
BOLLOM, C. (1978), 'Attitudes and Second Homes in Rural Wales', University of Wales Press, Cardiff.
DAY, G. and FITTON, M. (1975), Religion and Social Status in Rural Wales; 'Buchedd' and its Lessons for Concepts of Stratification in Community Studies, 'Sociological Review', vol.23, no.4, November, pp.867-91.
DOWNING, P. and DOWER, M. (1973), 'Second Homes in England and Wales', Publication No.7, Dartington Amenity Research Trust.
EMMETT, I. (1964), 'A North Wales Village', Routledge & Kegan Paul, London.
JACOBS, C.A.J. (1972), 'Second Homes in Denbighshire', Research Report No.3, Denbighshire County Planning Office, Mold.
JENKINS, D. (1960), Aberporth: A Study of a Coastal Village in South Cardiganshire, in Davies, E. and Rees, A.D. (eds), 'Welsh Rural Communities', University of Wales Press, Cardiff, pp.1-63.
LEWIS, G. (1970), A Welsh Rural Community in Transition, 'Sociologica Ruralis', vol.10, 1970, pp.143-62.
OSGOOD, C.E., SUCI, G.J. and TANNENBAUM, P.H. (1957), 'The Measurement of Meaning', University of Illinois Press, Urbana, Illinois.
PAHL, R.E. (1970), 'Whose City?', Longman, London.
PYNE, C.B. (1972), 'Second Homes', Caernarfonshire County Planning Department, Caernarfon.
TUCK, C.J. (1973), 'Second Homes', Merioneth Structure Plan, Subject Report 17, Merioneth County Planning Office, Dolgellau.

Chapter 5

THE PROVISION OF SOCIAL SERVICES IN RURAL AREAS

Gordon Grant

INTRODUCTION

Urban attitudes and theories concerning social work and social
administration today dominate the social services scene probably
more than at any time in the past. Central Government circulars
(Welsh Office, 1973), expensive research and intelligence activity
(Home Office Community Development Projects) and organisation
theory related to the development of social services all have an
extremely strong urban bias. Unlike some countries such as Canada
where major rural development plans have been drawn up by national,
regional and local government agencies the UK appears to be without
any kind of master strategy for social, economic or industrial
development in rural areas. The remainder of this paper will
therefore be primarily concerned to test the relevance of existing
policies and provisions concerning the personal social services to
the needs of rural areas. Empirical evidence is drawn from experience in Gwynedd, North Wales, particularly, and some comparisons
are drawn with relevant developments elsewhere.

SOCIAL INDICATORS AND SOCIAL NEEDS

In attempting to provide a more rational basis for the development
of resource allocation policies in the social welfare field both
central and local government agencies have increasingly turned to
the development of social need indicators. Though this process is
still in its infancy there are obvious lessons to be learnt in the
planning of social services, particularly in rural areas. Paradoxically large, sparsely populated areas have not yet been subjected
to the same amount of research as have inner city areas perhaps in
the misdirected belief that they do not possess social problems
meriting close study. In the last year or two emerging reports
(Monmouthshire County Council, 1974; Norfolk County Council, 1976;
Winrow and Priestley, 1976), have at last indicated that rural areas
do in fact possess varied and complex social problems whose resolution is not as straightforward as it may seem. This can be shown
for example in the case of Meirionnydd, the most sparsely populated

of the five districts in the County of Gwynedd.

Following a factor analysis of 34 census and non-census variables six principal components resulted and the factor matrix for the first three is shown in Table 5.1. Figure 5.1-5.3 depict the scale scores for each factor for the Meirionnydd district. The first factor is largely characterised by areas with elderly populations, single person households and low household room occupancies. Perusal of Figure 5.1 indicates that large areas to the south of the district are particularly marked by these characteristics. Considered in relation to physical isolation from mainstream public services, inadequate and costly transport systems which typify rural areas more and more one can begin to obtain a first notion of some of the problems likely to be encountered by dwellers in these areas. The second factor obviously separates out areas with poor housing conditions and again it can be seen that these are far from being restricted to the more densely populated areas of the district. Though being more difficult to explain, the third factor appears to identify areas where personal mobility is limited, linked with single person households, high population density and unemployment. In this particular regard Meirionnydd is obviously not so impoverished, judging by the number of parishes with low scores, by contrast to the remainder of Gwynedd.

The ramifications of some of these issues are discussed in more depth later on but the actual use of social need indicators appears to have a number of policy applications for the development of social services in rural areas:

1 as a means of weighting the severity or complexity of need for sub-units of geographically large areas,
2 as a means of identifying areas of unmet need,
3 as a method of evaluating resource allocation strategies adopted by social services and other departments,
4 as a means of developing typologies of rural areas and their parameters. This would assist further research in so far as sampling of rural areas could be done more objectively.

Without careful validation work the above-mentioned applications will remain at best a purely academic pursuit. An obvious way to start examining the predictive validity of any social need indicator is to collect data on patterns of demand on local services. Though demand characteristics will to an extent reflect a kind of administrative prevalence contingent upon the actual level of local services and facilities available it is a relatively straightforward way of beginning the exercise. Eventually this kind of information retrieval would have to be supplemented by surveys of need in the community in order to establish the 'true' rather than the 'administrative' prevalence of various types of disorder, handicap or social problem.

DEMANDS ON SERVICES

Within most Social Services Departments it is unusual to find record systems or registers of handicapped persons which facilitate the extraction of data for presentation in a spatial form. In most cases the smallest areal unit which can be used without recourse to

Table 5.1 Varimax rotated factor matrix showing variables with significant scores

	Factor 1		Factor 2		Factor 3
Variable description	Factor score	Variable description	Factor score	Variable description	Factor score
% pop. of pensionable age	0.93	% hh lacking/sharing bath	0.99	% hh with no car	0.89
% pop. aged 75+	0.82	% hh with excl. use amenities	0.98	% hh with 2+ cars	-0.79
% hh with <½ person/room	0.79	% hh lacking inside WC	0.93	% hh with 7+ rooms	-0.54
% pop. aged 0 - 4	-0.79	% hh lacking/sharing hot water	-0.92	One person pensioner hh/1000 pop.	0.49
One person pensioner hh/1000 pop.	0.70	% pop. Welsh speaking	0.55	One person hh/1000 pop.	0.49
One person hh/1000 pop.	0.69	% 5 year immigrants into area	0.35	% second homes	-0.48
% econ. active aged 45+	0.61	% hh council owned	-0.34	% hh council owned	0.48
% pop aged 5 - 14	-0.56			% hh vacant	-0.47
% hh with >1 person/room	-0.55			population density	0.47
Two person pensioner hh/1000 pop.	0.54			% E.A. seeking work	0.40
Fertility ratio	-0.53			Tourist bed places/1000 pop.	-0.38
E.A. males/1000 males 15+	-0.52			% hh unfurnished	-0.35
% hh owner occupied	0.47			E.A. married females/1000 females 15+	0.33
% hh council owned	-0.47				
% hh with >7 rooms	0.32				
% pop Welsh speaking	-0.30				
Eigenvalue 6.95		5.35		3.68	
% total variance 20.4		15.7		10.8	
Cum % total variance 20.4		36.1		46.9	

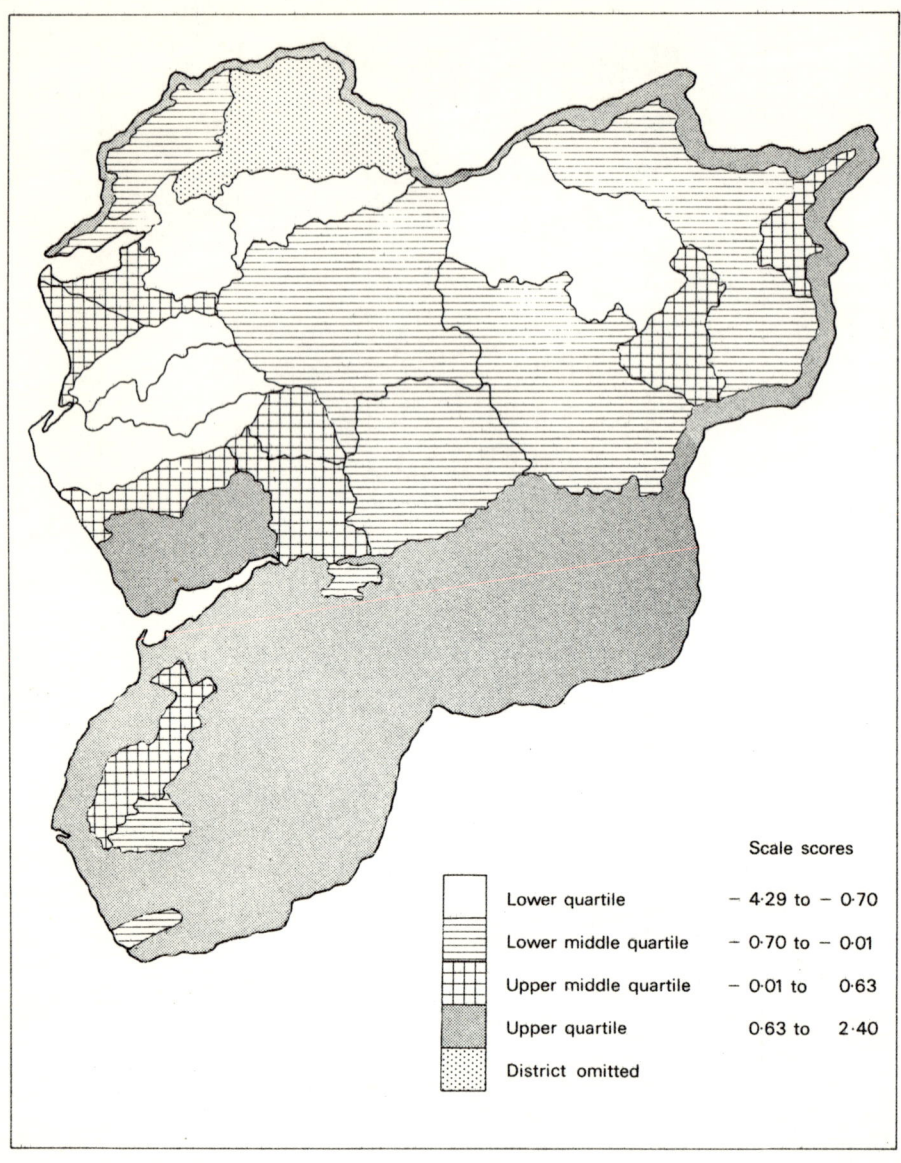

Scale scores

Lower quartile	− 4·29 to − 0·70
Lower middle quartile	− 0·70 to − 0·01
Upper middle quartile	− 0·01 to 0·63
Upper quartile	0·63 to 2·40
District omitted	

FIGURE 5.1   Scale scores for factor 1 (elderliness, single person
households, low room occupancies per household) −
district of Meirionnydd

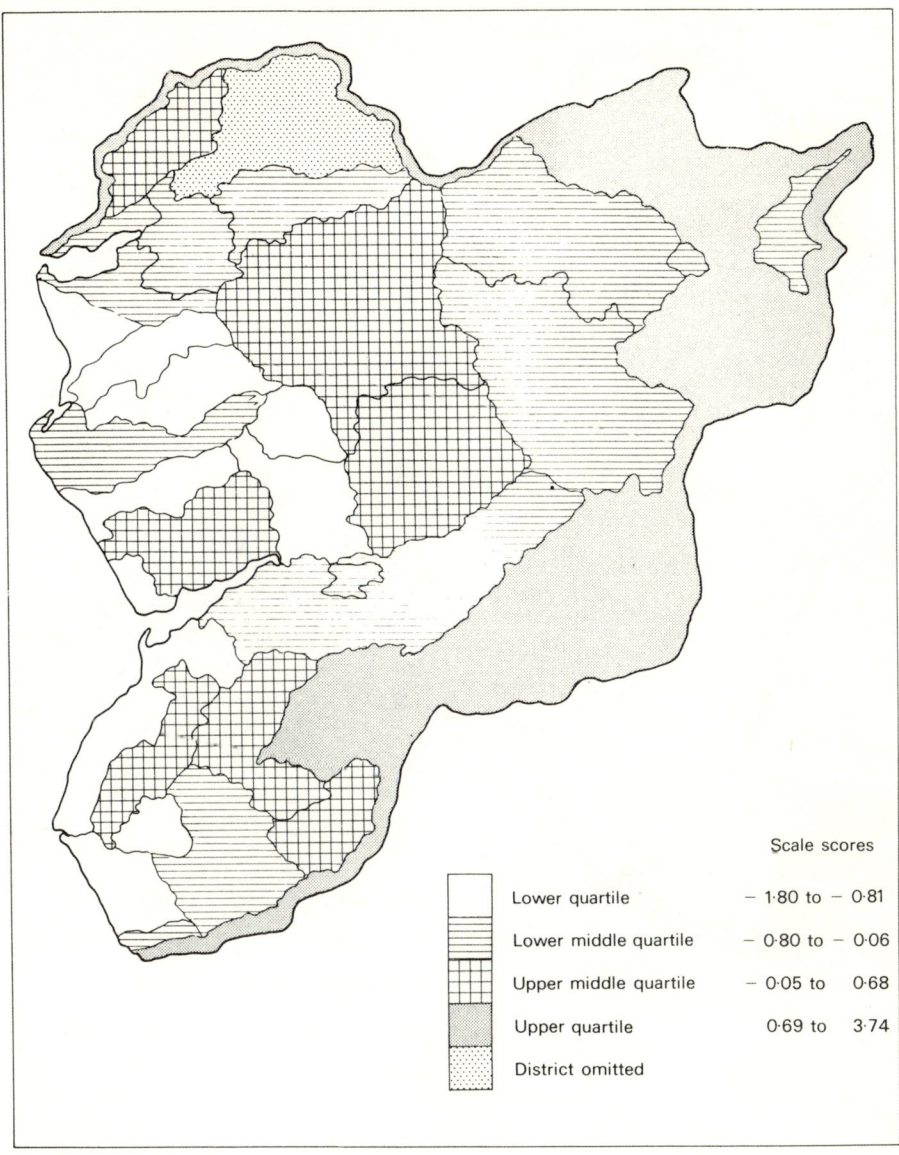

Scale scores

Lower quartile	− 1·80 to − 0·81
Lower middle quartile	− 0·80 to − 0·06
Upper middle quartile	− 0·05 to 0·68
Upper quartile	0·69 to 3·74
District omitted	

FIGURE 5.2   Scale scores for factor 2 (absence of housing amenities)
            – district of Meirionnydd

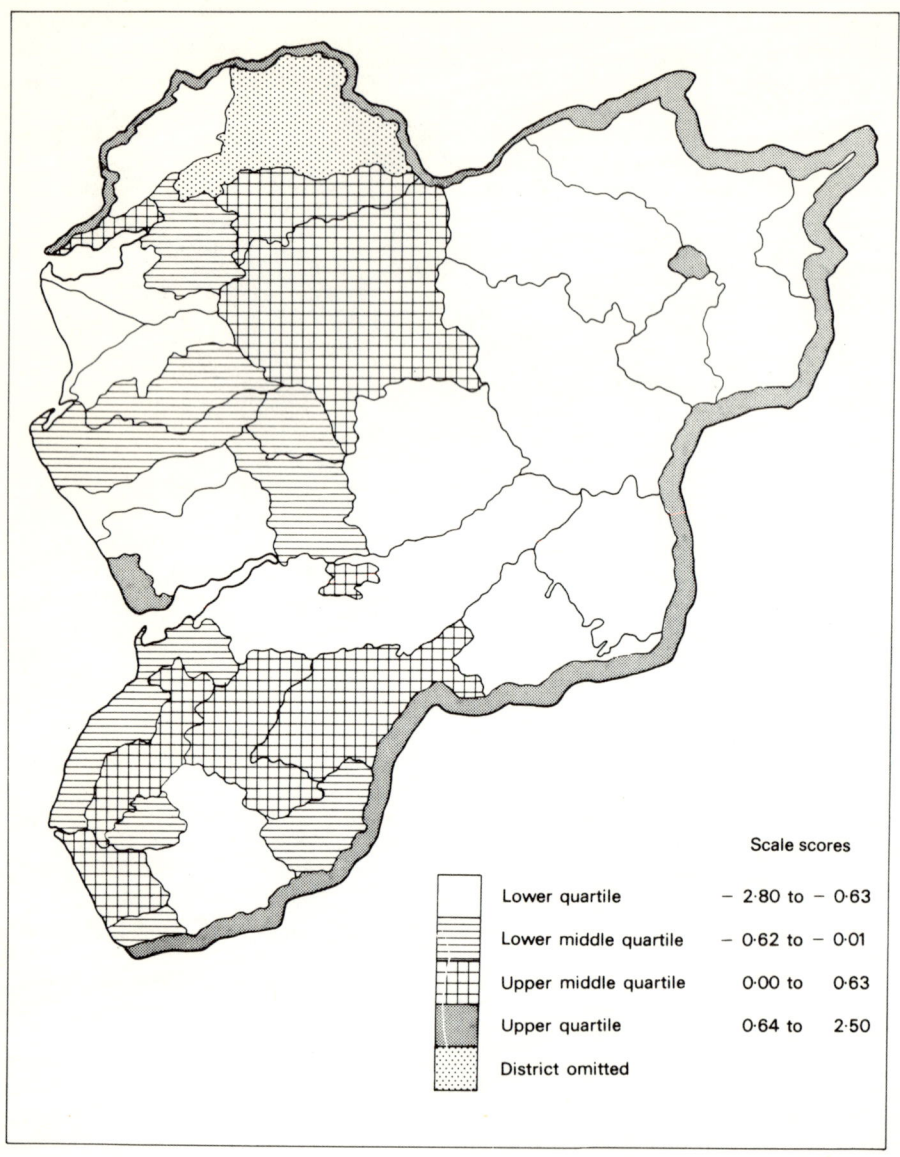

	Scale scores
Lower quartile	− 2·80 to − 0·63
Lower middle quartile	− 0·62 to − 0·01
Upper middle quartile	0·00 to 0·63
Upper quartile	0·64 to 2·50
District omitted	

FIGURE 5.3   Scale scores for factor 3 (low car ownership, single person households, population density, unemployment) - district of Meirionnydd

tedious research is, in county council areas, the district.   In
Gwynedd none of the five district council areas could conceivably
be classed as urban in character but nevertheless there is a reasonably wide variation in population density as Table 5.2 attests.
What is also apparent, however, is that the rate at which persons
are referred to the department does not vary unduly and there is no
obvious bias towards the most densely populated districts.   The
available evidence appears if anything to suggest that relative
demands on services are independent of both sparsely or densely
populated areas.   Even when individual urban areas are separated out
and compared on a similar basis no strikingly significant differences emerge.   In appearing to precipitate a very similar level of
social problems per head of population as more urban communities
rural areas are quite obviously far from being peaceful countryside
places as is the common public stereotype.

Table 5.2   Referrals to Gwynedd Social Services Department
            July 1974 - June 1975

Area	Population density per hectare	Total referrals	Referral rate per 1,000 pop	% of all referrals from pensioners
Arfon	1.30	1223	23	40.1
Aberconwy	0.82	1030	21	60.6
Dwyfor	0.42	686	26	55.4
Meirionnydd	0.20	633	21	61.6
Ynys Mon.	0.88	1414	22	57.3
Gwynedd	0.58	4986	22	56.3

    Available caseload information from within Gwynedd largely
supports this view.   In plotting Meirionnydd social work cases
which were receiving some form of social support the intercorrela-
tion between number of cases per head of population and population
density per parish or ward was so low as to be insignificant
($r = 0.28$, $p > .05$ for N = 31 where N is the number of areal units).
The association between these two indices was nevertheless positive
indicating a slight tendency for the rather more densely populated
areas to house more cases per capita.
    One way in which rural authorities could attempt to monitor wider
social trends would be to develop internal information systems which
have as their base, small geographical units such as community
councils or even grid squares.   One of the spin-offs is that information would be easier to integrate with other types of geographically
based data.

TOWARDS A NEW MODEL OF SOCIAL SERVICES IN RURAL AREAS

By and large Social Services Departments are fairly highly centralised agencies whose functions are ill-understood by the community
at large (Glastonbury et al., 1973; Hillingdon Social Services
Department, 1973). In large sparsely populated areas a key question
is to determine to what extent services ought to be decentralised in
efforts to bring services closer to the public. Even if this is
theoretically desirable the viability of alternative approaches will
have to be investigated. For example, it may not be feasible to
provide specialist services such as observation and assessment
centres or day centres for the mentally ill in the middle of thinly
populated areas, simply because unit costs are likely to be high.
The very role of area social work offices might well be reappraised
since their siting usually requires the public to travel long
distances. At the same time centralised public authorities probably have more than their fair share of problems attempting to
monitor social needs and cultural developments in their localities
simply because of their apparent remoteness from the community at
large.
     On a small scale some attempts are now being made to examine new
approaches to the delivery of services in rural areas. In collaboration with the Citizens Advice Bureau the Gwynedd S.S.D. is
attempting to investigate the effectiveness of a mobile information
service. A mobile van supplements static bureaux which are located
in the larger towns and it is aimed primarily at delivering an
information and advice service to the rural hinterland and other
nodal centres. Separate delivery systems are in various stages of
implementation, one involving a minivan which will be used to carry
an information and advice 'kit' which can be erected and displayed
in a variety of locations such as village halls, post offices and
community centres, whilst another involves the setting up of what
have become known as community links. Community links are key
persons, dispersed throughout the locality, who are trained both as
information distributors and advisers. Typically they would be
local people who already have established contacts in remote communities rather than outsiders who are mysteriously 'implanted' into
the community.
     These experimental services would not simply act as referral
points for persons in need of personal social services or other
services. They would have a very positive preventive role in so
far as more direct diffusion of information to rural dwellers is
likely to enhance the community's ability to act and make decisions
independently or urban based service centres. Continued monitoring
of schemes like these would also help to determine which system or
mix of systems is most suited to the needs of rural areas.
     In adopting urban models of practice rural departments have
attempted to provide decent facilities to receive and interview the
public, have a duty officer on hand and emergency out-of-hours
cover. Instead of pursuing such a passive policy rural social
services departments could develop a policy of positive out-reach
to villages and hamlets. This could begin with the establishment
of outstations, manned at fixed times during the week, at strategic
places which might include GP surgeries, health centres, community

centres, public libraries, if not in separate offices. Many rural departments have already developed this form of out-reach but information about the suitability of siting arrangements has yet to be properly evaluated. An alternative approach would be to have social workers operating on individual patches just as village PCs patrol their own 'beat'. Whilst on the one hand this would give the social worker the opportunity to develop first-hand information about local community needs it may on the other hand defeat the whole object of the exercise as his presence may be felt to be too immediate and too great a threat to the principle of confidentiality between worker and client. Having adopted this style of service delivery social workers would almost certainly be committed to generic caseloads and determination of the size of their 'patches' would be a prime consideration.

A further ploy would be to develop the practice of rural community development and to have workers engaged in active preventive and promotional work with both individuals and groups in rural areas. The scope for this work has not, it seems, been fully explored either within or outside Wales. The very term rural community work may be something of a euphemism in so far as so many of the problems of rural areas stem from local employment or rather the lack of it. Consequently the 'community work' emphasis might be placed on the promotion of work co-operatives such as have been launched in other parts of Gwynedd by local voluntary initiative (Dragon Times, 1975) or on the development of more traditional community industry schemes funded with central government money. As with his urban-based counterpart it would be the task of the rural community worker to operate alongside the rural dweller in appraising local problems, identifying needs, stimulating mutual support and promoting interaction with other agencies who have contributions to make to rural community development. This type of outreach programme will obviously require some considerable investment, for if work is to be intensive it will have to be focused on quite small geographical units.

Social Services Departments are legally bound to provide certain service packages whilst other facilities or more usually their precise mode of delivery may be developed to meet particular local needs. The outcome of legislation over the years is that the basic array of services provided by any department is likely to be extremely similar and there may outwardly be little to distinguish rural from urban social service departments. Whilst this may not be so surprising, the assumptions behind the precise role to be played by individual services, particularly residential establishments and day care centres, need reappraisal in the light of the special needs of rural areas.

Such establishments vary tremendously in the way they are managed, staffed and in their physical structure yet there are a number of elements which they have in common. They are usually uni-functional in that they typically provide care for fairly homogeneous groups of clients such as the elderly, children and mentally handicapped or mentally ill persons. Theory has it that certain client groups should not be accommodated within the same facility as this is thought to be contra-therapeutic. Accommodation of younger physically handicapped persons with the elderly is not

viewed with approval; mixing mentally handicapped children with
adults is still viewed by central government only as a last resort;
and combining day care or residential facilities for the physically
handicapped with mentally handicapped or mentally ill persons is
thought to create problems for the clients, their families and also
for care staff.

The economics of sparsity are such that in many cases it would
not be viable to establish totally separate residential facilities
for small homogeneous groups of clients classed according to need.
From a purely therapeutic point of view it is desirable not to have
establishments serving large catchment areas as this would inhibit
visiting patterns of families and friends and occasion transport
difficulties for those clients who require day care in alternative
establishments. For those clients living at home who attend adult
training centres, social centres and sheltered workshops the same
principle applies except that the relative inaccessibility of these
facilities would only serve to reinforce the client's handicapping
conditions. Solutions to these problems are not immediately
obvious and the various options available all have their own merits
and demerits. However some of the possibilities which can be
explored include the following:
  (a) multi-purpose static day care centres for single client groups,
  (b) multi-purpose static day care centres for several client
      groups,
  (c) day care centres offering limited residential accommodation,
  (d) mobile day centres modelled on the 'play-bus' idea,
  (e) residential complexes offering accommodation for a wide range
      of clients,
  (f) inter-agency establishments providing an array of services for
      the public.
  This list is by no means exhaustive but the permutations involved
need to be evaluated in terms of their therapeutic effectiveness,
cost, optimum size of catchment area and also from the standpoint
of what use could be made of any kind of establishment in sparsely
populated areas, i.e. their social utility as a community
resource.

COMMUNITY SUPPORT AND DOMICILIARY SERVICES

Under various legal enactments local authorities are obliged and
empowered to deliver a wide range of support services to elderly,
handicapped and distressed persons. Many of these basic services
not only supplement those facilities already described but they can
be construed as substitutable or preventive services aimed at
maintaining persons in their own homes and communities. Previous
work in this field (Wager, 1972) has amply demonstrated that with
prudent management of resources there are savings to be made in
providing the most appropriate mix of support services to elderly
clients, thereby reducing expenditure on costly residential services.

Paradoxically when Wales is taken as a whole it is the most
rural counties which appear to house the highest level of residential places for the elderly and within Gwynedd the same story holds
true for most rural districts. Whilst sheer coincidence cannot be

ruled out it seems that for some reason or another delivery of support services in sparsely populated areas is problematic. With the absence of adequate public transport systems, the lack of suitable road networks, and the relative absence of organised volunteer groups, homes for the elderly have to be relied on to a very great extent.

More direct use of volunteers is undoubtedly one way of improving the lot of isolated elderly clients and of reducing demands on establishments. In the larger towns and cities of the UK, it is quite commonplace to find groups of neighbours formed into 'good neighbour' schemes, but this notion appears not to have taken off within rural areas. Whilst, typically, a good neighbour is someone who may assist an elderly or handicapped neighbour with domestic chores and generally keep a watching brief over them, there is no reason why childminding, home help work, night sitting work or any permutation of these could not be carried out by neighbours. So often departments think of these services as separate entities each needing particular skills and personal resources, when in fact it may be feasible to think of a single person or family fulfilling some, if not all, of these functions. The 'gemeinschaft' quality of some rural communities would probably facilitate the promotion of this type of activity if indeed it is not happening already.

A classic case of urban models being adopted by rural departments can be seen in the case of the home help service. Pre-reorganisation Welsh authorities varied in the extreme in the way the service was staffed. Even within Gwynedd this can still be seen. Anglesey and Meirionnydd districts are staffed almost entirely by casual home helps. These are ladies who assist neighbours with domestic chores but their work lasts only as long as there is a local need for it. Usually a casual helper would have no more than three or four clients who live in the same community and in the event of her clients moving away or dying her temporary employment would cease. In most cases workers would put in no more than 20-25 hours per week. In the remaining districts the service is manned predominantly by permanent full- and part-time staff. The immediate implications of all this is that it becomes necessary to determine what is the optimum staffing mix for rural areas. Is it desirable for example to employ a large number of helpers who work only a few hours each week but with the probability of being able to recruit persons actually living in remote villages? Or is it still more practical to employ fewer persons but have them working full-time? If this latter option is taken up travelling costs will soar and workers will be less likely to know clients personally. If casuals are employed they will be local to the clients and nearer to hand in emergencies. On the other hand area organisers who employ casuals will have a task on their hands physically supervising that number of staff.

One of the other areas in which rural departments differ significantly from their urban counterparts is in the relative lack of pressure group interests. A positive benefit of active specialist voluntary associations in an area is the beneficial effect it has upon professional practice. Enthusiasm and expertise possessed by such groups has a way of transmitting itself to agency workers. Moreover it is often these groups who possess the funds, initiative

and freedom to experiment and pioneer new approaches to social work
and social services.   By and large rural Social Services Departments
do not have this type of challenge from outside so most of the
initiative has to be generated from within the organisation.   The
operations of specialist voluntary organisations can significantly
increase public awareness of the particular problems and needs of
clients of the organisation and thereby bring about a reduction in
social stigma for clients and their families.   This also leads to
the possibility of community domiciliary help and support to clients.

WIDER PERSPECTIVES

Quite obviously the social needs of rural areas and methods of
tackling them leave much still to be explored yet even to the
casual onlooker there are factors and social processes which now
sadly characterise rural areas more and more: depopulation, ageing,
unemployment, even disintegration of entire villages and their life
styles.   Such is the seriousness of these trends that the delivery
of existing social services becomes at best a palliative to the true
needs of rural areas.   By themselves departments responsible for
providing specific types of service become helpless when it comes
to tackling the real needs of the day.   Under existing structural
limitations there is a danger that even concerted attempts by single
agencies to deal with these issues will result in totally unbalanced
and unco-ordinated attempts to resolve basic problems and prevent
social disintegration.
     On one level there seems to be a need for local authorities at
least to develop a more corporate approach, specifically in the
case of rural areas, as the basic infrastructure provided in these
localities highlights the very interdependence of services.   For
example more rural employment has to be provided to make it feasible
for rural dwellers to remain in the locality but at the same time
schools and playgroups would have to be made available for children.
Adequate transport systems are needed to make it worthwhile for
industry to develop in rural areas and also to obviate the risk of
isolating persons in their own rural communities.   Continued depopulation is likely to result in disproportionately high demands on
local health and social services (Morgan, 1974) and the risk that
the residual population will not be able to organise itself to
overcome these problems.   Rural authorities therefore need urgently
to evolve plans for positive development in sparsely populated areas
but this can only be done if a truly corporate approach is adopted
and if the right resources are made available.
     Some encouragement that this may not entirely be wishful thinking
comes from Canada (Department of Regional Economic Expansion, 1973,
1974) in the form of the New Start programmes.   These were sponsored
by the Department of Regional Economic Expansion and Departments of
Education in an attempt to deal with a variety of human resource
development programmes.   Rural areas within a number of separate
provinces were selected in such a way that the disadvantaged population of the area would be sufficient in number to provide for a
variety of experimental training and community development programmes, but not so large as to render general area surveys and

programme administration unfeasible. Age and dependency characteristics, ethnic disparities, educational levels and economic factors
all formed a part of the criteria for the selection of areas. It is
impossible to list all the ingredients of the New Start programmes
but basic features which may have applications in rural Wales
included the following:

(a) Development of mobile centre projects to provide basic educa-
    tion, community and family counselling, home economics and
    trades training.
(b) Neighbourhood organisation projects designed to teach people
    how to define issues and become aware of strategies for dealing
    with them. Organisation of self-help groups, involvement of
    social agencies to give encouragement to disadvantaged groups
    in solving their own problems. Involvement of wider community
    with disadvantaged as assistants, advisers, instructors and
    enablers.
(c) Introduction of 'planned social change' programmes - through
    development of informational, technological and political
    linkages between the disadvantaged and the community at large.
    Specific programmes were aimed at: (i) studying the impact of
    an employment grant on the community, (ii) providing linkages
    to introduce adoption of new technology and new means of
    earning a livelihood, (iii) evaluate effects of a life skills
    course on community structural variables.
(d) Implanting community service centres to provide counselling,
    family assistance and child care, and community action
    projects.
(e) Introduction of programmes to promote increased mobility by:
    (i) establishing closer working relationships between socially
    and economically depressed rural communities and urban-
    industrial communities, (ii) co-ordinate activities of other
    agencies to share resources and experience, to avoid duplica-
    tion and present a credible image to community members.

These programmes commenced in about 1969 but already it seems
they have enjoyed a fairly high level of success in the specific
areas of concern. All have in common the notion of drawing the
community into full programme participation in identifying needs,
appraising priorities, and actually operating and evaluating programmes - a far cry from the traditional 'top-down' tradition of
programme provision for service consumers in this country.

In conclusion there are a number of points which bear some
repetition.

First, without the right kind of information about needs in
scattered rural communities, rural departments would appear to be
in danger of replicating urban models of practice which are usually
adopted by central government agencies. In particular departmental
information systems need some kind of geographic base which would
facilitate the plotting of rural community profiles over time.

Second, rural areas should be recognised as possessing certain
kinds of social problems which are inextricably linked with
declining employment, depopulation, retirement migration and a
generally poor level of infrastructure provision. So chronic in
nature are these problems that they require or seem to require a
positive long-term development policy. Some of the factors which

precipitate these problems have been outlined but what is now needed is the diversion of available funds away from urban to rural areas so that experimental development schemes can be introduced.   In the next decade or so rural renewal or perhaps rural development will become as popular a catch-phrase as urban renewal. This would of course be aided if planning for rural areas was the broad responsibility of a single agency instead of the partial interest of multifarious national and local agencies whose efforts are largely unco-ordinated.

Rural departments appear to need to re-think what kind of role their various services are going to have and the very system or method by which a service is made available will also need close scrutiny so that it maximises utility to the local community instead of to some central government circular or policy guideline.

It is to be hoped, too, that more economic and social research will be directed to the needs of rural areas for the available knowledge on which to base a truly effective delivery of social services in these areas is at best only embryonic. This, of course, is another challenge to rural departments who, because of their usual small population size in relation to metropolitan areas, do not typically possess the research specialists to provide the necessary input. Perhaps this will also provide some extra impetus for the establishment of more centrally funded research into the needs of sparsely populated areas, as well as leading to the recognition that rural areas have particular problems and characteristics which require a rather different kind of thinking about social administration and social work.

REFERENCES

DEPARTMENT OF REGIONAL ECONOMIC EXPANSION (1973), 'The human resources', Ottawa, Ontario.
DEPARTMENT OF REGIONAL ECONOMIC EXPANSION (1974), 'Social Development', Ottawa, Ontario.
'Dragon Times' (1975), Antur Aelhaearn, no.2.
GLASTONBURY, B., BURDETT, M. and AUSTIN, R. (1973), Community Perceptions and the Personal Social Services, 'Policy and Politics', vol.1, no.3, pp.191-211.
HILLINGDON SOCIAL SERVICES DEPARTMENT (1973), 'Attitudes and awareness of Hillingdon Residents to the Social Services Department', University of Birmingham Local Authority Social Services Research no.5, pp.33-43.
MONMOUTHSHIRE COUNTY COUNCIL (1974), 'Monmouthshire Social Malaise Study: An interim report on the distribution of social problems', County Planning Department, Newport.
MORGAN, R. (1975), Outmigration and the depressed area problem, in P.H. Ballard and E. Jones (eds), 'The Valleys Call', R. Jones Publications, Ferndale, pp.271-9.
NORFOLK COUNTY COUNCIL (1976), 'Social Indicators - Research Report', Social Services Department, Research Training and Personnel Division, Norwich.
WAGER, R. (1972), 'Care of the elderly - An exercise in cost-benefit analysis', Institute of Municipal Treasurers and Accountants.

WELSH OFFICE CIRCULAR, no. 50/1973 (1973), Urban Programme Circular No.9.

WINROW, M. and PRIESTLEY, M.M. (1975), 'Social and Economic Stress in Wales: A study of social deprivation and economic imbalance', Geography Department, St David's College, Lampeter.

Chapter 6

PERCEPTIONS OF THE VILLAGE SCHOOL

Roy Nash

At first sight the decision to close an old village primary school
and transport the pupils a few miles by bus to a larger modernized
school may not seem one of any great moment. Yet anyone with a
knowledge of the recent history of primary school reorganization in
rural Wales will understand that the decision is not merely about
where a score or so children will receive their education but has
wider implications for the future of the whole rural community.
The fate of these small schools can clearly be seen to be linked to
a larger struggle between competing groups with distinct ideological
positions. This struggle is concerned with the future development
of Welsh rural society.

It is a society that has been twice decimated by depopulation
since the 1930s.(1) Essentially it is an agricultural society and
more than two-thirds of all workers are employed in distribution
and agriculture.(2) Consequently the forces with a powerful voice
in urban society, industrial organizations and trade unions, are
absent and the social leadership of rural society lies with small
educated and articulate middle-class groups.

It is useful to differentiate three levels of leadership, first
of the locally based social, cultural and political institutions,
second, of the wider political authorities, and third, of the
nationally based cultural movements. In the Welsh-speaking villages
of North Wales the local organizations, the Village Hall Committee,
The Eisteddfod Committee, and the Urdd (Welsh Youth Movement) (3)
are run by the more educated and usually middle-class Welsh-speaking
men.(4) In most rural districts they are self-employed farmers, in
other districts skilled quarrymen or the proprietors of small
businesses predominate. Among these men will be found the deacons
of the chapel, the parish councillors and the managers of the village
school. A small number will represent the area on the district and
county councils. Their wives run the Ysgol Meithrin (5) (Welsh
Nursery School Movement) and the Women's Institute or its Welsh
counterpart Merched Y Wawr.

Only at community (parish) council level are the rural areas able
to control their own affairs. In almost all cases the district
councils with responsibility for housing and minor planning matters
have been formed to reflect the demographic character of the larger

county. Even in Gwynedd, the most rural of all the Welsh counties,
the rural population are in a minority. This is reflected in the
composition of the county council where rather more than half of
the councillors represent urban constituencies.(6) The county
council is responsible for education, social services, highways and
major planning, all of vital importance to the rural areas, and the
politically conscious among the rural population are fully aware
that the decisions affecting the future development of their communities will be made by the urban, probably anglicized, majority.

The Welsh-speaking rural people are understood to be the bedrock
on which Welsh culture stands. The remote hills and valleys are the
heartland of the Welsh people and those who live there are not alone
in recognizing this to be true. Social and political movements,
notably Cymdeithas yr Iaith Gymraeg (the Welsh Language Society)(7)
and Plaid Cymru,(8) are especially concerned with developments in
the rural areas. They are able through the publication of their
ideas in the press and through discussions in public meetings to
affect the opinions of local community leaders. Their specific
involvement in particular developments seen as potentially harmful
to an established community and its way of life is common. Although
as individuals they may have little or no personal contact with the
locality they are not seen by the community as outsiders but as
allies - Welsh-speaking Welshmen on their side. Once the pattern
of leadership is seen it is possible to examine more closely the
groups involved and their ideologies. Three groups can be recognized.
It will be shown how they become involved in the debate about
primary school reorganization.

Group 1 may be regarded as the established literary intelligentsia
- the llenorion. They are an older group of scholars, ministers of
religion, teachers and writers. Their concerns are with the preservation of the traditional values of Welsh life. They encourage and
support movements to give greater status to the Welsh language and
provide inspiration and financial backing for Cymdeithas yr Iaith
Gymraeg. During their lifetime they have witnessed the depopulation
of the rural areas and have a deep sense of loss at the results; a
generation of young people gone to work in the cities, the cottages
abandoned, the chapels weakened, the schools run down, and the Welsh
language eroded by English. Many have an attitude almost of resig-
nation. Historically they have failed to develop a convincing
critique of the basic weaknesses of the Welsh economy. Although
obviously conscious of English hegemony they have not understood
that this hegemony inevitably follows from the economic status of
Wales. The integration of the Welsh and the English economies
(which took place a long time ago) inevitably made the Welsh
economy marginal in a British context.(9) Unable to see how the
underlying economic problems can be solved their efforts have been
most effective in resisting obvious opponents: Water Boards proposing
to flood agricultural valleys, international companies planning to
mine in the mountainous areas, and local education authorities trying
to close village schools. As a group their influence on the major
cultural institutions of Wales is hard to over-estimate. The
National Eisteddfod Committee,(10) the Urdd, the University, The
Welsh Arts Council, for example, are all greatly influenced by them.
Perhaps most importantly they virtually control the Welsh-language

press.(11)   Their views are strongly represented on the county councils by members who usually sit for rural constituencies.

Group 2 occupy the positions of economic and administrative power. They are essentially technocrats. Fully aware of the marginal position of the Welsh economy they look to planning and development for solutions. The modernization of plant, the centralization of resources, the rationalization of uneconomic modes of production, and the inherent problems of transport.(12) are their major concerns. The same principles which make urban economies so successful would, in their view, do the same for Wales. Many live in the more urbanized areas of rural Wales and see the problems of rural Wales as contingent on the success of economic developments in Wales as a whole. They are a group of men in contact with the decision-makers in Cardiff, London and even Brussels. They relate to this wider society and are particularly conscious of the position of Wales in the EEC. Many county councillors clearly belong to this group.

Group 3 in many respects share the concerns of group 1, although more secular in outlook. Typically they are young professional workers, doctors, solicitors, architects, teachers and so on who intend to remain working in Wales. As a group they are critical of the solutions of the technocrats and see the survival of the Welsh language and culture as being dependent on the support of all rural communities. They are interested in the provision of small-scale local industries and self-help type organizations to solve the problems of housing and transport.(13) In many ways this group can be seen to relate to a very recent concern with alternative systems and technologies.(14) Wales is seen as a small country and is often explicitly compared with other small countries, Israel, Norway and Finland, for example.(15) Although without much formal representation on the county councils members of this group are particularly active in local politics and social events and have considerable influence. Besides being part of the bi-lingual community many young people with these views have frequent contact with each other through membership of the Welsh Language Society.

Although recognizable as distinct groups it is not necessarily the case that individuals will see themselves as belonging to one or another. The llenorion and the younger group of social activists do form relatively coherent groups. The technocrats are by far the most numerous and are perhaps for this reason less easy to regard as a group. Politically groups 1 and 3 are most likely to belong to Plaid Cymru, the Welsh National Party, while members of group 2 are equally likely to support any or none of the main political parties: Plaid Cymru has its share. It should be noted that this analysis is concerned only with groups that seek to give social leadership to the rural community. In many areas there are still powerful land-owning families referred to as Anglo-Welsh but so completely English in orientation that even though they may hold positions of influence (as school governors or Justices of the Peace, for example), they scarcely relate to the Welsh culture of the rural areas.

It will be useful at this point to relate the usual pattern of events which begins when a local education authority decides to re-organize a village school:

(a) The officers of the LEA prepare a scheme for the closure of what they term a non-viable school.
(b) The Development Sub-Committee (or other appropriate sub-committee of the Education Committee) study and accept the proposal after consultation with the school managers and teachers.
(c) The local community decides to oppose the scheme. It finds a spokesman (or spokeswoman) and oranizes: (i) a petition asking the LEA to reconsider its decision, (ii) coverage in the Welsh-language press, (iii) assistance from its emigrant middle-class, (16) (iv) agitation for a public meeting with the LEA and (v) lobbies its county councillor.
(d) A meeting, officially of the Development Sub-Committee, but invariably held in the school itself and treated as a public meeting makes the villagers' feelings known to the authorities. The effect of this meeting is always to harden resistance to the LEA's plans and almost always persuades the local councillor to change his views whatever his previous opinions.(17)
(e) The Education Committee debates the recommendations of the Sub-Committee. It may adopt the recommendation or it may reject it.
(f) The final decision is made by the Secretary of State for Wales.
(g) If the final decision is to close the school that is usually accepted by the community. On at least one occasion, however, teachers and parents have physically resisted the closure of the school and it has been necessary for the LEA to threaten legal action to enforce its will.(18)

This whole procedure may take a year or more.

In the argument about the reorganization of the rural primary schools the interested parties are the parents, school managers, the officers of the LEA, the Education Committee, and the Welsh Education Office. The arguments put forward by these groups in their dealings with each other arise from the distinct perceptions each has of the rural school and can be seen to relate to the ideological standpoints discussed above.

The rural school is seen variously as:
(a) a more or less sound and adequate physical structure,
(b) a social meeting place for the community,
(c) providing for pre-school children,
(d) more or less conveniently sited in relation to the village,
(e) having a curriculum which emphasizes the basic subjects preparatory for secondary school,
(f) having a child-centred curriculum where learning is dependent on a high level of resources and the availability of specialized teaching skills,
(g) more or less cost-efficient,
(h) an agency of cultural transmission,
(i) symbolic of the identity of the local society and a necessary resource for a viable community.

All parties are agreed that the school should be structurally sound, that it should serve as a meeting place for the community, and that it should provide pre-school facilities wherever possible. There is less agreement on other matters.

Parents are concerned that the school should be convenient,

preferably, in the village but in any case not far from it. A
school four or five miles distant is seen by parents as more than a
nuisance.   The buses or taxis may be involved in accidents on
narrow and winding roads; the teachers are much less easy to contact particularly where there is no bus service; for many children
the school day is appreciably lengthened by time spent waiting and
travelling; transport difficulties make pre-school admissions
difficult.   To the parents and managers the distance of the school
from the village is of great importance.   Others, though sympathetic,
are themselves less interested in this aspect.   The children will
almost certainly have to travel greater distances when they transfer to secondary school and in the view of the authorities the
disadvantages of a school distant from the village are outweighed
by educational benefits and by savings in cost.

   Parents regard primary schooling as preparatory for secondary
school work.   They therefore stress the importance of the basic
subjects: reading in Welsh and English, and number work.   They
expect the atmosphere to be homely and the teacher to be approach-
able but have no particular views about how he or she should teach.
School managers hold very similar views.   Most teachers and many
councillors also think of the primary school as essentially concerned with the basic subjects and though they often give considerable importance to environmental studies and music they do not
accept that pupils in very small schools are necessarily deprived
of resources or experience a restricted curriculum.   They certainly
do not accept that standards of achievement in small schools are
low; many assert the opposite.   Other authorities, the LEA officers,
the Welsh Education Office (especially the HMIs), and some councillors see things differently.   Their view of the curriculum is
wider than the basic subjects.   Primary education is seen as
something worthwhile in itself and not merely as a preparatory
stage for secondary school.   It is a concept of education which
implies a variety of resources and skills and the authorities are
aware that the two-room school cannot compare in these terms with
the larger school with its field, halls, library, workrooms and
associated equipment.   Nor can the two-teacher school match the
specialist skills - art, remedial, music, drama, and so on - available in the larger school.   These authorities are convinced that
pupils in larger schools achieve a higher standard than those in
small schools particularly in art, music and physical education,
but also in academic subjects.

   LEA officers, the Welsh Education Office and many councillors
necessarily see the schools in terms of expenditure.   They are
aware that economies of scale apply to education as much as to
anything else: the smaller the school the higher the relative cost.
Considerable savings are possible by what are seen by these authorities as small organizational changes.   Parents are little concerned
with the question of expenditure.   They suspect that there will be
no reduction in the rates demand no matter how much the LEA saves
on its educational budget.   Indeed, many parents, considering the
lack of village amenities, regard the money spent on running the
school as almost the only visible return for their rates.   Teachers
and managers, although able to appreciate the need for an economic
school system, argue that the amounts that might be saved are

relatively trivial in comparison with the total expenditure on
education.

The view that the village school should be particularly concerned
with transmitting and thus helping to preserve the culture of
rural Wales is held with deep conviction by teachers, managers,
many councillors, and recently, by an increasing number of people
in the LEAs and the Welsh Education Office. It is argued that the
small school serving a small local community is better placed to
succeed in this task than the larger school with a wider and less
homogeneous catchment area. To certain managers and councillors,
moreover, the school with only one or two teachers, who may live in
the village, is easier to observe and control, both formally through
the Board of Management and informally through ordinary social contact, than the school of six or seven teachers who may live
further away yet. The large 'area' school is thus seen as a threat
to the survival of the communities' way of life. The majority of
officials and many councillors disregard these arguments. The
aspiration for greater control over the school and its curriculum
is not regarded as legitimate and provided that the area school is
not actually sited in an English-speaking district they can see no
reason why it should be less Welsh in its cultural orientation than
the smaller school.

There is finally the view held by some councillors that the
school is a necessary resource for a viable community. That in
order for a community to continue to think of itself as such the
school is needed not only as an educational institution but as a
symbol of the community's commitment to its future. It is argued
that if the young children of a particular village are educated
elsewhere their ties with the village will be loosened to the point
where they no longer see themselves as belonging to their native
village. The loss of a village school is thus seen as a contributory factor in the decline of Welsh rural society - assisting
depopulation by making villages less attractive to couples with
young children, and depriving the village of yet one more facility:
no school; no shop; no chapel; no village. The official view,
shared by most LEA officers and many councillors, regards these
arguments as sentimentality. They point out that reorganization
with larger schools in 'key' villages (19) means that at least some
villages will be strengthened and if that is at the expense of
other smaller settlements that is only realistic. They argue that
these policies do not cause depopulation but are only a necessary
response to it.

These various perceptions may be displayed in grid form. This
model and the preceding analysis make it possible to see how the
debates between the protagonists involved in the recurring struggles
over primary school reorganization in rural Wales take a predictable
almost pre-ordained course. The built in misperceptions create a
lack of comprehension between those in favour of school reorganization and those against.

The LEA officers, supported by the Welsh Education Office and a
considerable part of their council, have an educational and economic
perspective which makes the need for school reorganization almost
self-evident. Parents, managers and teachers do not share this
view and see reorganization as an unnecessary inconvenience which

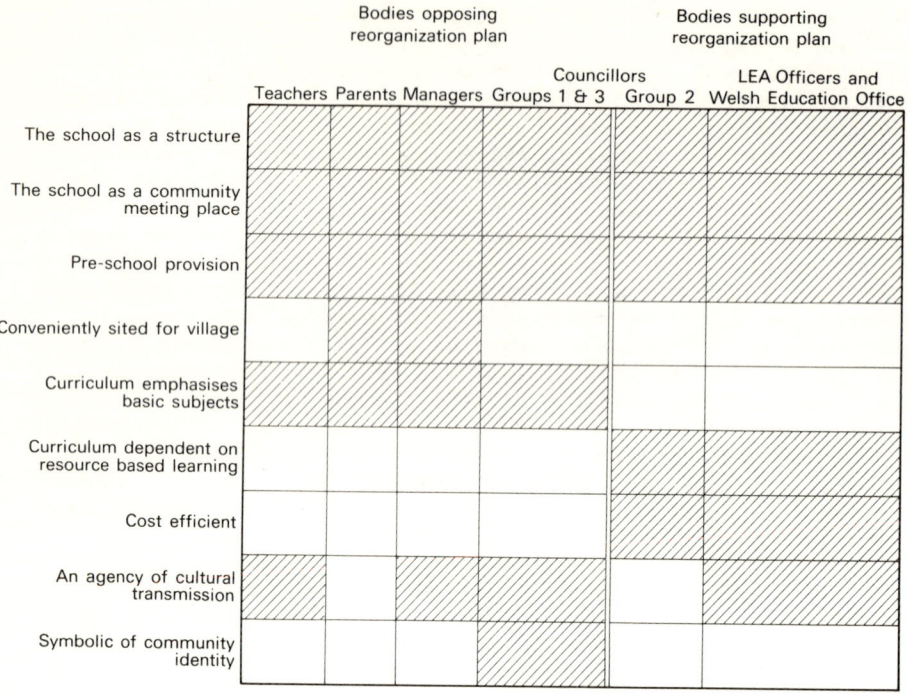

FIGURE 6.1   A model of the various perceptions held of rural
             primary schools by interested bodies

would certainly alter the kind of schooling their children receive
and possibly for the worse. Alone, parents and managers would
probably not be able to resist the LEA proposals but they have
found allies. The arguments advanced by intellectual groups may not
be fully understood by parents but since they are clearly ready to
take sides with the community they are welcomed as spokesmen and as
intermediaries in negotiations with the LEA. The LEA is seen by
many villagers as a remote authority with procedures that are
difficult for ordinary people to comprehend, but it is a bureaucracy
held in no awe by the middle-class.
     The implications this has for research may now be considered.
Research can usefully say how many rural schools there are, what
size they are, and what general condition they are in. It can say
how they are organized, what sort of curriculum they provide and
so on. This factual survey and description is necessary and
presents few difficulties. But only certain propositions - and
perhaps not the most important - are of the kind that can be
settled by empirical study. Assessing the quality of the teaching
and the curriculum is fraught with difficulty. The demand for
'objective' measures is impossible to meet. Even tests of reading
are suspect in many (perhaps too many) respects. Reports of
observations are still less 'objective'; a curriculum which seems

narrow and unimaginatively taught to an observer can be accepted, even highly regarded, by teachers, managers and parents. Again research can demonstrate how a school system might be reorganized and how much that reorganization might save the LEA on its educational budget. But it cannot say whether those savings are worth making. Empirical research has even less relevance to those who oppose school reorganization on cultural grounds. The questions they raise are resolvable, if at all, only by longitudinal studies which would necessarily report long after the time for making policy decisions has passed. All this suggests that the responsibility of a research worker is not only to his immediate sponsors but to all of those involved in the debate. It is his task to recognize and accurately report their concerns; to make his findings available to everyone; and, most importantly, to point out the limitations of his research methods.

This paper has attempted to show how an apparently unimportant side issue in the educational world is intricately bound up with much larger social questions. The debate over village schools can be seen as one particularly visible aspect of the debate about the future of rural Wales. Whether rural Wales will be seen as an area of planned land utilization with highly efficient agriculture and forestry, strictly controlled recreational use, and large economically sound villages connected by main roads to major towns: or whether it will be seen and developed as the homeland of a hard-pressed community dependent on the viability of its small scattered settlements for its cultural survival. These two views are essentially incompatible and we can expect to see the debate between the protagonists of each position and their struggle for the social leadership of the community grow increasingly intense as the problems of Welsh rural society grow greater.

NOTES

1 Almost all areas of rural Wales have lost some 20 per cent of their population between 1951 and 1971. The decline in completed family size, the ageing population, and the continuing movement of young people away from their home villages to find employment, will make a further decline in rural population inevitable. The tendency of retired people to move into certain districts does nothing, of course, to strengthen the schools.

2 In a typical rural area of south Clwyd, including a small market town with an industrial estate, the distribution of occupations is as follows: services 37.2 per cent, agriculture 26.4 per cent, construction and manufacturing both 11.5 per cent, utilities and transport 6.4 per cent, other forms of employment 7.2 per cent.

3 Urdd Gobaith Cymru (Welsh League of Youth), founded in 1922, is a bi-lingual youth organization which in addition to its local activities holds an annual camp and eisteddfod. It publishes five magazines in Welsh including two for learners of the language. It is particularly strong in the Welsh-speaking rural areas where it tends to be based in the schools.

4 Some recent data (reported at the 1976 Conference of the British

Sociological Association Sociology of Wales Study Group, at Gregynog, Powys) has been obtained by C. Wenger working in a small village in north-east Clwyd. She found that even in this village where Welsh speakers were in an actual minority the majority of the elected community councillors were Welsh speakers. Welsh speakers predominated in the administrative bodies of the village. Anglo-Welsh (born in the area but speaking only English) participated in voluntary associations particularly the play-group and the Women's Institute. English incomers had little involvement in the activities of the village: the men had a particularly marginal position.

5   Y Mudiad Ysgol Meithrin (Nursery School Movement) supports Welsh-medium nursery schools and pre-school playgroups. A growing number are being established in the rural areas.

6   There are 66 Gwynedd councillors of whom 34 represent predomin-antly urban constituencies. The neighbouring resort towns of Llandudno and Conwy alone have 9 councillors. Clwyd with the same number of councillors has only 22 representing the rural areas.

7   Cymdeithas yr Iaith Gymraeg was formed in 1962 following an influential speech on the condition of the Welsh language by the Welsh dramatist Saunders Lewis. It is essentially a move-ment of young people, often students, some of whom have been imprisoned for taking direct action against institutions they regard as harmful to the language.

8   Plaid Cymru is influential in the rural areas of north Wales. Two constituencies in the Gwynedd area have Plaid Cymru Members of Parliament. As yet, however, their presence on the county council is not large. Clwyd County Council seems to have no Plaid Cymru representatives.

9   Notable in this context is the uncertain future of the Shotton steel-making plant. More Clwyd workers are employed in making steel at Shotton (12,500) than are employed in agriculture (8,600). Shotton is regarded by the British Steel Corporation as uneconomic for reasons that apply to many industries in north and mid-Wales. In general Welsh industry is remote from its raw materials and markets, suffers from a shortage of skilled labour and has to overcome poor road and rail communications.

10 The National Eisteddfod is only the greatest of the eisteddfodau that take place every year in the Welsh-speaking areas of Wales. The Eisteddfod is a competitive festival of cultural events. A typical local eisteddfod held in a south Clwyd village annually at the end of June awards prizes for singing, piano playing, recitation, dance and original poetry including humorous verse. There are also classes for painting, sewing, knitting and cooking. Adults and children take part and the whole event starts soon after lunch and lasts to the early hours of the morning.

11 There are two national weekly newspapers *Y Cymro* and *Y Faner*. Equally important are the periodical magazines of which *Barn* is probably the most influential. Some weekly local newspapers have a Welsh edition and most others have at least a column or two in Welsh. Recently a few non-commercial local newspapers, for example, *Y Gadlas* in the Conwy valley, have been produced in Welsh.

12   Transport is an old problem.   Communications between north and
     south Wales are notoriously poor.   To travel by train from
     Holyhead to Cardiff it is necessary to go via Birmingham.
     There are just 20 miles of motorway (Chepstow to Cardiff) and
     many of the trunk routes, for example the A55 and the A552 the
     major roads from north Wales to the English North and Midlands,
     are hardly suitable for the heavy traffic they carry having
     only a single carriageway for most of their length.

13   One housing association *Cymdeithas Tai Gwynedd* has been partic-
     ularly influential in influencing policy.   The stage carriage
     bus services are finding it impossible to run economic routes
     in the rural areas and the service has been cut drastically.
     A number of solutions are being introduced in an attempt to
     provide alternative systems of transport.   One Clwyd community
     runs its own bus service with a small county grant, a second
     has a similar scheme using volunteer drivers, a third has a
     social car scheme organized by the WRVS for the use of infirm,
     handicapped and elderly persons.   Volunteer drivers use their
     own vehicles and receive a mileage allowance.   Many of these
     schemes were initiated by young people.

14   There is clearly a link at some level with the recent concern
     with environmental issues: the scarcity of resources, the need
     for conservation, and the desirability of small-scale industrial
     activities.   This is especially apparent in the events at
     Llanaelhaearn, a small village in Gwynedd, which has formed a
     co-operative and built a small factory in addition to producing
     handicrafts.

15   The comparisons are interesting.   Wales has an area of 8,017
     square miles, and a (1971) population of 2.7 millions.   The 1975
     UK Gross National Produce (per capita) was US $3,120.   The
     figure for Wales is not available but is undoubtedly lower.
     Israel is the most comparable with a land area of 7,992 square
     miles and a (1973) population of 3.2 millions.   The 1975 GNP
     (per capita) was US $2,165.   The figures for Norway are: land
     area 125,000 square miles, population (1975) 3.9 millions,
     GNP (per capita) US $4,735; and for Finland: land area 130,165
     square miles, population 4.7 millions, and GNP (per capita)
     US $3,661.   The comparisons with Israel are the more significant
     for Welsh speakers who note that over the last two or three
     decades, while Welsh has suffered a further decline, the
     Israelis have made Hebrew, a once dead tongue, their national
     language.

16   These are people who have been brought up and educated in the
     area but who have found it necessary to leave Wales to work.
     They maintain contact with their old community and can be a
     powerful assistance in times of stress.   A distinguished looking
     man who announces himself in a public meeting to discuss the
     future of a village school as 'John Roberts, Senior Registrar,
     St Jude's Hospital, London' and who points out that he and many
     of his fellows were educated in that school not to their
     noticeable detriment is heard with great respect and puts an
     argument difficult to counter.

17   Most county councillors see their role as being to represent
     the views of their constituents and will do so honestly and as

well as they are able. A councillor who did not take this
view would, of course, stand to lose the votes of an entire
village at the next election.

18   This occurred in 1970 at Bryncroes when the village school of
29 pupils was closed by the former Caernarfon LEA. Teachers
and parents refused to accept the notice of closure and only
capitulated after the threat of legal action from the LEA.
Feelings were aroused to such an extent that (with the exception
of one school with 20 pupils) neither Caernarfon nor its
successor authority Gwynedd has been able to close a village
school since.

19   'Key village' is a planning concept of some notoriety. These
are villages on good transport routes with potential for
expansion. Only in these villages will planning permission be
granted for housing and other developments. Settlements
without 'key village' status are expected to remain static or
decline. It is seen by many planners as the only realistic
policy but it necessarily means the extinction of many historically significant but now economically redundant small settlements.

20   Teachers as employees of the Education Committee are in a weak
position to take a leading part in a campaign against its
proposals although this does not always deter them.

21   The position of the Welsh Education Office may be changing. Its
recent publication of a report concerning the physical conditions of small rural schools suggests that it sees a place
for the two-teacher school in certain remote areas. Clwyd LEA
has clearly announced its policy to maintain village schools
wherever possible. Gwynedd LEA has made no policy statement
and although it is committed to implementing reorganization
plans drawn up by the former Merionethshire LEA it is clearly
in two minds about the wisdom of primary school reorganization.
The perceptions of LEA and Welsh Education Office officials
described in this paper are perhaps not quite so true today as
they were a few years ago. Nevertheless it seems that a
majority of both groups still favour reorganization.

Chapter 7

BLAENAU BOYS IN THE MID-1960's

Isobel Emmett

In this paper I shall explore the shared memory a number of young men have, in the mid-1970s, of their leisure lives in the mid-1960s and shall try to show the contribution made by the groups they formed to some kinds of social change.

My interest in this arose in the course of my writing a report on research I had made into leisure patterns of young people in the Manchester area in the mid-1960s. I had become interested in the routes of fashion change: in how a style of speech, clothing or music is initiated and spread through small groups of young people. When I was writing this report I lived in Blaenau Ffestiniog and I began to ask men in their mid-twenties what it had been like for them in Blaenau in the years around 1965; what clothes they had worn, music they had listened to, groups they had identified with, and how their particular adolescent rebellions had been initiated and influenced. This paper is based on those conversations and includes some speculations as to what was achieved by those rebellions.

Blaenau Ffestiniog is a small town in north Wales which grew up in the slate boom of the last century. Since the sharp decline in that industry, which accelerated after the Second World War, the town has suffered from the emigration of much of its population, a high unemployment rate, the deterioration of its buildings, and a reputation for rain and ugliness. It has one of the highest rainfalls in the UK. Slate tips dwarf the houses and shops; sheep walk down the middle of the High Street, past Woolworths and the Co-op, to graze in chapel grounds and front gardens or knock over and feed from dustbins in back alleys; decaying sheds and quarry machinery rusting on green hillsides complete a unique urban landscape.

In the slate quarries the workforce was solidly Nonconformist in religion, solidly first Liberal and then Labour in politics, a passion for choral singing stemming from the one allegiance and for serious discussion from the other. Quite formal discussion groups formed in the 'caban' where breaks from work were taken. A minute book from caban meetings in the Oakley Quarry in 1909 records resolutions passed on topics from 'Which is most important: the police or the bench?' to 'Why do we belong to different denominations in chapel?' and 'Should the Church be disestablished?'; and

debates on whether or not the House of Lords could be said to
represent in any sense slate quarry miners.   One quarryman said, in
this discussion, that because of the animal-like life that most of
the Lords had led for generations, without Godly grace, and because
their ancestry was so polluted, the fruits, the current members of
the House of Lords, could be no good.   Male voice choirs have
existed in the town since the early part of the century and the two
in existence now are very successful.   There is excellent singing
in the town's pubs.

In spite of their serious interest in public affairs and their
trade unionism, the radicalism of the quarrymen was limited in part
by their geographical and consequent political isolation; in part
by the Nonconformist church; in part by their poverty; and in part
by a sense of inferiority face to face with English bosses and landlords, an inferiority which coexisted with pride in being Welsh.

Between 1850 and 1950 small farmers and farm labourers in and
around Blaenau went to the same chapels as the quarrymen and were
part of the same community and culture.   Many small farmers worked
in the quarry during the day.   Perhaps a majority of the men had
experienced working on farms and in the quarries during their lifetime, so that there was no important distinction in lifestyles
between a group of miners on the one hand and a group of small
farmers and farm workers on the other hand.   Since the Second World
War there has been an increase in the prosperity of farmers and
such a division now exists, but it did not for most of the town's
life.   There were few professional or white-collar jobs and there
was and is remarkably little social differentiation in Blaenau, for
a town of its size.

Despite depopulation, Blaenau is still in 1976 the largest centre
of population in Meirionnydd.   Since the Second World War smaller
towns in the area have acquired swimming pools, theatres, art
centres, community centres, technical colleges, and sports fields
but Blaenau lacks all these amenities.   The secondary school has
playing fields and a small swimming pool but at the time of writing
these were not and had not been available to the general public.   In
Blaenau in 1971 the then Ffestiniog District Council refused to buy
the remaining local cinemas which had been closed down in the 1960s,
and since reorganization the new Merioneth District Council has
taken no action.   When the cinema closed down in the neighbouring
town of Bala the Merioneth District Council restored and opened it
and took over its running.

The neglect, indifference or powerlessness of successive generations of local and county councillors, MPs and central government
agencies, and their consequent failure to provide either work
prospects or leisure facilities for the town has for long been
accompanied by a certain apathy and feeling of hopelessness on the
part of the townspeople themselves, though this is now changing.

The Blaenau generation which reached adolescence in the mid-1960s
were all touched by the quarrymen's tradition.   Their parents,
grandparents or great grandparents had been quarrymen, small farmers
and farm workers; few of them had not at some time attended chapel
Sunday school; few families lacked some experience of silicosis.
They grew up speaking Welsh and inherited a Welsh tradition.   They
left school to face very poor work prospects in a town which saw

itself and was widely seen as dying, though that view has changed
and to the generation of which I am writing, Blaenau is a good town
worth fighting for.

Until September 1953 there were two secondary schools, a central
and a grammar school, in the town, which then merged into one comprehensive school. There was no opposition to comprehensivisation
in north Wales. The sparse and declining population made it common
sense. The radical tradition of a working-class area made it
politically attractive. And the virtual lack of a middle class in
north Wales meant there was no-one to organise or voice or even
think of opposition. One effect of this was that the teachers did
not have to struggle to prove, as they did elsewhere, that a comprehensive school was as good as or better than a grammar school.
They felt no challenge to discover new ways of teaching, new ways
of organising the school, the lessons or their content. They
continued to teach as they had always taught. The grammar school
had had some excellent teachers, one left Wales 'despairing' I was
told by one commentator 'of the revitalisation of Welsh cultural
life', another took a university post. Most of the remaining
teachers, aware of the scarcity of white-collar jobs in north Wales,
and the dearth of promotion prospects in teaching, were content or
felt obliged to work in a traditional fashion. Some pupils each
year went from the school to universities and colleges of education;
for these and for other fairly conforming pupils, the school worked
very well. But many of the teenagers of the mid-1960s left a
school which had offered very little. It was, and is, conventional:
it plays safe.

This generation met the distinctive adolescent sub-culture
characteristic of that time, through radio, records, television,
their trips to English cities, visits from young English people -
including the offspring of earlier emigrants from the town, and
from observation of the lifestyle of some English university drop-
outs of middle-class origin in villages and cottages in the
neighbouring countryside. The population of the town at that time
was 6,500. Everyone knew most other people in and around the town,
at least by sight. Of those who adopted anti-establishment values,
three distinctive groups grew up posing themselves against squares,
young and old. One group was called at first mods and later skinheads; another was called variously rockers, greasers or Hell's
Angels; and a third was called hippies.

I think that a smaller proportion of Blaenau's young people at
that time remained square than of the people in big cities. The
town was small and compact; everyone's behaviour, dress and speech
was and is part of a public performance - the audience comprising
the whole population of the town. Once the new styles were visible,
all the young people of the town were touched by them and by the
attitudes they were the expression of, and it needed stronger
pressures from parents in Blaenau than in Manchester to keep
children square and respectable. Some areas of Manchester can be
seen as distinctive small towns: a housing estate or block of flats
here; an old village still forming a local centre there; but such
communities are overlapping with each other and with less coherent
and self-aware collections of dwellings, and are far less inclusive
of all their inhabitants than is a discrete small town several miles

from any other town. For this reason, audiences for that part of
social life which occurs in public are smaller and more splintered
in a city than are audiences in a country town.

The accounts of that period given by members of the different
groups in 1975 were remarkably similar, if allowance is made for
some teasing, and some exaggeration arising from nostaligia and
glamorisation of the past.

HIPPIES

Sion Blewyn Coch (at the time of these conversations a farm worker):
It all started ten years ago in 1965 with the mods and rockers. We
were all together at school and knew each other. Then it started
breaking up into groups. Jacko and Dic Stripes and Brown and Twm
were mods. Dic Stripes had been to Manchester; he was two or three
years older and through him they had links with Manchester. They
all got scooters, wore a kind of uniform, their music was soul:
Otis Redding, that kind of stuff. They all went on to do something,
go to college, take an apprenticeship or something. Jacko went to
art school; Brown went away and trained to be an electrician or
something. They got on in the eyes of the world, got babies,
mortgages, good jobs. (Brown's comment: 'We did get qualifications
and settle down but not all of us are doing that well now.')
The rocks were led by Pedro. They were from the group who left
school at 15, never went out of Blaenau, went to work in quarries
straight away. A couple of Hell's Angels came from Manchester and
organised them into a chapter of Hell's Angels. They had all the
gear - leather jackets with sleeves chopped off, colours, they were
dirty and were supposed to roll in the mud, bite a chicken's head
and things like that. Some did bite a chicken's head off. (Pedro's
comment: 'One did bite a pigeon's head off.') They had more crash
helmets between them than bikes. They went to the Easy Rider cafe
and used that bit of town between the Easy Rider and the town's
Post Office. That was their patch. Pedro was really tough then -
if he wanted a particular girl he just got hold of her in a bear
hug whatever she thought about it. He knocked tables over and the
rest. Their music was Bill Haley, Chuck Berry, old fashioned rock.
(Pedro's comment: 'No, we liked the Stones then.')
We were in between. We thought we were individualists - we didn't
believe in uniforms - but we wore one, of course, looking back. We
didn't go out and buy orange corduroys but we got denim jackets -
Levi jackets and Levi trousers and had long hair. There were rows
about it at home - I suppose that's why I left home. Our music was
progressive rock. We were annoyed at people calling us hippies.
We didn't want to be categorised. We were individuals. There were
more cafes then, good ones. We kept separate from the mods and
rockers. Not that they would fight us, or each other. We all knew
each other too well to have gangs in the town, in that way. We'd
stay talking all night over two drinks; it was good. When people
called us hippies, dirty, et cetera, we would ask them what was a
hippy. No-one could say what a hippy was. Perhaps long hair and
drop-outs. We admired Joe Lord and Harry (two English boys) and
people like that. It took us a while to see it was all a big con.

If they got stuck they could fall back on their old man: get money
from somewhere. Joe Lord went around, really travelled, and we
looked up to him. But he always had middle-class contacts to stay
with. Zed and Y and me tried to set up communes in various places,
but of course they didn't work for us - we had no money at all.
By the time we realised, and got disillusioned, I suppose it was
then the social drinking turned to drinking for its own sake. And
now it's all just drinking to drink. All alcoholics.

The last statement was not true but it is true that all but one of
the speakers quoted here spent most of their spare time in pubs, as
did I, at the time the conversations took place.

Cratcho (unemployed quarryman):

I was never a hippy. But I suppose the people I hung around with
were called that. We used to go to the . . . hotel. It was run
by a nice couple. We had a room to ourselves: Wil Chips and the
rest. We'd play records, drink and talk. Talk about life. There
was a record player in the room. There wasn't a leader but if you
ask who I looked up to, I suppose Wil Chips. He wore a big black
hat and a woman's red coat. Everyone in Blaenau used to curse
him. He was far-out; he still is. It was a good time. But when
the new people came to the . . . hotel, they chucked us out.

Zed (coalman):

People made remarks about our long hair - were we trying to be
women and so forth, but quite a lot of us worked in the quarry and
so from the other men the antagonism couldn't be that great. They
judged us by what we did, not by what we looked like. They took
the mick out of us for our hair, yes, but we did the same work
that they did. Working side by side with people every day makes a
lot of difference. There was probably more hostility in the cities
against people like us.

MODS - SKINHEADS

Jacko (illustrator):

I was the leader of the mods first and then of the skinheads. I
ran away from home twice while I was at school. Once I went to
London and met some people and I thought they were mods. I was
wrong. But I copied them and I came back with these clothes on.
I bumped into Dic Stripes. He was a great friend of mine, still
is. Anyway he was at Bolton Tech then. He looked at me and said
'What are you trying to be?' I said, 'I'm a mod.' He said 'No,
you've got it all wrong. Look, I'll tell you what. You've got
the will and I've got the knowhow. Let's get together.' And
that's how it started. We went to Llandudno and bought our first
lot of gear and that was it. When we went to Pwllheli we were it.
We got hold of a parcel of razors - cut-throats - and we went to
Pwllheli and leaned up against the bar. The local boys came up
and we snapped them out and they ran. (Brown's comment: 'But
there were lots of times when it was us that ran away.')

Dic Stripes (fitter):

There was a bit of aggravation with the greasers. They became
rockers in opposition to us. There used to be dances in the Urdd
(the local branch of the Welsh Youth Movement). They'd get a group

from Rhyl which was really good. They played soul and we were
into soul then. They'd bring their girls along and we'd get in
with them to get to know their girls. There was a thing then for
dancing in a circle or a line. We'd dance in a circle and the
other girls of Blaenau would want to join in the circle. That
sometimes caused a bit of feeling. We didn't really used to sit
on the wall and stick our legs out and stop people passing - but
we looked as though we would.
Dic is out of the dance and describing street behaviour now.
We used to go to the Wheel in Manchester, to Rhyl, all over the
place. We had about three places in Blaenau where we'd meet. In
an old bus station that used to be where the Co-op is now; in a
garage at the bottom of Stac's house where we kept our scooters
and had parties; and in an old railway shed. Some of the best
times were going to Rhyl and places like that - there'd be mods
from everywhere; everyone on a scooter would wave at you. And of
course fights sometimes between us and the rockers that gathered
there. I knew a bloke in Stockport, really THE top mod there.
Benjy, the King of Stockport. When we went to Pwllheli and there
were gangs or they shouted at us we'd let it go. But when Benjy
came down and we went to Pwllheli he wouldn't let it pass.
Mind you, I think the rebellion had already started in Blaenau
before these groups got going. I was in school with Wil Chips and
Zed (two who later became hippies) and we were all into the Stones
and got on well.
Jacko:
Dic was the first to get a scooter. He used to come from
Manchester with accessories for the scooters. At that time I was
ashamed of being Welsh. But when I went to art college the students there were so middle class, that started me coming back to
being Welsh.
Brown (electrician):
We wanted to be different - that was the main thing. It was a way
of being different. Jacko and I shaved off our hair once. We
used to go to the cafe - six of us; that was the real group. We
were anti-Welsh because Welsh people were square, Wales was
square. You couldn't be with it if you were Welsh. There isn't
that feeling now. But the hippies weren't anti-Welsh and nor
were Pedro's lot (the Hell's Angels). We were more friendly with
the hippies because we used to go to some of their parties. And
of course they were friendly with everyone then. That was their
thing.

ROCKERS - HELL'S ANGELS

Pedro (grinder - unemployed at the time of the conversations):
Almost everybody in Blaenau were greasers. Greasers wore leather
jackets, full of studs. Hell's Angels wore leather jackets and
over them denims with no sleeves with the colours embroidered on
them, but no studs. Greasers were clean, though they had greasy
hair and weren't as tough as the Angels. Oh, I must have been
about 18 then. Anyway, fifteen of us went to Manchester on a
trip. One of us knew one of the Angels in Manchester so we got

off the bus in Piccadilly and went to the cafe and he said they
wanted a Welsh chapter and we would be suitable. We weren't called
Hell's Angels, but 1 percenters. Our colours were 1 percent and
the word Wales and in between a flying wheel. One percent was a
section of Hell's Angels. Ifan was leader and me and a bloke from
Dolwyddelan were seconds - Sergeant-at-arms we were. We got going
after the mods and quite late on I got a 600 - no insurance, no
tax. The others in Blaenau had bikes - four out of five of them
and about six blokes came over from Pwllheli every weekend and
sometimes we'd go to Manchester. We ran Blaenau. We were
expected to keep off other gangs from our territory. Jacko was a
skinhead and we got on well together. They were always respectable
- they had short hair, but not really short like the skinheads in
Manchester (Jacko's comment: 'You can't have it shorter than no
hair at all!') and not the chrome caps and spikes on shoes.
(Jacko: 'Skinheads didn't wear toe-caps.') We used to fight with
the straights and there was a gang of greasers used to come down
from Talsarnau and we used to do them in when they came down to
Blaenau. That's when the dance was closed down in Blaenau. I
was barred from there ten times, I suppose. If you were a Hell's
Angel you weren't supposed to take it from people, but the others
did. If someone said to me 'You're a bastard' I'd hit them. The
others would take it. Ifan wasn't hard enough to be our leader.
He was certainly hard enough physically but he was soft-hearted.
So Gai said he'd be leader but this wasn't on. Gai went to
Manchester and said he wanted to be leader. There should have
been a fight between the old leader and the challenger but Ifan
was fed up. He'd been chucked out of his house for being an
Angel. So he wouldn't go down to being just one of the blokes.
He and most of the others sent in their colours. They were
always doing me for actual bodily harm, offensive weapons, disturbing the peace, and so forth. People in Blaenau thought of me
as the only real Hell's Angel. Once I was done for offensive
weapons; I'd jumped off a motor bike and had a crash helmet on.
I suppose the helmet was the offensive weapon. After a lot of
suspended sentences I went inside and that was that. The end of
it. When we packed up, the skinheads packed up, more or less.
Everyone, the young kids from 12 upwards were making their mothers
buy leather jackets. But there were more of the hippies than
there were of us, the real group. I suppose our group lasted
about three years.

In the conversations from which these quotations are extracts
and in others, it transpired that three rebellious groups grew up
in the mid-1960s composed of young boys who all knew each other.
There is general agreement about who was attached to each group.
To be a mod or a Hell's Angel was to make a firmer commitment than
was made by those described as hippies. The mods and Hell's Angels
accepted the labels and endeavoured to act in ways that conformed
to their notion of what a mod or a Hell's Angel should be. Those
described as hippies did not accept their label in the same way, and
no conformity was required of them, though some occurred. The
number of boys having a more or less loose attachment to the hippy
philosophy and style was, therefore, larger than the groups of
Hell's Angels and mods, the former being a formally structured

group, the latter being a very small and informally structured
group.

Many people, including Jacko himself, looking back, saw Jacko
as leader of the mods and skinheads, but he shared that position
with Dic Stripes and Jacko felt that Dic's influence was crucial.
Jacko was in the district more of the time than was Dic, and still
lives in the town, whilst Dic lives in an English city. Most
people, looking back, saw Pedro as leader of the Hell's Angels and
from his own account it is clear that whilst he never formally held
that position, he shared Ifan's leadership and in the daily interaction with people of the town, superseded it. The transformation
of Pedro and his group from greasers to Hell's Angels was initiated
by Manchester acquaintances. The hippies did not see themselves as
a gang; by definition were non-combative,(1) although as individuals
and in pairs they got involved in fights; and they did not like the
idea of, or the word, leader. But all the ex-hippies of Blaenau to
whom I spoke saw the English drop-outs as models, and some saw the
Welsh, Blaenau boy Wil Chips as the initiator amongst themselves.
Of the English drop-outs named to me by hippies as influential in
some degree, all but one have now conformed by going back to higher
education and professional careers. Joe Lord is still in the
district, being now seen as a lonely eccentric. Wil Chips works
in England and has been involved in arranging Pop concerts.

Thus the immediate stimulus to form the groups came from outside
and the music, speech, gestures, clothes and styles which were the
manifestation of adolescent rebellion at that time, came from
outside Wales. The Blaenau boys adapted that raw material to their
own situation, limited means and Welsh culture. The hippies devised
a Welsh hip vocabulary. Only in the case of the mods was there a
rejection of Wales and of the Welsh language. That rejection was
temporary. All the ex-mods I met speak Welsh for preference;
Jacko is a fervent nationalist and most of those mentioned above
support Plaid Cymru.

In making this short study, my original aim was to find first a
concrete illustration of the impact of the events of the mid-1960s
on the lives of specific people; and second, a concrete illustration
of the routes by which changes in fashion travel, and become modified. This first aim was satisfied. I knew the English drop-outs
who had been influential on the hippies; I met an English Hell's
Angel who had been a contact of the Blaenau Angels; I heard much
of Benjy, the King of Stockport, who had been influential on the
mods. I had acquired some insight as to how important the mid-
1960s had been for my informants and for changes in customary
behaviour between parents and teenage children in Blaenau. But
the enquiry had aroused my interest beyond its first goal, and I
have since gone on to reflect on whether or not the conversations,
some of which are reported above, help towards an understanding of
social change in Wales.

In the opening paragraphs of this paper I referred to its
content as an exploration of a shared memory which a group of young
men have, in the mid-1970s, of their lives in the mid-1960s.

The exact truth and validity of the accounts and the

representativeness of the speakers, interest me less than do their
current significance to the speakers and to others.

The accounts were responses to my expressed interest by young
men seen, in the first instance, separately and alone. In each
case, the amount of enquiry or explanation I needed to make in
order to start the conversation was minimal. I knew the speakers
well or quite well before the enquiry. Several of the conversations
took place when the speakers happened to be in my house casually
visiting. A hint of the topic I was interested in was enough to
set off very long monologues and in several cases the speakers took
up the topic again and again when they saw me. I showed the
speakers and others involved in the groups, drafts of what I wrote
and I have recorded in parentheses some of their comments. The similarities between the first received accounts which came from Sion
Blewyn Coch (hippy), Pedro (Hell's Angel) and Jacko (mod) were
remarkable to me. In many later conversations with the speakers,
their wives and girlfriends and other members of the groups, I
received no impressions which made me doubt the honesty or the
general rightness of the picture painted. From a participant in
the conference whose proceedings form the subject of this book, a
native of Blaenau and, in his own words 'a square' in the mid-1960s,
I received the comment that I had got the picture of those times
'just right'. For the young adults in Blaenau in 1976 whom I know,
the shared memory described above is a valid account. This version,
this myth (2) of the past, is shared by more than the speakers. It
may have been fashioned in the course of many encounters between
the participants, over a number of years. It was not so fashioned
in the early months of 1975 by interactions between my informants.

I have no accurate measure of the proportion of teenagers living
in the town in the mid-1960s who could be said to be represented by
the speakers here recorded. Nor have I an accurate measure of the
degree to which the speakers were typical of those who felt and
dressed like them. There was and is a 'square' Blaenau. There are
now in Blaenau young men and rather more young women between 20 and
30 years old who attend chapel fairly regularly, but they are very
few. The first year of the sixth form of the school contained, in
1966, 21 out of a school population of 529 and in 1976, 29 out of a
school population of 647. The girl guide movement has members
between 20 and 30.(3)

Almost by definition my speakers were not typical of the town's
population in the mid-1960s. They were rebels, they were to some
extent precursors of the future; they were to some extent victims
of a market drive to dip into the pockets of a group with new
spending powers. Some sociologists see that generation of adolescents as solely the latter: victims of a phase of capitalism. If
this view is correct, the rebellion, aspects of which I have given
accounts of, will have no lasting significance; it will not have
changed anything of importance. I do not accept that view; I think
it contributed to change in three important ways: to the change in
parents' and teachers' behaviour towards young people; to the change
in the view young people in Welsh-speaking Wales have about Welsh
culture; and to the change in the view that Blaenau people had of
their own town, which is part of a general move towards decentral-
isation and grass-roots political action.

CHANGE IN INTER-GENERATIONAL BEHAVIOUR IN BRITAIN

Adolescents in the 1960s were treated more as a separate section of
society than they had been before. This treatment partly reflected
the division between generations which increase with the increasing
pace of social change. It partly reflected the fact that a section
of the commercial world magnified that division and spread by
national networks of communication the changes in musical taste,
dress and speech initiated by young people. This commercial activity
in turn reflected the new relative affluence in the post-war boom of
adolescents whose wages, whilst they were single, were largely
available for spending on leisure.
    The current climate of opinion was one in which conventional
beliefs were being questioned; the population of Britain as a whole
was less inclined than hitherto it had been to do what it was told,
to accept as 'better' or 'fit to lead' those in positions of
leadership and power, and more sceptical about what it read. That
climate of opinion; child-rearing theories which stressed the
humanity of young people and the filtering down of those theories
to the majority of parents; and the fact that young people formed a
market; all strengthened the timeless, perpetual revolt of teenages
against their parents, which has always stemmed from the different
life situations of parents and teenage children. Teenagers existed
in a trap; their bodies told them they were grown up; the newspaper
spoke of pupil power; but another part of the economy, speaking
through the education system and through industry, said 'You will
not succeed in the world unless you stay on at school, go to
university, or in other ways extend your period of dependence.'
    In addition, events in the USA, from the James Dean cult, through
the beat and hippy movements, to the Vietnam war protests and
student drop-outs, fed rebellious values into the consciousness of
British adolescents and this input in turn was magnified by the
national networks of communication and by commercial exploitation.
In 1965 the pressures encouraging the recognition of adolescents as
a distinct sub-culture were particularly sharp. National service
was abolished in 1961 and the last national serviceman had left the
forces by the end of 1962. Between January 1956 and June 1966 the
pay of juvenile workers increased significantly faster than that of
other workers. For example, the weekly wage for juveniles in
manufacturing industries increased by 61.2 per cent (the hourly
rate by 76.8 per cent) but that for male workers in those industries
by only 47.8 per cent (the hourly rate by 61.8 per cent).
    American influences had been strong in films, music, language
and dress for some years, but now the supremacy of the Beatles
symbolised the strength of native, corner-boy cultures.
    Adolescents shared a common life situation, having largely
escaped parental control but not yet subject to the social constraints of full maturity, including their own parenthood; and were
at a stage where friends of the same age, the peer group, are a very
important influence. As they became treated as a separate section
of society and perceived themselves in that way, they themselves
sought for ways to distinguish themselves from adults and from those
who accepted adult values and adult authority. The values differed
not so much in substance from adults' values as in the order of

priorities. A general agreement about what are virtues is not
useful since virtues conflict with each other: the dictates of
honesty conflict with the dictates of loyalty; caring for your own
children prevents you from giving to the poor. Thus people hold
different values to the extent that they have different priorities,
and to say they value a quality is meaningful only to the extent
that they pay the cost of valuing that quality, which is to reject
its opposites. Young people value some things more than adults do
because they dislike more intensely the vices which spring from the
lack of these qualities. The content of adolescent values was not
only an affirmation of certain virtues such as sincerity, personal
freedom, gaiety and novelty but also a rejection of others which
have high priority for adults.

The reaction from the adult world was very sharp. The first
young men to wear shoulder-length hair were regarded by many adults
as literally sick in the mind, perverse and in need of treatment.
A revulsion only slightly less strong was felt for girls who wore
long skirts during the day.

That period can be seen as one in which teenagers battled hard
to break up the widespread belief that acceptance of received
values, styles of behaviour, was in itself a virtue. Other rebellious groups, religious and political, had fought and were fighting
that battle on particular issues: women's votes, acceptance of
Fascism by British leaders, the use of atomic weapons; and on very
general and fundamental issues: the necessity for Socialism to
replace Capitalism, for instance. There have always been dedicated,
serious minorities whose members spend all their spare time
intentionally trying to change the society in which they live. In
the mid-1960s a large section of a whole generation, without overall
organisation or plan, fought a battle on a wider, though more
shallow front, than others and won a decisive victory.

The generation who were adolescents in the late 1960s succeeded
in breaking down conventions of dress and hair-style and at the
same time won recognition of their right to more independence than
previous generations, as adolescents, had had. Those reaching
adolescence in later years have not met with the same resistance to
their bids for freedom as faced the young in 1966. The decisiveness
of the 1960s victory had a more far-reaching consequence. The
adolescents of the late 1960s were the model, not only for those
younger than themselves, but also for many older than themselves
who in the ensuing years took advantage of the outcome of the battle.
Some followed the young in their choice of language, dress, hair
and smoking to declare themselves not square, not conventional, not
'dead'. Others recognised that many old rigidities as to what was
'not done' by this or that age-group, class or gender were ended and
took advantage of this fact to build their own self-images from a
wider range of raw materials.

These superficial changes were not all that was left when the
adolescent sub-culture declined. A catch phrase for what it
ushered in is 'the permissive society'. A more important legacy
was its help in spreading to wider groups than ever before the
habit of questioning received values. People are less likely than
they were before the war to do something because they are told it
is good for them.

The rebellion of the Blaenau boys was part of this important movement. They helped, in their own place, in their own distinctive way, to successfully claim for young people an earlier independence than their parents and teachers had achieved; to have their opinions taken into account; to have wider rights to act in the ways they thought correct.

THE CHANGE IN YOUNG WELSH PEOPLE'S VIEW OF THEIR CULTURE

Social movements of the kind I am discussing occasionally crystallise and make visible the constant but often imperceptible process of social change. One of the significances of the movement was that in Welsh-speaking Wales it helped to create a new non-square, non-deferential Welshness.

In the 1950s and early 1960s, when the impact of television was first being felt in Wales, the future of the Welsh language and culture looked dim. The unemployment rate in north Wales (4) was high. It had long been the case that fluency in writing and speaking the English language was a necessity for most white-collar jobs. Thus there was economic pressure on young people to speak English and to move out of Wales. The chapel, for so long a carrier of the Welsh traditions, had lost most of its force. Plaid Cymru at that time seemed the property of intellectuals and returned exiles who, realising they had lost irremediably the treasure of their native heritage, in so far as to come into that inheritance involved interacting easily with working quarrymen and farmworkers, sought to assert their Welshness by formal political action.

What turned the tide? Some of the responses to the threats to the culture were well publicised. Saunders Lewis gave his powerfully seminal BBC lecture in February 1962. In 1966 the Welsh Committee of the Arts Council of Great Britain became a much more independent Welsh Arts Council. In 1965 the Welsh Books Council, which from 1962 to that date had existed as a voluntary organisation, was reformed with subsidies from the Arts Council. Gwynfor Evans was elected for Parliament in a by-election of 1966. But without changes at the grass roots these events either would not have taken place or would have occurred without important effect.

The generation which came to adolescence in the mid-1960s, happening to hit the world wide adolescent movement and respond to it in ways some of which are described above, could at that period, have opted for anglicisation. The music they listened to was English and American. The books they read were English.

Whatever the labels hippy, mod and rocker represented elsewhere, in Blaenau the three groups who for a time accepted these labels represented, amongst other things, different responses to the prospect of anglicisation.

Three alternative styles of rebellion were available from outside and were picked up in one case by the solid manual working base of Blaenau's population; in the second case by some of those who were using school at the same time as rebelling; and in the third case by a group of those already further than the others in their own private rebellion. One of the important things members of all

three groups had in common was that they not only picked up ideas
from outside but adapted them, used them, assimilated them to
their own Welsh small-town lives and were not dominated by them.

Purists of the Welsh language said the language would be killed
by the incorporation into it of English borrowings. But the
language would be much more likely to die if it were not sufficiently flexible to assimilate and adapt to serve its own purposes
vocabulary from outside. Welsh cultural purists expressed views
ranging from 'If the chapel dies, the culture dies' through 'to
be Welsh, singing must follow in the old tradition' to 'there
cannot, by definition, be Welsh pornography'. But Dafydd Iwan,
Lolfa (5) and the Blaenau boys and their like showed, on the
contrary, that only if you had modern popular music, pin-ups,
Hell's Angels and hippies IN WELSH could you keep young people
faithful to the culture. The Hell's Angels seem to have felt no
temptation to become anglicised; they spoke English with their
Manchester equivalents, incorporated technical and jargon words
about motor bikes and the movement into their own speech patterns,
and continued to speak Welsh among themselves. They were firmly
embedded in the life of the town and carried on, in a new style,
an already existing pattern of behaviour. The hippies, using, for
a time, a commune set up by English drop-outs, entangled in philosophical arguments and reading English books and magazines,
consciously faced and consciously resisted the temptation to
become anglicised. The mods, finding their identity as mods most
clearly in gatherings of other scooter riders in Manchester and at
the seaside towns, felt and for a time succumbed to the temptation.
But members of all three groups supported each other in their
Welshness: they could not speak English to each other, certainly
not in Blaenau; and the town itself supported them in their Welshness. For although some of the boys had difficulties at home and
at school; some left home and several got into trouble of a more
serious kind, breaches with the family were temporary, and the
overwhelming majority interact a great deal with their families.
Zed's comment: 'They took the mick out of us for our hair, yes, but
we did the same work that they did. Working side by side with
people every day makes a lot of difference' illustrates that at
the height of their rebellion, the boys' normalcy, as well as their
novel ways, was visible to the whole community. Now, ten years on,
most of the boys still do not dress conventionally, but though
still distinctive, they merge into the population as a novel but
still Welsh component of a very Welsh community.

In 1960, to a stranger entering Blaenau on a Sunday, the predominant sight was bright-hatted women going to or from chapel,
accompanied by middle-aged and elderly men in suits and hats, with
a few men in working clothes setting off with fishing rods. Now,
in addition to those, the same stranger would see the informants
quoted above and their friends, bearded, dressed in denims, hitch-
hiking to a county which has Sunday opening; and their descendants,
in the styles of the 1970s, taking over the streets but failing for
the most part to shock.

CHANGE IN THE VIEW THAT BLAENAU PEOPLE HAVE OF THEIR TOWN

In the above section I argue that there has been a change in the
social components of the town. There has also been a change in how
the town is perceived by its population. Many inhabitants of other
villages and towns in Gwynedd express the view that Blaenau is
dead, and a few believe that this is just as well. For many years
some such negative view was reflected in Blaenau people's own
perception of their town. Several processes have contributed to
that view being transformed. A number of English people, finding
houses in the town relatively cheap, moved in and having done so
found its unique visual qualities and the friendliness of its
people an incentive to stay and enthuse about it. Quarry tours
and other tourist attractions have made Blaenau people look again
at a town which foreigners will travel, and pay, to see. Such an
altered perception snowballs. Once the slogan 'Black is beautiful'
had been announced in America, increasing numbers of negroes found
a new beauty in their own people. Once the feeling 'Blaenau is
beautiful' found expression, increasing numbers of Blaenau people
felt a new pride in their town.
    To these strands of change can be added another. The Blaenau
boys of this paper, having won, with some panache, the right to be
themselves and to be Welsh in a different way from the way of their
fathers, were equipped to fight a new battle. They had rebelled
against some traditions, retained others and transformed still
others and in doing so had to some degree made the town their own.
In the process, having acted as a group and learned the strength
that comes from group action, they acquired, as a by-product of
their rebellion, experience which they could use more intentionally
in the town's life. They intend to stay in Blaenau: it is their
town and it is good. Some of them are finding their way into local
political action and are trying to make the town a better place to
grow up in.
    Thus the mid-1960s rebellion, in this town at least, was not
merely an example of big business manipulating young people. It
made important contributions to social change in three distinct
ways.

NOTES

1 I heard much teasing reference, from members of the other groups,
   to the hippies' slogan 'Peace, man'.
2 I use the term myth not to imply that Blaenau people peculiarly
   make myths of their past but to refer to the fact that all our
   versions of our past are in some way fashioned by us and can be
   seen as myths, often used to justify or account for present
   behaviour.
3 I adopt these crude indicators of squareness, not to suggest
   that a person who goes to chapel or belongs to the guide movement
   or who stays on at school is necessarily square but rather because
   these activities are approved by adult society and a person who
   does several of them will probably be regarded as square by his
   or her peers.

4   I confine myself to North Wales since I am unfamiliar with
    other Welsh-speaking parts of the country.
5   A small Welsh publishing venture which produces with-it Welsh
    posters and books.

Chapter 8

ETHNIC AWAKENING IN THE FIRST WORLD: THE CASE OF WALES

Bud Khleif

INTRODUCTION

The post Second World War era is marked by ethnic awakening in the First World. Groups long dormant or thought to be dead have begun to assert their cultural rights, language rights, and community rights. In this assertion, '"culture" is brandished as a magic word, embracing the total life and aspirations of a group' (Thomas, 1973a:21). This is true, for example, of the five Celtic groups in Britain and France (the Scots, Welsh, Northern Irish, Cornish, and Breton) and of the Basques in Spain and France. Paradoxically, it would seem, whereas the Third World is intent on *de-tribalization* as a prerequisite for creation of national unity, the First World is going through a stage of *re-tribalization* in the interest of decentrality. But this paradox is more apparent than real: independence movements within the First World are but an extension of, and a sequel to, those of the Third World; for it is the under-developed regions of the overdeveloped world, what may be termed 'the Third World within the First World,' that are currently asserting their autonomy (Khleif, 1974:1).

The twentieth century, the American Century, marks the heightened entrance (in some cases, re-entrance) into history of heretofore diverse, isolated, or acquiescent groups: tribal and farm populations in the hinterlands of Asia, Africa, and Latin America; old 'non-state nations,' e.g., Wales, Corsica, and Quebec; and non-Protestant 'White Ethnics' and 'Third-World Americans' in the USA. What is common to all these groups is that they have developed new rising elites after 1945, an assertive new middle-class, anti-colonial in character, aware of its past, bent on consolidating its future. Indeed, in the First World, North America itself is a case in point, e.g., the *Quiet Revolution* in Canada, that is, the post-1945 waning of the political and social influence of the Catholic Church in Quebec and the stress on self-reliance, achievement, and ethnic pride on the part of French Canadians (cf. Rioux, 1971; Trent, 1975). In the USA, this era signifies the emergence especially of non-Protestant 'White Ethnics' into full political and occupational equality (Henry A. Kissinger and Daniel Patrick Moynihan are meteoric examples), an era celebrated in two well-known books, *The*

Decline of the WASP (i.e., the rise of the non-WASP, Schrag, 1970)
and *The Rise of the Unmeltable Ethnics* (i.e., defiance of Anglo
particularism and cultural hegemony, Novak, 1971). A not unrelated
example in Western Europe is the ethnic resurgence of the Celtic
Fringe, e.g., in Scotland and Wales, against the English centre.
In a word, ethnicity is part of a global structural change.
   We now come to the central hypothesis of this paper, namely, that
ethnicity, to be viewed as a worldwide phenomenon (one is tempted to
say, in global Kissingeresque manner: with a world map spread
before one's eyes) *is to be located in the transformation of group
relations as a result of change in the systems of labor in the post-
industrial society, a transformation associated not only with
external but also with internal decolonization*. This applies in
particular to the First and Third Worlds. It is perhaps a useful
framework for examining seemingly diverse phenomena: the transition
from the Pax Britannica, for example, to the Pax Americana; the
relation between the populations of politically independent but
economically dependent states and multinational (actually 'trans-
national') corporations; the civil rights movement, student movement, and women's movement especially in the post-1965 era; the
series of externally induced civil wars since 1945; the politics
of non-violence; and the politics of ethnicity.

ETHNICITY AS AN ESTATE

Ethnicity could be viewed as part of an older system of labor, a
pre-capitalist division of labor, indicative of the *Staende* (estates
or status-groups) preceding the *Klassen* (social classes) in Weber's
sense of the terms, a sort of persistence which is mobilizable in
socio-political and socio-economic group transformations, an aspect
of a seemingly never ending de-tribalization/re-tribalization progression. Ethnicity is a matter of stratification, a macro-
sociological variable equal to class and race; it is 'an aspect of
the fusion of status order with the political order, while class is
a dimension of the relationship of the economic order to the
political order' (Horowitz, 1976:224).
   Ethnicity is indicative of new social forms; it is a function of
an imperfect integration of societal layers, of blocked assimilation.
If society, in Robert E. Park's terms, is defined as a group of
competitive groups that are in temporary balance (1921:665), then
ethnicity could be understood as a strategy of new generations of
subordinated groups to alter the traditional balance of power, the
peace treaty (so to speak), the definition of reality imposed by
dominant groups (Khleif, 1972). In this sense, then, ethnicity is
dependent on structural conditions, on positions to which groups
are relegated in the social structure, on definitions of the situation in which groups find themselves (cf. Yancey et al., 1976).
   In this paper, we view ethnicity primarily as a political phenomenon, analyzable in terms of its interconnections with socio-
economic arrangements, a vehicle for getting political power and
defending economic interests, a strategy for change (cf. Charsley,
1974; Cohen, 1969; Cohen, 1974:xv; Zolberg, 1976). We argue that
the post-1945 new middle class, the new intelligentsia in Wales and

elsewhere, has used its ethnicity as a tool for recreating its
sense of distinctiveness, a rallying point for unity amidst com-
petitiveness with other groups, a symbol of a quest for economic
advancement. The post-1945 ethnically assertive middle class has
attempted, through an ideology of nationalism, to present its
interests as general interests and thus influence or mobilize large
segments of the population.

Obviously, ethnicity is of two kinds. We are concerned here with
the ethnicity of the oppressed, the subordinate, the minorities -
not that of the oppressor, the dominant, or the majorities. In
other words, what is at stake is the ethnicity of the Welsh and
similarly situated groups, an ethnicity connoting a sense of deprivation, historical injustics, a search for roots, and a quest for
socio-economic advancement - not the ethnicity of the English or
culturally hegemonic groups, an ethnicity that for those outside it
looms large as a massive reality, an all-permeating ideology,
taken-for-granted, unquestionably privileged, or seemingly so.

We see ethnicity as part of a large framework of stratification.
We do not subsume ethnicity under class but look at both as inter-
locking elements that are at times in conflict, at others in full
reciprocity. We consider the *ethnic* factor - the 'estate' factor
in Weber's terms - as having quite often a force of its own, as
having consequences in its own right, as augmenting or counteracting the effect of class, as forcing the person to take a stance
between what he sees as his position vis-à-vis his cultural community and his relation to the marketplace.

Obviously, not all members of the new middle class in the Third-
World regions of the First World are engaging in ethnic assertion.
Some are vociferously anti-ethnic, regarding ethnicity as a form
of self-ghettoization, a total institution (in Goffman's terms) that
impedes their social mobility, a curb on their sense of individuality
and personal autonomy (Woolfe, 1974; Patterson, et al., 1975;
Basham, 1976). Some deny their ethnicity or suffocate it deliberately; others live it only privately at home (Kalčik and Hawes,
1976); others, in the third or fourth generation of assimilation are
estranged from their ethnicity and feel uncomfortable when confronted
with it (Wilkes, 1976). But what is important to remember is that a
considerable number of the post-1945, new middle class is militant
about its ethnicity and that for them ethnicity serves a dual purpose: it is an expression of upward striving as well as a context
for social bonds and solidarity. This is precisely the class that
has supplied a requisite ideology for cultural regeneration, for
'consciousness raising' amongst the general population.

ETHNICITY AS COMMUNITY

Ethnicity can be regarded as a search for roots, for identity, for
creation of Gemeinschaft in the midst of Gesellschaft, for coping
with issues of alienation in a mass society. The resurgence of
ethnicity cannot only be understood as a tool for social mobility
but also as a widespread quest for community, a search for authenticity in the face of the overwhelming forces of modern life that
are thought to be conducive to depersonalization, bureaucratization,

and unresponsiveness on the one hand, and to glorification of the
trivial, the violent, and the absurd on the other.   'Too little,'
in the words of Novak (1976:v), 'stands between the solitary individual and the bureaucratic power of the large modern state;
intermediate social bonds have been weakening - family, kinship,
group loyalties, churches, neighborhoods, regions'; hence, the
importance of ethnicity in putting the person in touch with himself,
his history, and his cultural kin.

The increasing emphasis on ethnic identity may be a self-
protective response to the increasing homogeneity of modern life,
to an oppressive uniformity.   Increasingly, more and more people
especially in the First World look alike, think alike, and eat
alike: an emphasis on ethnicity, on an ancestral language, for
example, is an emphasis on something that cannot be bought or
mass-produced.   An emphasis on ethnicity, on unique cultural
elements, will probably increase with international levelling in
consumption, production, and scientific-technical processes (cf.
Schoek, 1969:355, cited by Goehring, 1975:64).

We think the preceding formulations are useful. We would like
not only to view them in a worldwide context and fundamentally
anchor them in the notion of systems of labor and the exigencies
associated with the recreation of such systems, but also locate
them essentially in the post-1945 socio-economic transformations
that are collectively known as the 'post-industrial society'.

ETHNICITY AND THE POST-INDUSTRIAL SOCIETY

The world as we know it began in the nineteenth century. The 'White
Peril,' as Black American writers termed it in the 1960s, was a
process of relentless racial and socio-economic hegemony that
culminated around 1850 into turning the whole globe into a single
social system serving an industrial culture radiating out of
Western Europe and North America. It was Western colonialism that
consolidated the world into a single social system serving the needs
of Western industrialism (Worsley, 1973:50-3). This explains the
historical intersection of the First World and the Third World, as
we call them today, and especially the enclaves of the Third World
in the First World itself. For during the decades preceding the
First World War (the 'first imperial war'), Western Europe nations,
by exacting greater cultural conformity from various population
strata in their own periphery created some of the 'ethnic problems'
seen in them today (Zolberg, 1976:33). The Education Act of 1870
in Britain, for example, made English the compulsory language of
instruction throughout the Celtic Fringe, thus almost killing the
Welsh language as a vehicle of indigenous culture.

It is useful to think of significant transformations in the
world system as affecting the resurgence or dormancy of ethnicity
and to regard a given country as merely *a sub-unit in the world
system*.

The fundamental structural change in the nature of industrial
society in the West occurred, however, after 1945, a distinct
transformation, the major features of which are perhaps two: (a) the
emergence of trans-national corporations as worldwide entities

affecting the economy and stratification system of the nation-
state; and (b) the death of old empires and the rise of new ones.
What Scotland, Wales, Cornwall and Northern Ireland were to England
are now what the countries of Western Europe are to North America:
a 'Celtic Fringe' writ large, a North Atlantic Fringe. What this
essentially means is the following:

(a) a transformation of the occupational structure of the First
    World, e.g., an increase in white-collar occupations and in
    rising expectations; and

(b) the extension of industrialization into hitherto isolated
    peripheries, giving rise to the sort of heightened conscious-
    ness that had much earlier been associated with the industrial-
    ization of centers but which here took on an 'ethnic'
    character.

    Examples are the post-Second World War asbestos strike in
    Quebec, some aspects of which helped later on to trigger off
    the 'Quiet Revolution' among French Canadians, and the more
    recent strike of the 'Joint Français' in Brittany, which is
    thought to have contributed to consolidating the Breton ethnic
    consciousness (Zolberg, 1976:34-5).

In other words, the accelerated industrialization and bureaucratization of peripheral regions of the First World after 1945,
of Third-World enclaves therein, has resulted in increased restless-
ness of heretofore subordinate groups - a case of disruption of
the colonial order *within* after it had been disrupted without.

The emergence, after 1945, of what Gorer (1975) terms the 'skilled
working class' in Britain accounts partly for ethnic resurgence in
the Celtic Fringe, that is, for an enhanced solidarity of a
deprived group, for an increased consciousness of group identity.
The emergence of a new middle class completes the picture, in the
sense that it is usually the middle class which supplies the
requisite ideology and articulates identity consciousness. We will
deal with such emergence in some detail.

A number of writers in Europe and North America have referred to
the post-1945 fundamental structural changes in the nature of
industrial society in the West by various labels: the 'post-
capitalist' society (Dahrendorf, 1959:272); the 'post-bourgeois'
society (Lichtheim, 1963:194), the 'post-modern' society (Etzioni,
1968:vii); the 'neo-capitalist' society (Mallet, 1975:68,115); and
especially the 'post-industrial' society (Touraine, 1969; Bell,
1973:51-4, 112-19; Kleinberg, 1973). Bell deftly summarizes the
characteristics of the post-industrial society:

In descriptive terms, there are three components; in the economic
sector, it is a shift from manufacturing to services; in technology, it is the centrality of the new science-based industries;
*in sociological terms, it is the rise of new technical elites
and the advent of a new principle of stratification*. From this
terrain, one can step back and say more generally that the post-
industrial society means the rise of new axial structures and
axial principles: *a changeover from a goods-producing society to
an information or knowledge society*; and in the modes of knowledge, a change in the axis of abstraction from empiricism or
trial-and-error tinkering to theory and the codification of
theoretical knowledge for directing innovation and the formulation
of policy. (Bell, 1973:487, emphasis added)

For Bell, (a) the occupational structure is the key to the
social structure; (b) class is based on technical knowledge; (c)
the new 'knowledge class', or 'men of information', is the dominant
element of the post-industrial social structure (Janowitz, 1974:
231-3).

In the post-industrial society, the key institutions are those
that are concerned with the production and distribution of knowledge,
not with the production of material goods. The new 'knowledge
class,' what some people have called 'educated labor,' is of central
importance in the political economy (Flacks, 1972:86-7).

The new 'knowledge class' is a university-produced class. In the
post-industrial society, 'the university ... has now become the
arbiter of class position' and 'has gained a quasi-monopoly in
determining the future stratification of society' (Bell, 1973:410).
Whereas the first industrial revolution inverted the traditional
ratio of agricultural to industrial workers, the second industrial
revolution - the cybernetic revolution of the post-industrial
society - is inverting the ratio of manual to intellectual workers,
making organized intelligence the chief productive force (Schelsky,
1961:33; Garaudy, 1970:22,61). Between 1955 and 1965 for example,
the college student population especially in Europe and America
doubled in some countries, in others tripled (cf. Banks, 1972:20).
More people have been employed in teaching and research and in sales
and services rather than manufacturing; more MAs and PhDs produced.
The traditional university orientation moved from 'class' to 'mass';
the university became a 'knowledge factory'.

What has all this got to do with ethnicity? The post-industrial
society marks the advent of a new system of labor, a system where
the new 'knowledge class' is prominent. The new 'knowledge class'
is heavily ethnic: pro-Welsh, Welsh-speaking Welshmen in Wales;
pro-Quebec, Joual-speaking Frenchmen in Canada ('Joual' is Quebec
French, not standard or Parisian French); self-assertive, post-1945
university-trained professional class of non-WASPs (Catholics and
Jews) in the USA. It is precisely this new middle class, this
intelligentsia, which is spearheading ethnic resurgence, that is,
using ethnicity (ethnic boundaries, markers and signs of exclusivity
and belongingness) as an instrument of social change. In a word,
ethnicity is a function of higher education in the post-1945 era.

APPLICATION TO WALES

We are now ready to pull together three essential points and present
them in relation to Wales: a rising middle class as an agent of
ethnic revitalization, its use of language as the supreme mark of
ethnicity, and its quest for community. Our data are based on our
field work in Wales during 1973-4.

The new middle class in Wales is a middle class mostly appearing
after 1945 (Khleif, 1974:19-21; 1975:106-9). The current leaders
of Welsh opinion are overwhelmingly sons and daughters of coal
miners, agricultural workers, steel workers, shop keepers, and minor
civil servants, but especially of coal miners. These leaders are
mostly school masters, clergymen, and university lecturers,
occupational categories highly prized in a country like Wales with

its traditional emphasis on education. They come, for the most
part, from rural areas both north and south but not typically from
Cardiff or Swansea, although they may live there now. They are all
Welsh-speaking and, in a small country such as Wales, know each
other very well. Their Welshness sets them apart, for to have
spoken Welsh at home, a generation ago, meant that the person by
definition was working-class. They are very proud of their Welshness, of their ability to speak Welsh, of their ability to 'live a
full Welsh life'. They consider their knowledge of Welsh a badge
of achievement, for it differentiates them from other middle-class
men as well as working-class men who are English monoglots.

In Wales, the new university-trained class has been a reinforcement of the Llenorion, that is, the cultured or literary class
(ministers, teachers, civil servants), which used to be a much
smaller class before the Second World War.

This new class, this Welsh-speaking middle class, only a generation removed from working class, has retained a tradition of nonconformity and political awareness. Members of this class have a
sense of loyalty to a Welsh past, a working-class past, for as one
informant put it, 'It is a betrayal for a coal-miner's son to vote
Conservative.' It is an awareness of exploitation by a foreign
power and resistance to alienation from their own cultural heritage.

Members of the new class have a sense of community retained from
the days of their childhood. 'In my childhood,' said an informant,
    Welsh life was village life, as it mostly is now. You thought
    in terms of the village, and usually these villages grew around
    a coal mine ... Co-operation was essential in village life. In
    the coal-mine, when you worked underground, you had to work with
    a fellow miner, a partner, and learned to do things in a spirit
    of interdependence .... But there has been a big difference
    since 1945: things people used to do together are no longer done
    together.... The focal point used to be the workmen's hall and
    the chapel. Now the focal point is the pub. But for non-
    drinkers, there is not much of a social life left. This explains
    the erosion of the language, because social contacts kept the
    language alive - now people live within their own families. They
    watch television, they stay mostly at home.... Television is a
    threat to community.

The new Welsh intelligentsia is faced with a trinity of interlocked issues: land, language, and community ('Gwlad,' 'Iaith,' and
'Cymdogaeth' Khleif, 1974, 1975). We have already touched upon the
'community' issue. In the fight against bigness and its corollaries
of impersonal, elusive, or tentacular administration; in decrying
the trivializing and dehumanizing pressures of modern industrial
society, the Welsh have had eloquent spokesmen who have inextricably
linked cultural regeneration with the maintenance of community (cf.
Thomas, 1971; Evans, 1973). Welsh cultural nationalism - with its
emphasis on community, language, authenticity - has been characterized by Morgan (1971:171) as being almost 'a crusade ... against
the twentieth century itself' - a long overdue crusade perhaps!

The issue of 'land' is an issue of both 'community' and territoriality of language. Indeed, the Welsh have a rather mystical
word, which is 'Cydymdreiddiad': the mutual interpenetration of land
and language. The issue of land is that the bastions of Welshness

in the heart of Wales, many Welshmen feel, are being eroded.

Loss of Welsh-speaking communities through purchase, commercial pressure, expropriation, and inundation by the English has been aptly referred to by Welsh writers as the problem of 'erosion of the core', and 'theft of the environment' (Price, 1971:16; Evans, 1973: 136-7; Betts, 1976:39-54).

But it is the issue of language which is the supreme issue in Wales, an issue that mobilizes the total population pro and con. Language problems bring to the fore socio-economic and personal conflicts; they have both a social-structural and a social-psychological dimension.

I would like to discuss the social-psychological aspect of language under the rubric, 'language as identity'; the social-structural aspect, under 'decolonization and internal colonialism'. The two aspects are intertwined; in Wright Mills's terms (1959), 'public issues' are precursors of 'private troubles'.

LANGUAGE AS IDENTITY

Language denotes status - it is an index of social rank, of the capacity to command deference. An inferior language means an inferior person, a psychologically handicapped one, perhaps an economically circumscribed one also. An attack on one's language is but an attack on one's personal integrity and on one's group integrity, for the person is essentially a reflection of his group affiliations. Destruction of culture starts with destruction of language.

As Daniel Corkery, the Irish scholar, has said: *'Languages do not die natural deaths; they are murdered, and their murderers are those who would destroy the soul of the nation'* (quoted in Thomas, 1966:73, emphasis added).

The intersection of language as identity and the necessity of de-colonizing the self in the interest of authenticity, that is, the inseparable unity of the social-structural and social-psychological, is best expressed by the radio message of Zaïre's President Mobutu Sese Seko, heard over the Voice of Zaïre Radio several times a day: 'I no longer have a borrowed soul; I no longer have a borrowed way of looking at things; I no longer talk a borrowed language' (quoted by Ellington, 1973:20).

In this context, a native language can thus be seen as a language of regeneration, an indispensable tool for cultural resurgence. It is no wonder that in Brittany, Scotland, Cornwall, and Wales - to cite but Celtic examples - a number of writers when grown up did chuck the metropolitan language that they had learned as an adopted tongue at home in favor of a suppressed ancestral language that they had to acquire as adults and turn into a major, at times the sole, vehicle of their literary output. This is true, for example, of Morvan Lebesque in Brittany (1970, 1973); of Hugh MacDiarmid in Scotland (1973); of Tim Saunders in Cornwall (1976); and of Bobi Jones (197), 1974) and Chris Rees (1973) in Wales - to mention but very few.

If an ethnic group can be meaningfully defined as essentially one that shares a historic memory, then a good deal of the Welsh

historic memory can be said to revolve not only around their
deliberate impoverishment by the English but the suppression of
their language as well.   The highlights of the history of the
suppression and revival of the Welsh language (Khleif, 1975:45-102,
146-63) are as follows:

1   Deliberately, as a provision in the Act of Union of 1536, which
    incorporated Wales into England, English became the only
    official language in Wales.   Welsh ceased to be the language
    of administration.

2   Ironically, on the basis of an Act of Parliament, the Book of
    Common Prayer was translated into Welsh in 1567, the Bible in
    1588 - a move designed not merely to Protestantize the Welsh
    but to forestall their co-operation with England's Catholic
    enemies.   The language was preserved: a tradition of reading
    the Bible in Welsh developed.

3   From the seventeenth century onwards, Welsh had the status of
    a despised and ridiculed language, spoken only by the 'Gwerin'
    (common people), not by the English or Anglicized gentry of
    Wales.   As a result, many prejudice words against the Welsh and
    the language entered English (see the complete 'Oxford New
    English Dictionary', vol. 10, under 'Wales' and 'Welsh';
    Khleif, 1975:27-8).

4   The Methodist revival in Wales in the eighteenth century gave
    a boost to the Welsh language: the 'Circulating Schools' and
    the 'Sunday Schools' helped to create a reading public in Wales
    and keep the language alive.

5   Two drastic blows were dealt the Welsh language (by the English)
    in the nineteenth century: (a) the 1847 'Report of the Royal
    Commission of Inquiry into the State of Education in Wales',
    and (b) the 1870 Education Act.   The former blamed all of
    Wales's ills, real or imagined, on the Welsh language, defamed
    and libelled the Welsh, and thus 'stung Welsh nationalism
    alive' (Coupland, 1954:195).   The latter made English the sole
    medium of instruction in schools in Wales and prompted some
    teachers to terrorize their monoglot Welsh charges into acquis-
    ition of English as the sole working language through making
    them wear around their necks, when caught speaking Welsh, a
    device known as the 'Welsh Not', a piece of wood suspended by
    a string, which the child could not get rid of until he in turn
    caught another child speaking Welsh to pass it on to him, thus
    avoiding being severely punished at the end of the day.   Such
    practices left deep wounds in the Welsh psyche.

6   In 1939, the first bilingual school in Wales was established in
    Aberystwyth.   There are now close to 70 bilingual schools
    throughout Wales, a symbol of ethnic pride.   These schools are
    controlled by the new middle class, the Welsh-speaking intel-
    ligentsia.

7   The Welsh Courts Act of 1942 and the Welsh Language Act of 1967
    gave the Welsh language 'equal validity' alongside English but
    did not make it an official language.   There are a few hours a
    week of Welsh programs on TV and radio but no TV channel
    devoted to Welsh and no fully Welsh-medium college as yet.

8   According to the 1971 Census, only about 21 per cent of the
    approximately 2½ million population of Wales speak Welsh.   The

steady decline of Welsh speakers in Wales has prompted both Plaid
Cymru (the Welsh National Party) and in particular the Cymdeithas
yr Iaith Gymraeg, (the Welsh Language Society, established in
1962 and composed chiefly of college-age youth) to exert tremendous efforts towards winning increasing support for the use of
Welsh in daily life. As a result, the Government has been
induced to issue bilingual official forms for use in Wales and,
amongst other things, to set up bilingual road signs throughout
both the English and the Welsh-speaking parts of Wales.

THE ISSUE: INTERNAL COLONIALISM

An emphasis on language is usually an emphasis on something else -
on dignity, identity and economic power. Socio-economic fights can
be carried out under a linguistic guise; language as 'culture' lends
the necessary symbolism.

   Language is expressive of social stratification, of inexorable
dominance and subordination representing the 'fated mutuality', the
'relentless reciprocity', of two interlocked ethnic groups, forging
a unity out of their dichotomy:

   The industrial and agricultural experience of the past confronted
   Welsh-speaking, Nonconformist, Liberal wage-earners and tenant-
   farmers with *Anglicized*, Anglican, Tory landlords and employers,
   as were Welsh workers elsewhere in Wales. *English and Welsh were
   almost synonymous with landlord and tenant or capital and labour.*
   As has often been pointed out, Disraeli's description of
   employers and employed as two nations applied literally to
   Wales. (Frankenberg, 1971:91, emphasis added)

   We have maintained that in the post-1945 era, a useful way to
understand the resurgence of ethnicity on a worldwide basis is to
think of it first and foremost as a socio-economic and socio-
political issue and to see it rooted in the post-industrial society,
in the breakdown of older European nation-states in the First World,
in the transformation of empires at the end of the Second World War;
in short, in the notion of successive decolonization. We would like
to explore this notion further in relation to Wales, beginning first
with a theoretical account.

INTERNAL COLONIALISM AS A FRAMEWORK FOR EXAMINING ETHNICITY

A colonial analysis of the inner workings of an advanced industrial
society such as Britain or the USA is only of recent vintage among
sociologists (Khleif, 1972:12-13). In America, for example, the
notion of internal colonialism was first suggested in relation to
the South and to White Southerners (Odum, 1936; Arnall, 1946);
applied to Mexicans in Texas and California (McWilliams, 1946);
then deliberately applied to Black and White relations in the 1960s
(Cruse, 1967 and 1968; Clark, 1965; Carmichael and Hamilton, 1967).
It was Robert Blauner, however, heavily influenced by the work of
such Afro-French writers as Frantz Fanon (1966) and Albert Memmi
(1967), who, in a ground-breaking paper (1969), introduced 'internal
colonialism' as an analytical concept into American social science.

'Internal colonialism' was applied by Joan Moore (1970) to Mexican Americans and their historical experience; she contrasted its features in New Mexico, Texas and California. In a later work (1972), Blauner extended the notion of 'internal colonialism' to apply to all non-Whites in America: Blacks, American Indians (currently self-named 'Original Americans' or 'Native Americans'), Mexican-Americans ('Chicanos'), Puerto Ricans, Chinese-Americans, Filippinos, and for important socio-economic reasons - the whitest of Whites, the purest Anglo-Saxons, White Appalachians, Khleif (1972) examined the utility of 'internal colonialism' among other notions American sociologists use for conceptualizing race and ethnic relations.

In Britain, the only sociologist to use 'internal colonialism' as an organizing concept has been John Rex (1973, 1974). He is concerned with development of a typology of colonial situations, external and internal, grounded in both history and sociology. In Canada, 'internal colonialism' has been applied to the Quebec situation by Marcel Rioux (1969, 1971) and by Milner and Hodgins (1973). In South America, Pablo Gonzáles-Casanova (1965) and Rodolfo Stavenhagen (1965) have written on the underdeveloped nature of peripheral regions in relation to the core, on the rural hinterlands of Mexico and Brazil and their inhabitants. It is especially the work of these two Latin-American writers that has inspired the American sociologist, Michael Hechter (1975), to apply the internal colonialism analogy to the Celtic Fringe and to examine systematically its historical manifestations in the period 1536-1966.

Hechter emphasizes that when high-status socio-economic roles are reserved to core members (e.g., the English) whereas peripheral group members (e.g., the Welsh, Scottish, or Irish prior to 1922) are denied access to these roles, the stratification itself then contributes to the maintenance of cultural differences between core and periphery and even to development of further differences (1973: 323).

In his review of Hechter's 1975 book, 'Internal Colonialism: The Celtic Frings in British National Development, 1536-1966', a Welsh literary writer, Paul Luke (1976:52-3), though finding fault with the terminology and stance of American sociology, finds the colonial analogy applicable to Wales and deftly summarizes one of Hechter's main arguments - an argument, one may add, indicative in part of the historical development of some of the currently self-alienated Anglo-Welsh, though perhaps not intended by Luke as such:

> The social mobility of the natives is severely circumscribed, the more able being *admitted to elite positions solely on the proviso that they forego their subscription to the impoverished native culture*.... In essence, 'internal colonialism' is a theory about the problem of nation-building or rather nation-maintaining, when there are regional economic disparities which coincide with cultural and ethnic boundaries, the problems of what Hechter calls a *'cultural division of labour'*. (Luke, 1976:52, emphasis added)

To what extent do Welshmen, not to mention other Celts, think of their socio-political situations as that of internal colonialism - of forced entry (conquest), cultural destruction (linguistic suppression), and administration from the outside (socio-economic control by London) so that they feel they are *subjects* in the original, not

merely citizenship sense of the word?   The answer is: to a great
deal.

According to D. J. Davies, Welsh resources (coal, iron, tinplate,
and water for major English cities) are commandeered by the English;
used chiefly in their interest, not Welsh interest; so are Scottish
products (1958:84).   P. B. Ellis contends that Celtic nations are
subjugated nations, the 1536 Act of Union an act of colonial annex-
ation (1968:42-7, 55-60).   Gwnfor Evans describes Wales as an
underdeveloped country inside Britain, as a colony; it is not even
represented on the Union Jack; English efforts have been aimed at
'proletarianising of an ancient community', at uprooting the Welsh
from their history, language, culture, and land (1973:38, 134-8).
Ceinwen Thomas and others speak of Wales as a 'subject nation'
(Lloyd, 1950:60 passim).   Ned Thomas speaks of the Welsh as a
subject people; his book explores the issues of ethnocide, suppressed
language, and feelings of inferiority, and highlights how, for the
colonized self, the immediate preoccupation is restoration of self-
respect (1973:13, 61, 76, 95, 121-2).   Indeed, Sir Reginald
Coupland's book on Welsh and Scottish nationalism (1954), for a long
time the only available book on the subject and still a major
reference, was written as part of its author's interest in independence movements in the British Empire, a topic about which he had
already published some important work.   The similarity of internal
and external colonialism could not have escaped Sir Reginald,
although he opted to treat Scottish and Welsh nationalism as a self-
contained case.

Various indices of 'internal colonialism' are apparent in the
facts and figures gathered by Gwynfor Evans in response to his
queries in Parliament when he was first elected an MP, 1966-8
('Black Paper on Wales', Book 3, 1969).   Examples are the expenditure on health, education, housing, and other services in Wales
as compared on the same basis with England.   A particular feature
that has infuriated Welshmen is the dismantling of various sections
of the Welsh railway needlessly, thus destroying a workable and
inexpensive transportation system ('Welsh Freedom': the Maiden
Speech of G. Evans in Parliament on 26 July, 1966).   A distinct
stratificational and occupational feature with far-reaching demographic consequences is that whereas Wales is dotted with teachers
colleges that turn out annually a lot of teachers for the English
market, it has only two polytechnic colleges.   This is seen as a
deliberate plan, retardation of the scientific-technical progress of
Welshmen and a 'huge subsidy' to England ('Black Paper on Wales',
Book 3, 1969:46).

Gwynfor Evans, president of Plaid Cymru, the Welsh National Party,
re-elected to Parliament in 1974, seems to have become even more
insistent on referring to Wales as an internal colony:

The British are not a nation at all.   Britain is a State.   It is
those who wish Scotland and Wales to continue as *internal British
colonies* who are insistent on calling Britain a nation....
Whitehall is the heart of the British Establishment, but Westminster politicians have an important place in it.   *Deraciné
Scotsmen and Welshmen,* such as Mr. Roy Jenkins, are among its
most ardent admirers, foremost in the ranks of those who are
determined to prevent the ancient nations of Wales and Scotland

enjoying any measure of national freedom. (excerpt from a letter
by Gwynfor Evans, MP, House of Commons, to the 'Manchester
Guardian Weekly', 4 October 1975, appearing under the heading,
'Is Britain a Nation or a State?', emphasis added)

'Deraciné Scotsmen and Welshmen', i.e., natives uprooted from
their traditional culture (culturally 'neutralized', so to speak,
across one or more generations, that is, 'Anglicised' Celts) tend
to be more English than the English. In allegiance and identity,
they are part of the governing elite, not the natives. For every
colonial situation, internal or external, seems to have three
feudal-type estates, caste-like in character: (a) the colonizer;
(b) assimilated and assimilatable natives; and (c) the colonized.

The intermediate layer in any colonial situation, be it external
or internal is, in its psychology and allegiance, best exemplified
by what Macaulay in the nineteenth century deliberately *created* in
India at the height of the British Empire: 'a class who may be
interpreters between us and the millions whom we govern - a class
of persons Indian in blood and colour, but English in tastes and
opinions, in morals and intellect' (quoted by Worsley, 1973:52).

Mutatis mutandis, the same may be true of the creation, historically, of a pro-English intermediary class in Wales, Scotland, and
Northern Ireland - in England's own backyard.

We can say that the new ethnicity in Wales is precisely an
attempt at upsetting both the cultural (in Hechter's terms) and the
material division of labor; it is an index of social change.

CATECHISM FOR IDENTITY: THE WELSH-WELSH AND THE ENGLISH -
AND THE ANGLO-WELSH IN BETWEEN

We have maintained that the pro-Welsh, Welsh-speaking, new middle
class in Wales is particularly a post-1945 phenomenon, a counter-
balance to the traditionally pro-English, usually anti-Welsh
language, Macaulay-type, intermediary class of Anglo-Welshmen.
Internal colonialism has created in Wales a 'torn consciousness',
an identity split between those for whom Welshness without language
is unthinkable (the pro-Welsh Welsh speakers) and those whose
Welshness, they think, is undiminished if it is English-based or
pro-Englishry (to reactivate an old word) oriented. To the former,
Welsh - in the words of a 1682 pamphlet (Fishlock, 1972:54-5) - is
not to be 'English'd out of Wales'; to the latter, Welsh - as
Matthew Arnold wrote in 1866 - seems to be the 'curse of Wales'.

There is competition and resentment between the pro-Welsh Welsh
and the Anglo-Welsh, with English settlers in Wales not an uninter-
ested party. But the basic drama is played out not so much between
the English and the Welsh as between the two categories of Welshmen
who confront the issue of language and identify face to face daily:
the pro-Welsh Welsh and the Anglo-Welsh.

Is Welshness possible without the Welsh language? Is a Welshman
who does not speak Welsh equivalent to an Englishman who does not
speak English? Because he speaks English but is not an Englishman,
is the Welshman who does not speak Welsh neither psychologically
British nor Welsh, that is, essentially a 'marginal man'? Such
questions point to the interdependence of language and identity in

Wales, to issues of torn consciousness, ambivalence, self-hatred and language hatred, and split or suppressed identity that are part of the legacy of Wales' long association with England; indeed, of the post-colonial legacy everywhere.

Parallels from Canada come to mind: the bifurcation of Anglo-Canadians and Franco-Canadians on the basis of language. Historically, different types of nationalism even within the same group were associated with different types of languages: whereas in Eastern Europe prior to the First World War, the 'Jewish Labor Bond of Russia, Lithuania, and Poland' emphasized Yiddish, the Zionist movement emphasized Hebrew, the two languages subsequently colliding in what came to be known as 'Riv Haloshoynes' (language conflict), with Hebrew becoming the language of daily life among those who chose to be non-Diasporized (Fishman, 1968:49-50; Milosz, 1975: 345-8). In a larger sense perhaps, language conflicts at times are a collision of ethnicity with social class, of the status order with the pull of the marketplace, or, in Weber's terms, of estate solidarity with class solidarity. The situation in Wales is a case in point, with the full outcome not yet known.

The Welsh language is seen by the pro-Welsh Welsh as the last remaining vestige, the crucial symbol, of their solidarity. As an informant put it:

The language is an essential part of our self-confidence. Without the language, the non-Welsh speaking person in his heart of hearts faces a dilemma: he is a *Welshman without having much Welshness*. At one time, the community could carry him, but when the community is breaking down, he has to carry his Welshness in himself, and the language is what gives him that. (5/30/74 Field Notes)

The 'community is breaking down' in the transition from an industrial to a post-industrial society. In the same way that the sociology founding fathers in Europe - e.g., Toennies, Durkheim, and Weber - were faced in their day with the task of accounting for the passing of Western European society from pre-industrialism to industrialism, current, post-1945, sociologists are faced with the task of accounting for the passing of the First World from an industrial to a post-industrial society (cf. Sauvy, 1956; Schelsky, 1961; Ellul, 1964; Touraine, 1969; Mallet, 1969; Garaudy, 1970; Bell, 1973; Kleinberg, 1973). Wales exemplifies the dilemmas and opportunities of the new, post-industrial class in the First World, the university-trained class in search of community and authenticity in *detente* or *entente* with ethnicity and social mobility.

REFERENCES

ALLEN, Irving Lewis (1946), WASP - From Sociological Concept to Epithet, 'Ethnicity', 2(June):153-62.
ARNALL, E.G. (1946), 'The Shore Dimly Seen', Philadelphia: Lippincott.
BANKS, Olive (1972), 'The Sociology of Education', New York: Schocken Books, no.SB-367.
BARNET, R.J. and MÜLLER, R.E. (1971), 'Global Reach: The Power of the Multinational Corporation', New York: Simon & Schuster, Touchstone Books.

BASHAM, Richard (1976), 'Ethnicity as a Total Institution', Boulder, Colorado: Dept of Anthropology, University of Colorado, mimeo., 15 pp.

BELL, Daniel (1973), 'The Coming of the Post-Industrial Society: A Venture in Social Forecasting', New York: Basic Books.

BLAUNER, Robert (1969), Internal Colonialism and Ghetto Revolt, 'Social Problems', 16(Spring):393-408.

BLAUNER, Robert (1972a), Colonized and Immigrant Minorities, pp.243-58 in P.I. Rose (ed.), 'Nation of Nations', New York: Random House.

BLAUNER, Robert (1972b), 'Racial Oppression in America', New York: Harper & Row.

CARMICHAEL, S. and HAMILTON, C. (1967), 'Black Power', New York: Random House.

CHARSLEY, S.R. (1974), The Formation of Ethnic Groups, pp.337-68 in A. Cohen (ed.), 'Urban Ethnicity', London: Tavistock.

CLARK, K.B. (1965), 'Dark Ghetto', New York: Harper & Row.

COHEN, Abner (1969), 'Custom and Politics in Urban Africa', London: Routledge & Kegan Paul.

COHEN, Abner (ed.) (1974), 'Urban Ethnicity', London: Tavistock.

COUPLAND, Sir Reginald (1954), 'Welsh and Scottish Nationalism: A Study', London: Collins.

CRUSE, Harold (1967), 'The Crisis of the Negro Intellectual', New York: Morrow.

CRUSE, Harold (1968), 'Rebellion or Revolution', New York: Morrow.

DAHRENDORF, Ralf (1959), 'Class and Class Conflict in an Industrial Society', Stanford, California: Stanford University Press.

DAVIES, D.J. (1958), 'Towards Welsh Freedom: Twenty-Seven Articles', edited by Ceinwen H. Thomas, Cardiff: Plaid Cymru.

DULONG, Renaud (1975), 'La Question Bretonne', Paris: Cahiers de la Fondation Nationale de Science Politique, no.196.

EDWARDS, Owen Dudley, et al. (1968), 'Celtic Nationalism', London: Routledge & Kegan Paul.

ELLINGTON, John (1973), What is Authentic?, 'Africa Report', vol.18, no.4, pp.20-2, July-August.

ELLIS, P.B. (1968), 'Wales: A Nation Again!', London: Tandem Books, no.3332.

ELLUL, Jacques (1964), 'The Technological Society', New York, Knopf.

ETZIONI, Amitai (1968), 'The Active Society', New York: Basic Books.

EVANS, Gwynfor (1969), 'Black Paper on Wales', Book 3, Cardiff: Plaid Cymru.

EVANS, Gwynfor (1973), 'Wales can Win', Llandybie, Carmarthenshire, Wales: Christopher Davies.

FANNON, F. (1968), 'The Wretched of the Earth', New York: Grove Press.

FISHLOCK, Trevor (1972), 'Wales and the Welsh', London: Cassell.

FISHMAN, J.A., et al. (eds) (1968), 'Language Problems of Developing Nations', New York: Wiley.

FLACKS, Richard (1972), On the New Working Class and Strategies for Social Change, pp.85-98 in P.G. Altbach and R.S. Laufer (eds), 'The New Pilgrims: Youth Protest in Transition', New York: David McKay.

FRANKENBERG, Ronald (1971), 'Communities in Britain: Social Life in Town and Country', Baltimore: Penguin Books.

GARAUDY, Roger (1970), 'The Turning Point', London: Fontana Books.

GOEHRING, Heinz (1975), Comments on Ross, Jennie-Keith, 'Social Borders: Definitions of Diversity', 'Current Anthropology', 16 (March):64-5.

GONZÁLES-CASANOVA, Pablo (1965), Internal Colonialism and National Development, 'Studies in Comparative International Development', 1(4):27-37.

GORER, Geoffrey (1975), English Identity over Time and Empire, pp.156-72 in G. De Vos and L. Romanucci-Ross (eds), 'Ethnic Identity: Cultural Continuities and Change', Palo Alto, California: Mayfield Publishing.

HECHTER, Michael (1973), The Persistence of Regionalism in the British Isles, 'American Journal of Sociology', 79(September): 319-42.

HECHTER, Michael (1975), 'Internal Colonialism: The Celtic Fringe in British National Development, 1536-1966', Berkeley, California: University of California Press; and London: Routledge & Kegan Paul.

HOROWITZ, Irving Louis (1976), Book Review of N. Glazer and D.P. Moynihan (eds), Ethnicity: Theory and Experience, Harvard University Press, Cambridge, Mass., 1975, 'American Journal of Sociology', 82(July):221-5.

JANOWITZ, Morris (1974), Book Review of Daniel Bell, The Coming of the Post-Industrial Society: A Venture in Social Forecasting, Basic Books, New York, 1973, 'American Journal of Sociology', 80(July): 230-6.

JONES, Bobi (1970), Why I write in Welsh, 'Planet', 2(October-November):21-5.

JONES, Bobi (1974), The Roots of Welsh Inferiority, 'Planet', 22 (March):53-72.

KALČIK, Susan and HAWES, Bess Lomax (1976), In Celebration of Ethnicity, 'International Educational and Cultural Exchange', 12(Summer):9-14.

KHLEIF, Bud B. (1972), A Socio-Cultural Framework for Understanding Race and Ethnic Relations in Schools and Society, paper read at the annual meeting of the Society for Applied Anthropology, Montreal, Canada, 7 April, 1972, mimeo. 25 pp.

KHLEIF, Bud B. (1974), Ethnic Boundaries in Welsh-English Relations, paper read at the annual meeting of the Society for the Study of Social Problems, Montreal, Canada, 24 August, mimeo., 25 pp.

KHLEIF, Bud B. (1975), Ethnic Boundaries, Identity, and Schooling: A Socio-Cultural Study of Welsh-English Relations, Washington, D.C.: National Institute of Education, lithographed, 462 pages. (Available in microfiche or hard copy as #ED-108-517 and #FL-006-988 from: Center for Applied Linguistics, ERIC Clearinghouse on Languages and Linguistics, 1611 North Kent Street, Arlington, Virginia 22209. Also obtainable on an inter-library loan from: Dimond Library, University of New Hampshire, Durham, New Hampshire 03824.)

KHLEIF, Bud B. (1976a), Cultural Regeneration and the School: An Anthropological Study of Welsh-Medium Schools in Wales, 'International Review of Education', 22(2):177-92.

KHLEIF, Bud B. (1976b), The Political Economy of Language Problems: Wales, Quebec, and Other Cases, paper read at the annual meeting of the Society for the Study of Social Problems, New York, 29 August, mimeo., 30 pp.

KLEINBERG, B.S. (1973), 'American Society in the Post-Industrial Age: Technocracy, Power, and the End of Ideology', Columbus, Ohio: E.E. Merrill.
LEBESQUE, Morvan (1970), 'Comment Peut-on Être Breton?', Paris: Editions du Seuil.
LEBESQUE Morvan (1973), Becoming a Breton, translated from the French by Eileen Holt, 'Planet', 17(April–May):3–20.
LICHTHEIM, George (1963), 'The New Europe: Today and Tomorrow', New York: Basic Books.
LLOYD, D.M. (ed.) (1950), 'The Historical Basis of Welsh Nationalism: A Series of Lectures by A.W. Wade-Evans, T. Jones Pierce, Ceinwen Thomas, A.O.H. Jarman, D. Gwenallt Jones, and Gwynfor Evans', Cardiff: Plaid Cymru.
LUKE, Paul (1976), The Ideal Research Site (Book Review of Michael Hechter, 'Internal Colonialism: The Celtic Fringe in British National Development, 1536–1966', Routledge & Kegan Paul, London, 1975), 'Planet', 30(January):52–3.
MACDIARMID, Hugh (1973), Saunders Lewis and the Real Thing, 'Anglo-Welsh Review', vol.22, no.55, pp.153–60, Autumn.
MCWILLIAMS, Cary (1946), 'North from Mexico', New York: Harper & Row.
MALLET, Serge (1969), 'La Nouvelle Classe Ouvrière' (The New Working Class), Paris: Editions du Seuil.
MALLET, Serge (1975), 'Essays on the New Working Class', edited and translated by D. Howard and D. Savage, St Louis: Telos Press.
MEMMI, Albert (1967), 'The Colonizer and the Colonized', Boston: Beacon Press.
MEMMI, Albert (1971), 'Dominated Man: Notes towards a Portrait', Boston: Beacon Press.
MILNER, S.H. and HODGINS, H. (1973), 'The Decolonization of Quebec', Toronto: McClelland & Stewart.
MILOSZ, C. (1975), Vilnius, Lithuania: An Ethnic Agglomerate, pp.339–52 in G. De Vos and L. Romanucci-Ross (eds), 'Ethnic Identity: Cultural Continuities and Change', Palo Alto, California: Mayfield Publishing.
MOORE, Joan W. (1970), Colonialism: The Case of the Mexican Americans, 'Social Problems', 17(Spring):463–72.
MORGAN, K.O. (1971), Welsh Nationalism: The Historical Background, 'Journal of Contemporary History', 6(January):153–72.
NOVAK, Michael (1971), 'The Rise of the Unmeltable Ethnics', New York: Macmillan.
NOVAK, Michael (1976), On Cultural Ecology: The United States as Nervous System of the Planet's Cultures, Preface to Richard Gambino, 'A Guide to Ethnic Studies Programs in American Colleges, Universities, and Schools', pp.v–ix, New York: The Rockefeller Foundation, Working Papers on Ethnic Studies, May, mimeo., 39 pp.
ODUM, H.W. (1936), 'Southern Regions of the United States', Chapel Hill, N.C.: University of North Carolina Press.
PARK, Robert E. and BURGESS, Ernest W. (1921), 'Introduction to the Science of Sociology', Chicago: University of Chicago Press.
PATTERSON, Orlando (1975a), Ethnicity and the Pluralist Fallacy, 'Change', vol.7, no.2, pp.10–11, March.
PATTERSON, Orlando (1975b), Rejoinders, 'Change', Summer, pp.4–7, 70–2.
PRICE, D.L. (1971), Wars of National Liberation, 'Planet', 7(August–September):13–20.

REES, Chris (1973), No Welsh as a Child, 'Meithrin', no.4, p.3, Easter.

REX, John (1973), 'Race, Colonialism, and the City', London: Routledge & Kegan Paul.

REX, John (1974), 'Sociology and the Demystification of the Modern World', London and Boston: Routledge & Kegan Paul.

RIOUX, Marcel (1969), 'La Question du Québec', Paris: Editions Seghers.

RIOUX, Marcel (1971), 'Quebec in Question', translated by James Boake, Toronto: James-Lewis & Samuel.

SAUNDERS, Tim (1976), Why I Write in Cornish, 'Planet', 30(January): 29-33.

SAUVY, Alfred (1956), 'Le Tiers Monde' (The Third World), Paris:PUF.

SCHELSKY, H. (1961), Technical Change and Educational Consequence, pp.31-6 in A.H. Halsey et al. (eds), 'Education, Economy, and Society', New York: Free Press, Macmillan.

SCHOECK, Helmut (1969), 'Kleines Soziologisches Woerterbuch', Freiburg im Breisgau: Herder.

SCHRAG, Peter (1970), 'The Decline of the WASP', New York: Simon & Schuster, Touchstone Books.

STAVENHAGEN, Rodolfo (1965), Classes, Colonialism, and Acculturation, 'Studies in Comparative International Development', vol.6, no.1.

THOMAS, Ceinwen H. (1966), The Welsh Language, 'Journal of the Faculty of Arts, Malta University,' vol.3, no.2, pp.73-101.

THOMAS, Ned (1973a), Culture, Community, Territory, and Survival, 'Planet', 17(April-May):21-4.

THOMAS, Ned (1973b), 'The Welsh Extremist', Talybont, Cardiganshire, Wales: y Lolfa.

TOURAINE, Alain (1969), 'La Société Post-Industrielle', Paris: Denoël.

TRENT, John (1975), National and Class Interests in Multi-Ethnic Societies: The Case of Nationalist Groups in French Canada, Ottawa, Canada: University of Ottawa, mimeo.

WEBER, Max (1968), 'Economy and Society' (Wirtschaft und Gesell-schaft), edited by C. Roth and C. Wittich, New York: Bedminster Press.

WILKES, Paul (1976), Rejoining the Slovak Community, 'New York Times', 6 August.

WOOLFE, Ray (1974), Second Time Around, 'Planet', 24-5(August): 87-90.

WORSLEY, Peter (1973), 'The Third World', London: Weidenfeld & Nicolson.

YANCEY, W.L., ERICKSEN, E.P. and JULIAN, R.N. (1976), Emergent Ethnicity: A Review and Reformulation, 'American Sociological Review', 41(June):391-403.

ZOLBERG, Aristide R. (1976), Culture, Territory, Class: Ethnicity Demystified, paper read at the annual congress of the International Political Science Association, Edinburgh, 16-21 August, mimeo., 38 pp.

Chapter 9

ETHNICITY AND SOCIAL ORGANIZATION IN NORTH-EAST WALES

G. Clare Wenger

The concept of 'ethnic group' has been recognized since the earliest
writings on complex societies, dating back to Herodotus 2,500 years
ago; and the existence, nature, problems and persistence of ethnic
groups have been of continued interest. The term 'ethnic group' as
generally used in the social sciences designates a biologically and
culturally distinct aggregation of people between whom exist
established patterns of communication and interaction and who are
marked off from other aggregations of the same order by social
boundaries. Ethnographic interest, until recently, centred on
descriptions of ethnic cultures, distinctions between cultures and
the acculturation of members of one group to another. Subsequently,
the problem of defining the boundaries of ethnic groups received
considerable attention.

The equation of one people, one language, one culture, which
seemed valid in the consideration of isolated groups, became
problematical as soon as researchers became aware of and interested
in contiguous cultures which displayed varying degrees of similarity
and/or diversity. The concept of the culture area (Kroeber, 1939;
Wissler, 1938) which included different groups with similar cultural
forms and related languages but discrete ethnic identities was the
thin end of the wedge for the one people-culture-language model. As
soon as interest centred on the boundaries, the model lost its
effectiveness.

Approaches to the solution of boundary definition, most using
language as a prime criterion (e.g. Narroll, 1964), proved
fruitless. One of the first to point out the inconsistencies
between language and ethnic group was Edmund Leach in his introduction to 'Political Systems of Highland Burma' (1954) and subsequently
several papers and a conference (Helm, 1968) were generated in
consideration of this problem and a plethora of ethnographic
illustrations of the problem were provided.

For instance, the situation in Australia was described (Sharp,
1958), where groups sharing very similar cultures and speaking
mutually intelligible dialects have no uniting political or social
organizational ties and consider themselves to be separate ethnic
groups. The opposite situation has been found in the Amazon Basin
(Sorensen, 1968), where members of a tribe of exogamous patrilocal

clans speak the language of their particular clan in addition to the
tribal language, which is also spoken by other clans not affiliated
with the tribe.   Wives retain their own patri-clan language and a
status quo of multi-lingualism and unselfconscious switching is an
integrated part of social organization.

The criterion of cultural difference to define ethnic boundaries
has been questioned independent of language.   Moerman (1965), for
instance, in asking the question 'Who are the Lue?' finds that in
comparing traits said by the Lue to be distinctive, with traits
present in the contiguous culture, very few are in fact diagnostic-
ally Lue.   Barth (1969) has even suggested that ethnic difference
or identity may precede cultural difference and that cultural items
are adopted to symbolize ethnicity.   This tendency has been
observed to include dialect differentiation among blacks in the USA
to set themselves apart from whites as black became beautiful
(Burling, 1970).

Gradually, the classificatory model of ethnic group has been
replaced by an interactional model.   Ethnic groups are now more
frequently seen as a form of social organization.   Ethnic membership is used symbolically to channel or form social relationships
and to express an individual's self-concept vis-à-vis others.
Ethnic identity may develop out of regionalism or may acquire a
new salience in the face of international events or of social
change which affects the relationship between a minority ethnic
group and the majority society.   The culture may change and ethnic
identity remain stable, as among the Hawaiians.   The culture may
be the same, ethnic identity the same, but language different, as
occurs in Southern Nigeria.   So although ethnic categories take
cultural differences into account, there is no simple one-to-one
relationship between ethnic units and cultural similarities and
differences.

The homogenizing effect of modern society, it has been suggested,
will result in the assimilation and disappearance of ethnic differences.   However, experience now indicates that even in the absence
of overt physical or racial characteristics, i.e. visible ethnicity,
ethnic categories remain significant for those who are categorizing.
The fact that membership has been observed to be negotiable and
manipulable suggests that ethnic categories are in fact being used
symbolically.   The diacritics of ethnic affiliation can be displayed
selectively in accordance with rules of appropriateness in the same
way as dress, speech style, dominance or submission may be employed
in the presentation of self.

We can consider the ethnic group as a core symbol in the model
symbolic system of a society and in the individual symbolic systems
of members of a society.   By symbolic system here I am referring to
that patterned set of symbols, the interrelationship of which is
determined by a philosophical or metaphysical belief system, which
seeks to orient the individual bearers of the system, in an ordered
way, to the experience of living.   As a core symbol, the ethnic
group is itself, in turn, represented by other symbols such as
language, badges, loyalties, etc. in a web of connotative meanings.
The success of such core symbols, as Lloyd Warner (1959, 1961) and
Victor Turner (1969) have shown, derives from their diffuseness -
Turner calls it multi-vocality or their polysemic nature - that is,

they mean different things to different people in different contexts, while maintaining a precise referant meaning. A wide range
of connotative meaning accrues to the symbol but any one act of
interpretation or response selects specific facet(s) for immediate
salience.

If we look at some of the ways in which ethnicity affects social
organization, the symbolic use of the concept of the ethnic group
becomes clear. The following discussion is based on fieldwork done
in a rural community in north-east Clwyd with a Welsh-speaking
population of approximately 27 per cent. Not only are community
members categorized as Welsh (meaning Welsh-speakers), Welsh-but-
they-don't-speak-it (whom I shall refer to as Anglo-Welsh) and
English (a residual category), but certain spheres of social interaction are also categorized implicitly as Welsh-speaking, Anglo-
Welsh or ethnically neutral. What I want to do is to describe some
of the ways in which ethnicity affects or is interwoven into
specific areas of social organization. From discussion of specific
data on the life of a small community, the multivocality of the
meaning of ethnicity will be demonstrated. It will be shown how
the meaning of Welshness is different for different people and that
the quality of that difference shifts according to context,
audience and situation so that different facets of Welshness are
salient at different times.

If we are to consider ethnicity as one of the central symbols in
a symbolic system, we can infer that in the affective realm of
religion, where similar orienting symbols abound, a certain amount
of cognitive overlap might be expected. This in fact is the case
in the Welsh context. The relationship between ethnicity and
religious denomination has a long history in Wales. The link
between the Welsh and Nonconformity has been well documented and
the point has been made that although chapel going remains part of
the stereotype of the Welsh, many who identify themselves as Welsh
are members of the Anglican Church of Wales. While there appears
to be a general understated antagonism in the community between the
church and the chapels, this is generally not stated in ethnic
terms.

The Rector feels that giving services in Welsh is a waste of
time because hardly anyone comes; in spite of the contradictory
evidence recorded in the 'Register of Services', which indicates
comparable numbers of communicants in Welsh and English. Several
self-professed Welsh speakers remarked that they attended the English
services at the Church in spite of being Welsh speakers. It was
also suggested that many Welsh speakers do not go to the Welsh
services because they cannot understand the Welsh used and it was
suggested by older informants that some Welsh speakers went to the
English services because they 'won't admit' they understand Welsh.
Other Welsh-speaking informants stated that they always tried to
attend the Welsh Church services because they felt uncomfortable
about the low attendance. 'It's always the same half dozen of us
there', they stated. And, 'I go for shame's sake.' And at the
same time, a few members with a limited understanding of Church
Welsh said they occasionally attended the Welsh services because
they liked to hear the language used.

Two conflicting attitudes seem to be represented here. On the one hand, some of the older generation, including the Rector and other Welsh speakers, see Welshness as a stigmatized category from which they choose to disaffiliate; on the other hand, a predominantly younger group, including some whose Welsh is rudimentary, attend Welsh-language services in a symbolic gesture of ethnic loyalty.   In other words, attendance of younger members is motivated not by the need to communicate with one's god in one's mother tongue, but in order to communicate ethnic solidarity.

For many, religious experience and ethnic identity appear to belong to the same mystical sphere of experience; they are both things that are known or felt but hard to put into words; and, as illustrated, there is an emotive overlap of religion and ethnicity. As often happens, the subtleties of human affairs are seen clearly through the eyes of children as shown in the following anecdote. The young granddaughter of an English informant attends a convent school run by a Roman Catholic order.   Her mother was born in Wales and her father is Oriental and a Hindu, who has become involved in local nationalist politics.   On a feast day in the Catholic calendar, one of the nuns at the school was trying to separate the Protestants from the Roman Catholics so that the latter could attend a special Mass.   Turning to this seven-year-old child, she asked, 'What religion are you?'   'Well', the little girl explained, 'I was christened for the chapel on the hill and my Daddy's a Hindu, but I'm really a Welsh Nationalist.'

Within the village it happens that those who are anxious about the fate of the language are also chapel members.   However, since it was found that denominational affiliation was of an ad hoc nature, it must be assumed that involvement in or support of the language movement would be more easily sustained within a religious body having Welsh-speaking members only, whereas the Church membership is predominantly English speaking.   In these circumstances, a language movement supporter might be expected to gravitate towards the chapel if not already a member.   Some churchmen have suggested that support for the language by chapel congregations is an attempt to bolster flagging Methodism.   On the other side of this debate, those involved in the language movement point with regret to the failing chapels, which they see as a fading outlet for oral expression in the national language.

In these ways, religious disagreement and ethnic attitudes can become confused and at times it is difficult to decide whether an individual is antagonistic because an institution is Nonconformist or because it is Welsh; or whether a person's affiliation is to a denomination or an ethnic group.   As the case of the little girl referred to above illustrates, it is often difficult for the members to make the same distinction.

The March Meeting, held by the Welsh Presbyterian Chapel, which in the past was an inter-chapel eisteddfod, part of a local cycle, has in recent years, become a concert in which two other Presbyterian chapels, one Welsh and the other English, take part.   Formerly, of course, all the proceedings, in accordance with consensual appropriateness constraints, were conducted in Welsh and there are those who feel that this precedent should be continued.   Within the last two or three years, as the numbers of English and Welsh speakers become more and more equal, this has generated a certain amount of

tension. This was finally brought out into the open when an
officiating Deacon of the chapel switched to English during the
1973 meeting and announced that he had realized that a lot of 'our
friends from the chapel on the hill have not been able to understand what is going on and I think that if we invite them and they
are kind enough to come and participate, then we should make sure
they understand what's happening.' He then proceeded to conduct
the remainder of the programme translating as he went along; maintaining the symbolic use of Welsh, since all present understood
English.

In keeping with the definition of the Welsh chapel as being
within the Welsh-speaking domain, all verbal performances at the
March Meeting had been offered in the Welsh language even by the
English chapel members. In 1974 two or three English incomer
children from the English chapel performed in English. This
appeared to offend a few of the older Welsh members and according
to the mother of the English children, the minister gave sweets to
all the Welsh-speaking children and ignored the English children!

What seems to be happening here is that with the erosion of
Welsh speaking, Welsh chapel activity is becoming impinged upon by
the Anglo-Welsh domain. As a result, there is a conflict of
expectations; the appropriateness constraints of a Welsh-speaking
sphere being inappropriate in an Anglo-Welsh sphere and vice versa.
This conflict becomes inevitable where the concensual definition of
domain begins to break down. The interplay of unity and exclusion
produces a tension experienced by both sides: the non-Welsh speaker
happy to be invited but feeling not quite accepted and the Welsh
speakers proud of their heritage yet anxious for its survival in
the face of the encroachment of the dominant English-speaking
culture. This tension between members of the different chapels is
also experienced within the Sunday School of the Welsh chapel as
more and more children speak Welsh as their second language and are
more fluent in English. While their elders decry the erosion of the
use of Welsh, the Anglo-Welsh parents of many of these children
frequently see attendance at Welsh Sunday School as a worthwhile
exposure to the Welsh language for their children in a predominantly
English-speaking environment. Another example of the confusion
between religious and ethnic commitment.

At times when community solidarity is ritually enacted, such as
the annual Service of Unity and at Christmas, not only do members
of both conformist and Nonconformist congregations join together in
religious expressions of good will to all mankind, but care is also
taken to ensure a balance of ethnic affiliation between participants
and a balanced bilingual programme. This ritual use of Welsh is
scrupulously observed even when more than half of the congregation
does not understand the content. Any suggestion to omit this
observance, it is predicted, would be as vociferously rejected by
the Anglo-Welsh as by the Welsh speakers. And recent tombstones in
the community cemetery are only very slightly more frequently
English than Welsh, testifying that in a population of only 27 per
cent Welsh speakers, the Welsh language as a symbol is more powerful
than the number of its bearers indicates. For some, it may be not
only an ethnic symbol but also a religious symbol.

In terms of religious activity then, the Welsh language as the

most salient badge of ethnicity can be seen as a mechanism for both
schism and unity. Whereas the use of English in the Welsh domain of
the Welsh chapel is perceived as inappropriate by some and Welsh
seen as the symbol of the integrity of the group; the carefully
balanced use of the two languages in community rituals may be seen
as symbolizing the presence of two ethnic groups in the community
and as an acting-out of community solidarity. It is also evident
that ethnic distinction is being used to talk about other distinctions, including group affiliation, insider/outsider, Welsh speaker/
non-Welsh speaker. In order to understand what is the underlying
significance of statements about ethnicity, an interactor needs a
wealth of background information acquired only through long residence
in the community.

Due to certain factors of historical development and community
attitudes, the decision-making bodies of the community, i.e. the
Parish Council, etc. are composed of virtually all Welsh incumbents,
most of whom are also Welsh speakers. Community attitudes reinforce
this state of affairs and the various bodies fall into the Anglo-
Welsh domain, where ethnic affiliation and loyalty may be overtly
expressed, albeit most frequently in English. In this context, the
Welsh are conceived of as those who speak Welsh and local-born
Anglo-Welsh. These secular authorities see themselves very much as
guardians of the local community, particularly against outside
incursions of interference and incoming residents see them in the
same light. In this context, 'the Welsh' and 'the locals' are
synonymous, and 'we Welsh' is used to refer to the Gemeinschaft.

In contrast to the community decision-making bodies and the
Welsh chapels, the voluntary associations are composed of a broader
cross-section of parish residents. There is a high salience of
ethnic membership within the former, for instance, the frequent
allusion to 'the' or 'we Welsh' and concern for of marked use of
the ethnic language. A very different pattern may be observed in
the context of voluntary association. While ethnic membership has
low overt significance in these contexts, prescribed avoidance of
cleavage along ethnic lines appears to be an ideal form of
behaviour which is not always easy to sustain.

In the Youth Club all verbal interaction is conducted in English
and while it is possible that Welsh pop records may occasionally be
played, I heard none. Conversation is predominantly anecdotal and
predictably concentrated on school, friends and personal relationships. Ethnic membership is not an overt concern during any
activity.

Although ethnicity is not an overt aspect of interaction at the
Youth Club, it seemed that its members could not be unaware of
ethnic distinctions which were being made in the community all the
time, if only as something with which their elders were concerned.
In order to find out more about their feelings on this topic, a
meeting was arranged for several interested members to come to the
leader's house (also the house of a member) for a discussion and
the proceedings were recorded. The transcript shows well the ambivalence of the young people towards the ethnic categories in the
community.

The group ranged in age from thirteen to seventeen, mostly
incomers, all of whom were non-Welsh speakers, as were the hosts.

(There are only four or five Welsh-speaking children who are members of the Youth Club, but it is difficult in a small community to draw any conclusions from this as most Welsh-speaking children I met or heard about were not in this age range.) The following summarizes the course of the discussion. Initially, only two in the group of seven identify themselves as English; they have been in the parish for two years or less. The others were born else-where but feel they have lived in the community 'all their lives', i.e. they identify with the parish and they say they are Welsh. The chief distinctions made are between residents and outsiders, as in a comment about holidaymakers. At first, they appear to see little difference between English and Welsh people, but as the discussion continues their perspective shifts. Gradually, they admit that there is a difference between English and Welsh but that it is limited to the older generation and does not apply to their own age group. Later, the group begins to speak of those children who go to the bilingual school as different from themselves. At first they base this distinction on class - the only overt use of this concept encountered in the community - but as the discussion progresses, differences are stated more and more along ethnic lines. Those in the group gradually oppose themselves to another group which they are calling 'Welsh', composed of Welsh speakers. When reminded that they had at first said that they themselves were Welsh, they hastily add that it is not necessary to speak Welsh to be Welsh. When asked what being Welsh means for them, the talk shifts to discussion of another group - a separate English category - with the youth group again defined as the Welsh group. Establish-ing membership of themselves and others in this Welsh group involves them for a considerable time. It is obvious that they want to call themselves Welsh, to belong to and be accepted by the community. But as the talk moves on, the contrast between the Youth Group and the Welsh-speaking schoolchildren, now being referred to as 'the Welsh', becomes more and more emphasized. Additionally, that minority who identified themselves initially as English, take over more and more of the conversation. At one point a schism develops between the Welsh and English within the discussion group; but when they realize what is happening, confront-ation is quickly averted. The group re-establishes unity and a joke releases and dissipates the residual tension.

It is evident that 'Welsh' is being used to describe two differ-ent categories: those who speak Welsh and those who are identified with the locality. For the Anglo-Welsh there is a situational pendulum effect, depending on the context, and ethnicity may be a very ad hoc identification, sometimes based on language and some-times on locality or origins. Even youngsters who have come from England as children call themselves Welsh, and while they may say that this is for 'convenience', it is evident from what else they say that being accepted as a bona fide member of the local community is the effect sought. Even those who claim English ethnicity use the pronoun 'we' in an ethnic context to talk about the parish vis-à-vis other English incomers. As one of the young people said of Welsh speech characteristics in English, 'After a while you pick it up.' The same may perhaps be said of ethnic identification. Some young married people in their early twenties, who came to the parish as children and who have put down roots in local jobs, told me that they now feel completely Welsh and hope that their children will learn to speak Welsh.

It is obviously important to maintain the unity of the peer group as the avoidance of overt antagonism in the discussion illustrates. In other social situations, one could imagine those who identify as Welsh taking a stronger Welsh stance, for instance, in a group composed of themselves and Welsh speakers; and, those who identify as English expressing more overtly derogatory opinions of the Welsh, for instance, in a group including holidaymakers from Liverpool.

A similar procedure was followed in speaking to children who attend the bilingual school. The results were comparable. Early in the discussion, the division between English and Welsh is made strictly along the lines of school attendance, but in other contexts they are willing to extend the Welsh category to include non-Welsh speakers. Those who attend the bilingual school, however, see less difference between the English and the Welsh. While both sets of young people feel that English/Welsh differences are greater in the older generations, Welsh-speaking children see less difference between themselves and their English-speaking peers. This may be a reflection, on the part of Anglo-Welsh adolescents, of their ambivalent situation as being 'not really Welsh'. The different school backgrounds, however, could contain the seeds of polarization for in both discussion groups, the two participants who felt most strongly for or against Welsh identity and concerns gradually took over and dominated the conversation.

For all these young people, being Welsh is seen primarily as an affiliative category. At the same time, they describe a clear division between those who attend the different medium schools. In this context, ethnic labels are used to distinguish between the two subgroups; whereas older people are, in some contexts, using them to distinguish between those who are committed to the community and those who are not. Each group appears to be using ethnic labels symbolically to make distinctions which are useful in their particular realm of experience. In other words, the same labels are used repeatedly to refer to different things. They are used differently by different people in similar contexts and they are used differently by the same people in different contexts. The absence of ethnicity as an issue within the Youth Club does not imply that the categories are unimportant, but rather than a moratorium on their use or salience exists in the club context. In other words, if ethnic labels can be used to distinguish factions, it is necessary to avoid their use to maintain unity within the club.

A similar pendulum effect on ethnic identification is observed in the Women's Institute. In deciding upon recommendations to the local delegate to the national Annual General Meeting in London, for instance, the question of Common Market restrictions on dressed poultry was raised. The reaction was one of 'why should they tell us what to do in our own country', i.e. Great Britain. In another situation, the problem of Welsh rate relief was discussed and 'this country' became Wales; 'Why should we subsidize England?' 'We' can be 'we in Great Britain' one moment and 'we in Wales' the next.

This shift was witnessed to take place several times in the course of a single meeting.

To preserve the unity of the group, however, it is important to avoid ethnic division or even friction and overt instances of this avoidance were observed. One member of the Institute was a known nationalist. In private she expressed concern over the Anglicization of the community. One day, after the conventional singing of 'Jerusalem', urging the building of Jerusalem in 'England's green and pleasant land', I asked her if this sentiment was not incongruous. Although she registered a certain amount of disgust, she did not pursue the topic and no other member ever commented on the words as inappropriate.

On early acquaintance, one member made sure that I perceived her as a Welsh speaker by such devices as Welsh tag questions and 'spontaneous' reactions to the weather, etc. Within the role of President of the WI, however, she maintained an objectivity which at times leaned in the other direction. When announcing a regional event, she had received a programme which indicated a fairly traditional English offering and commented, 'I'm glad to see that it's in English; when I saw 'Noson Lawen', I thought, Ooh dear, I hope it's not all in Welsh, otherwise it would be a poor show for those of us who aren't too good in Welsh. But, anyway, it's in English, so that's all right.'

For some members, the complicated web of appropriateness constraints results in unresolvable conflict. The farmers' wives are predominantly Welsh speakers and often share kin ties with other farmers' wives. They are the only group who use Welsh among themselves, consistently, in the company of other members. Frequently they will apologize for this usage to non-Welsh speaking members. In the context of the WI they experience an obvious conflict in appropriate choice of code, since the relationships and the social situation make incompatible demands.

While the Women's Institute exists as an area where ethnic differences are minimized, it also exists contiguously and simultaneously with other spheres of parish life. When different spheres overlap ethnicity may come to the surface. At the Christmas service in the formal religious domain, this surfacing is accommodated easily enough by the symbolic use of both languages in the ritual, but in the informal farming and kin spheres, conflicts are less easily resolved. As could be predicted, it is easier for the Anglo-Welsh member to adapt, since they at least have a foot in each camp; the Welsh speaker has the option of interacting in all spheres but finds the transition to an ethnically neutral sphere more difficult and for the English member, an understanding of the various spheres becomes possible only after years of residence and assimilation.

As the above examples of contextual ethnicity demonstrate, like all good symbols, ethnicity may be many things to many people in many contexts. Variation can be observed in: definition of ethnic categories; salience of ethnicity depending on the social sphere; contextual appropriateness of the use of ethnic symbols and even the appropriateness of specific symbols, viz. language. Ethnic behaviour is not merely an idiosyncratic matter but also a situational one. One point is clear: the English/Welsh dichotomy is used by Welsh speakers and non-Welsh speakers alike as a reference point for judgment of a variety of linguistic and non-linguistic behaviours.

The importance of the Welsh language as an ethnic badge has already been discussed, and is reflected in proverb, fiction and non-fiction. The old saying 'Nid Cymro heb Gymraeg'(2) dies hard but as the language recedes, the term 'Cymro Cymraeg',(3) which is heard more and more frequently, appears to acknowledge the fact that there are Welshmen who do not speak Welsh. In Flintshire, it is accepted by the majority that it is possible to be Welsh without the language. Even so, the language is seen as a valuable ethnic asset and as a result members are prone to overestimate their linguistic ability. Forty-one per cent of my initial sample said they spoke Welsh. Each informant who had claimed to be a Welsh speaker was visited by a research assistant who used only Welsh. The percentage of informants who were able to converse completely in Welsh then dropped from 41 per cent to 27 per cent of the total sample.

It is, of course, possible that failure to speak Welsh in these contexts may have resulted from other than linguistic factors. On the other hand, all these informants were observed to speak some Welsh in limited, formalized or ritual contexts, such as greetings, exchanges about the weather, enquiries about health, offers of hospitality and other routine daily matters. To say that they speak Welsh, therefore, is not inaccurate, but a matter of degree. Some admitted that they would not like a 'real Welsh person' to listen to them. Obviously, a person such as the Welsh-speaking interviewer, who addresses strangers in Welsh, must be 'a real Welsh person', no one else would be so foolish! If you are con- cerned about the quality of the Welsh you speak, you choose an appropriate audience. Several of these non-fluent speakers were not ashamed to speak some ritualized Welsh to me, whom they per- ceived ultimately as Anglo-Welsh.

The language is, in fact, 'used' by all members of the community. It may, at one extreme, be used by antagonistic incomers as a symbol of stigma. It can be used as a linguistic code with a wide range of intensity - from merely singing the national anthem to serving as the medium for as much interaction as possible. It can, as demonstrated, be used to include or exclude and to accept or reject. It is used by most as the symbol of Wales' heroic past and claim to separate integrity. Many purists would reject peripheral uses of the language as real use at all, but in a community where only 27 per cent speak Welsh, there must be few who do not use some Welsh in some way every day of their lives - even if that use is merely as a cognitive marker of an ethnic category.

Having looked at some aspects of ethnicity in a border community, it becomes eminently clear that the traditional definition of an ethnic group fails in most respects to describe the situation. The assimilation theory of ethnic groups, which supposes that ethnic differences lose their importance and gradually fade in modern industrial societies, seems to find tacit support among those champions of Welsh integrity who bemoan the Anglicization of Welsh culture. On the other hand, while the Welsh way of life, partic- ularly in the borders, may suffer the effects of cultural homogen- ization in this age of the global village, ethnic identity and ethnic pride appear to be experiencing an intensification (Bourhis and Giles, 1974; Tajfel, 1974). Social change, including the erosion of the use of the Welsh language, appears to take the form of, not a shift to English (or even British) identification, but a redefinition of Welshness. In other words, the reference group remains the same but the personnel and the symbols of membership change.

It is interesting to find, for instance, that while those over fifty are far more likely to use Welsh speaking as a sine qua non for inclusion in the Welsh ethnic group those under twenty never suggest that this is a necessary criterion. They say of their Anglo-Welsh peers: 'They are just as Welsh as us'. Both Welsh speakers and Anglo-Welsh under the age of approximately forty overtly express more loyalty, concern and support for Wales as an entity than do those who are older. Political issues such as the Kilbrandon Report, Welsh-language television programming, Welsh water, etc. also receive more sympathetic consideration from younger community members. In other words, the salience of specific ethnic *markers,* such as language, may be less for younger members, but the salience of the ethnic group is greater. What appears to happen is that adjustments are made in the symbolic systems of individuals so that the symbol of the ethnic group remains, but the secondary symbols, diacritics or markers change. In terms of social organization, the function of the ethnic group is unchanged. It functions as a multivalent symbol, whose facets are sufficiently diverse to satisfy all who seek meaning. It is both an ascribed and an affiliative category, which serves as an orienting principle for the individual, a common cause for ethnic institutions and a rallying call for propagandists.

The lack of concensus about secondary symbols, however, can lead to ambiguity and misunderstanding. Plaid Cymru (4) and Cymdeithas yr Iaith Gymraeg (5) have very little overt support in Clwyd. The vote for Y Blaid (6) has never quite reached 5 per cent in a general election and informants suggested that these organizations were only for Welsh speakers and, in addition, politically suspect! Support for the aims of these organizations, however, when they were presen- ted in a neutral context, was considerable and identification with the Welsh ethnic group was claimed by all who could produce even the flimsiest of legitimizing credentials.

Looking at ethnic groups as symbolic categories rather than aspects of social structure results in different questions being raised. Interest inevitably shifts from boundaries, membership criteria and inter-ethnic conflict or assimilation to consideration of such things as what makes a particular ethnic category a success- ful symbol; under what circumstances may we predict an intensifica- tion - or even emergence - of ethnic consciousness; what causes a shift from negative to positive ethnic image; or, why do ethnic categories persist in situations where previous theory would predict assimilation.

In summation, it is contended that while the traditional defin- ition of ethnic group delineates some of the most usual core attributes, it does not go far enough. A more analytically satis- fying approach to the phenomenon can perhaps be found in treating it as a symbolic category. Such an approach would focus on the meaning of ethnic labels for the community and the individual using them; the ways in which ethnic membership is symbolized by the use of ethnic markers; how and by whom ethnicity is being used to talk about other factors; and the ways in which internal and external change affect the dimensions, symbols and salience of ethnic identification. From this perspective, which could perhaps be broadly termed a social organizational approach, the added knowledge of the dynamics of ethnicity should lead to a richer understanding of ethnic groups; to more informed and creative policy decisions affecting their membership; and to an explanation of both the persistence over time, the emergence and the demise of specific groups.

NOTES

1 The research upon which the bulk of this paper is based was
   supported by grants from the National Institute of Mental
   Health, Washington, DC, whose help is hereby acknowledged.
2 'No Welshman without Welsh.'
3 'Welsh (speaking) Welshman.'
4 Welsh Nationalist Party.
5 Welsh Language Society.
6 The Party.

REFERENCES

BARTH, Frederic (1969), 'Ethnic Groups and Boundaries', London,
George Allen & Unwin.
BOURHIS, Richard and GILES, Howard (1974), Welsh is beautiful, 'New
Society', 21, 15-16.
BURLING, Robbins (1970), 'Man's Many Voices', New York, Holt,
Rinehart & Winston.
HELM, June (ed.) (1968), 'Essays on the Problem of Tribe', University
of Washington Press, AES Monograph.
KROEBER, A.L. (1939), 'Cultural and Natural Areas of Native North
America', Berkeley, California, University of California Press.
LEACH, Edmund R. (1954), 'Political Systems of Highland Burma',
Cambridge, Mass., Harvard University Press.
MOERMAN, Michael (1965), Who are the Lue? Ethnic Identification in
a Complex Civilization, 'American Anthropologist', vol.67, 6,
pp.1215-30.
NARROLL, Raoul (1964), Ethnic Unit Classification, 'Current
Anthropology', vol.5, no.4.
SHARP, Lauriston (1958), People without Politics, in 'Systems of
Political Control and Bureaucracy', Verne Ray (ed.), Seattle,
University of Washington Press.
SORENSEN Jr, Arthur P. (1967), Multilingualism in the Northwest
Amazon, 'American Anthropologist', vol.69, no.6, pp.670-84.
TAJFEL, H. (1974), Social identity and intergroup behaviour, 'Social
Science Information', 13, 65-93.
TURNER, Victor W. (1969), 'The Ritual Process', Chicago, Aldine.
WARNER, W. Lloyd (1959), 'The Living and the Dead: A Study of the
Symbolic Life of Americans', New Haven, Yale University Press.

WARNER, W. Lloyd (1961), 'The Family of God: A Symbolic Study of Christian Life in America', New Haven, Yale University Press.
WISSLER, Clark (1938), 'The American Indian', New York, Oxford University Press.

Chapter 10

NATIONAL IDENTITY IN SOUTH WALES: SOME PRELIMINARY DATA

Howard Giles and Donald M. Taylor

Corrado (1975) has examined the social history of Wales from the time the nation was conquered and incorporated into the English political system to the present day. Currently, only about 25 per cent of Welshmen speak their national tongue which has seen its greatest erosion during this century. Although Welsh has an official status in Wales, it is not, in reality, given equal status with English in all walks of life in the principality. Furthermore, it is undoubtedly true that the status afforded a Welshman and his national language in the UK has been a consensually inferior one (Thomas, 1973). Until fairly recently, many Welshmen felt that an important strategy for securing an adequate social identity was to attempt 'to pass' as an individual into the dominant, English social group (cf. Tajfel, 1974), for example, by losing their Welsh-language skills, assuming an English accent, Anglicizing their names, moving into England, and so forth.

However, for reasons as yet undefined, there has been a sudden awareness in the late 1960s that such 'individualistic' strategies of linguistic and cultural assimilation are not the only possibilities open to Welshmen. For some, the plight of Welsh as a language is comparable with the plight of Wales as a nation (Khleif, 1975). In this light, it might be said that such Welshmen perceive themselves more as members of a national group than as detached individuals within a society. For these then, the low status of Welsh is perceived to be unjust and illegitimate and no longer acceptable; alternatives are sought. To this end, and as a first step towards a redefinition of Welshness, a number of Welshmen are assuming a new pride in their bilinguality and changing their names into Welsh ones, while others are now acquiring their national tongue as a symbol of their Welsh allegiance. In addition, a Welsh Language Society (Cymdeithas yr Iaith Gymraeg) is taking social action to improve the status of the national language in Wales, while the Welsh nationalist party (Plaid Cymru) and its ideas are beginning to flourish (Hearne, 1975).

Empirical research also attests to a positive evaluation among Welshmen for speakers of the Welsh language. Bourhis and Giles (1976) found, in a naturalistic study, that Welsh bilinguals reacted more favourably to a request for help when it was voiced in Welsh

rather than English. During the interval in a Cardiff theatre,
those attending a Welsh dramatic performance were invited to help
the management by co-operating in a short audience survey. This
information was transmitted to them via the loudspeaker system;
some nights in Welsh, and others in English. It was found that
almost three times as many Welsh bilinguals completed the questionnaire when the plea was made in Welsh than in English (cf. Sharp,
et al., 1973; Lewis, 1975).

Such positive reactions to Welsh-language speakers have also been
found among English-only speaking Welshmen. Bourhis, Giles and
Tajfel (1973) asked three groups of Welshmen to listen to and
evaluate on certain personality traits of various Welshmen they
would hear reading a passage of prose on tape. These three groups
were: (a) Welsh-English bilinguals, (b) those who were learning the
Welsh language, and (c) Welshmen who could neither speak the Welsh
language nor were learning it. Actually, the passages were read by
the same two male bilinguals in the following guises:(1) in Welsh;
in English with a BBC-type (Received Pronunciation:RP) accent; in
English with a south Welsh accent. Perhaps rather surprisingly,
there was no evaluative divergence between the different groups of
Welsh listeners in their reactions to the speakers on tape. Whether
the listeners could speak Welsh or not did not seem to matter in the
sense that all groups upgraded the Welsh language speakers on most
traits. For example, on the scale, 'How much I'd like to be like
that speaker', all groups of listeners preferred to attain the image
of a Welsh speaker rather than model themselves after the supposedly
high prestige, RP-accented speaker. These findings suggest that the
Welsh have a favourable image of themselves as a group; they do not
appear to seek a prestigious mode of speaking English. Even those
Welshmen who could not speak Welsh reflected this view.

Interestingly, this study also showed that the Welsh accent
could also serve as a marker of national identity. On some traits
(e.g., trustworthiness, friendliness and sociability), the mere
possession of a Welsh *accent* was as effective in eliciting a positive
reaction from the listeners as speaking the Welsh language itself.
In another study, Bourhis, Giles and Lambert (1975) found that Welshmen take a relatively favourable view of Welshmen broadening their
Welsh accent (in English) in a public radio interview with an RP-
accented interviewer. Indeed, Bourhis and Giles (1977) have found
that certain Welshmen tend to broaden their accents in English as a
symbol of their national allegiance when others question the value
of the Welsh language.

Empirical studies then suggest that Welshmen value their national
group membership and its language highly. Moreover, the focus of
the contemporary social change developing in Wales outlined earlier
has been mainly in terms of the Welsh language. With such an
emphasis on affective aspects of Welsh identity, there has been
little attention paid to its cognitive and structural components.
The present paper is concerned with a preliminary attempt to specify
the dimensions which constitute national identity for people in
south Wales.

A METHOD FOR STUDYING WELSH IDENTITY

In order to study group identity, a method is needed which, according to Taylor (1975) is (a) sensitive to the subtleties and complexities of social categories in the context concerned, (b) relatively simple for people to perform, and (c) minimizes the possibility for people to bias their responses in terms of social desirability or acquiescence. The studies to be reported here involve the use of a procedure which seems to satisfy, at least partially, these criteria.

The first step in the procedure is to prepare, through informal elicitation procedures, an over-inclusive list of labels which represent the potential social and national reference groups with which a Welshman could identify. To this list is added the control label, 'Myself'. Respondents are then presented with these stimulus concepts (of which 'Myself' is one) two at a time in all possible combinations. For each pair, the respondent is asked to judge on a scale the degree of similarity between the two stimulus concepts. This is a relatively simple judgment for respondents to make and yet the data can be analysed so as to reveal important dimensions of Welsh identity. Since respondents make judgments of all possible pairs of concepts, it is possible to generate a mean similarity matrix analogous to a correlation matrix. A multidimensional scaling analysis (Shepard, 1962; Kruskal, 1964) can then be performed. The objective of non-metric multidimensional scaling is to map a set of stimuli into a set of points in a metric space such that stimuli which are similar are close together, and those which are dissimilar are distant from each other in that space. In terms of Welsh identity, those reference groups placed close together are perceived by Welshmen to be relatively similar whereas those placed far apart are perceived as different. By focusing special attention on the position of each of the concepts relative to 'Myself', inferences can be made regarding the national identity of respondents.

A study by Taylor, Bassili and Aboud (1973) using this multidimensional scaling procedure provides an illustration of the type of dimensions which can emerge in some multi-ethnic situations. The study examined how the factors of geography (living in Quebec vs. living outside Quebec), language spoken (French vs. English) and cultural background (born of French- vs. English-Canadian parents) interact in the process of ethnic identity in Quebec. It was found that language spoken for both English- and French-Canadians was more important than cultural background as a dimension of ethnic identity. For instance, French-Canadians would identify more closely with an English-Canadian who spoke French mainly than a French-Canadian who spoke only English. Moreover, it was clear that the respondents identified more closely with those who were linguistically similar even though this meant not identifying with the people with whom one shared the same geographical space. One important feature of Quebec is that French is a functional language spoken by the vast majority of French-Canadians and hence it is not surprising perhaps that language is a particularly salient feature of their ethnic identity. It is possible however that this relationship between language facility and ethnic background need not be so strong in all cultural backgrounds (cf. Giles, Taylor, Lambert and Albert, 1976).

THE WELSH STUDIES

In Wales of course about three-quarters of the population cannot
speak their national language. Yet given the fact, as shown
previously, that Welshmen appear to evaluate Welsh-sounding representatives of their own cultural group very favourably, it may well
be that English-only speaking Welshmen consider cultural background
to be the most important feature of their identity since they have
no Welsh-language skills upon which to rely. For Welsh bilinguals
on the other hand, it might be expected that language (as with the
Canadian groups) would emerge as a salient feature of their Welsh
identity. Another factor that could prove to be an important
variable in Welsh identity is geographic residence, particularly
in view of the fact that south and north Walians are isolated from
each other by mountainous ranges and poor transportation links.

    With this in mind, Giles, Taylor and Bourhis (1977) examined the
roles of language (Welsh vs. English), cultural background (being
born of Welsh vs. English parents) and geographic residence (living
in England vs. north Wales vs. south Wales) as dimensions of
identity. Two groups of Welsh students attending a college in
south Wales - 22 Welsh speakers and 22 English-only speakers -
were provided with twelve stimulus concepts by taking combinations
of the above three factors. For example, the list included, 'A
Welshman living in England who speaks only English' and 'An Englishman living in north Wales who speaks Welsh'. To this list was
added the anchor stimulus, 'Myself'. They were then required to
make similarity judgments between all possible combinations of these
13 concepts.

    Multidimensional scaling analyses (MDSCAL) of these data showed,
as expected, that language was read out as the most important
dimension of Welsh identity for the bilingual sample (Khleif, 1975).
They identified, for example, more closely with an Englishman who
could speak Welsh than a Welshman who could not speak the national
tongue. Cultural background played a subordinate role in the
sample's identity profile with geographical residence having little
effect on these respondents' judgments. For Welsh bilinguals then,
identity seems clear. They perceive themselves as extremely close
to other Welsh-speaking people in general, and particularly to those
whose cultural background is Welsh. The subject sample in this
study comprised of students and it is of course necessary to
replicate these findings with other groups of bilingual Welshmen
from a variety of social classes.

    The expectation that cultural background would be read out as the
most salient dimension of identity for the English-only speaking
sample was however not met. Again, the configuration for this group
appeared to be largely influenced by the linguistic variable with
the cultural background and geographical factors playing subordinate
roles. In other words, these Welshmen identified most closely with
speakers of English and not with other Welshmen. Indeed, they seem
to feel socially distant from those who do speak Welsh. Yet,
according to previous data reported, such Welshmen do find Welsh-
speaking Welshmen more desirable on a number of affective dimensions
than their English-speaking counterparts. Thus, the majority of
Welshmen may be faced with the problem of feeling psychologically

distinct from a social group to whom they feel attracted.

These results (together with those from Quebec) indicate that language spoken may be a dimension of fundamental importance for group identity (cf. Fishman, 1977; Giles, Bourhis and Taylor, 1977). While both samples of Welshmen appear to be homogeneous in their appreciation of Welsh linguistic skills, it would appear that they are heterogeneous in their identity profiles and even appear to consider themselves psychologically distinct from each other. Moreover, it would seem, from these data at least as if cultural affiliation is not a crucial variable for English-only speaking Welshmen. Could it be that many Welshmen who cannot speak their national language find difficulty in defining Welshness in terms *other* than linguistic? Hence, could it be that Welshmen without bilingual skills find it very difficult to identify themselves realistically as 'Welsh'?

Thus far, however, we have been dealing with the dimensions of national identity as if they were static givens under what have been admittedly socially sterile conditions. Perhaps it is the case that identity profiles are context-specific and that one could discover situations in which cultural affiliation was very salient for English-only speaking Welshmen. In addition, it may be that this group's apparent lack of identification with 'Welshness' was due in some measure to the limited range of stimulus concepts offered the respondents. Had the multidimensional scaling procedure provided a less restrictive range of Welsh and English social groups with which to identify and had it included notions of nationalism, cultural affiliation may have been more pronounced for the mono-lingual sample.

In order to counteract these problems to some degree, a follow-up study was conducted by us in collaboration with Nick Gadfield (UWIST, Cardiff) and John Christian (McGill University, Montreal) with English-only speaking 17-year-olds attending a high school in south Wales. This study attempted to take into account the fact that different social contexts may tap different identity profiles and incorporated a more varied range of stimulus concepts within the procedure. It was expected that cultural affiliation would now become more salient for these Welshmen when the stimuli incorporated concepts relating to nationalism and this effect would be accentuated in a context where English-Welsh conflicts were highlighted (cf. Tajfel, 1959; 1972).

Two groups of respondents co-operated in the study. One of these groups (24 respondents) had cultural affiliation made salient for them by being required to write an essay on how Welsh identity had suffered through English domination over the last century (the Salient condition). The other group of 26 respondents (the Neutral condition) wrote an essay unrelated to English-Welsh relations (industrial pollution).(2) After completing these essays, both groups were presented with ten stimulus concepts and asked to form an impression of each. The concepts were: 'A Welshman who can speak Welsh'; 'A person deeply concerned about the environment'; 'An Englishman who can speak only English'; 'A Cornish Nationalist'; 'A Welshman who can speak only English'; 'A person deeply concerned with the survival of Welsh identity'; 'An Englishman who can speak Welsh'; 'A Welsh Nationalist'; 'A person who advocates British unity';

'Myself'. Two dimensions adopted in the previous study – cultural
background and language – were reflected in this list along with
concepts related to nationalism and the themes of the essays. The
respondents were then presented with the stimulus concepts two at
a time in all possible combinations. For each pair, the respondents'
task was to judge the similarity between the two stimuli on 9-point
rating scales (very similar – very different).

   The same multidimensional scaling analysis (INDSCAL; Carroll and
Chang, 197); Ramsay, 1975) was adopted for use on the data from
both samples of respondents. In each case, the similarity ratings
were best represented along the same two dimensions.(3) It is
interesting to note that the structure of dimensions of national
identity remain the same under quite different conditions, e.g.,
when intergroup conflict is made salient and when it is not. The
first dimension appeared to represent an English culture – Welsh
culture dimension in that for both samples, 'An Englishman who
speaks only English' and 'A person concerned with British unity'
anchored one pole while 'A Welsh Nationalist' and 'A person concerned with the survival of Welsh identity' are at the extreme of
the opposite end.

   Despite the structural similarity of identity profiles between
the two conditions, differences did emerge between the positioning
of the stimulus concepts for the two samples (see Figure 10.1).

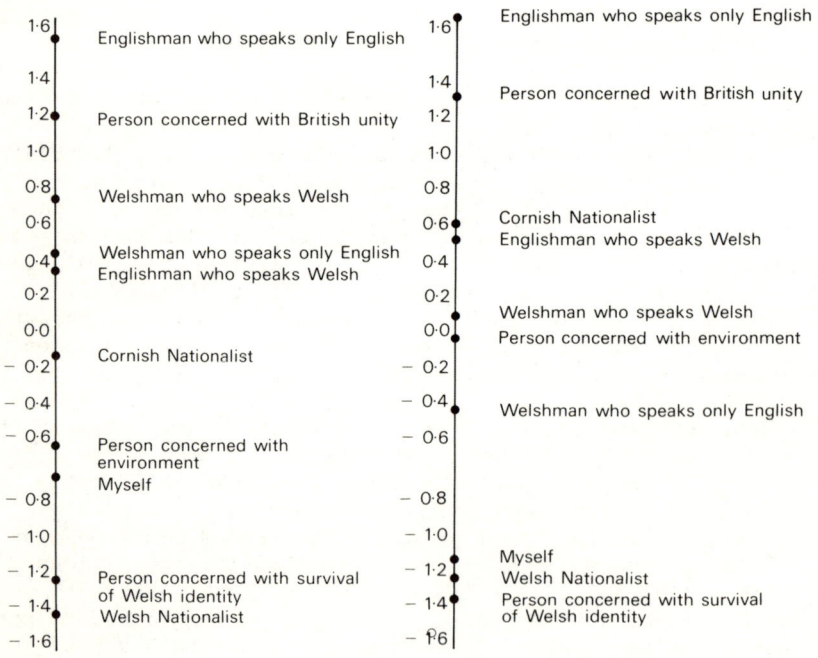

NEUTRAL CONDITION   SALIENT CONDITION

FIGURE 10.1 Results of INDSCAL for Dimension 1 for both groups of
            Welshmen

For instance, there was a close association between 'Myself' and 'A person concerned with the environment' for respondents in the Neutral condition, while for those in the Salient condition, the latter concept was placed at the origin.   Thus, there is good evidence that the experimental manipulation had been effective. In addition, it can be seen that 'Myself' shifted towards the 'Welsh' concepts (e.g., 'A Welshman who speaks only English', 'A Welsh Nationalist') were closer to 'Myself' while all the English concepts (e.g., 'An Englishman who speaks Welsh', 'A Cornish Nationalist') were more removed from 'Myself' in the Salient condition than the Neutral condition.

The second dimension that emerged from the analyses can be interpreted as a radical separatist-conservative integrationist dimension.   It was anchored at one end with the concepts, 'A Cornish Nationalist' and 'A Welsh Nationalist' and at the opposite pole by 'Myself', 'A Welshman who speaks English' and 'A person concerned with British unity'.   Again, there was an important difference in the arrangement of stimulus concepts along this dimension for respondents in the two conditions (see Figure 10.2). Whereas there is some distance between 'Myself' and 'A Welshman who speaks English' in the Neutral condition, these two concepts converge in the Salient condition.

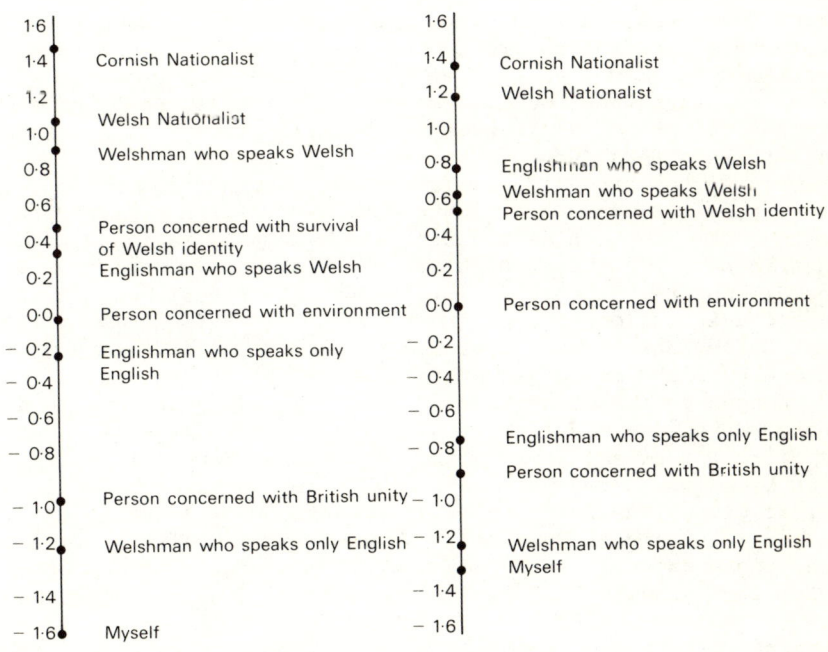

NEUTRAL CONDITION   SALIENT CONDITION

FIGURE 10.2   Results of INDSCAL for Dimension 2 for both groups
              of Welshmen

Thus, language did not emerge as a dimension of Welsh identity for these respondents under these conditions. However, it is probably the case that the inclusion of stimulus concepts such as 'Cornish' and 'Welsh Nationalist' which were not included in the previous study, highlighted the political and national character of the stimulus groupings. It would be interesting to determine whether the same two dimensions would have emerged for other English-speaking samples in Wales as well as for Welsh bilinguals.

Having described each of the two dimensions separately, it remains to interpret the meaning of the simultaneous operation of them for the respondents. The emergence of two dimensions demonstrates the complexity of ethnic categorization in which people may identify with certain features of their national group and not with others. Respondents in the present case felt themselves to be similar to 'A Welsh Nationalist' on Dimension 1. Since this dimension was based on a Welsh culture - English culture distinction, it would seem that it is the Welsh cultural ideals of the Welsh Nationalists that respondents found attractive. Yet at the same time, these Welshmen felt they were very distant from a Welsh Nationalist on the radical separatist -conservative integrationist dimension (Dimension 2). On the one hand these students identified strongly with the survival of Welsh culture while, on the other, they felt little affinity for more radical (separatist-type) manifestations of Welsh identity. Furthermore, they associated themselves with British unity, but not to the extent that they were willing to sacrifice the Welsh culture. The fact that these Welshmen were cautious about the way in which Welsh cultural traditions are preserved, and were concerned about the social costs involved in their maintenance, may help explain why respondents in the previous study did not allow the cultural background factor to assume prominence in relation to the other possibilities offered them.

These findings strongly suggest that identification with the Welsh national group is multidimensional and not an all-or-none dichotomy. It has been shown that Welsh identity is susceptible to changes in social context which are manifest not in the structure of the dimensions conceptualized, but rather in terms of the arrangement of concepts along these dimensions. In the final study, making salient Welsh-English conflicts led to a closer affiliation with Welsh ingroups and an accentuated polarization of English outgroups. Other changes in the perception of Welsh-English relations, and indeed other entirely different social concepts, may well induce quite different alterations in the nature of national identity. Just as relations between England and Wales can never be considered as static givens, neither can Welsh identity be assumed to be a stable, unidimensional constant. Nevertheless, scaling procedures such as those adopted herein may provide a useful methodological tool for further empirical explorations of national identity in Wales.

The preliminary data reported here should be heartening to those who are interested in maintaining and developing a sense of national pride in Wales. But it should also sound a note of caution as regards national unity. Both of the studies on identity reported here suggest that Welsh-speaking, and English-only-speaking, Welshmen consider themselves dissimilar from each other. Relations

between these two factions could then become tense if speakers of
Welsh on the one hand become intolerant of a lack of Welsh bilinguality in other Welshmen and if non-Welsh-speakers on the other
refuse to co-operate with demands made by those who can speak Welsh.
We cannot, as yet, talk of a homogeneous 'Welsh identity'.

NOTES

1 This procedure is termed the 'matched-guise' technique (see
   Giles and Powesland, 1975).
2 This technique of making intergroup relations salient was based
   on empirical work by Eiser (1974). It has also been adopted
   successfully in a recent study by Bourhis, Gadfield, Giles and
   Tajfel (1976) who investigated south Welsh adolescents' reactions to anti-Welsh and anti-English humour (cf. Chapman, Smith
   and Foot, 1977). A content analysis of the essays written in
   the study reported in this paper showed that respondents in the
   Salient condition of necessity focused upon Welsh-English
   relations, while this topic never arose in respondents' essays
   in the Neutral condition.
3 Because there were ten stimulus labels, a solution of greater
   than two dimensions would be quite unstable and in fact a very
   stable two-dimensional solution appeared to provide a more
   substantive interpretation than one- or three-dimensional
   solutions (cf. Christian, Gadfield, Giles and Taylor, 1976).

REFERENCES

BOURHIS, R.Y., GADFIELD, N., GILES, H. and TAJFEL, H. (1977), Context
and ethnic humour in intergroup relations, in A.J. Chapman and H.
Foot (eds), 'It's a Funny Thing, Humour', Oxford: Pergamon, pp.261-6.
BOURHIS, R.Y. and GILES, H. (1976), The language of cooperation in
Wales: A field study, 'Language Sciences', 42, 13-16.
BOURHIS, R.Y. and GILES, H. (1977), The language of intergroup
distinctiveness, in H. Giles (ed.), 'Language, Ethnicity and Inter-
group Relations', London: Academic Press, pp.119-35.
BOURHIS, R.Y., GILES, H. and LAMBERT, W.E. (1975), Social consequences
of accommodating one's style of speech, 'International Journal of the
Sociology of Language', no.6, 55-72.
BOURHIS, R.Y., GILES, H. and TAJFEL, H. (1973), Language as a
determinant of Welsh identity, 'European Journal of Social
Psychology', 3, 447-60.
CARROLL, J.D. and CHANG, J.J. (1970), Analysis of individual differ-
ences in multidimensional scaling via a N-way generalization of
'Eckart-Young' decomposition, 'Psychometrika', 35, 282-319.
CHAPMAN, A.J., SMITH, J. and FOOT, H. (1977), Language, humour and
intergroup relations, in H. Giles (ed.), 'Language, Ethnicity and
Intergroup Relations', London: Academic Press, pp.137-69.
CHRISTIAN, J., GADFIELD, N., GILES, H. and TAYLOR, D.M. (1976), The
multidimensional dynamic nature of ethnic identity, 'International
Journal of Psychology', 11, pp.281-91.
CORRADO, R.R. (1975), Welsh nationalism: An empirical evaluation,
'Ethnicity', vol.2, 360-81.

EISER, R. (1974), Attitudes and the use of evaluative language: A two-way process, paper presented at Conference on Research Paradigms and Priorities in Social Psychology, Carleton University, Ottawa, July.

FISHMAN, J.A. (1977), Language and ethnicity, in H. Giles (ed.), 'Language, Ethnicity and Intergroup Relations', London: Academic Press, pp.15-57.

GILES, H., BOURHIS, R.Y. and TAYLOR, D.M. (1977), Towards a theory of language in ethnic group relations, in H. Giles (ed.), 'Language, Ethnicity and Intergroup Relations', London: Academic Press, pp.307-48.

GILES, H., TAYLOR, D.M. and BOURHIS, R.Y. (1977), The dimensions of Welsh identity, 'European Journal of Social Psychology', vol.7, 29-39.

GILES, H., TAYLOR, D.M., LAMBERT, W.E. and ALBERT, G. (1976), Dimensions of ethnic identity: An example from Northern Maine, 'Journal of Social Psychology', 100, 11-19.

GILES, H. and POWESLAND, P.F. (1975), 'Speech Style and Social Evaluation', London and New York: Academic Press.

HEARNE, D. (1975), 'The Rise of the Welsh Republic - Towards a Welsh Theory of Government', Talybont, Wales: Y Lolfa.

KHLEIF, B.B. (1975), 'Ethnic Boundaries, Identity, and Schooling: A Sociocultural Study of Welsh-English Relations', mimeo., University of New Hampshire, Durham.

KRUSKAL, J.B. (1964), Multidimensional scaling by optimizing goodness of fit to a non-mettri hypothesis, 'Psychometrika', 29, 1-27; 115-30.

LEWIS, G. (L975), Attitudes to language among bilingual children and adults in Wales, 'International Journal of the Sociology of Language', no.4, 102-26.

RAMSAY, J.O. (1975), 'Two Algorithms and Various Statistical Models for Multidimensional Scaling by Maximum Likelihood', mimeo., McGill University, Montreal.

SHARP, D., et al. (1973), 'Some Aspects of Welsh and English: A Survey of Schools in Wales' (School Council Research Studies), London: Macmillan.

SHEPARD, R.N. (1962), Analysis of proximities: Multidimensional scaling with an unknown distance function: I & II, 'Psychometrika', 27, 125-39; 219-46.

TAJFEL, H. (1959), Quantitative judgment in social perception, 'British Journal of Psychology', 50, 16-29.

TAJFEL, H. (1972), La categorization sociale, in S. Moscovici (ed.), 'Introduction à la Psychologie Sociale', Paris: Larousse.

TAJFEL, H. (1974), Social identity and intergroup behaviour, 'Social Science Information', 13, 65-93.

TAYLOR, D.M. (1975), Ethnic identity: some cross-cultural comparisons, in J.W. Berry and W.J. Lonner (eds), 'Applied Cross-Cultural Psychology', Amsterdam: Swetz & Zeitlinger, 168-73.

TAYLOR, D.M., BASSILI, J. and ABOUD, F.E. (1973), Dimensions of ethnic identity: An example from Quebec, 'Journal of Social Psychology', 89, 185-92.

THOMAS, N. (1973), 'The Welsh Extremist', Talybont, Wales: Y Lolfa.

Chapter 11

AGGREGATE STUDIES OF LANGUAGE AND CULTURE CHANGE IN WALES

Harold Carter and Stephen Williams

1 INTRODUCTION

Since the earliest census returns dealing with the Welsh language were published it has been the custom to construct maps depicting the spatial pattern of change (Southall, 1895; Williams, 1937; Thomas, 1956; Jones and Griffiths, 1963; Bowen and Carter, 1974; 1975). From these maps inferences have been drawn as to the processes operative in the changes taking place. Such studies have clear limitations and there are cogent arguments for the direct evaluation of attitude and behaviour from sample populations, rather than for the abstraction of factors causing language loss (or gain) from the consideration of spatial patterns at different historical stages. Even so the hypotheses to be considered in behavioural studies and the problems to be solved must be derived from the initial analysis of aggregate data. This paper consists of two closely related studies based on such aggregate data and aims to identify, at a fairly gross level of generalization, some of the forces which condition language decline, and by implication, culture change.

2 Y FRO GYMRAEG AND THE 1975 REFERENDUM ON THE SUNDAY CLOSING OF PUBLIC HOUSES IN WALES

In 1969 one of the present authors published a paper entitled 'The referendum on the Sunday opening of licensed premises in Wales as a criterion of a culture region' (Carter and Thomas, 1969). In that paper, as the title suggested, it was maintained that the Sunday opening issue has a close relationship with the notion of Welsh cultural identity. Indeed, it was argued that voting in the referenda of 1961 and 1968 could be used as a surrogate for an attitude survey to traditional aspects of the Welsh culture complex. In that paper this contention was justified by a discussion of the original Sunday Closing Act which was a private member's bill introduced during Gladstone's second ministry. It received its second reading on 4 May 1881 (Parliamentary Papers, 1881). Consideration of the contemporary social scene would suggest that the

origins of the Act lay in three nuclei, none of which was completely
separate from the others. The first of these was that of the
influence of religious Nonconformity with its ascetic views on
alcohol in general and its insistence on Sunday observance. That
alcohol should be consumed at any time was abhorrent to the devout
chapel goer; that it should be consumed on Sunday in premises open
for that purpose was well high intolerable. The second nucleus of
support lay in the national aspirations which in Wales were becoming
increasingly articulate in the latter part of the nineteenth century.
The circumstances surrounding this growth of national feeling, of
cultural awareness, have been fully documented elsewhere (Jenkins,
1935; Jones, 1950; Williams, 1950), but it is worth repeating and
stressing here that the Sunday Closing Act was the first occasion
(apart, possibly from the Act of Union itself and the acts of the
translation of the Bible and the Prayer Book) on which the then
Imperial Government was prepared to treat Wales as a separate unit.
Gladstone, himself, seems to have been conscious of the need for
this sort of treatment for Wales, for in his speech on the occasion
of the second reading he referred both to the somewhat shabby
treatment which Wales had received in the past, particularly in
relation to Church appointments, and to the desirability of the
Government's discovering whether there was a distinct Welsh
opinion on any specific issue, and if so, taking note of it (Parliamentary Papers, 1881). It is not surprising, therefore, that Welsh
feeling, which was largely Nonconformist in outlook, should have
regarded the Act both in content and background, as a tremendous
advance in its long struggle for national recognition. To these
sources of support must be added that from the third nucleus, for
it was a Liberal Government which was prepared to sponsor the Bill
and Gladstonian Liberalism seems to have been particularly attractive
to Welsh Nonconformity (Morgan, 1960). With support from these
three nuclei of opinion it is not surprising to find that on this
issue at least, the Principality seems to have been unusually firmly
united. The introduction of the Bill and the passing of the Act
represent the recognition at that time of the existence of a
definite culture area, not only internally by the people themselves
but externally by the Government at Westminster, and in this lies
its significance.
    During the 80 years that have elapsed since the Sunday Closing
Act, this culture has, through a variety of circumstances, been
subject to a steady and continuous erosion. Factors such as the
decline of the Welsh language, movements of population, the secularization of life and the impact of mass media of communication, have
all played their part in this process. Thus, while Welsh people
generally have been conscious of the decreasing 'Welshness' of their
country, it has been very difficult for them to take any practical
steps to remedy this situation without becoming involved in political ideas and actions which might be termed 'extremist'. But the
Referenda of 1961 and 1968 provided a specific issue on which a
definite stand could be taken without necessarily involving such
wider and less clear issues as, for example, self-government or the
compulsory use of the Welsh language in schools and public affairs.
To many people Sunday Closing was an expression of the cultural
separateness of Wales (a separateness which need not involve

political nationalism) as indeed it was to Gladstone himself in 1881.

In the examination of the 1961 and 1968 Referenda close links were demonstrated between the results, both the proportion voting and the proportion voting dry, and the degree of Welshness as measured by the proportion of Welsh speakers at the 1961 census. In consequence the latest Referendum in 1975 raises three issues:

a   Do the relationships established for 1961 and 1968 still hold good?

b   Do the Referendum returns confirm the patterns of decline of traditional Welshness which appeared in the 1971 census of the language?

c   Is Y Fro Gymraeg, Welsh-speaking Wales, a distinctive Welsh region?

Before examining these questions a brief explanatory note is needed. A referendum is held every seven years if there is a local demand which is defined as a requisition for a vote signed by 500 people eligible to vote in local government elections. In 1968 and 1971 the votes were held on a county basis. In 1974 the local government structure was changed and the 1975 referendum was held on a District basis. Polls were held on 5 November 1975 in 18 of the 37 District authorities in Wales (Figure 11.1). This situation presents a standard geographical problem, for between 1971 and 1975 the areal basis of the referendum had changed, and also in just over half the areas there was no contest, so that the data produced related to only part of the country. The real problem, however, is that direct comparability is lost since only three areas (Anglesey, Ceredigion and Montgomery), where polls were held, covered the same area in 1968 and 1975. It is now possible to turn to the three questions posed by the latest referendum.

a   Do the 1961 and 1968 relationships still hold good?

There is little doubt that the basic patterns identified in 1961 and 1968 are still clear (Table 11.1). In spite of the so-called ecological fallacy the correlations set out can be accepted at face value as showing a close relation at the aggregate scale between Welsh-speaking, dry-voting and the commitment to vote.

Table 11.1 Correlations between Welsh-speaking, dry-voting and percentage voting

	Welsh-speaking	Dry-voting	Poll
Welsh-speaking	1.0	0.925**	0.684*
Dry-voting		1.0	0.788*
Poll			1.0

** Significant at 0.1% level.
* Significant at 1.0% level.

The only other positive and significant correlations with dry-voting, out of the other seventeen selected variables set out in the

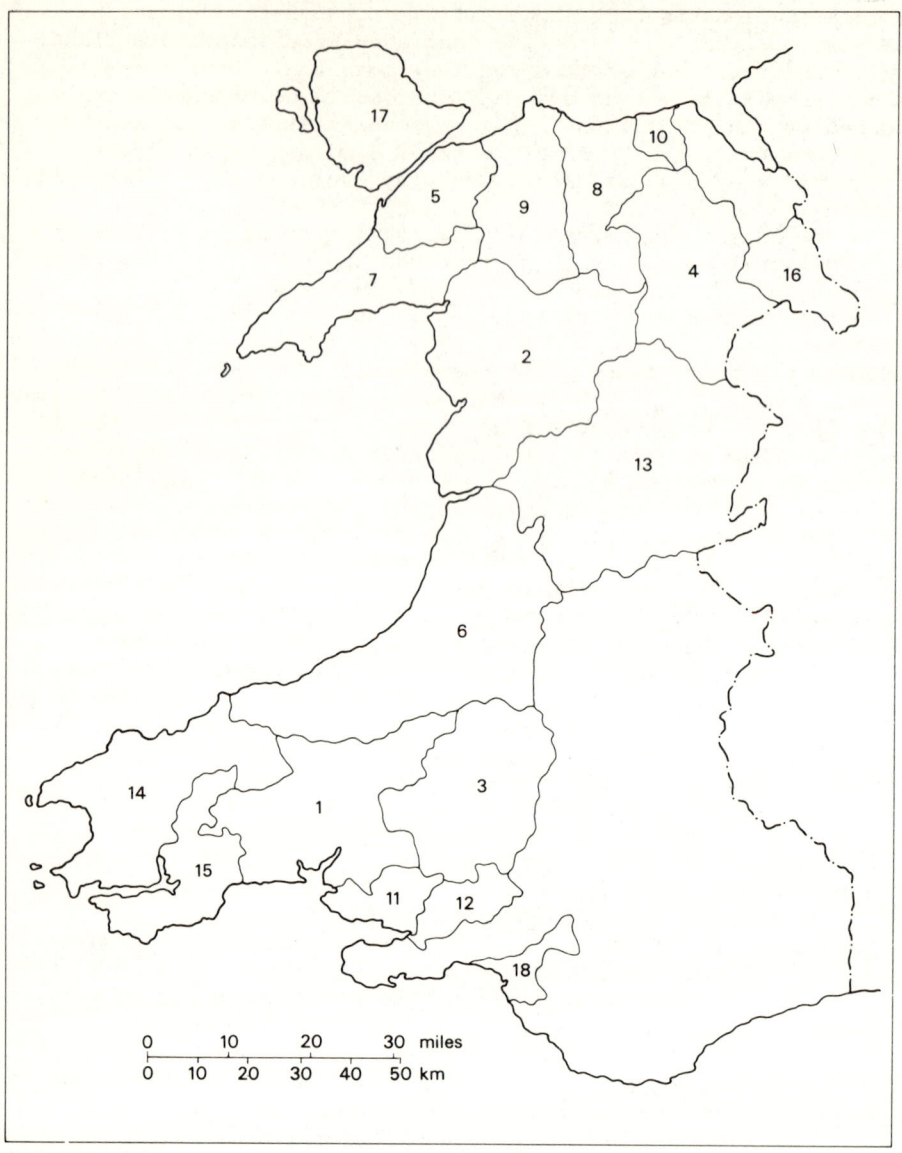

FIGURE 11.1   Districts in which the Referendum on the Sunday Closing
of Licensed Premises was held in 1975 (for identification of Districts see Figure 11.3)

appendix, were employment in agriculture (0.458, significant at the
5 per cent level) and also Social Class 1 (0.604, significant at 1
per cent level). The rural nature of the language/dry-voting
complex is as expected, but of greater interest is the Social Class
1 relation. This would seem to suggest on the one hand the
professional-elitist association of that complex and on the other
its contrast to the working-class, wet areas of the Anglo-Welsh
industrial parts of the country.

b Does the referendum confirm a pattern of decline?

An examination of the returns from the 1971 census of the Welsh
language in Wales reveals a clear pattern of decline (Bowen and
Carter, 1974; 1975). The total Welsh figures showed a decrease of
some 5.2 per cent in those able to speak Welsh. More significant
are the variations within this overall decline for examination of
the distribution pattern of decline reveals not only continued
erosion along the main Welsh-English divide but also a tendency for
the core area of Welsh speaking itself to break up. The main forces
involved can be identified as the growth of resort and retirement
functions, and suburban extension from towns into the surrounding
rural areas, in Wales Anglicization is a feature of the rural-urban
fringe. In addition any form of intrusive economic development
results in a decline in the *proportion* of Welsh speakers if not in
their absolute numbers. The crude areal basis of the Referendum,
that is by District (Figure 11.1) as against the parish basis of
the language census, makes it difficult to use it effectively to
assess decline, but the general process is shown in Figures 11.2a
and 11.2b. Figure 11.2a shows the results of the 1975 poll and
Figure 11.2b the general pattern of retreat of the 'dry frontier'
over fourteen years. The problem of the comparability of areas has
been indicated, but four areas can be isolated and the percentage
vote in the three referenda related (Table 11.2).

Table 11.2 Per cent voting dry in comparable areas

	1961	1968	1975
Anglesey (Môn)	76	66	54
Cardigan (Ceredigion)	74	64	59
Montgomery (Trefaldwyn)	57	41	29
Merioneth (Meirionnydd)*	76	66	57

* The former county of Merioneth and the District of Meirionnydd
  are not strictly comparable. Edeyrnion R.D., formerly part of
  Meirioneth, was transferred to Glyndwr District in the new
  county of Clwyd.

The uniform decrease of 10 per cent between 1961 and 1968 for the
three strongly Welsh areas of Anglesey, Ceredigion and Meirionnydd
has not been simply replicated in the period 1968-75. Anglesey

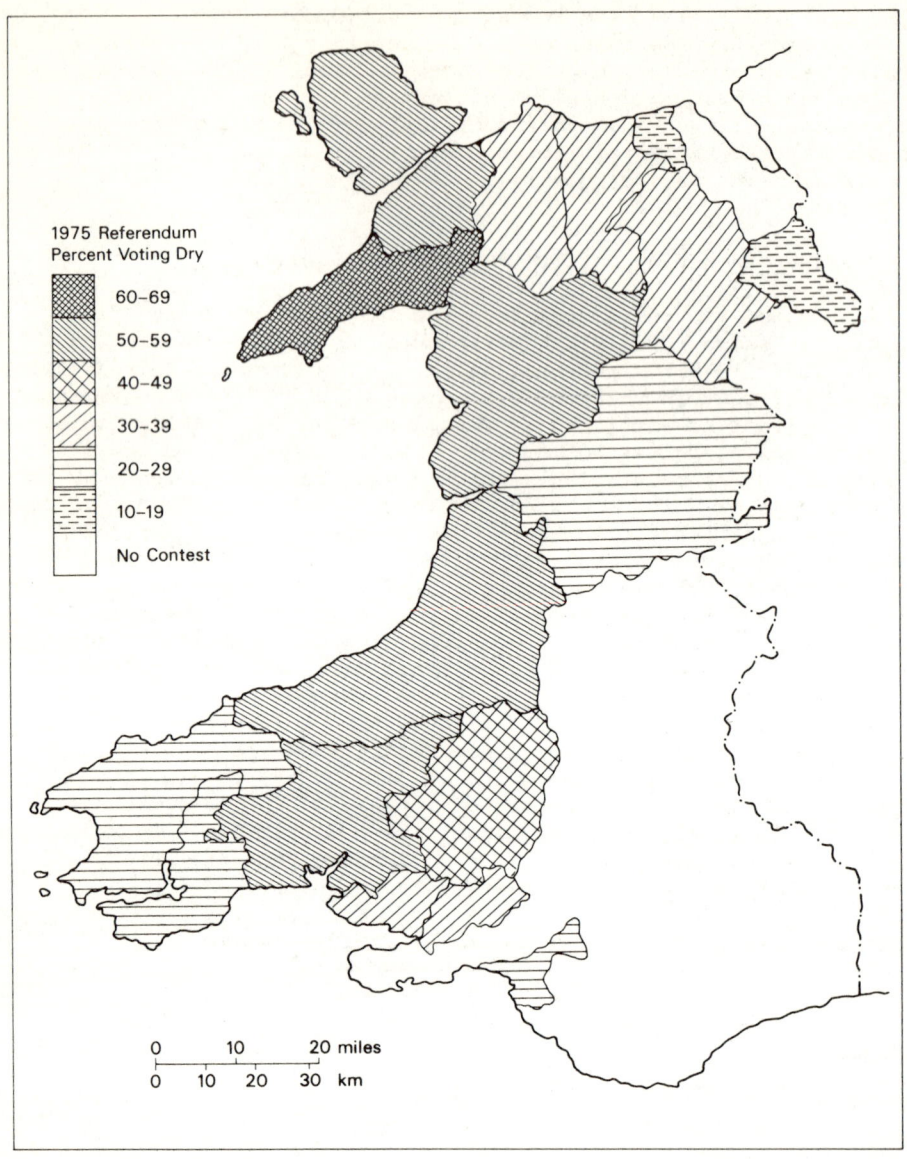

FIGURE 11.2a Voting in the 1975 Referendum

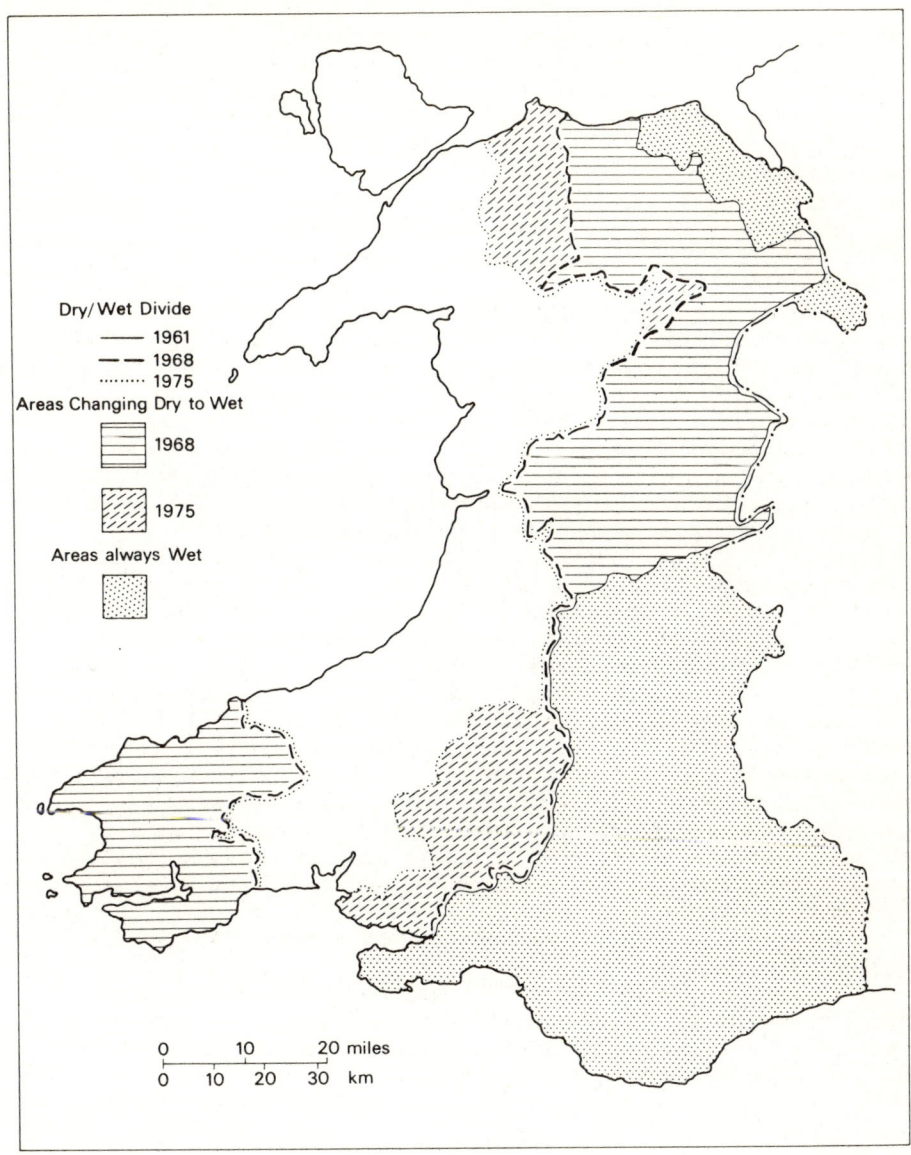

FIGURE 11.2b 'Wet' and 'Dry' Areas in Wales 1961-75

especially stands out, for the transfer of rural, Welsh-speaking
(77 per cent) Edeyrnion out of Meirionnydd could possibly account
for that District's slight variation from Ceredigion. This sharp
decline in Anglesey is in keeping with language evidence for
between 1961 and 1971 the Welsh-speaking percentage fell from 75
to 65 compared with a fall from 75 to 68 in Ceredigion. Some
Anglesey parishes recorded decreases of as much as 21 per cent
(Llanfair-Mathafarneithaf fell from 67.9 to 46.9). All this is a
clear reflection of economic development on the island, including
the establishment of a nuclear power station and an aluminium
smelter as well as an increase in the resort and retirement
function and a marked spill-over of suburbanization from Bangor.

The progressive isolation of the traditional Welsh culture
complex is clearly displayed in Figure 11.2b. The divide between
wet and dry has pushed westwards until only what has been called
'fortress Wales' remains. In the more recent period from 1968 to
1975 it was fairly evident that once Aberconwy as a District, with
only 39 per cent Welsh-speaking and strong tourist association, was
detached from inclusion within the old county of Caernarfon it would
turn wet. Again the highly industrialized and urbanized District
of Llanelli, although with a fairly high percentage of Welsh
speakers (59), was predictably a dry loss. The major unexpected
shift was the new District of Dinefwr where some 79 per cent of the
population are Welsh speaking, the next highest after Dwyfor. But
only 47.5 per cent voted dry on a fairly high poll. It is true
that this was the nearest vote to the critical 50 per cent divide,
but even so with an urban population no higher than Ceredigion it
would seem to have more in common with the dry culture core than
the wet fringe. On the other hand the District includes a distinctive industrial area in the Amman valley where, as in Llanelli, the
link between Welsh speaking and dry voting is modified. Also it is
situated on the divide and provides evidence, as does the language
(Carter and Bowen, 1974), that there is a distinctive spatial
character to the pattern of decline. In spite of the mass media
geographical contiguity still seems a factor in promoting change
for it ensures the physical mixing of populations with different
language backgrounds.

The general conclusion must be that the referendum results
confirm the evidence of the decline of traditional Welshness.
Simple extrapolation of the 1961-75 trends suggests that insofar
as the closing of pubs on Sunday is a distinctive element, it will
have disappeared from all Districts, apart from Dwyfor, by 1990.

c   Y Fro Gymraeg, a distinctive Welsh region?

The expression 'the traditional Welsh culture complex' has been used
in the first two sections of this discussion. Its use demands some
form of explanation and a consideration of whether a core region
variously called 'Inner Wales', 'Le Pays de Galles', 'Welsh Wales'
or 'Y Fro Gymraeg' can be identified.

In order to examine these points a number (18) of relevant
variables was assembled (see Appendix 1). Although these were
related mainly to socio-economic characteristics, it must be admitted

that the determining factor was the possibility of conversion to the District basis.

An 18 x 18 matrix of Districts and variables was set up and subjected to a principal component analysis. A varimax rotation was also introduced but since little change in the output results, and the stability of the components was confirmed, the following discussion is based on the PCA.

The first five components produced eigenvalues of over one (6.45, 4.44, 1.90, 1.28 and 1.13) and the cumulative percentage variance explained by these was 35.84, 60.52, 71.09, 78.18 and 84.47. The first four components seem capable of reasonable interpretation.

Table 11.3   Loadings on component 1

Positive		Negative	
Dry Voting	0.337*	Industrial Employment	0.280
Per cent Poll	0.322	Pop. Change 1951-61	0.274
Welsh Speaking	0.319	Youth	0.252
Voting in local elections	0.315	Urban pop.	0.228
Agric. Employment	0.254	Social Class 5	0.224
Social Class 1	0.241		

* These are eigenvectors. The more usual loadings are calculated by multiplying by the square root of the eigenvalues.

Component 1 quite clearly identifies what has been termed the traditional Welsh culture complex (Table 11.3). It is characteristically associated with high Welsh-speaking, dry-voting rural areas with an elderly population. Two points require comment. The association of Social Class 1 confirms the points already made when correlations were considered (p.147). The second is that general voting in elections is also associated and this suggests that the simple explanation that the people voting are concerned about the culture is too simple, for they seemingly turn out to vote on other issues as well; perhaps it is more a reflection of a small-scale and concerned society.

Table 11.4   Loadings on component 2

Positive		Negative	
Elderly	0.398	Social Class 5	0.263
All amenities	0.358	Industry	0.233
Employment; service distrib.	0.351		
Five-year movers	0.321		
Pop. change 1961-71	0.318		
Owner occupiers	0.237		
Urban	0.231		

Component 2 (Table 11.4) defines a tourist and retirement complex. Employment in the service and distributive trades, which was intro-duced as a representation of tourism into the variable list, appears and is associated with the elderly, owner-occupiers, and recent movers and an urban environment.

Table 11.5   Loadings on component 3

Positive		Negative	
Five-year movers	0.413	Owner-occupiers	0.278
Social Class 1	0.416	Urban	0.247
Young people	0.405	Elderly	0.207
Pop. change 1961-71	0.338		

Component 3 (Table 11.5) is rather enigmatic but interesting. The movement characteristic, together with the association of young people and high social class, when also the negative urban and elderly association are taken into account, suggest a suburbaniza-tion identity. The anomalous feature is the negative loading of owner-occupiers since it would seem that a complex of young families of high social class moving into the rural fringes of towns would show a high positive owner-occupier characteristic. Again it is possible that the large, mixed Districts on which the analysis is based may be responsible. Thus the towns of Ceredigion, especially Aberystwyth, are characterized by marked suburban expansion into areas classed as rural but this is only one feature of the District. It must also be added that converted into a usual loading the value is 0.38 and loadings below 0.5 are usually ignored. If this procedure were followed all the negative loadings would be discounted.

Table 11.6   Loadings of component 4

Positive		Negative	
Welsh decline	0.685	Agriculture employment	0.423
Welsh-speaking	0.306		

Component 4 (Table 11.6) is a Welsh decline component on which Welsh speaking must load significantly since decline cannot take place unless there is already a clear Welsh-speaking proportion. The negative loading of agriculture suggests that this identifies the heavy losses suffered by the language between 1961 and 1971 in the urban areas.

    If this analysis of the principal components abstracted from the variables is accepted then the conclusions drawn from examination of the referendum vote and the language census are confirmed. There would seem to be a rural Welsh culture component with the remainder illustrating the critical impact upon it which is being made by retirement and tourism, by suburbanization and in the urban indus-trial areas.

This interpretation can be given a spatial context by the examination of:

1   The maps of dry voting and changes in voting 1961-75 (Figures
    11.2a and 11.2b).
2   Factor scores recorded on component 1 which was seen as ident-
    ifying Welshness.
3   A clustering procedure (Ward's Error Sum) based on scores on
    the first three components (Figure 11.3).

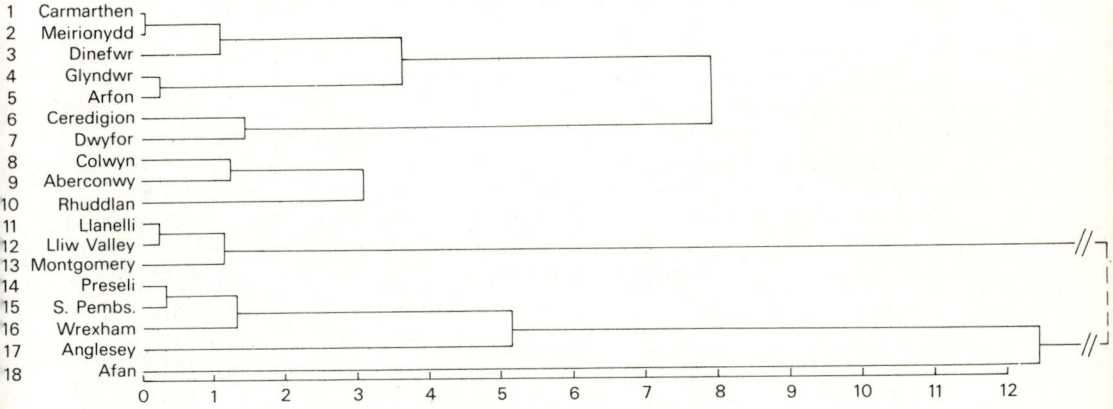

FIGURE   11.3   Grouping of Districts (Ward's error sum)

The general results from this analysis are presented in Table 11.7.

Table 11.7   Districts characterized by 'Welshness' measures

1 Dry Areas, 1975 Figures 11.2a and b	2 Welsh Cluster at 3 Groups Figure 3	3 Factor scores on component 1	4 Percentage Welsh speaking
Dwyfor	Dwyfor	Dwyfor	Dwyfor
Ceredigion	Ceredigion	Ceredigion	Dinefwr
Meirionnydd	Meirionnydd	Meirionnydd	Arfon
Carmarthen	Carmarthen	Carmarthen	Carmarthen
Arfon	Arfon	Dinefwr	Ceredigion
Anglesey	Dinefwr	Arfon	Meirionnydd
	Glyndŵr		

1 Each list has been stopped at six members to correspond to the
  dry area.
2 The Welsh cluster was started at Dwyfor and built up from that
  District. The process of clustering means that seven Districts
  have to be included.

All the evidence identifies a clear culture core, Y Fro Gymraeg, which is dominantly Welsh in speech and rural in character. It is essentially the dry-voting area. There are three areas which appear to be marginal either by inclusion or exclusion.

(a) Anglesey or Ynys Môn. To suggest that Anglesey is in any way marginal in a Welsh culture context would seem to be ridiculous, but all the evidence shows that it is an area where traditional patterns have been severely eroded. It recorded a high increase in non-Welsh born population between 1961 and 1971. It is equally interesting politically in that it is the only part of the core represented by a Labour Member of Parliament. All the other areas came under Plaid Cymru held constituencies apart from Ceredigion which has a Liberal Member. The figures for the last election are given in Table 11.8

Table 11.8 Percentage votes for the main parties at the last Parliamentary election, 1974

Constituency	Labour	Conservative	Plaid Cymru	Liberal
Anglesey	41.6	23.8	19.1	15.5
Caernarfon[1]	34.1	12.6	42.6	10.6
Cardigan	35.2	9.5	13.1	42.2
Carmarthen[2]	38.1	5.7	45.1	10.4
Merioneth[3]	31.0	11.1	42.5	15.4

1   This does not correspond with the county.
2(a) Although having the same name this is not the same in extent as the new District of Carmarthen.
  (b) A British Party candidate polled 0.7 per cent of the votes.
3   This corresponds with the old county but not with the new District.

This evidence demonstrated Anglesey's variation from the other constituencies. Not only is the Labour vote higher but also the Conservative vote is almost double that of any of the others, while the combined Plaid Cymru-Liberal vote is 20 per cent less. This Anglesey voting pattern has far more in common with the Anglicized constituencies of the fringe than with those of the Welsh core.

(b) Dinefwr. This area appears to belong to the core on everything but the dry vote. It has already been suggested that the industrial character of part of the area might be responsible for its detachment.

(c) Glyndŵr. This District, formerly part of Denbighshire, is caught up in the cluster of Welsh Districts. Here the explanation would seem that it is a large and marginal area where characteristics both of core and margins appear. It is significant that the former Edeyrnion R.D., with a high proportion of Welsh speakers (77 per cent), was transferred from the old

county of Merioneth to Glyndŵr District in the 1974 reorganization.

3 THE SOCIO-ECONOMIC CHARACTERISTICS OF AREAS AND THEIR RELATION
TO LANGUAGE AND LANGUAGE CHANGE

This section examines at a general level the types of environment
in which the Welsh language exists (Welsh language taken as a 'hard'
indicator of culture). The principle object is to try to identify
those factors which are producing changes in the Welsh cultural
milieu and which may produce more potent changes in the future.
    With this object in mind the analysis aims to produce a region-
alization of Wales based on two distinct but related approaches:
 1 A classification of Wales based on a set of census measures, the
    overall aim being to find those dimensions which best characterize
    and summarize Wales in socio-economic terms.
 2 Relating the above classification to both proportion Welsh
    speaking and particularly to per cent change in Welsh speaking
    during the period 1961-71.
    Both stages of the analysis utilize the multivariate statistical
technique of Principle Component Analysis (PCA), which from a
specific data set statistically derives the major sources or
dimensions of variation, and relates in a parsimonious way the
initial variables and units of observation to these major dimensions
of variation.
    Fifty-one units of observation were used (Figure 11.4), that
number being arrived at by the amalgamation of Rural Districts and
Urban Districts, a procedure which produced a more continuous
spatial framework than if RDs and UDs were considered separately.
Twenty-nine variables were selected from the 1971 100 per cent and
10 per cent censuses, which can be considered as representing five
main groups, namely, demographic, economic activity, mobility,
social class and amenities. The matrix of intercorrelations
between the twenty-nine variables (R mode)\was analysed by means
of PCA. Eight factors were extracted with eigenvalues greater than
1.0, which also corresponded to Cattels scree test. However, in
empirical terms and particularly in terms of interpretability only
six were retained for varimax rotation. The rotated component
loadings are presented in Table 11.9. Only loadings over ±0.3 are
given. The first five components together account for 64 per cent
of the total variables contained in the initial data set. Thus, by
using PCA to examine the intercorrelations the initial 29 variable
data set has effectively been reduced to a 5 'variable' set while
losing only 36 per cent of the variance.
    At this point, therefore, it is possible to turn to an examina-
tion of the first stage of the analysis and the substantive results
produced by the statistical manipulations. The first factor is in
effect a general factor and, as such, can best be described in the
terms of an urban/rural dimension. The positive loadings provide
the urban flavour while the negative are essentially rural in
character loading particularly highly on agriculture and selected
deprivation indices. If the negative component scores are examined
for this factor (see Table 11.10) then the areas which stand out

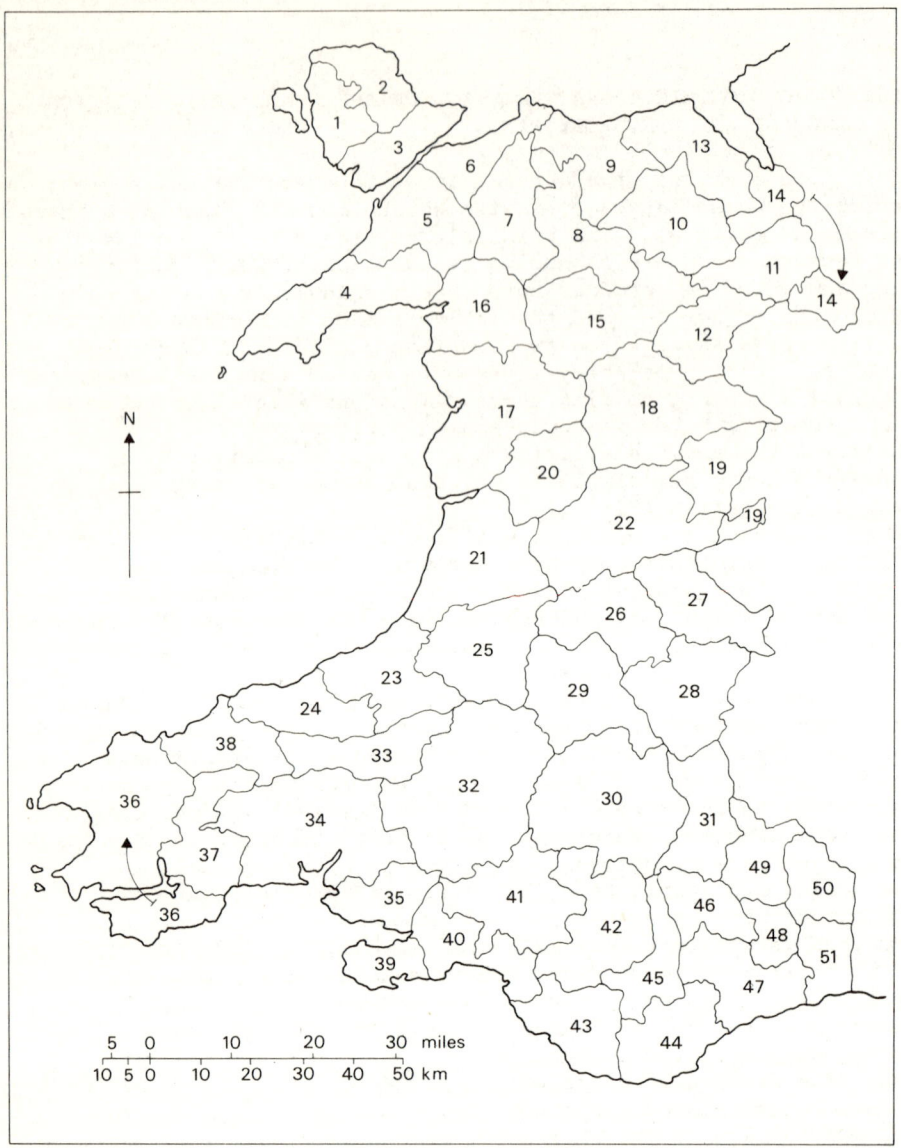

FIGURE 11.4   Areas used in the socio-economic study (for
              identification see Appendix 2)

Table 11.9 Principal component analysis with varimax rotation of six components

		Factor 1	2	3	4	5
1	% pop. change 1961-71	0.438	-0.518	0.558	-0.314	
2	% of pop. in urban areas	0.471				
3	% 14 and under	0.303	-0.796			
4	% 15 - 24			0.556	0.577	
5	% over pensionable age		0.853			
6	% econ. act. females					-0.665
7	5 yr into migrants			0.842		
8	5 yr within migrants				0.780	
9	Births/000		-0.495			
10	Deaths/000		0.638			0.313
11	% females	0.449	0.433			
12	% active but unemp.			-0.322		0.515
13	% Social Class I			0.891		
14	% Social Class II	-0.405		0.574		
15	% Social Class IV				0.581	
16	% Social Class V		-0.465		0.498	
17	% of emp. in agric.	-0.827			-0.313	
18	% of emp. in mining			-0.320	0.429	
19	% of emp. in manufac.	0.654	-0.509			
20	% of emp. in construct.					0.795
21	% of emp. in utilities	0.313				0.549
22	% of emp. in distrib.	0.311	0.571	0.469		
23	% of emp. in govt.					
24	Education level			0.860		
25	% of H/H without bath	-0.748		-0.355		
26	% of H/H without w.c.	-0.893				
27	% of H/H without cars	0.381		-0.368	0.721	
28	Hotel rooms/000 pop.		0.691			
29	Divorce/000 of pop.	0.776				
	Eigenvalues	6.89	4.63	3.17	2.20	1.77
	% explanation	23.8	16.0	11.0	7.6	6.1
	Cumulative %	23.8	39.8	50.7	58.3	64.4

most clearly are Tregaron, the Aberystwyth area, Machynlleth and Llanfyllin while in the south Llandovery and Llandeilo exhibit similar profiles.

The second factor explains 16.0 per cent of the variance and in general terms can be designated a factor of 'age and low growth'. The positive loadings reflect a weak socio-economic structure with demographic imbalances in the proportion of old people, female ratio and deaths/OOO; also loading highly are hotel rooms/OOO of population and those engaged in distributive trades. The negative end of the dimension illustrates the 'low growth' characteristics associated with areas which exhibit this patterning of variables (Table 11.9). This factor therefore represents a resort/retirement function particularly prevalent in coastal areas of Wales. The positive component scores illustrate this quite clearly, especially along the north Wales coast, that is, the Llandudno - Colwyn Bay - Prestatyn resort area.

Factor 3 which accounts for 11.0 per cent of the variance can be labelled 'high class, inmigration, growth' or more contentiously, a 'suburbanization' factor. The variables which give the distinctive character to the positive end of the dimension are those which refer essentially to a young, highly educated and highly mobile population generally associated with the higher social class categories. This in fact defines that section of the population which has the greatest propensity to move and which also characterizes the type of person that one would expect to find moving into a suburban environment. From an examination of the factor scores four main areas are worthy of mention. First, Aberystwyth and environs emerges quite clearly as having the highest score, this is an obvious point to make as Aberystwyth is one of the principle nodes in the mid-Wales region and as such is a selected growth point plus the fact that the tertiary sector is already well developed. Second, the coastal areas abutting the Menai Straits on the island of Anglesey. This is principally a result of suburban expansion from the Bangor area and also is a result of developments on the island itself, for example the establishment of a nuclear power station and the existence of Ministry of Defence establishments. Third, the Gower, an area of high amenity value which in recent years has been characterized by suburban development spreading west from Swansea. This feature can also be seen in the valley areas to the north of Swansea, while Port Talbot has a similar pattern of development. What appears to be happening therefore is that there is an informal development of the 'Swansea Bay city' idea, resulting in an extension of the urban sphere of influence into the surrounding rural and semi-rural areas. Fourth, similar suburban developments can also be seen in the Cardiff and Monmouth areas, especially in the Cwmbran region. Here, there exists in effect a development axis along a corridor linking Pontypool-Cwmbran and Newport, closely related to new town developments and to the activities of the British Steel Corporation in the area.

The fourth factor, which explains 7.6 per cent of the variance, has positive loadings generally associated with an urban and industrial context, i.e. short-distance migration, without cars, but more specifically, in this instance the variable mix relates to urban areas which are 'running down' or are experiencing low growth.

Table 11.10   Factor scores of +1.0 and above

Factor 1		Factor 2	
(9) Colwyn Bay*	+2.01	(6) Bangor-Llandudno	+2.46
(6) Bangor	+1.60	(17) Dolgellau	+2.08
(47) Newport	+1.49	(9) Colwyn Bay	+1.98
(44) Cardiff	+1.48	(4) Lleyn	+1.75
(13) Upper Deeside	+1.25	(21) Aberystwyth	+1.28
(40) Swansea-Port Talbot	+1.11	(26) Rhayader-Llandrindod	+1.27
(43) Cowbridge-Bridgend	+1.07	(16) Ffestiniog-Deudraeth	+1.18
(51) Chepstow	+1.11		
(49) Abergavenny			

Factor 3		Factor 4	
(21) Aberystwyth	+4.72	(21) Aberystwyth	+3.14
(39) Gower	+1.79	(46) Tredegar, Bedwellty, etc.	+2.31
(48) Pontypool-Cwmbran	+1.64	(41) Ystradgynlais-Pontardawe	+2.16
(3) Menai Bridge-Aethwy	+1.45	(42) Taff-Cynon-Rhondda	+1.71
		(11) Wrexham	+1.00

Factor 5	
(2) Twrcelyn	+2.41
(37) Narberth	+2.08
(16) Ffestiniog-Deudraeth	+1.67
(38) Cemaes	+1.24
(1) Valley	+1.62
(5) Caernarfon-Gwyrfai	+1.24
(25) Tregaron	+1.24

* In most cases the place names above refer to composite retions
  rather than to specific areas - see Figure 11.4.

In terms of the factor or component scores the Aberystwyth region,
somewhat unexpectedly, comes out highest. This tends to illustrate
the general point that as a result of selective development in a
small-scale urban economy there tends to be a significant degree of
inequality between different sections of the population even in an
area the size of Aberystwyth. Other areas which also score highly
on this component include Pontardawe and Ystradgynlais, while the
industrial areas of Ebbw Vale in south Wales and Blaenau Ffestiniog
in north Wales also score highly.

The fifth factor, which is the final factor to be examined,
contains 6.1 per cent of the initial information and has high
positive loadings on those engaged in construction and utilities,
unemployed, deaths/OOO and those in social class V. This tends to
point to areas which are declining or have declined demographically,
while also exhibiting a limited economic base. The high loadings
relating to construction and utilities may be explained to a large
extent by reference to the existence of capital investment in major
construction projects in certain parts of the Principality which
entail large numbers being engaged in directly related and ancillary
occupations. An examination of the component score tends to confirm
this general view. The Twrcelyn area of Anglesey, for example, contains nuclear power station installations, while Tregaron contains
two large construction concerns. Lleyn also has a number of labour
intensive construction projects several of which are related to
infrastructure development.

The second stage of the analysis related the proportion of Welsh
speakers and the change in the percentage speaking Welsh between
1961 and 1971 to the five initial factor scores for the fifty-one
areas discussed above, by means of a factor analysis of a 7 x 7
matrix (the 5 factor scores together with language and language
change). The results are shown in Figure 11.5.

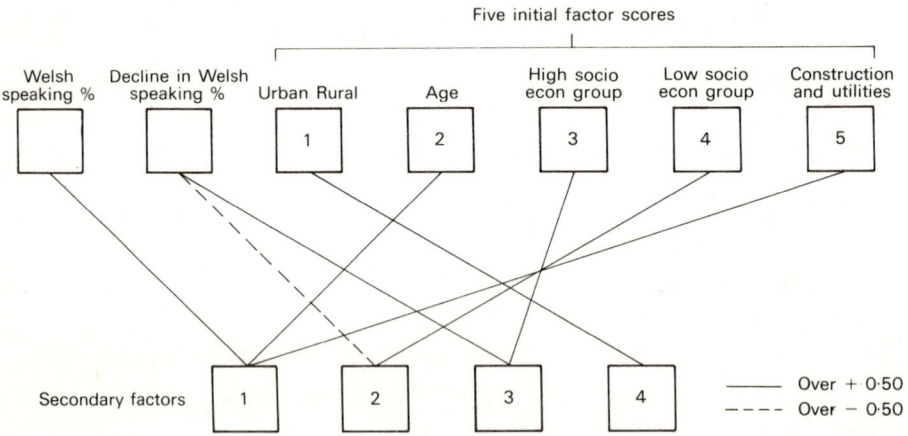

FIGURE 11.5   Diagram to illustrate the relationships between initial
              factor scores and Welsh data using a secondary factor
              analysis

This secondary analysis reveals that a positive statistical relationship exists between the initial factors two and five, that is between the age factor and the construction and utilities factor, and the Welsh-speaking proportion. Briefly this situation suggests that the Welsh language is essentially a rural phenomenon although its non-urban character may be lessening though not significantly so. It is lodged in an environment of limited economic potential. These are the areas which have attracted the attention of government agencies and within which major capital investment has been made. These may temporarily halt depopulation but it is significant that the association of large capital works with small rural communities could be seen as the exact opposite of what is needed to retain a cultural character.

The second feature identified from this secondary analysis is the positive relation between what has perhaps rashly been called the 'suburbanization' factor and the decline of the language (Figure 11.5). This association of highly mobile adults of the higher social classes with language decline seems to bear out conclusions derived from univariate studies (Bowen and Carter, 1974; 1975) that such suburbanites are generally non-Welsh (despite the existence of the 'Nouveaux Welsh') and are active in the erosion of the language at the urban-rural interface.

A further relationship also needs some comment for the second 'secondary' factor is positively related to the fourth initial factor which was identified as having a low socio-economic status industrial characteristic. It is also negatively related to the change in the percentage of Welsh speakers. This is partly fortuitous for the Anglicized industrial areas already had low percentages of Welsh speakers in 1961 and therefore could not record high losses in the intercensal period. To some extent, therefore, this identifies the already Anglicized areas of the south and north east, although there are clear exceptions.

4   CONCLUSIONS

The conclusions to these two brief studies can be set out under three headings - Factual, Interpretive and Speculative.

I   Factual

(a) A core area of traditional Welsh Wales - Y Fro Gymraeg - exists as a fairly clearly defined region within the country but it is rapidly approaching a stage of fragmentation.
(b) All the evidence confirms that the period 1961-71 was one both of decline and retreat. Spatial shrinkage is still dominant but, as indicated in (a) above, the point is now imminent at which a continuous residual core is likely to be lost.
(c) In decline, retreat and fragmentation certain major forces are operative.
    (i) There is a general decline (retreat) at the margins. This
        suggests that some critical situation might exist, a tipping
        point, below which change becomes rapid. This is seemingly

confirmed by the fairly rapid transition across the Welsh-English divide and by the examination of the pattern of frequencies of Welsh-speaking proportions. To confirm this the individual histories of a number of areas would have to be traced and no further evidence is offered here.

(ii) Suburbanization, or the spread of housing out of the small country towns, now seems to be an active force in the transformation of rural, Welsh-speaking Wales. It may be the critical interface.

(iii) Tourism, with which retirement and second home holding are closely associated, is clearly coincident with areas of change.

(iv) The language holds its own less effectively in heavily urbanized and industrial areas.

(v) i, ii, iii and iv are all related to situations where Welsh- and English-speaking populations are mixed.

II Interpretive

(a) The process of decline can be related to the notion of cumulative causation (Myrdal, 1957) and especially relevant is the implication of the first secondary factor of the second analysis which related employment in construction, the elderly and the language. The areas most strongly associated with the language are rural in character and the traditional economic base was subsistence farming. However, with the coming of merchandized, capitalist farming the shedding of labour, in a situation where no alternative employment was available, led to age specific outward migration, the younger people moving, to leave a demographical structure which is unbalanced; even natural decrease has followed in consequence. All this produces reactions in poorer services, degraded infra-structures, and a spiral downward in terms of economic attractiveness; that is a process of downward cumulative causation sets in so that an already economically deprived area becomes further impoverished. At this point investment tends to move to large capital projects which can best use these thinly peopled lands - nuclear power stations, hydro-electric schemes and water storage schemes for example. These are the worst possible investments for they are labour intensive only in the construction period when they attract large non-Welsh speaking influxes. In operation they provide no extensive employment base. Moreover the very rurality of depopulated country attracts seasonal second home owners or permanent retired people alien to the indigenous culture. The loss of Welsh in this way becomes an integral part of the downward spiral.

(b) At the other end of the rural-urban scale the language was maintained in the small industrial village, but in order to survive at present it has to become the language of the cities and a medium of modern bureaucracy. There seems little prospect of its future vitality if it is inextricably linked to the folk society, the elderly and the past. The close association of the language and the dry Sunday ties it to the old rural and village tradition rather than directs it towards a reinvigorated future.

(c) The last two points are sometimes taken to imply that there are

straightforward solutions given the political will. The survival
and increase of the language could be ensured if its preservation
became one of the primary ends of rural planning, although even so
the incompatibility of development on the one hand and the preservation of the language on the other is not always fairly faced. In
the same context it is argued that Welsh can become the medium of
bureaucracy by the compelling of its official use in the administration of both local and national government.

III   Speculative

Such views as have just been outlined and speculation as to the
future suggest a more deeply lying problem. If one accepts that
dominant trends in contemporary Western Society are a growing
specialization in occupations, growing geographical mobility and a
growing local and regional dependence on surrounding area, then all
are apparently destructive of minority language (Lunden, 1974).
That is, the mixing of populations with contemporary mobility as
identified in paragraph 4-c above, as well as the impact of modern
bureaucracy, destroy rather than enhance linguistic diversity. If
a communications theory of urban growth is tenable then those communications can multiply and intensify effectively only in a common
medium. All this means that the decline of the Welsh language must
be seen as an aspect of broad changes in Western society, which
include the increasing scale of social contacts, the impact of
non-place realms of communication and operation, as well as direct
physical mobility. All these produce conditions which are greatly
different from the circumstances in which Welsh flourished. They
constitute a contemporary environment which cannot be changed
simply by legislation: they imply that most of the actions taken,
and proposed, strike quite ineffectively at symptoms and so nothing
to alter the major social changes, from which language decline
follows.

APPENDIX 1   VARIABLES USED IN SECTION 2

All are percentages.

 1. Dry voting 1975
 2. Poll 1975
 3. Voting in local elections
 4. Welsh speaking 1971
 5. Decline in Welsh speakers 1961-71
 6. Population over 65 1974
 7. Population under 15 1974
 8. Heads of households in Social Class I 1971
 9. Heads of households in Social Class 5 1971
10. Moving into LA areas in last 5 years 1971
11. Population change 1951-61
12. Population change 1961-71
13. Agricultural employment 1971
14. Industrial Rate values of total rateable value 1973

15. Urban population (resident in M.B.s and U.D.s in 1971)
16. Exclusive use of housing amenities 1971
17. Employed in service and distributive trades 1971
18. Owner occupiers 1971.

APPENDIX 2   LIST OF AREAS USED IN SECTION 3 (SEE FIGURE 11.4)

 (1) Valley-Holyhead
 (2) Twrcelyn-Amlwch
 (3) Menai Bridge-Aethwy
 (4) Lleyn
 (5) Caernarfon-Gwyrfai
 (6) Bangor-Llandudno
 (7) Vale of Conwy-Bettws-y-coed
 (8) Vale of Conwy-Llanrwst
 (9) Colwyn Bay-Aled
(10) Ruthin-Denbigh
(11) Wrexham
(12) Ceiriog
(13) Upper Deeside
(14) Lower Deeside
(15) Bala-Penllyn
(16) Ffestiniog-Deudraeth
(17) Dolgellau-Towyn
(18) Llanfyllin
(19) Welshpool-Montgomery
(20) Machynlleth
(21) Aberystwyth
(22) Newtown and Llanidloes
(23) Aberaeron-Lampeter
(24) Cardigan-Teifiside
(25) Tregaron
(26) Rhayader-Llandrindod Wells
(27) Knighton
(28) Radnor-Painscastle
(29) Builth
(30) Brecon
(31) Hay-Crickhowell
(32) Llandovery-Llandeilo
(33) Newcastle Emlyn
(34) Carmarthen
(35) Llanelli-Kidwelly
(36) Haverfordwest-Milford Haven-Pembroke
(37) Narberth
(38) Cemaes
(39) Gower
(40) Swansea-Port Talbot
(41) Pontardawe-Ystradgynlais
(42) Taff-Cynon-Rhondda
(43) Cowbridge-Bridgend
(44) Cardiff
(45) Caerphilly-Pontypridd-Llantrisant
(46) Tredegar, Bedwellty, etc.

(47) Newport
(48) Pontypool-Cwmbran
(49) Abergavenny
(50) Monmouth
(51) Chepstow

REFERENCES

BOWEN, E.G. and CARTER, H. (1974), Preliminary observations on the distribution of the Welsh language at the 1971 census, 'Geog. Journal', 140, 432-42.
BOWEN, E.G. and CARTER, H. (1975), The distribution of the Welsh language in 1971: an analysis, 'Geography', 60, 1-5.
CARTER, H. and THOMAS, J.G. (1969), The referendum on the Sunday opening of licensed premises in Wales as a criterion of a culture region, 'Regional Studies', 3, 61-71.
EMERY, F. and WHITE, P. (1975), Welsh speaking in Wales according to the 1971 Census, 'Area', 7(1), 26-30.
JENKINS, R.T. (1935), The development of nationalism in Wales, 'Sociological Rev.', 27, 163-82.
JONES, D.G. (1950), National movements in Wales in the nineteenth century, 'The Historical Basis of Welsh Nationalism', Cardiff.
JONES, E. and GRIFFITHS, I.L. (1963), A linguistic map of Wales: 1961, 'Geog. Journal', 129(9), 192-6.
LUNDEN, T. (1974), Linguistic minorities in a world of communications, unpub. prelim. version.
MYRDAL, G. (1957), 'Rich Lands and Poor', New York.
SOUTHALL, J.E. (1895), 'The Welsh Language Census of 1891', Newport.
THOMAS, J.G. (1956), The geographical distribution of the Welsh language, 'Geog. Journal', 122, 71-9.
WILLIAMS, D. (1950), 'A History of Modern Wales', chaps XVI and XVII, London.
WILLIAMS, D.T. (1937), A linguistic map of Wales, 'Geog. Journal', 89(2), 146-57.

Chapter 12

LINGUISTIC DECLINE AND NATIONALIST RESURGENCE IN WALES: A CASE STUDY OF THE ATTITUDES OF SIXTH-FORM PUPILS

Colin Thomas and Colin Williams

The declining use of the Welsh language and the resurgence of Welsh nationalism have emerged as major social issues in Wales over the last decade. This has expressed itself in the growth of a variety of organisations developed to reverse the linguistic decline and these have been closely associated with, but not in all cases completely commensurate with, the ideal of the political separation of Wales from the UK. The processes of social change operating in this situation have been inferred from the ecological analysis of published data relating to the concept of the 'culture region' (Carter and Thomas 1969), the use of the language (Bowen and Carter, 1975), and the development of Welsh nationalism (Taylor, 1973). This paper aims to supplement the valuable information provided in these studies by adding an exploratory behavioural dimension to the analysis. The attitudes of sixth-form pupils to the Welsh language and to Welsh political identity were tested in order to contribute to an understanding of the processes of linguistic and political change and their implications for the future. It was considered that the attitudes of the current generation of school leavers were likely to be an important indicator of the nature of the processes of change because the socialisation of this group to life in Wales has occurred within the context of the lively debate surrounding these issues over the last ten years and because this group will soon form the next socially and politically active generation.

Social scientists investigating the socialisation of young people suggest that their systems of values and associated attitudes to most aspects of life are closely related to the socio-cultural environment in which they have lived (Richert, 1973). Of prime significance are considered to be the influences of the family, the school and religious and social organisations, as they interact with information received from the mass media and the personal attributes and experiences of the individual (Rose, 1965). The importance of this concept in the current context is clear. The ecological studies indicate that cultural distinctiveness, the strength of the language and political allegiance in Wales demonstrate considerable spatial variations, a consequence of the sequence of historical events (Jones, 1967). This has created a

complex spatial pattern of socio-cultural environments within which
the socialisation of the sixth formers has occurred and these are
considered likely to influence their attitudes to the language and
to national separatism.

THE SPATIAL CONTEXT

The 1961 Census revealed that only 26 per cent of the population
spoke Welsh compared with 49.9 per cent at the beginning of the
century. This motivated a number of individuals and organisations
in Wales to call for action to arrest the process of contraction
and decline (Thomas and Williams, 1976). However, despite this
activity, the Welsh-speaking population had declined to 20.8 per
cent by 1971. The spatial pattern of decline is summarised in
Figures 12.1 - 12.3. The decline in the eastern half of Wales
associated with the spread of Anglicising influences westward
continued in a north-south belt from Flint and east Denbigh through
eastern Montgomery, Radnor and Brecon to the western mining valleys
of Glamorganshire. The suggestion of a second decline front moving
eastward from the area of long-standing English influence in south
Pembroke was also evident in 1971, while a similar tendency could
be noted from the coast inland in south Carmarthen, north and west
Cardigan, Merioneth and Anglesey. It was particularly apparent
that the greatest losses were recorded in the areas characterised
by 'moderate' percentages of Welsh speakers (40-70 per cent)
(Figure 12.3). Significantly, stabilisation was apparent in only
two restricted areas: the Lleyn Peninsula to Snowdonia; the uplands
of eastern Merioneth and the adjoining Denbighshire uplands of
Mynydd Hiraethog; both amongst the most remote and most sparsely
populated areas in Wales.
     In contrast, during the last decade the Welsh Nationalist Party
(Plaid Cymru) has grown significantly (Butt Philip, 1975). Initially, in the interwar and early postwar period it functioned as a
predominantly cultural nationalist pressure group, primarily aiming
to secure legal rights for the language and to safeguard Welsh
culture rather than to promote political separatism (Morgan, 1972).
More recently, in an attempt to develop a broader based political
support, Plaid Cymru has developed commitments to regional economic,
social and political policies. However, it is apparent from recent
general elections that Plaid Cymru's strongest support was still
restricted to parts of the Welsh-speaking cultural core area (Figure
12.4). In industrial south Wales support was still spasmodic and at
a substantially lower general level.

THE HYPOTHESES

The hypotheses examined in this paper emerge from the preceding
discussion. It was evident that the proportional decline and
spatial contraction of the Welsh-speaking population in the period
1961-71 had maintained long-established trends. Particularly, it
was apparent that the decline had been greatest in the areas characterised by 'moderate' levels of Welsh-speaking in 1961 (40-70 per

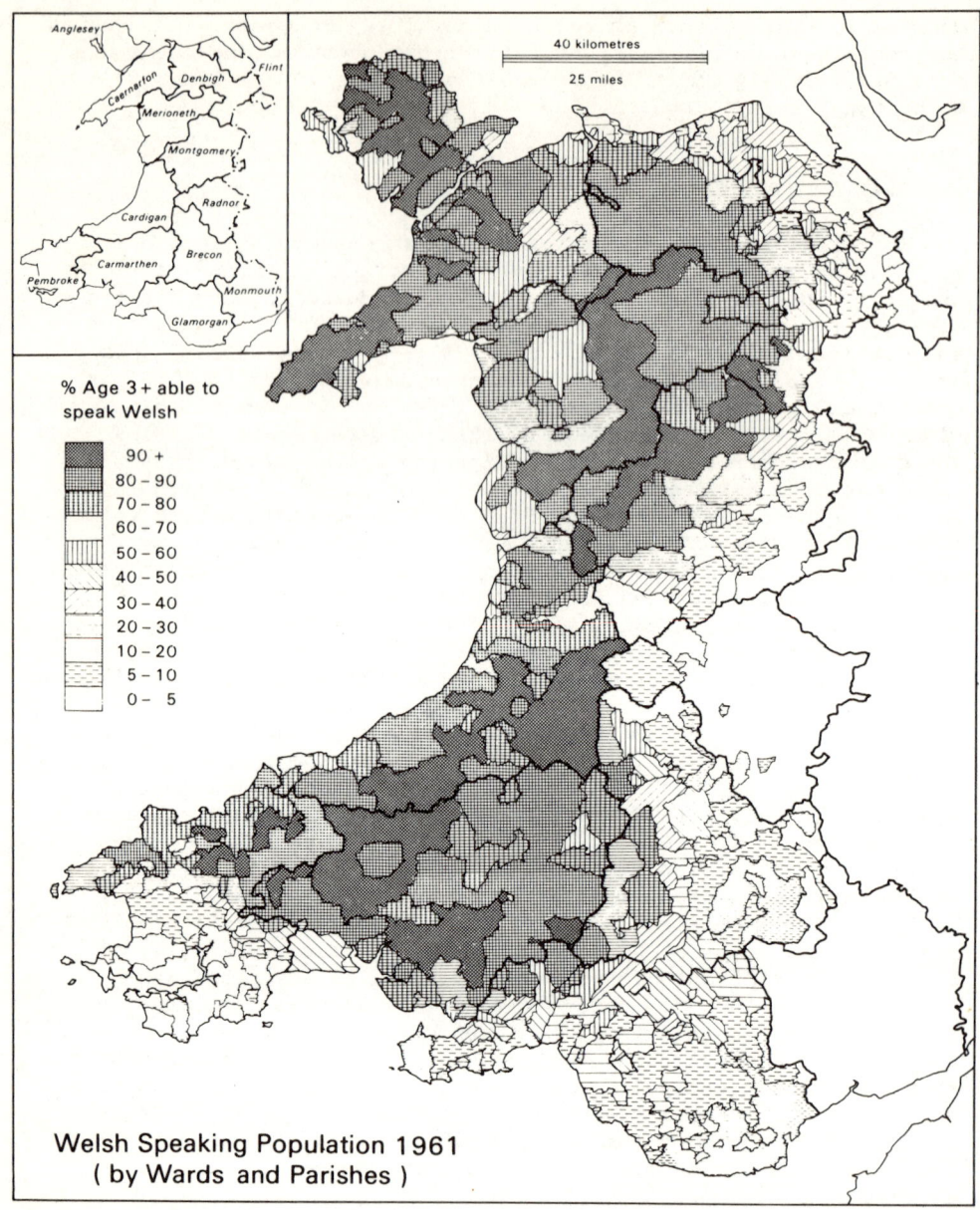

**Welsh Speaking Population 1961
(by Wards and Parishes)**

% Age 3 + able to
speak Welsh

	90 +
	80 – 90
	70 – 80
	60 – 70
	50 – 60
	40 – 50
	30 – 40
	20 – 30
	10 – 20
	5 – 10
	0 – 5

40 kilometres

25 miles

Anglesey
Flint
Caernarfon   Denbigh
Merioneth
Montgomery
Radnor
Cardigan
Carmarthen   Brecon
Pembroke   Monmouth
Glamorgan

FIGURE 12.1

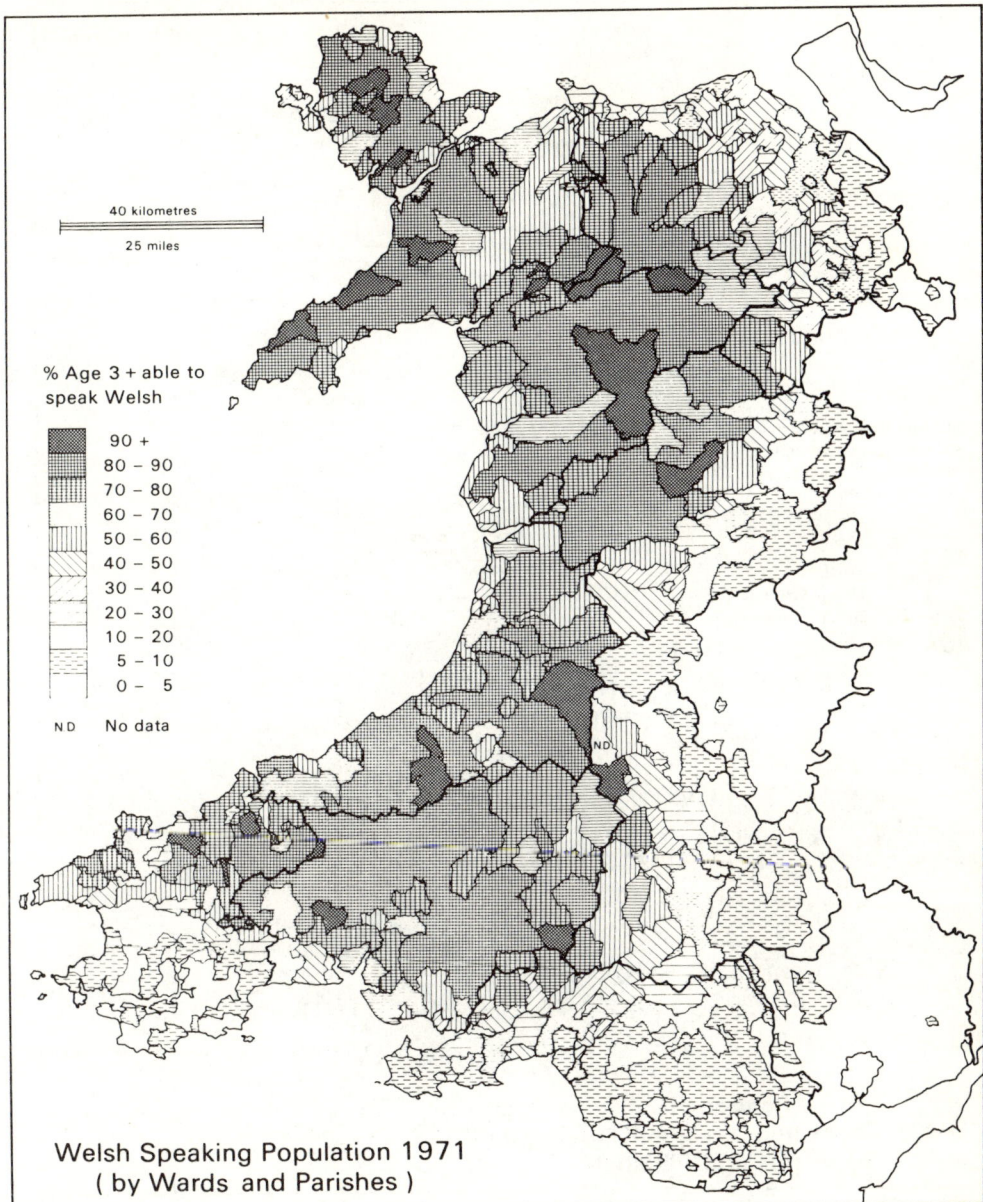

% Age 3 + able to
speak Welsh

90 +
80 – 90
70 – 80
60 – 70
50 – 60
40 – 50
30 – 40
20 – 30
10 – 20
5 – 10
0 – 5

N D   No data

Welsh Speaking Population 1971
(by Wards and Parishes)

FIGURE 12.2

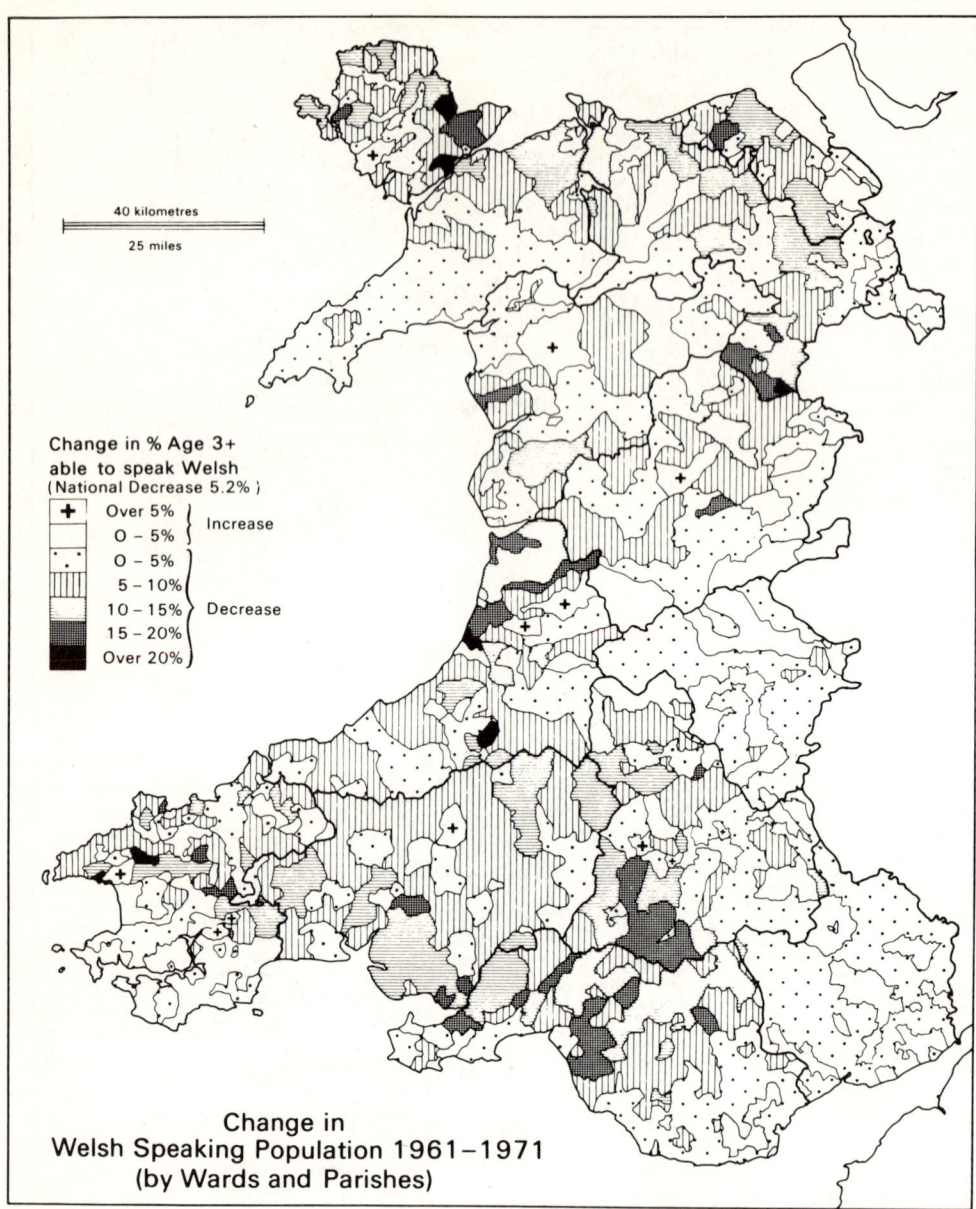

Change in
Welsh Speaking Population 1961–1971
(by Wards and Parishes)

FIGURE 12.3

Percentage Votes for Plaid Cymru

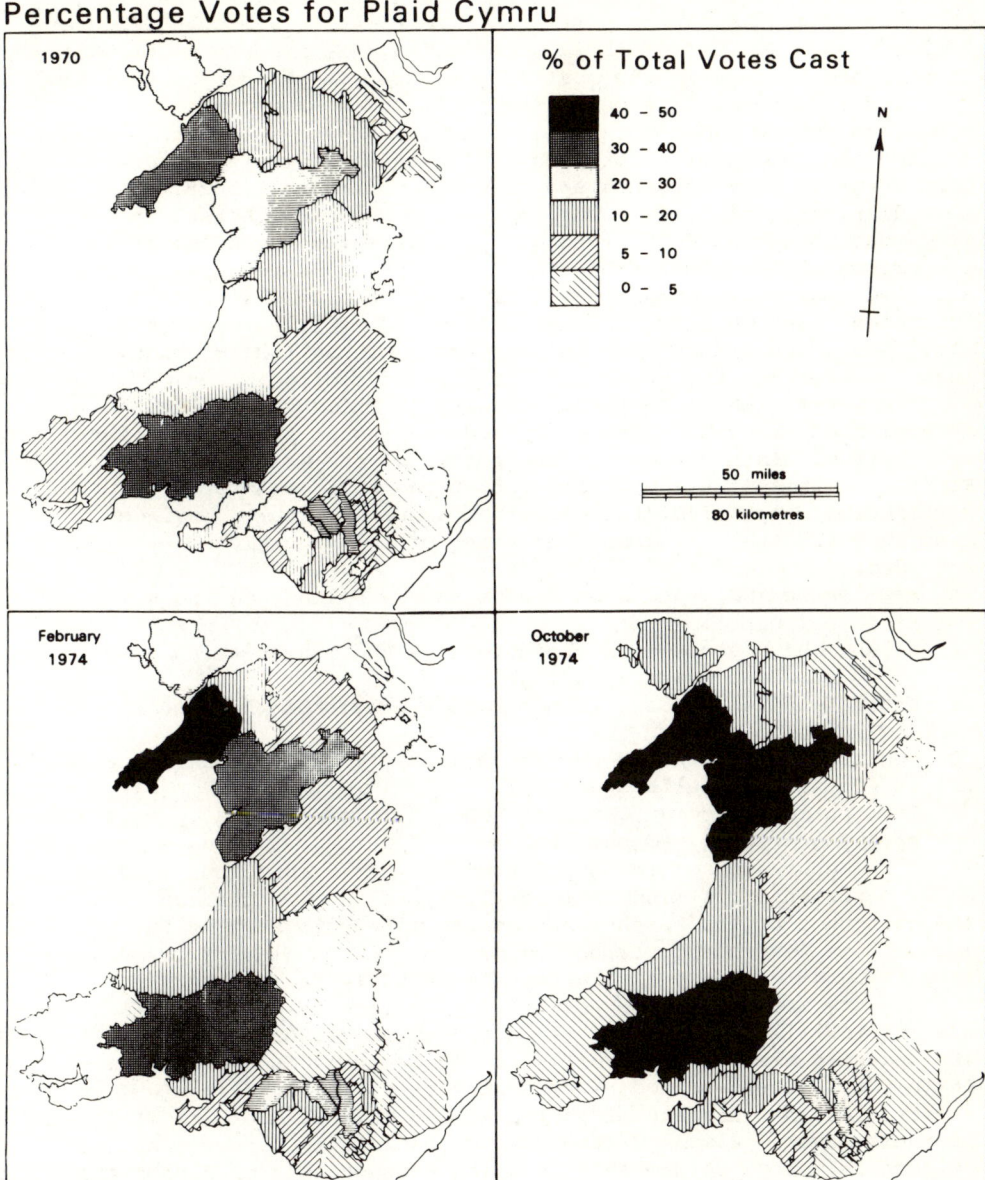

% of Total Votes Cast

40 – 50
30 – 40
20 – 30
10 – 20
5 – 10
0 – 5

N

50 miles
80 kilometres

1970

February 1974

October 1974

FIGURE 12.4

cent), mainly located in a broad north-south belt extending along the eastern margin of the core area from Flint to Pembroke (Figure 12.3). Bowen and Carter (1974) considered this feature particularly significant because in the most recent inter-censal period they had expected that the influence of the English-language dominated mass media would have reduced the relationship between the pattern of decline and geographical propinquity to the Anglicising forces. Consequently, they hypothesised that the continued importance of a spatial pattern of decline was related to the fact that it is in the areas where the Welsh language is only spoken by a 'moderate' proportion of the population that it begins to be rejected as the accepted medium of communication and that once this process is initiated there quickly follows 'a slow and tacit acceptance of attitudes which acknowledge the supremacy of English' - which, in turn, accelerates the process of linguistic decline.

This paper aims to test the validity of this hypothesised mechanism of linguistic change by undertaking an analysis of the attitudes of sixth formers to the status of the Welsh language. For this purpose the sample population was divided into five distinctive categories, relative to the socio-cultural environment in which they lived and the kinds of schools which they attended:

A English-medium schools in predominantly Welsh-speaking areas (+ 70 per cent).

B Welsh-medium schools in predominantly English-speaking areas (< 40 per cent Welsh speaking).

C English-medium schools in moderately Welsh-speaking areas (40-70 per cent).

D English-medium schools in predominantly English-speaking areas (< 40 per cent Welsh speaking).

E English-medium Roman Catholic schools in predominantly English-speaking areas (< 40 per cent Welsh speaking).

If the character of the local socio-cultural environment is a major determinant of linguistic decline, it is hypothesised that the attitudes to the Welsh language are likely to be most favourable amongst the respondents attending category A schools and to become less favourable progressively towards category E. Category A schools are located in the Welsh-speaking core area and, while they are not formally constituted as Welsh-medium establishments, most of the teachers are Welsh speaking and the language is a significant influence in the classroom (see next section). Thus, it might be anticipated that for the sixth formers in this category, most facets of their lives would be Welsh-culture reinforcing rather than culture changing, so probably creating a favourable predisposition towards the Welsh language. Pupils in category B schools are at the outset presumed likely to demonstrate attitudes similar to those in category A. Although they live in predominantly English-speaking areas, the development of the schools that attend reflected favourable attitudes to the maintenance of the language by a strongly motivated group, and significant proportions of the teaching staff are considered to share similar attitudes. Also, the parents sending their children to such schools are usually Welsh-speaking and have strong positive feelings themselves towards the maintenance of the language. However, it is possible that the attitudes expressed by pupils in category B schools might be less favourable than those in category A because a considerable proportion of the social life of the former is conducted in a wider English-speaking context.

From the point of view of Bowen and Carter's hypothesis the category C sample is critical. Most of the schools are located in areas characterised by 'moderate' percentages of Welsh speakers. However, while a considerable proportion of the pupils of these schools are from Welsh-speaking homes, the schools are located in the significantly less-Welsh towns and the normal language of instruction is English. It is considered that if the hypothesised mechanism of linguistic decline is valid then category C respondents should demonstrate attitudes which are significantly more favourable to the increased supremacy of English, and more detrimental to the continued use of Welsh, than attitudes expressed by respondents in categories A and B.

In contrast, the category D schools are all located in predominantly English-speaking areas. Here most facets of normal day-to-day life are conducted in the English language and the majority of sixth formers have no more than a passing acquaintance with Welsh, although most will have learnt the language in the early years of their secondary school careers. It is presumed that this background will tend to result in a greater indifference to the maintenance of the language. Such tendencies are considered likely to be accentuated in the category E sample. The pupils of the Roman Catholic schools also live in a predominantly English-speaking environment and a knowledge of the typical Welsh-speaking cultural traditions is likely to be even less-well developed because the majority of the pupils are the descendants of the children of Roman Catholic immigrants attracted to the employment opportunities of industrial south Wales, initially from Ireland and England, but more recently from Italy and Poland.

It was also apparent that the greatest support for Plaid Cymru and the only parliamentary seats won during the recent period of nationalist resurgence were within the Welsh-speaking culture core areas. Thus, it is initially presumed for the purposes of this analysis that attitudes favourable to national separatism are likely to be most evident amongst sixth formers in category A schools and, like the attitudes to the language, to become progressively less favourable towards category E. However, since the general level of support for Plaid Cymru has been significantly less than the ability to speak the language, attitudes favourable to Welsh political separatism are not expected to be as well marked. This forms the second hypothesis to be tested in this study.

The schools included in the study were subjectively chosen in accordance with the requirements of the five categories, while including as wide a range of locations as possible. The choice was made with reference to the distribution of the Welsh-speaking population 1961 (Figure 12.1) and the Welsh Office map of secondary schools in Wales (Welsh Office, 1972). In all, 22 schools participated in the study, the number constrained by the time and cost involved in the survey. The sample was drawn from a total 165 schools with sixth-form pupils.

The schools were not chosen by a scientific random sampling procedure because of certain practical considerations. Specifically,

the overall number of schools in categories A and B were not considered large enough to adopt such a procedure. In addition, the
problems associated with the initial classification of the many
potentially marginal cases in the remaining three categories, in
the absence of easily available information relating to school
catchment areas, and prior to the publication of the 1971 census
data, was considered prohibitive. Thus, no claim is made that the
resulting survey constitutes a completely representative appraisal,
but rather than the conclusions reached are exploratory and broadly
indicative of the situation under review.
     The survey was conducted in 1973-4 and a respondent administered
questionnaire in English or Welsh was offered. The first part
obtained information designed to indicate whether the five categories of sixth formers defined, differed significantly in terms of
the socio-cultural milieux in which they lived.

THE SOCIO-CULTURAL CHARACTERISTICS OF THE SAMPLE POPULATIONS

In general, the backgrounds of the five categories of sixth formers
varied in accordance with the requirements of the analysis, although
the neat gradation in the degree of 'Welshness' implied in the five-
fold categorisation demonstrated significant deviations.
     The ability of the parents to speak Welsh accorded directly with
the expected pattern (Table 12.2). In category A, over 70 per cent
of the parents were recorded as fluent in Welsh and this was only
marginally less in the case of category B. A significant reduction
to the expected 'moderate' figure was demonstrated by category C,
while D and E clearly indicate a predominantly English-speaking

Table 12.1 Socio-cultural characteristics of the sample population:
Pupils' Welsh fluency*

Category	Parents fluent in Welsh		Parental encouragement to pupils learning Welsh	Welsh first lang.	Biling. Eng./ Welsh	Little Welsh	No Welsh
A (n = 80)	Father	73.7	88.7	53.7	15.0	22.5	7.5
	Mother	70.0					
B (n = 96)	Father	67.7	96.8	58.3	28.1	13.5	0
	Mother	72.9					
C (n = 315)	Father	55.2	61.2	21.5	15.2	38.4	23.4
	Mother	45.4					
D (n = 224)	Father	11.6	29.9	1.3	1.3	35.2	61.1
	Mother	10.2					
E (n = 101)	Father	1.0	23.7	0	2.9	16.8	80.2
	Mother	1.9					

*Percentages of respondents

family situation. This pattern is generally repeated for the
degree of parental encouragement to their children to learn Welsh.
However, in all cases the level of parental encouragement significantly supersedes the degree of parental fluency. This might be
considered a promising sign for the maintenance of the language
except that, significantly, the differential is least in the critical
category C - drawn from the areas in which the language is hypothesised to be under the most active erosion. The extremely high
figure of 96.8 per cent recorded for category B reflects the special
circumstances associated with the children attending Welsh-medium
schools.

The promise for the maintenace of the language associated with
parental encouragement is only partially reflected in the ability
of the children to speak Welsh. In the Welsh-speaking core area (A)
nearly 69 per cent of the sixth formers are recorded as speaking
Welsh as their first language or speaking Welsh and English equally
well, a figure very similar to the level of parental fluency (Table
12.1). Significantly, the pupils in the Welsh-medium schools (B)
although living in English-speaking areas, record 86 per cent in
these two categories, over 16 per cent greater than the level of
parental fluency and clearly attesting to the efficiency of these
schools in assisting the promotion of the Welsh language. However,
it is again the areas where the language is under greatest pressure
that the least promising situation is demonstrated. In the category
C schools the ability of the pupils to speak Welsh falls approximately 15 per cent below the parental level, while the low parental
levels in the predominantly English-speaking areas is further
reduced to an insignificant level for the children.

The degree to which the teaching of Welsh formed part of the
school curriculum also varied considerably between the categories
(Table 12.2). In the category A schools 81 per cent of the pupils
were taught Welsh for more than five years and this figure, not
unexpectedly, increased to 99 per cent in the category B schools.
This was substantially reduced to 63 per cent for category C and to
22 per cent and 9 per cent for D and E respectively. The teaching
of subjects other than Welsh through the medium of the Welsh

Table 12.2 Socio-cultural characteristics of the sample population:
Welsh at school*

Category	Years of secondary school Welsh								No.'A' level subjects studied via Welsh			
	0	1	2	3	4	5	6	7	0	1	2	3
A	5.0	0	0	7.5	5.0	50.0	13.7	17.5	68.7	21.2	6.2	2.5
B	0	0	0	0	1.0	40.6	52.0	6.2	28.1	20.8	31.2	19.7
C	8.2	2.5	5.0	15.5	5.0	47.9	8.8	6.3	85.0	10.1	3.8	0.6
D	29.02	0	14.7	28.1	5.3	18.3	3.5	0.4	97.3	2.2	0	0
E	55.4	10.8	18.8	1.9	2.9	3.9	1.9	3.9	97.0	1.9	1.0	0

* Percentages of respondents

language is clearly only really important in the category B schools, although still significant in category A schools.

It was suggested earlier that in addition to the family and school situation the development of the system of values and the associated attitudes of young people are also closely related to the influence of religious, cultural and political organisations which form part of the wider socio-cultural context in which they live. Historically, it has been indicated by Bowen and Carter (1975) that since the eighteenth century the formal promotion of the Welsh language was closely related to the promotion of religion in general and to Nonconformity in particular. Since that time the chapel has been an important element in the development and subsequent mainten- ance of the linguistic and cultural distinctiveness of Wales. However, with the secularisation of life in the twentieth century the importance of the religious dimension in the socialisation of the young has been declining. Nevertheless, the Church still forms a significant element in the lives of sixth formers in Wales and serves to differentiate further the socio-linguistic background of the five categories of the sixth formers.

The influence of the Welsh Nonconformist chapel is most important for the pupils in category B and A schools (57 per cent and 45 per cent respectively) (Table 12.3). Clearly the relationship between an ability to speak Welsh and continued adherence to Welsh Noncon- formity is still highly significant. Both regular church attendance and the importance of the Welsh Nonconformist tradition decline substantially through categories C and D. The religious background of the pupils in category E schools is obviously completely differ- ent from all the others. The influence of the Roman Catholic Church has served to maintain a strong regular attendance (87 per cent). However, while for this group the Church is likely to be an important influence upon socialisation generally, in terms of language it is likely to have reinforced the importance of the English language.

Membership of Welsh social and cultural organisations serves to further differentiate the groups (Table 12.3). Probably of greatest significance in this respect is the influence of Urdd Gobaith Cymru (The Welsh League of Youth). Traditionally the organisation has been strongest in the Welsh core area and the levels of membership demonstrated in this study faithfully replicate the sequence which has become familiar in this section. Considerable strength is apparent in category A schools (83 per cent), which is again super- seded in the Welsh-medium schools (B) (97 per cent). This gives way to a moderate membership in category C schools (55 per cent), becoming significantly less important in the English-speaking peri- phery (D and E, 40 per cent and 30 per cent respectively).

Membership of Welsh political organisations, again as might be expected in a youthful population, is almost insignificant, although a 15 per cent membership of Plaid Cymru amongst the pupils of the schools in category A is obviously worthy of note. However, this does not suggest that a Welsh national identity is not important amongst the sample population. The sixth formers were asked to state their nationality and interesting results emerged (Table 12.3). A high proportion of pupils in the Welsh core area considered them- selves Welsh (71 per cent), a figure closely similar to those fluent in Welsh. This was superseded in the Welsh-medium schools (95 per

Table 12.3   Socio-cultural characteristics of the sample population: religion, cultural and political societies, nationality*

Category	Regular attendance at place of worship						Urdd membership	Membership Plaid Cymru	Nat. stated		
	Not attend	English Nonconf.	Welsh Nonconf.	Bilingual Nonconf.	C of E	Roman Cath.			Brit.	Eng.	Welsh
A	38.7	1.2	45.0	1.2	11.2	1.2	83.7	15.0	17.5	7.5	71.2
B	27.0	4.1	57.2	0	9.3	2.0	97.9	3.1	4.1	0	95.8
C	44.4	2.5	24.7	0	22.2	4.4	55.8	2.2	26.9	9.2	59.6
D	57.1	10.2	6.2	0	20.9	3.1	40.6	1.3	22.7	9.4	64.3
E	2.9	0	8.9	0	0	87.1	30.7	3.9	18.8	5.9	72.3

* Percentages of respondents

cent), a figure 10 per cent higher than those recorded as fluent in
Welsh. This tends to suggest that for this group the combination
of a strongly Welsh background in the home and at school results in
a far stronger Welsh national identification than would otherwise
have been the case, although this has not been transferred into the
explicitly political arena, considering their low level of membership of Plaid Cymru.

In the other categories Welsh national identification did not
decline in the expected manner. While only 59 per cent of the sixth
formers in category C considered themselves Welsh, this rose to 64
per cent in category D and, even more unexpectedly, to 72 per cent
in category E, a figure higher than that returned in the Welsh-
speaking core area. This appears to suggest that in a predominantly Welsh-speaking situation there is a strong tendency for
linguistic and national identity to be equated, but elsewhere
national identity appears to be far more closely related to a
general regional-cultural awareness rather than to be dependent
merely upon language.

In summary, it is apparent that the socio-cultural backgrounds
of the respondents varied broadly in accordance with the requirements of the analysis. The only major anomaly was illustrated by
category B. Despite the location of the schools in predominantly
English-speaking areas, the concept behind their development
resulted in the pupils being subject to far stronger, specifically
Welsh influences in the home, at school, in the Church and through
the more organised aspects of their social life than would normally
have been the case.

THE ATTITUDE PROFILES

The participants in the study were presented with 21 stimulus
statements to which they could respond according to a five-point
attitude scale ranging from strong agreement to strong disagreement (Table 12.4). Attitude profiles were then constructed from
the mean responses of the five categories of pupils for each of the
statements (Figures 12.5 and 12.6). These were considered to conveniently summarise the variations in attitudes for the purposes of
the first stage of the analysis.

(1) Attitudes to the Welsh language

The attitude profiles for the eleven statements (1-11) relating to
the future use of the Welsh language and its place in the education system of Wales are illustrated by Figure 12.5. Each profile
indicates considerable variations in attitude between the respondent
categories, the average range of the mean responses covering 23 per
cent of the scale.

Only one statement produced the hypothesised progression from A
to E. This concerned the ability of the individual to bring about a
change in the status of the Welsh language (1). As expected,
category A pupils expressed the strongest disagreement with the
suggestion of individual ineffectiveness, while category B pupils
similarly tended to oppose the statement. In contrast, category C

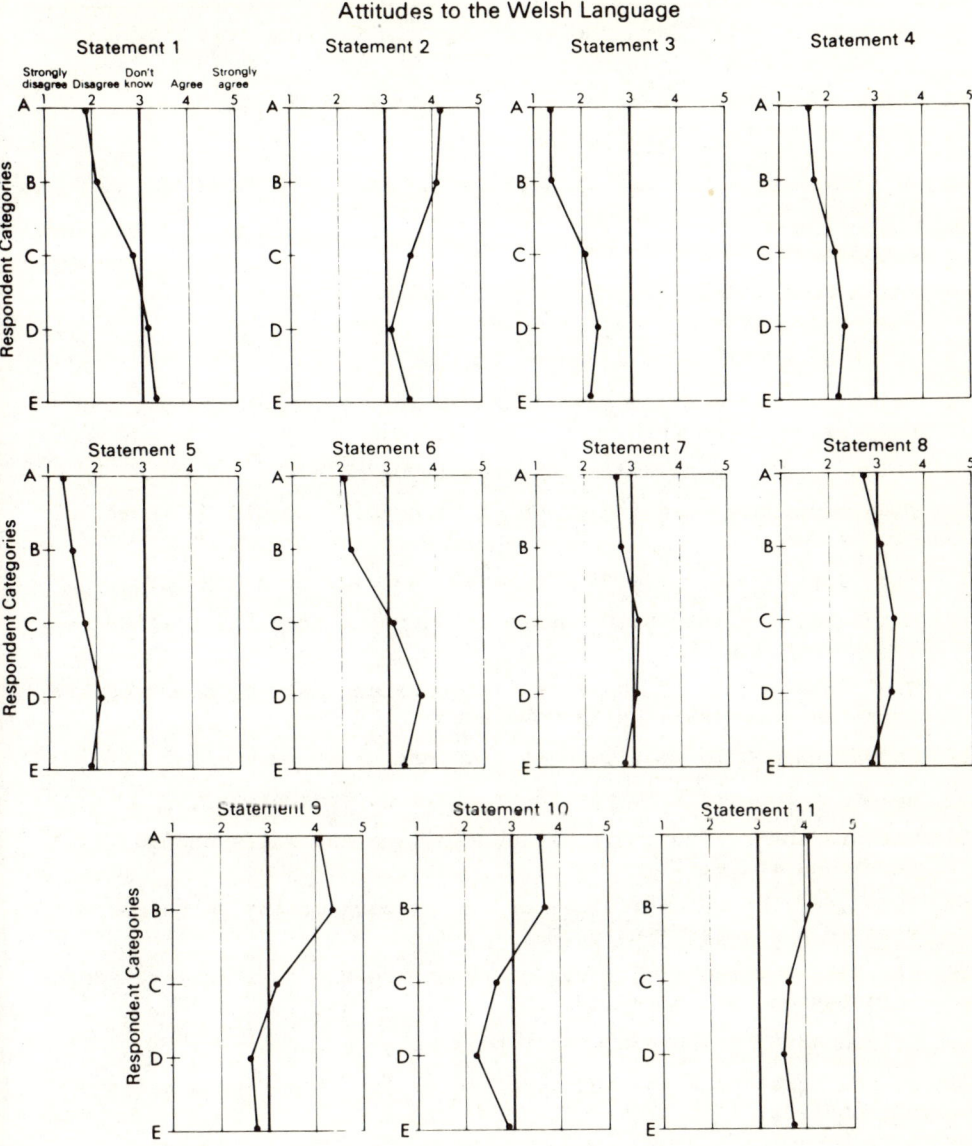

Attitudes to the Welsh Language

FIGURE 12.5

Table 12.4 Stimulus statements

---

1 There is nothing I can do to change the present status of the Welsh language.

2 Welsh people should be able to speak the Welsh language.

3 It is a waste of time to learn Welsh.

4 An increase in the use of Welsh would be a bad thing for life in Wales.

5 English should be allowed to completely displace Welsh.

6 It is more useful for children in Wales to learn another European language rather than Welsh.

7 Welsh is a difficult language to learn.

8 Welsh people should not speak Welsh in the company of English people.

9 Welsh should be the main language in Wales.

10 The compulsory teaching of Welsh in schools should be increased considerably.

11 The continued decline of the Welsh language is a bad thing.

12 A further decline in the Welsh language is inevitable if Wales remains in the UK.

13 The preservation of the Welsh language can only be achieved if there is a separate Welsh Government.

14 The Welsh people should be self-governing if they wish.

15 Wales is too small to have a separate Government.

16 The present relationship between England and Wales should remain as it is.

17 The people of Wales are better off as part of the UK rather than as a separate State.

18 There is nothing much I can do to change the political relationship between Wales and the UK.

19 If you speak Welsh you should be a Welsh nationalist.

20 If you care about the future of Wales you should be a Welsh nationalist.

21 Wales is strongly dependent upon England.

---

pupils were markedly less opposed to the statement and within the grou demonstrated marked ambivalence (40 per cent disagreeing and 31 per cent agreeing). As anticipated, category D and E respondents tended to agree with the statement, suggesting an acceptance of their perceived inability to change the socio-political status of the Welsh language.

Five additional profiles also indicated the hypothesised progression for categories A to D (2-6). The statements concern the

current and future use of the Welsh language. The first (2) was
strongly supported by both category A and B pupils, but the strength
of agreement declined progressively for category C and D. Statements 3, 4 and 5 elicited similar patterns of response, but in these
instances they were the mirror image of profile 2, indicating
greatest opposition from categories A and B. The latter clearly
favoured an increase in the future use of Welsh and did not think it
a waste of time to learn the language, whereas the 'moderate' Welsh
category C and the predominantly English-speaking category D were
significantly less favourably disposed towards an increase in the
use of the language. Even so, the significantly Welsh-speaking
categories were not separated from the English-speaking respondents
by the neutrality line, indicating a general degree of tolerance on
the part of the non-Welsh speakers towards the use of the Welsh
language.

However, with respect to the fifth, rather more specific statement, in this group a somewhat different situation was indicated.
Statement 6 attempted to measure the utility of learning Welsh
compared with learning another European language. The same general
pattern of responses was evident, but here there was a strong
opinion divide between the pupils living in a predominantly Welsh-
speaking environment (A and B), who disagreed with the statement,
and those living in the areas where the language is under pressure
(C) or spoken by only a small minority (D and E). Clearly, a toler-
ant attitude to the continued use of the language gave way to a
marked polarisation of opinion regarding its utility in the wider
European context. It might be suggested that the differences in
the responses between statements 3, 4 and 5 and the more specific
statement 6 was the result of a conflict generated between an underlying loyalty to the minority language and its associated cultural
distinctiveness, even by those unable to speak the language, and
the realisation of its limited practical utility. A similar finding
has also been illustrated amongst a sample of primary school
children in Wales (Schools Council Research and Development Project,
1973). Significantly, in the current study the polarisation did not
occur between the groups with a substantial proportion of Welsh-
speakers (A, B and C) and the English-speaking groups (D and E).
Instead, the aggregate response of the category C pupils was rather
more akin to the attitudes of the English-speaking respondents than
to the predominantly Welsh-speaking categories (A and B). This
tends to support the operation of the hypothesised mechanism of
linguistic decline and highlights the central importance of the
moderately Welsh-speaking areas (C) in this process.

The attitudes of the Roman Catholic sixth formers (E) was the
most unexpected element in this group, and indeed throughout the
remainder of the study. Their responses were distinctly more favourable to the Welsh language and its users than was anticipated from
the contextual data. A consistently reactive attitude was demonstrated, which resulted in the great majority of cases in an average
response more similar to the 'moderately' Welsh category C than to
any other (Figure 12.5). This unexpectedly high degree of tolerance
cannot adequately be explained by the information presented in this
study. It may be that their attitudes are the result of an over-
reaction on the part of a religious minority anxious to be integrated

into the perceived Welsh community. This is a phenomenon identified
by other researchers working in the host-immigrant situation, where
the immigrants in an attempt to be fully accepted, conform zealously
to the perceived norms and value system of the host society, if
these are not in direct conflict with the most valued of their own
principles (Handlin, 1969). Equally, the reaction need not necessarily be based upon a Roman Catholic self-interest motivation, but
might result more simply from a sympathetic tolerance towards a
linguistic minority by a religious minority. However, in the absence
of direct information on this point the explanations offered must
remain speculative.

A third set of two profiles (7 and 8) is essentially a subgroup
of the last, with the additional feature of category D demonstrating
similar but reactive attitudes to category C. The first statement
(7) attempted to gauge whether the respondents considered Welsh a
difficult language to learn. The more objective rather than emotive
nature of this statement relative to those already considered, not
unexpectedly, elicited a less variable range of responses. This
profile appears to result from the tendency of the fluent Welsh-
speakers to disagree with the statement, probably reflecting the
ease with which they learnt Welsh as a first language in a familiar
home environment. In contrast the English-speaking respondents tend
to express Welsh-learning experiences that were gained predominantly
in the classroom, experiences that were not often reinforced by
contact with spoken Welsh in the home. Hence, the element of difficulty involved in learning a second language. The slightly anomalous
response of category D is difficult to reconcile with this explanation, but a tentative alternative can be offered. The unexpectedly
low average response of category D (3.02) results from 37 per cent of
the respondents disagreeing with the statement despite the fact that
this category exhibited a low-level of Welsh fluency. It may be that
the 35 per cent of category D respondents claiming to 'speak only a
little Welsh' consider themselves sufficiently differentiated
linguistically from the majority of their fellow members of this
group and from their English-speaking social environment to express
this difference in an unexpectedly high degree of disagreement with
this statement (Table 12.1). Clearly, such a reaction would not be
expected from those able to 'speak only a little Welsh' in the
category C sample, where 36 per cent of the respondents were completely bilingual. Hence the anomalous similarity of categories C
and D.

The same general pattern of responses occurred for statement 8,
which suggested that Welsh people should not speak Welsh in the
company of English people. Two possible reactions were anticipated:
either disagreement with the statement, indicating a strong degree
of language loyalty and a conviction that it is correct to use Welsh
in such situations, or agreement, based upon ideas of good manners,
which are likely to be associated with language switching to accommodate the outsider. The responses to this statement are considered
a critical indicator of the future strength of the Welsh language,
since it might be suggested that the process of language-switching
to accommodate majority language users is an important social element
of the mechanism by which minority languages decline in general use.

As expected, category A respondents were the strongest advocates of language loyalty, although significantly a marked polarisation occurred with 46 per cent disagreeing with the statement and 36 per cent agreeing. Thus, even in the Welsh-speaking core area considerable evidence of attitudes conducive to the decline of the language occur. The attitudes expressed by category B pupils were on average even more deferential (45 per cent agreeing). This suggests a greater degree of language tension within the bilingual school sample and can possibly be related to the fact that while most of their school and home experience advocated the maintenance of Welsh as the first language, their wider social experience demands that they switch to English. However, probably the most significant finding is that category C pupils registered the highest mean favourable score (3.44) with 60 per cent in favour of language-switching. This constitutes positive support for the contention of Bower and Carter (1974) that it is in the 'moderately' Welsh areas that attitudes most conducive to the increasing supremacy of the English language are likely to be found.

Category D pupils were, as might be expected, in general agreement with the statement since it was in their direct interests that Welsh speakers should switch to English. However, the general level of support is less than anticipated (3.26), falling significantly below the mean response of category C (3.44). In fact, 33 per cent of the predominantly English-speaking respondents disagreed with the statement. Possibly this results from a tendency for some individuals to express attitudes contrary to their self-interests in deference to the minority language, although there is no evidence to support this explanation.

The fourth set of profiles approximately maintains the expected gradation, again demonstrating the reactive attitude of category E, but also including a tendency for category B to take the extreme position anticipated for category A (9, 10 and 11). This effect is most marked in the case of statement 9 which suggests that 'Welsh should be the main language in Wales'. Since this ideal directly reflects the aim of the cultural nationalists, whose pressure in the post-war years led to the creation of the Welsh schools movement and the extension of Welsh-medium education into Anglicised areas, it is not surprising that the strongest support came from the Welsh-medium schools sample (B). Fully 90 per cent of the category B sample supported this statement, the majority favouring it very strongly, a full 20 per cent higher than the category A pupils. This difference, it is suggested, can be attributed to the heightened Welsh-speaking identity of category B pupils. The other three categories varied their support approximately in accordance with the expected gradation with category C marginally in favour and category D and E crossing the opinion divide to disagree with the statement. A similar situation is demonstrated for statements 10 and 11 which respectively concern the extension of the teaching of Welsh in schools and the possible decline of the Welsh language. The evidence of these three statements indicates that the pupils attending Welsh-medium schools develop markedly positive attitudes towards the language which surpasses those expressed by pupils resident in the Welsh-speaking area (A) on a significant number of language oriented issues.

The analysis of the attitude profiles has indicated a general progression from category A to D, modified in detail when related to specific statements, but consistently displaying a reactive Roman Catholic element (E). However, a more detailed examination of the complete distribution of responses between the respondent categories reveals additional evidence relevant to the hypothesised mechanism of linguistic decline. A series of chi-square tests of the variation in the pattern of responses between adjacent respondent categories was undertaken for each of the stimulus statements. The difference between categories A and C was also investigated since the relationship between the attitudes expressed in the Welsh-speaking core area and the areas characterised by 'moderate' levels of Welsh speech was considered critical to the analysis (Table 12.5).

Table 12.5   Attitudes to the Welsh language (1)

Categories	Statements										
	1	2	3	4	5	6	7	8	9	10	11
A-B	8	10	2	13	11	10	0	7	17*	18*	7
B-C	36**	29**	29**	16*	11	37**	8	12	76**	48**	11
A-C	27**	29**	28**	27**	26**	40**	12	36**	50**	46**	23**
C-D	15*	13	9	8	5	30**	5	41**	22**	15*	7
D-E	9	6	3	2	4	4	17*	5	2	21**	6

(1) Chi-square values for the contingency tables of pairs of categories of sixth-formers against the five-point attitude scales

Chi square: 9.49 significant at 0.05 level with 4 degrees of freedom.
         * 13.28 significant at 0.01 level with 4 degrees of freedom.
        ** 18.46 significant at 0.001 level with 4 degrees of freedom.

Overall, the differences between the patterns of response of categories A and B were slight. In contrast, the differences between the pattern of responses of categories B and C were much greater. In six cases the difference was significant at the 0.001 level and in one other at the 0.01 level. This suggests that the category B respondents were significantly more inclined to express attitudes favourable to the maintenance of the Welsh language than their category C counterparts, although the difference was not strong in every case.

More significantly, an even clearer break occurred between categories A and C. In ten of the eleven cases the difference was highly significant at the 0.001 level. In effect, the 'moderately' Welsh-speaking category C respondents displayed a much stronger tendency towards the acceptance of attitudes conducive to the increasing supremacy of English than those from the Welsh-speaking core area. This lends considerable support to the operation of the hypothesised mechanism of linguistic decline. The relationship between the patterns of response of categories C and D also tends to support this contention. In only three cases are the differences significant at the 0.001 level (6, 8, 9) and in two others at the 0.01 level (1, 10). In the remaining six cases the pattern of responses of the moderately Welsh-speaking category and the predominantly English-speaking category do not differ markedly. Clearly, while there are considerable differences in the degree of 'Welshness' exhibited by these two categories, this is not reflected in commensurate differences in attitudes conducive to the continued strength of the Welsh language.

The relationship between the patterns of responses of the remaining two categories D and E do not contribute appreciably to the analysis of the hypothesis under review. For the most part the responses of the Roman Catholic group tend to be similar to those of the predominantly English-speaking category, although in two instances statistically significant differences are recorded at the 0.01 level, a reflection of the tendency towards the expression of reactive attitudes already noted for the Roman Catholic respondents.

Thus, while the analysis generally supports the expected pattern of progressively declining attitudes favourable to the maintenance of the Welsh language, it also indicates some interesting variations and confirms the critical position of category C.

(2) Attitudes to Welsh political identification

The sixth-formers' attitudes to the two statements concerning the relationship between the Welsh language and separatism (12 and 13) and the eight concerning Welsh political identity (14-21) differ significantly from those to the language (Figure 12.6). However, the mean responses are just as variable as those illustrated in the previous section.

None of the profiles accords precisely with the expected pattern, although a significant degree of support for the suggested hypothesis was provided. The most general pattern which recurred in seven out of the ten cases, illustrates the hypothesised progression for categories A to D. The respondents in category A were most likely, and those in D, least likely to agree with statements suggesting that the maintenance of the language is closely related to the degree of political separation of Wales from the UK (12 and 13). Similarly, for five additional statements (14, 15, 16, 17, 18) those in category A expressed attitudes more favourable to the development of a separate Welsh political identity in descending progression to category D. Significantly, in the latter four cases, in which the statements have explicitly separatist connotations, the pupils living in the Welsh core area (A) and those attending Welsh-medium schools (B) were divided from categories C and D by the neutrality line on the attitude profiles.

In all seven cases category E again deviated significantly from the expected pattern. In fact, in most cases the attitudes of category E respondents were more akin to those with predominantly Welsh backgrounds (A and B) than to those with more similar socio-cultural backgrounds (D). Presumably, the explanation for this

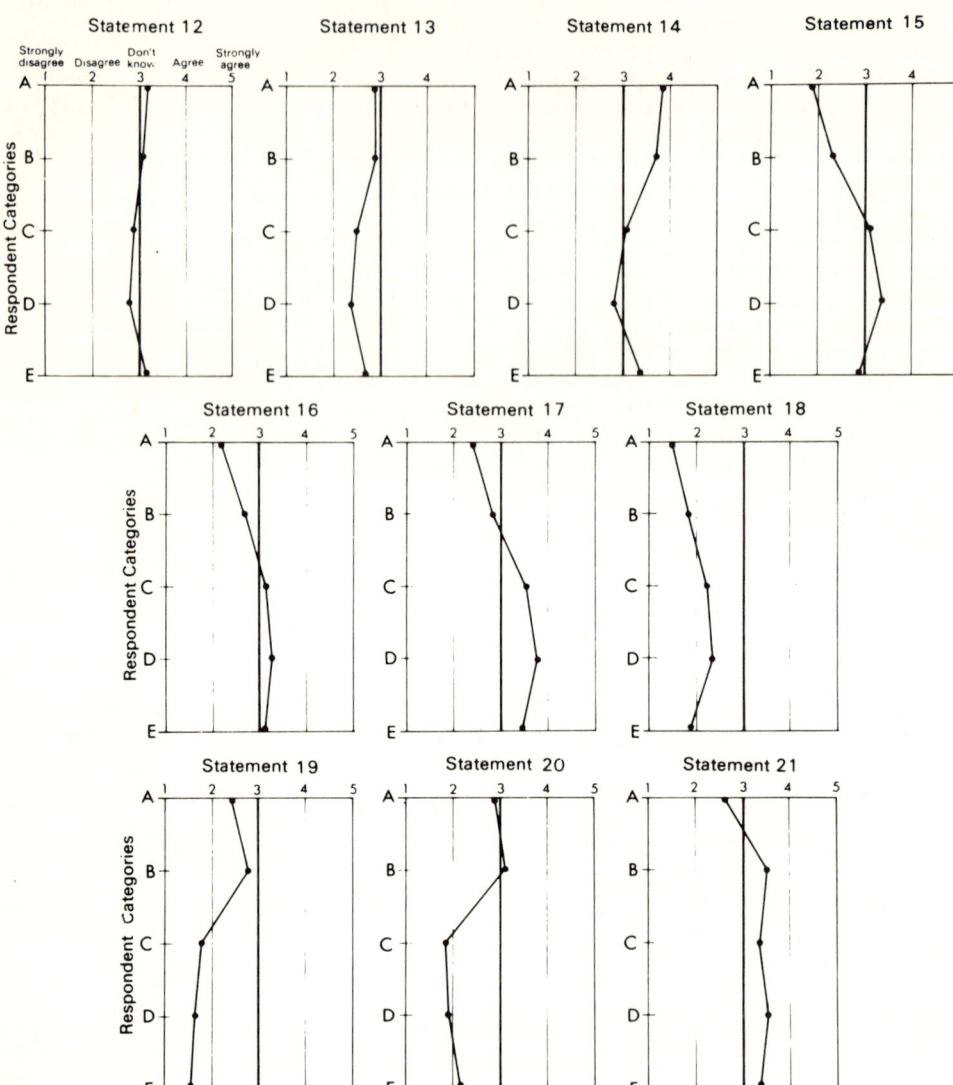

Attitudes to Welsh Political Identification

FIGURE 12.6

strongly reactive effect is similar to that discussed in the previous section.

Statements 19 and 20 are significantly different from the others in this section. Instead of attempting to obtain responses to the general concepts of language maintenance and political separatism they were specifically designed to elicit the respondents' attitudes to the Welsh nationalist movement (Table 12.4). In both cases there was a tendency for each of the five categories to disagree with the statements. In fact, even the slight aggregate agreement of category B with statement 20 (3.01) was not indicative of support for the statement, but rather that an abnormally high proportion of responses to this statement (30.2 per cent) were placed in the 'don't know' category. Clearly, the sixth formers participating in this invest-igation did not consider that proficiency in the Welsh language and caring for the future of Wales need be equated with a necessity to support the Welsh nationalist movement. This suggests that Welsh nationalism has not enlisted the support of the majority of Welsh-speaking sixth formers.

However, the profiles for these two statements differed only slightly from those already discussed in this section. Contrary to the expected pattern, the category B respondents disagreed signif-icantly less with statement 19 and marginally less with statement 20 than the category A respondents. At first sight this might be taken to suggest that the pupils in the Welsh-medium schools (B) expressed attitudes more favourable to Welsh nationalism than those living in the Welsh-speaking core area (A). On closer examination this appears to be partly illusory because it is the result of significantly higher percentages of the responses of category B recorded in the 'don't know' category rather than to a truly positive expression of support. For statement 19, 21.8 per cent of the responses were so recorded, while this rose to 30.2 per cent for statement 20, compared with figures consistently below 10 per cent recorded for the other four categories. It may well be that the partly artificially created Welsh-speaking environment of the pupils in these schools has resulted in a greater degree of indecision on overtly nationalist issues, albeit falling short of majority support, than might other-wise have been expected; although this explanation cannot be verified by the information available at present. Nevertheless, it does suggest that the category B pupils do not have a greater orientation to the Welsh nationalist movement than those from category A, despite the apparently contradictory attitude profiles.

The remaining statement (21) which suggests that Wales is strongly dependent upon England, has resulted in an attitude profile which is markedly different from those already discussed. The category A respondents tended to disagree with the statement and this differen-tiates them from the other four categories who are all in moderate agreement. This result provides additional support for the conten-tion that the pupils from the Welsh-speaking core area are most likely to demonstrate attitudes favourable to increased Welsh separa-tion. However, the response of category B cannot easily be reconciled with the earlier findings, since a response closer to that of A might have been anticipated. It might tentatively be suggested that the statement has elicited an emotive antipathetic

response from category A pupils who live in areas where an overt
dependence is not obvious. This is clearly different from the,
possibly more objective, response of the other four categories, who
live in areas where the English economic and social influences are
far more obvious to the observer. The fact that the mean responses
of categories B to E are uncharacteristically similar with respect
to this statement might be considered to support this contention,
although this explanation is clearly tentative.

Thus, in general the aggregate attitudes to the statements
relating to Welsh political identity followed the hypothesised
progression from category A to D, although again category E demonstrated a significant deviation from the expected pattern in almost
every case. Clearly, it seems that support for political separatism
amongst the respondents is strongest in the areas and amongst the
groups subject to the strongest Welsh cultural influence, rather than
being a more widespread politically based phenomenon. This tends to
support the second hypothesis investigated in this paper. In
addition, it was also apparent that support for the formally organised Welsh nationalist movement by the pupils from a predominantly
Welsh-speaking environment or attending the Welsh-medium schools
was much weaker than the expressions of support for the maintenance
of the language.

An additional important difference between the attitudes expressed
in the two sections is revealed by chi-square analyses of the variations in the patterns of responses between the five respondent
categories (Table 12.6). In the previous section the favourable
attitudes expressed towards the maintenance of the language by categories A and B were for the most part very similar with a tendency
for category B to surpass the support of A on a number of statements.

Table 12.6 Attitudes to Welsh political identification (1)

Categories	Statements									
	12	13	14	15	16	17	18	19	20	21
A–B	31**	4	1	17*	8	6	6	13	16*	21**
B–C	3	14*	28**	25**	10	26**	10	43**	79**	7
A–C	26**	10	39**	47**	43**	45**	25**	29**	43**	35**
C–D	3	5	15*	7	1	1	4	7	10	8
D–E	15*	2	16*	6	3	7	9	1	5	3

(1) Chi-square values for the contingency tables of pairs of
    categories of sixth-formers against the five-point attitude
    scales.

Chi square: 9.49 significant at 0.05 level with 4 degrees of
                 freedom.
            * 13.28 significant at 0.01 level with 4 degrees of
                 freedom.
           ** 18.46 significant at 0.001 level with 4 degrees of
                 freedom.

However, for the statements relating to political separatism the
attitudes of categories A and B did not demonstrate an equivalent
degree of similarity. In two instances (12 and 21) the patterns of
responses were significantly different at greater than the 0.001
level, in another two cases (15 and 20) at the 0.01 level and in a
further one case (19) at the 0.05 level. In each instance it was
apparent that the respondents from the Welsh-speaking core area (A)
were significantly more inclined to express attitudes favourable to
increased welsh political separatism than those attending Welsh-
medium schools. This suggests that the socio-cultural environment
of the Welsh-speaking core area, where Plaid Cymru has achieved its
most significant successes in recent years, is far more conducive
to the development of attitudes favourable to Welsh separatism than
the combined influence of the school and home environment of the
pupils attending the Welsh-medium schools. This would appear to
detract from any suggestion that a Welsh-medium school policy *unduly*
disposes the pupils towards Welsh nationalism.

Similar to the previous section the differences between the
patterns of responses of categories B and C were markedly greater
than those between A and B. In five instances the difference was
significant at well beyond the 0.001 level, three of which statements have explicit separatist (14, 15, 17) and the remaining two
(19, 20) explicit nationalist connotations. Thus, while the pupils
from the Welsh-medium schools do not express such strong separatist
attitudes as those from the Welsh-speaking core area, they are
nevertheless significantly more separatist in orientation than the
pupils from the areas of 'moderate' levels of Welsh speech.

Again, even more significantly, the differences between categories
A and C were the most marked. In nine out of the ten cases the
differences were significant well beyond the 0.001 level. Thus,
the major opinion divide between the pupils living in a predominantly
Welsh-speaking environment (A) and those living in the areas of
'moderate' Welsh speech (C), already noted with reference to the
statements concerning the language, was repeated for the statements
relating to Welsh political identification. This provides additional
support for the second hypothesis and suggests that the critical
significance of the category C respondents demonstrated for the
attitudes to the language issue was also apparent with regard to the
question of political separatism.

In contrast, in no case does the difference between categories C
and D or D and E reach the 0.001 significance level and in the
great majority of cases no major difference is recorded (Table 12.6).
This indicates that outside the Welsh-speaking core area and the
Welsh-medium schools, despite the aggregate tendency for a decline
in support for Welsh separatism and nationalism to occur, the three
categories express patterns of response which tend to be similarly
unfavourable to increased Welsh political separatism. This is
slightly different from the situation illustrated for the statements
relating to the language, where in a number of cases the moderately
Welsh-speaking category C expressed significantly more favourable
attitudes to the maintenance of the language than the predominantly
English-speaking categories. Clearly, on the question of political
separatism there is a greater polarisation of attitudes between
those subject to predominantly Welsh-speaking influences (A and B)
and the remainder (C, D and E).

CONCLUSIONS

The mechanism for linguistic decline suggested by Bowen and Carter
(1974) has been provided with considerable support in this study.
The general decline of attitudes favourable to the continued use of
the Welsh language from category A to D, the major opinion divide
between categories A and C, and the considerable differential in the
relative ability of the parents and sixth formers amongst the category
C sample to speak Welsh all point in this direction.

It was also apparent that the special circumstances associated
with the Welsh-medium schools (B) resulted in the development of
attitudes favourable to the continued health of the language in
predominantly English-speaking areas. This was reflected in a
significant positive differential between the ability of the parents
and pupils to speak Welsh. However, whether the school and its
associated influences or the home background, or a complex combination of both these factors provide the explanation for these effects
has yet to be determined. The resolution of this problem will
require a more detailed behavioural investigation than that undertaken in the current study.

In addition, the pupils from English-speaking Roman Catholic
schools consistently demonstrated unexpectedly favourable attitudes
to the maintenance of the Welsh language. A tentative explanation
for this was suggested, but again this behavioural tendency requires
additional investigation before a satisfactory explanation can be
offered.

The attitudes to Welsh political separatism were, in general,
similar to those for the language, and were in accordance with the
hypothesised pattern. Again the most favourable attitudes were
expressed by pupils in category A schools and became less favourable
to category D, while the most significant opinion divide again
occurred between categories A and C. The positive influence of the
Welsh-medium schools was also apparent and the unexpectedly favourable attitudes expressed by category E. However, attitudes favourable to separatism were not nearly as pronounced as those for the
maintenance of the language. In general, whatever the category of
pupils, their attitudes could not be interpreted as indicative of
strong support for the ideals of Welsh nationalism, but merely as
inclinations towards separatism. Also, in contrast to the attitudes
to the language, the category A respondents were significantly more
favourable to separatism than those of category B. This suggested
that the overall socio-cultural context of the Welsh-speaking core
area was a more important determinant of positive attitudes to separatism than the school alone. Thus, the evidence presented is broadly
in accordance with the hypothesis that support for political separatism amongst this youthful age-group has a stronger cultural rather
than a political basis.

A number of implications derive directly from these conclusions.
The evidence suggests that it is highly likely that the use of Welsh
will continue to decline in the future, particularly amongst sixth
formers living in the critical category C situations, but also amongst
the remaining Welsh-speakers in the predominantly English-speaking
areas. In contrast, the situation appeared relatively stable in the
Welsh-speaking core area, while positive expansion in the use of

Welsh was recorded only amongst the pupils attending Welsh-medium schools. Clearly, practical policies designed to arrest further linguistic decline would be most effective if applied to areas characterised by 'moderate' levels of Welsh speech, where further erosion of the language appears most likely to occur in the short term and where the decline in attitudes favourable to the mainten-ance of the language were most critical. It might be suggested that one mechanism by which a degree of stabilisation could be achieved would be via the extension of formal Welsh-medium education within such areas, in order to complement the effect of the 'moderately' Welsh home backgrounds of the pupils. This suggestion presumes that the school-based influences favourable to the maintenance of the Welsh language have a substantial effect, independent of and additional to the home background. This contention was not irrefut-ably demonstrated in the study. However, the fact that the sixth formers in the Welsh-medium schools developed attitudes which in some cases were significantly more favourable to the language than those expressed by pupils living in the Welsh-speaking core area and that the children become uncharacteristically more proficient in Welsh than their parents, tends to suggest that, even if only acting as a mechanism by which parental attitudes are put into effect, a partially independent school effect exists. It also appears that such a policy would have the additional effect of giving further impetus to attitudes favourable to Welsh political separatism, although the effect is likely to be less well marked than in the case of the language.

Finally, a note of caution should be reiterated at this point. The conclusions reached in this investigation relate to a limited number of schools in Wales. It is possible that they constitute an unrepresentative sample, although there is no clear evidence to suggest that this is the case. Nevertheless, the findings can only be regarded as tentative in the absence of a more comprehensive coverage.

REFERENCES

BOWEN, E.G. and CARTER, H. (1974), Preliminary observations on the distribution of the Welsh language at the 1971 census, 'Geographical Journal, 140, 432-41.
BOWEN, E.G. and CARTER, H. (1975), The distribution of the Welsh language in 1971: an analysis, 'Geography', 60, 1-15.
BUTT PHILIP, A. (1975), 'The Welsh Question', Cardiff, University of Wales Press.
CARTER, H. and THOMAS, J.G. (1969), The referendum on the Sunday opening of licensed premises in Wales as a criterion of a culture region, 'Regional Studies', 3, 61-71.
HANDLIN, O. (1969), Historical perspectives on the American ethnic group, in H.A. Bailey and E. Katz, 'Ethnic Group Politics', Columbus, Ohio, Merrill.
JONES, E. (1967), The changing distribution of the Celtic languages in the British Isles, 'Transactions of the Honourable Society of Cymmrodorion', 22-38.
MORGAN, K.O. (1972), Welsh politics, in B. Jones (ed.), 'The Anatomy of Wales', Cardiff, Gwerin Publications.

RICHERT, J.P. (1973), Political socialization in Quebec: young
people's attitudes toward government, 'Canadian Journal of Political
Science', 62, 303-13.
ROSE, R. (1965), 'Politics in England', London, Faber & Faber.
SCHOOLS COUNCIL RESEARCH AND DEVELOPMENT PROJECT (1973), London.
TAYLOR, A.H. (1973), The electoral geography of Welsh and Scottish
nationalism, 'Scottish Geographical Magazine', 89, 44-52.
THOMAS, C.J. and WILLIAMS, C.H. (1976), A behavioural approach to
the study of linguistic decline and nationalist resurgence: a case
study of the attitudes of sixth-formers in Wales, Part 1, 'Cambria',
vol.3, no.2, 102-24.
WELSH OFFICE (1972), Map: Secondary Schools in Wales, 1:250,000,
W/63/72.

Chapter 13

LANGUAGE AND ASPIRATIONS FOR UPWARD SOCIAL MOBILITY

Glyn Williams, Ellis Roberts and Russell Isaac

One of the areas of investigation in the relatively new field of the sociology of language involves the role of the socio-cultural setting which governs the factors that determine the dominance of one language over another in a bilingual environment. Particularly prominent in such investigations is the importance of language as a means of achieving upward social mobility. In Canada it has been demonstrated that there is a greater incentive to become bilingual for French- rather than English-language speakers (Lieberson, 1970; Canada, 1969). Upward mobility for the French-Canadian involves a need to learn the English language in order to open up more employment opportunities than exist for the monolingual French speaker. The simplest and most persuasive explanation for the asymmetry of bilingualism and occupations involves the differential social power in economic organization. Such an explanation has been forwarded by Angle (1976) in his study of bilingualism in Puerto Rico where he found that the domination of the commercial sector of the Puerto Rican economy by mainland companies resulted in a tendency towards bilingualism among those who were employed in this sector.

Such studies of language discrimination suggest that language groups can provide valuable information about the dynamics of status groups of which language groups are one type. Weber (Gerth and Mills, 1974: 187) has indicated that closed status systems need not be based upon class lines but rather upon some criteria such as language which cuts across class lines. As has been suggested above such status groups depend upon a stable distribution of economic power. However language groups differ from most status groups, especially with reference to closure, in that it is easier to enter the group by learning the language or to leave it by rejecting the language. Thus the identity marker of group membership is largely a matter of individual decision. This of course implies that there exists a suitable school instruction policy and a favourable structure of the labour market which can influence the individual decision concerning language acquisition.

The above examples from Canada and Puerto Rico refer to the adoption of the English language as the vehicle for occupational mobility. This was also the tendency where the prestigious language domains were dominated by the English language, this dominance being

heightened by institutions which generated a stigmatic connotation
for the Welsh language. Thus children were punished for speaking
Welsh in the schools while their parents were persuaded that the
Welsh language interfered with the learning of the English language
and thereby with their child's occupational potential. During the
depression of the 1930s, and indeed since then, the scarcity of
employment opportunity within Wales meant that the search for work
inevitably took Welsh people to England where a knowledge of the
English language was essential. It has also been suggested that
the experience of the depression persuaded parents not to view education as a preparation for industrial employment but rather to think
of the secondary schools and the institutions of higher education as
the basis for counteracting the economic/industrial insecurity
(Central Advisory Council for Education, 1965). Clearly the official
policies which derived a measure of support from the economic conditions were not geared towards generating bilingualism but rather
to stimulating direct language substitution or a deculturation which
involved linguistic assimilation.

Of late there has been a strong movement to increase Welsh-
language loyalty and to expand bilingualism. The earlier policy of
stigmatization had been so successful that the main objective of the
revitalization movement has been to generate respect for the Welsh
language in a number of public and private domains. While the work
of various pressure groups, most notably Cymdeithas yr Iaith Gymraeg
(Welsh Language Society), has been primarily responsible for the
recent reorientation, the decentralization of certain functions from
London to Cardiff has also played an important role.(1) Thus the
expansion of the broadcasting media and various aspects of the civil
service within Wales has served to create more high-status employment
within Wales, many of these positions carrying a Welsh-language
qualification. The pressure groups in turn have acted by agitating
for a wider use of the Welsh language by public bodies, this serving
not only to focus attention on the language and the language issue
but also to expand the number of employment domains requiring a
Welsh-language qualification. Such being the case the question
arises of how this trend relates to the wider socio-cultural setting
within Wales.

Most of the recent studies of the Welsh language in Wales have
tended to involve a socio-psychological perspective focusing upon
attitudes towards language,(2) with social variables being relegated
to a secondary role in such studies. Our objective in the present
study was to focus more attention upon such social variables
although the relevant attitudinal features could not be ignored.
The changes which we have described above suggest two main hypotheses.
First, if the new employment opportunities which carry the Welsh-
language qualification tend to be prestigious or middle-class occupations then it is to be expected that those working-class parents
who have aspirations for their children which involve upward social
mobility (3) are more likely to encourage the learning of the Welsh
language or the retention of the Welsh language than are those
parents who do not hold such aspirations for their children. Thus
it is from among this group of parents that we would expect children
attending the bilingual schools to be drawn. This of course carries
the assumption that such parents are cognizant of the value of the

Welsh language for upward inter-generational mobility. However, it is clear that despite these new developments the Welsh language has a limited value, being restricted to Wales. Watson (1964) has discussed social mobility in terms of what he refers to as 'spiralists' and 'burghers', the former being a person who combines social and geographical mobility and the latter viewing social mobility in terms of a more restricted spatial context, being tied to a more localized community. Thus our second hypothesis maintains that those parents who send their children to the bilingual schools for reasons of mobility aspirations are more likely to view the social mobility of their children as 'burghers' rather than 'spiralists' although there may well be a tendency for spiralism to involve migration within Wales.

   In order to test these hypotheses we selected two groups of forty working-class parents, evenly distributed by gender and chosen randomly from among the parents of children attending two primary schools, one being a bilingual school and the other teaching exclusively through the medium of English.(4) These schools were both located in the Rhondda Valleys, an area with a predominantly working-class population and which, as we shall see below, is an area that has been subject to a high degree of Welsh-language erosion and depopulation during the past few decades.

LANGUAGE IN THE RHONDDA (5)

The demographic growth of the Rhondda Valleys resulted from the expansion of the coal industry during the 1870s. The first new levels were sunk during the 1850s and by 1861 the population of the Rhondda stood at a mere 3,035. Ten years later this figure had increased to 23,950. The subsequent demographic growth is shown in Table 13.1. Much of the early growth resulted from inmigration

Table 13.1 Demographic growth of the Rhondda 1861-1911

Year	Population	Year	Population
1861	3,035	1891	88,351
1871	23,950	1901	113,735
1881	55,632	1911	152,781

Source: Lewis (1974:202).

during the 1860s and 1870s from the neighbouring Welsh counties and during the subsequent two decades from the substantial influx of people from outside Wales. Despite the non-Welsh origin of much of the population it is suggested that most of the male population was absorbed linguistically to Welsh via the work situation. The subsequent years until 1920 saw a continuation of the movement of population from England to the Rhondda with the flow from the Welsh counties being important only during certain periods, e.g. at the turn of the century.

There is little doubt that the place of origin of the inmigrating population had a profound influence upon language behaviour although it is difficult to estimate the diverse influences on language retention and language conversion. In 1901 the percentage of monoglot Welsh speakers in the Rhondda was 11.4 per cent with a further 53.2 per cent being bilingual and the remaining 35.4 per cent being monoglot English speakers. Ten years later the respective figures were 6.2 per cent, 50.7 per cent and 43.1 per cent. Even within this decade there was a distinct trend towards bilingualism and a certain erosion of the Welsh language.

The main reason for the erosion of the Welsh language lay in the educational institutions and in the attitudes towards the Welsh language that had developed during the earlier decades but which were particularly damaging at this time. The Welsh language was held to be the main obstacle to 'progress' and 'national (sic) integration' (Lewis, F.W., 1974:212). Thus the following statement appeared in a government report on education published in 1852:

> Whatever encouragement individuals may think it desirable to give
> to the preservation of the Welsh language on grounds of philo-
> logical or antiquarian interests, it must always be the desire of
> a Government to render its dominions, as far as possible, homo-
> geneous, and to break down barriers to the freest intercourse
> between the different parts of them. Sooner or later, the differ-
> ence of language between Wales and England will probably be
> effaced ... and they are not the true friends of the Welsh people,
> who, from a romantic interest in their manners and traditions,
> would impede an event which is socially and *politically* so desir-
> able for them. (Quoted in Lewis, C.W., 1974:212.)

This was the basis of official policy in the Rhondda schools during the second half of the nineteenth century and it is little wonder that the language data for 1911 indicates that Welsh-language erosion was already very much advanced among the children of school age (Table 13.2).

Table 13.2   Language ability, Rhondda Urban District 1911

Ages in years	Number speaking			
	English only	Welsh only	English & Welsh	No statements
3.0-4.9	5,145	451	2,688	740
5.0-9.9	9.464	465	8.186	539
10.0-14.9	7,242	313	7,705	365
15.0-24.9	13,017	635	14,738	151
25.0-44.9	19,394	1,833	25,136	34
45.0-64.9	5,849	1,845	10,438	1
65	945	658	1,805	0
Totals	61,056	6,200	70,696	1,830

Source: Lewis (1974:210).

Such a policy was promoted to such an extent that it gained support among many of the parents who were led to believe that the English language was the essential ingredient of upward social mobility and that a knowledge of the Welsh language hindered the child's ability to learn the English language. Although a token gesture to the Welsh language was made by the introduction of it as a class language in 1893 it was not until the beginning of the century that language began to be taught with any emphasis in the Rhondda and even then of course all of the teaching in the schools was through the medium of English. That the Welsh language survived as anything more than a vernacular language during this period was the result of the activities of the chapels which numbered 151 and which had a seating capacity of 85,105 in the Rhondda Urban District in 1914 (Lewis, E.D. 1974:120). Here the children were taught to read and write in their native language and the Sunday Schools, the various religious and secular activities associated with the chapels were almost exclusively conducted in Welsh. There is here something of a contradiction in that it was largely through the Welsh-language institutions such as the chapels and the adult education classes that the workers were encouraged: 'to inculcate in their children a respect for education in general and for grammar school education in particular' (Lewis, C.W. 1974:247). Yet the official policy was to emphasize the English language at the expense of the Welsh language in formal education.

Despite the limited introduction of the Welsh language into the school curriculum at the turn of the century the position of the Welsh language continued to deteriorate (Table 13.3).

Table 13.3 Proportion of the enumerated population (over two years of age) speaking Welsh at successive censuses, 1911-71, Rhondda Municipal Borough

Year	Percentage speaking Welsh only	Percentage speaking English only
1911	4.4	50.8
1921	3.0	42.5
1931	1.1	45.4
1951	0.4	29.0
1961	0.5	23.7
1971	1.1	12.5

Source: Lewis (1974:217).

Despite the establishment of two bilingual primary schools in the Rhondda in 1950, schools in which the main medium of instruction was Welsh, the decline in the number of people able to speak Welsh in the Rhondda continued. With only 196 out of 15,810 schoolchildren in the Rhondda claiming to speak Welsh as their first language in 1951 it is apparent that if anything was to be done to arrest this decline urgent steps had to be taken. However the establishment of

two schools with a limited enrolment is not going to have a profound
effect upon the above figures and the demand for an expansion of such
educational facilities had to come from among a substantial number
of the local population. What has been suggested in the introduction
is that the circumstances which are likely to generate such a demand
have developed in an incipient form through the relationship between
Welsh-language ability and the possibility of upward social mobility.
It was in order to learn more about this apparent change in the
status of the Welsh language from the perspective of the local population in the Rhondda that this study was undertaken.

THE FINDINGS

The choice of school which the parents sent their children to was
not an open-ended one for all parents sampled. The policy of the
educational authorities with reference to the applications for
places in the bilingual school is that all children over the age of
five must be accepted. While there has been some difficulty in
accommodating those under five years of age the policy would suggest
that some parents may well have been misled into believing that the
same difficulty applied to the older children. The local education
authorities are certainly aware of the demand for an expansion of
bilingual education at the primary level and plans were in hand to
open a third such school until the financial constraints that have
been recently imposed on educational spending resulted in the
shelving of the project for such a school. The knowledge of the
restricted access also appears to inhibit some parents from applying
for places. Among the NW group was a subgroup consisting of 17 per
cent of the total parents who would have preferred to send their
children to the bilingual school and their responses to many of the
questions were similar to those of the W group rather than those of
the other NW group parents. This tends to promote a greater congruence between the response patterns of the two groups than would
otherwise have been the case.
   There was a substantial difference in the reasoning of the parents
from each group with reference to the selection of the school which
their children would be sent to. Among the parents from the W group
two reasons dominated their selection process. The first was
related to their attitude towards the language as a language, i.e.
the language in its emotive context. This was expressed in a
variety of forms including an expression of the feeling that Welsh
children throughout Wales should be given an opportunity to speak
the 'mother tongue', that the children should be given an opportunity
to learn the language which they themselves were denied, etc. The
second reason related to an evaluation of the quality of the education offered at the bilingual school, an evaluation which had a
strong tendency towards a future orientation. Such an evaluation
was based on a number of criteria including the student/teacher
ratio, a 'friendlier environment' which created a greater enjoyment
of the school and education among the children, the quality of the
bilingual secondary school which the children from the primary school
would eventually attend.
   In contrast the parents from the NW group had a far more practical

orientation in their selection of school, an orientation that was
far more present and self-oriented rather than future and child-
oriented. Thus it was expressed in terms of the proximity of the
school to the home, this being an element of convenience for both
the parent and the child, that it was the 'natural' school for their
children to attend since it was the 'local school'. The other
feature of this response set was the absence of choice that we have
already referred to, this sometimes being expressed in terms of a
desire for an alternative choice but more generally in terms of a
passive acceptance of the 'status quo'.

The persistent reference to the Welsh language in the responses
of the W group and the absence of such statements among the other
group suggests that the two groups have contrasting attitudes
towards the Welsh language. In order to evaluate this difference
attitude profiles for each group were constructed on the basis of
responses to the following five stimulus statements (Table 13.4):

Table 13.4 Stimulus statements

---

1 Welsh people should be able to speak Welsh.
2 Learning Welsh is a waste of time.
3 Welsh should be the first language in Wales.
4 It would be more valuable for children in Wales to learn a
   European language other than Welsh.
5 Welsh language teaching should be expanded in schools in Wales.

The ascription of values to the various response categories (from
'agree strongly' = +2 to 'strongly disagree' = -2) allowed us to
assign scores to each individual and to the groups in general. From
these scores the respective group attitude profiles were constructed
(Figure 13.1). This demonstrates quite clearly that while there was
a basis for agreement between members of the two groups with reference to statement 2, there was a tendency to disagree on the other
four statements, with members of group W tending to show a strongly

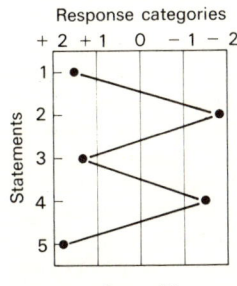

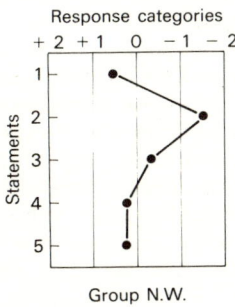

Key: + 2 — Strongly agree
     + 1 — Agree
       0 — Don't know
     − 1 — Disagree
     − 2 — Strongly disagree

Group W.   Group N.W.

FIGURE 13.1 Attitude profiles

positive attitude towards the Welsh language as expressed in all
five statements. Members of the NW group on the other hand tend to
be less sure in their responses. Thus while there is a high degree
of tolerance for the learning of the language among the members of
this group they tend towards the opposite attitudes of the W group
when it comes to the prominence of, and attention afforded to the
Welsh language in Wales.

The other interesting feature of this orientation towards the
Welsh language among the members of the W group is their orientation
towards Welsh-language institutions and to their own language backgrounds. Of the parents in this group 65 per cent had at least one
parent who spoke Welsh fluently but only 7 out of the 40 parents
claimed to be fluent themselves. Yet 21 of these parents (mainly
the mothers) were learning the Welsh language, partly in order to
stimulate their children to learn it. Similarly 12 of the 40
families sent their children to Welsh chapels although they themselves
did not attend the chapel. In addition 25 per cent of these parents
indicated that their children belonged to secular Welsh-language
institutions such as the Urdd (Welsh League of Youth).(6) This would
suggest that there is a third generation return, not only to the
language but also to the cultural institutions and that the support
for the teaching of the Welsh language in the schools is only part
of a much wider reorientation towards the language and culture which
serve as symbols of a heightened ethnic awareness.

Further probing into the value of Welsh-language education produced interesting responses. Among the W group parents such education was recognized as an identity marker associated with a heightened
ethnic awareness, a point that received considerable support from NW
group members. W group parents expanded upon their references to
educational quality claiming that the bilingual schools throughout
Wales were superior in terms of the quality of education offered.
Such a judgment was based on a number of criteria. It was held by
several parents that bilingual education served to 'make the mind
more flexible', or served as the basis for facilitating the learning
of a third language. Also the belief held by 72.5 per cent of the W
group parents and 27.5 per cent of the NW group parents that discipline in the bilingual schools was superior was significant, especially since only 50 per cent of the NW group disagreed with this
view, and even among those who did disagree it was not so much a
disagreement with the superiority of the discipline but rather an
expression of the relative importance of the role of the school as
an agent of discipline among the young. The importance of this
discipline was seen by the majority as its importance in the formation of the child's personality which involved a deference to
authority which was couched in terms of 'respect' which, for some
at least, was the essential ingredient of educational success and
'getting on in the job'. On the other hand many of those who did
not send their children to the bilingual school denied the value of
Welsh-language education and some went as far as to claim that it
adversely affected English-language ability and undermined political
beliefs!

The most interesting suggestion in response to the query about the
value of Welsh-language education involved its role in the creation
of wider employment opportunities. Among the W group parents 87.5

per cent subscribed to this view compared with 52.5 per cent of the
NW group parents. In many cases the nature of the employment was
specified as being associated with the media, local government,
tourism, government administration or teaching, all of them being
significantly middle-class occupations. Among those who held this
view the value of the language was seen within the context of a
highly restricted and competitive job market in a declining area
with the language serving to open up a few more job opportunities,
especially of the type which offered an alternative to their own
experience of 'working down the pit'. Such instrumentality has been
referred to by Lockwood and Goldthorpe in the context of inter-
generational mobility (Goldthorpe et al., 1968). Half of the NW
group parents denied the value of the Welsh language in terms of
employment potential. In a sense perhaps they were more realistic
in claiming that the number of jobs which carried a Welsh-language
qualification were limited in number, that a knowledge of the Welsh
language without intellectual ability was of little value and that
other criteria were more important as job qualifications. Certainly
few parents from either group would send their children to the
bilingual school in the blind belief that a knowledge of the Welsh
language alone would guarantee a good job. Rather it is the *combination* of a positive attitude towards the language in identity terms,
a belief in the superiority of the bilingual educational institution
and the *possibility* that the Welsh-language ability might help to
widen the job market which underlie the preference for Welsh medium
education. Thus the language is seen as both means and end in both
ideological and instrumental terms.

The responses of the W group parents to the query as to the value
of a bilingual education suggests that there is a tendency among
members of this group for the holding of middle-class occupational
aspirations for their children, at least in ideal terms. This issue
was pursued directly and the responses are summarized in Table 13.5.

Table 13.5   Ideal occupational aspirations for children

Occupations	Group W parents		Group NW parents	
	Boys N*=34	Girls N=37	Boys N=32	Girls N=31
High professional: lawyer/MD/ architect/dentist, etc.	17	6	5	2
Low professional: teaching/media/ planning/bank/civil service, etc.	10	9	5	4
Skilled/semiskilled: craft/military/ carpenter/baker/industrial/mechanic	5	8	21	15
Manual/unskilled	0	0	1	5
Don't know/doesn't matter	2	4	0	5

* N varies since not all respondents had both sons and daughters.

The difference between the aspirations of the members of the two
groups is clear with 50 per cent of the W group parents having upper
professional occupational aspirations for their sons and a further
29.4 per cent having lower professional occupational aspirations for
their sons compared with figures of 15.6 per cent and 15.6 per cent
for the parents from the NW group. Only 14.7 per cent of the W group
parents viewed skilled occupations as desirable for their sons compared with 65.6 per cent of the NW group parents among whom a further
3.2 per cent were satisfied with unskilled or manual labour for their
sons. Among the W group the mothers had higher aspirations for their
sons than did the fathers. Both groups had lower aspirations for
their daughters than for their sons but to a greater degree among the
W group parents.

When asked about the expected occupations of their children the
same difference is again apparent (Table 13.6). Among the W group

Table 13.6   Expected occupations of children

	Group W parents		Group NW parents	
Occupations	Boys N*=34	Girls N=27	Boys N=32	Girls N=31
High professional: lawyer/MD/ architect/dentist, etc.	15	3	1	1
Low professional: teaching/media/ planning/bank/civil service, etc.	5	7	0	2
Skilled/semi-skilled: craft/baker/ military/carpenter/industrial/ mechanic	5	4	14	6
Manual/unskilled	1	4	6	9
Don't know/doesn't matter	8	9	11	13

* N varies since not all respondents had both sons and daughters.

parents the expected occupations are quite close to those aspired for
but with some scaling down from lower professional employment categories to skilled employments and a considerable number of 'don't
know' responses. A similar tendency to scale down and to express
'don't know' responses is found among members of the NW group.
Among the W group parents 57.5 per cent confirmed their aspirations,
a further 11.5 per cent scaled down, 1.5 per cent scaled upwards and
the remaining 29.5 per cent gave 'don't know' responses. The comparable percentages for the NW group were 40 per cent, 20.6 per cent,
1.6 per cent and 37.8 per cent.

Thus there is some confirmation for our initial hypothesis. There
appears to be a greater tendency for the parents of the children
attending the bilingual school to have higher occupational aspirations for their children than the parents of the children who attended
the English-language school. This difference was one which involved
a difference between parents who looked to an upward inter-
generational social mobility and those who did not have such

aspirations for their children. The W group parents recognize that
within a restricted job market the possibility of achieving such
upward mobility is limited but that it is increased somewhat by the
acquisition of the Welsh language as a qualification for such employment and by gaining access to what is felt to be a superior educational opportunity. This contrasts with members of the other group
who are less instrumental in their educational attitudes and have
lower aspirations for their children in terms of their future
employment.

Given the above tendency among the W group parents it is reasonable to expect that if the Welsh language plays such a central part
in their aspirations on behalf of their children that they will view
the desired social mobility in terms of a geographic limitation
focusing upon Wales. The converse does not necessarily hold for the
NW group of parents since the absence of a Welsh-language ability
does not preclude local job opportunities.

The migration and employment histories of the respondents indicated that in only two of the eighty families had the head of the
family been employed outside Wales and that in only six cases had
the family head been employed outside the valleys. Thus the work
experience of virtually all of the respondents was by and large a
local one. However, there was a greater tendency for the parents
from the NW group to express a willingness to relocate outside Wales
if a better job opportunity was offered them (Table 13.7). Thus
40 per cent of the members of this group compared with only 12.5 per
cent of the W group parents expressed such a willingness. This
willingness to relocate was also apparent with reference to other
spatial alternatives with 51.5 per cent of the NW group parents

Table 13.7 Willingness to relocate if a better job offered

| | W group parents | | | | NW group parents | | | |
| | Fathers | | Mothers | | Fathers | | Mothers | |
	Yes	No	Yes	No	Yes	No	Yes	No
More than 20 miles	5	14	8	13	9	11	12	8
Outside Wales	1	18	4	17	5	15	11	9
Outside Britain	2	17	1	20	3	17	6	14

compared with 29.5 per cent of the W group parents being willing
to move more than twenty miles from their present location to obtain
such an opportunity, and 22.5 per cent of the NW group and a mere
7.5 per cent of the W group parents being willing to relocate outside
Britain if such an opportunity were offered. A difference also
appears in response to the query as to how the parent would feel if
their child's eventual occupation took them outside Wales, with 45
per cent of the W group parents and 27.5 per cent of the NW group
parents expressing an unhappiness about such a possibility. Indeed
several of the W group parents expressed this dissatisfaction in
terms of a feeling that the children should remain in Wales either
to take full advantage of the educational facilities which they had
been given or to further the language cause or, in their terms, 'to

help the language'. Thus again there is some confirmation for the second hypothesis.

CONCLUSION

In conclusion there is some evidence to suggest that the policies of the language lobby are beginning to pay off. The demand for official activities to be conducted through the medium of Welsh has created a demand for those who hold a Welsh-language qualification. This, together with other factors, has served to raise the status of the Welsh language and also to heighten the Welsh identity, a process which involves, among some people, a re-evaluation of the self in terms of the symbolic value of the Welsh language as an identity marker of ethnic status. The two aspects of subjective assessment (of the self and of the future direction of Welsh society) has resulted in a tendency to stress the importance of the Welsh language in terms of upward social mobility via the use of the bilingual schools. Yet if the authorities are not to be accused of tokenism involving the use of public conscience money there must be a further expansion of such bilingual education in order to meet the increasing demand.(7) Similarly there is little room for complacency among the language supporters. Although significant, the demand is limited. The public employment domain is similarly limited and if the conversion process is to continue the private economic employment domain must also be persuaded, this obviously being a much more difficult task.(8) Furthermore one suspects that the process described above is by no means universal in Wales. In many parts of north Wales the orientation is towards Merseyside rather than the national capital and the Welsh language tends to retain its stigmatic connotation as a marker of low socio-economic status. In such areas the expected tendency would for members of the working class to 'pass' by emphasising the standard language associated with the source of political and economic power in an attempt to enhance their individual status. Viewed in this context the effort to 'rescue' the Welsh language has a long uphill fight ahead of it.

NOTES

1 In many respects this is akin to the development of a new indigenous elite which occurred with the decolonisation of Africa (see Little, 1965).
2 See for example the discussion of recent work pertaining to Wales in Giles and Powesland (1975:74-8).
3 This does not imply the existence of a heightened class consciousness but merely an awareness of the value of middle-class occupations. Indeed the study indicated that most of the respondents perceive the Rhondda as a basically classless society, although a difference is recognised between 'workers' and 'professionals' they are adamant that this has little to do with social relationships nor status allocation.
4 In the following discussion the parents whose children attend the bilingual school will be referred to as the W group and the

parents whose children attend the English-medium school will be
referred to as the NW group.
5 Most of the information included in this brief summary derives
from C. W. Lewis (1974).
6 This is despite the fact that many of the parents had children
who were too young to attend such institutions. Several such
parents indicated that their children would attend when old
enough.
7 In fairness to the education authority which the study area was
administered by they have opened three new bilingual primary
schools during the past year. However other authorities have
been far less responsive and the supporters of bilingual education often find their requests either ignored or referred elsewhere.
8 Thus, for example, the taxation office at Bangor which serves a
predominantly bilingual area received only seven applications
for Welsh-language taxation forms from among the approximately
3,000 employers which it serves.

REFERENCES

ANGLE, JOHN (1976), Mainland control of manufacturing and reward for
bilingualism in Puerto Rico, 'American Sociological Review', vol.41,
no.2, pp.289-307.
CANADA (1969), Royal Commission on bilingualism and biculturalism,
1969, vols 3A, 3B, 'The Work World', Ottawa.
CENTRAL ADVISORY COUNCIL FOR EDUCATION (WALES) (1965), 'Science in
Education in Wales Today', HMSO, London.
GERTH, H.H. and MILLS, C.W. (1974), 'From Max Weber: Essays in
Sociology', Routledge & Kegan Paul, London.
GILES, H. and POWESLAND, P.F. (1975), 'Speech Style and Social
Evaluation', Academic Press, London.
GOLDTHORPE, J.H., LOCKWOOD, D., BECHHOFER, F. and PLATT, J. (1968),
'The Affluent Worker: Industrial Attitudes and Behaviour', Cambridge
University Press.
LEWIS, C.W. (1974), The Welsh language, in K.S. Hopkins (ed.),
'Rhondda Valley Past and Future', Maddock, Ferndale, pp.179-235.
LEWIS, E.D. (1974), Population changes and social life 1860 to 1914,
in K.S. Hopkins (ed.), 'Rhondda Valley Past and Future', Maddock,
Ferndale, pp.110-28.
LIEBERSON, S. (1970), 'Language and Ethnic Relations in Canada',
Wiley, New York.
LITTLE, K. (1965), 'West African Urbanization: A Study of Voluntary
Associations in Social Change', Cambridge University Press.
WATSON, W. (1964), Social mobility and social class in industrial
communities, in M. Gluckman and E. Devons (eds), 'Closed Systems and
Open Minds', Oliver & Boyd, London, pp.129-56.

Chapter 14

DOMAIN AND REGISTER IN THE USE OF WELSH

Pat Clayton

1 INTRODUCTION

This paper focuses on the concepts of domain and register and
explores the application of these concepts as analytical tools in a
research study whose overall objective was to examine erosion and
maintenance factors in the use of a minority language - in this case,
Welsh. The research was conducted amongst the residents of a small
north Wales village and the sample included all those who had some
command of both Welsh and English languages. I hesitate to describe
these respondents as bilingual since most were considerably more
fluent in Welsh than in English. In this community there are no
ethnic group identity problems such as those identified by other
papers in this volume. The issue of Welshness is clear: if you are
Welsh, you speak Welsh, if you do not speak Welsh, you are not
Welsh. The non-Welsh speaking Welshman is an unknown phenomenon in
this area, but is believed to inhabit the ethnic limbo of mid- and
south Wales.
   Focusing on the community under study, the research collected
empirical data to examine the respondents' language background and
development. A fairly homogeneous pattern emerged, of a group of
people who had spent their early years in remote north Wales villages
as monoglot Welsh. They were increasingly but differentially exposed
to English as consumers (1) of that language, and developed in
varying degrees some 'producer' command of English in relation to
some social contexts.
   In theory people who speak two languages have a choice of which
they speak to whom and under what circumstances. In practice both
social contexts and role relationships are more language bound than
they are language free. By focusing on language behaviour in
domains, it is possible to examine whether in any way domain boundaries also represent differentials in language behaviour in two
aspects: (i) whether any domains are language bound, and what, within
domains are catalysts for language shift from Welsh into English;
(ii) whether these differentials and language shifts are related to
variables already identified as language erosion and maintenance
factors.
   In this paper domains (2) represent the institutionalised contexts

relevant to the lives of the respondents in the community under
study. The concept has been in use since 1934 (Fishman, 1972) as
an operational device for exploring language maintenance and language
shift amongst bilinguals in various social contexts. The number of
domains identified is usually a variable of the social organisation
of the linguistic group (3) or community under study.

The concept of register (Whiteley, 1971) is a functional variant
of language in the same way that linguistic codes (Bernstein, 1971-4)
are a functional variant of language. Register can be used in two
ways - (i) to describe a kind of language which is related to a
particular social context, for example it may represent the 'in-
group' jargon of a particular social or occupational group; (ii) to
refer to a scale of qualitative use of language - e.g. as scale from
'high' Welsh such as might be used in a religious domain to 'low'
Welsh which might be the kind of 'pidgin' language (4) used characteristically in a shopping situation.

While both uses of the term imply the drawing of boundaries around
certain social contexts, it is the second use of the concept which
is applied in this study. Thus an additional element was added to
the original objective to study the way in which differentials in
language behaviour related to domain boundaries, namely to explore
the relationship between register and domain, and whether in fact
register might be a major differential between domains.

2   EROSION AND MAINTENANCE FACTORS

While in many parts of Wales, the education system has a historical
responsibility for language erosion, the influence is not universal.
In the area where this research took place, primary education is
through the medium of Welsh, and it is the secondary system which
represents the greatest English influence. The emphasis which
national and local government has placed on English in education has
made English the language of literacy and social mobility. This has
contributed both to a decline in the standards of written Welsh and
to the general undervaluing of the Welsh language by at least two
generations of young people.

Population migration has also contributed to language decline.
This refers both to the out-migration of Welsh speakers and to the
in-migration of English speakers. Both at inter-group level, as in
the industrial areas of the south and the north-east of Wales, and at
inter-personal level, as the English migrant came to the heartland,
first as visitors then as residents, this migration eroded the
language. Mixed Anglo-Welsh marriages are seen as a by-product of
population migration and this was seen by respondents as a contributing factor in language decline.

The influence of the media, especially television, is strongly
felt to be erosive to the Welsh language. Whilst television is seen
as exposing Welsh speakers at an early age to English the respondents
were also conscious of the displacement effects television viewing
has had on Welsh cultural activities. Such Welsh television programmes as do exist are often criticised for low standards and dull-
ness of content. Equally, in written Welsh in books, magazines and
newspapers a lack of breadth is emphasised. Some respondents claimed

there were not enough good Welsh authors to interest the serious
reader and conversely there was an interesting appeal on behalf of
pulp fiction consumers for 'more Welsh rubbish'.

Where technology penetrates, language erosion follows. What
Fishman (1972) calls the languages of wider communication, that is
the major world languages, tend to lead to technological innovation
adding words associated with technology to their own languages which
are then borrowed along with the technology by minority languages.

Both technology and the media are major contributors to the
process of linguistic borrowing. Many words and phrases are borrowed
from English into Welsh and are absorbed into common usage before
the Welsh-language lexographers can produce an equivalent word in
Welsh. Linguistic borrowing and the presence of many loan-words in
a minority language hasten the erosion process at a lexical as well
as a social level.

The historical development since the 1536-40 Acts of Union of an
Anglicised squirearchy has established a tradition in Wales that
English was the language of law and administration in Wales. Political and economic status and power, and any social mobility has
always been associated with English in Wales. For three centuries
the only status Welsh speakers could achieve in their own language
was through literary, religious and cultural channels. Thus the
acceptance of Welsh as a low-status language by its own speakers, a
condition reinforced by the 'Blue Books' report on education in
1845,(5) has contributed to the erosion of the language. The cumulative effects of education, the media, technology, and increasing
English language bureaucratisation during this century have continued
this reinforcement and many of the 'gwerin' (the ordinary people) of
Wales have been only too anxious to rid themselves of the language
which they have been encouraged to perceive in low-status terms.

Finally the weakening of the influence of the chapel is seen as
an erosion factor. Religion in Wales has always played an important
role in language maintenance in both qualitative and quantitative
respects. Erosion in language reflects secularisation. Once again
the concept of displacement is relevant since the activities which
replace chapel-going are unlikely to expose people to the high
quality of Welsh associated with the chapel.

Many of the maintenance factors identified in this study represent
the adaptive strategies of the Welsh to these erosion factors, with
changing policies and attitudes in local government towards Welsh in
education and Welsh as a prerequisite in many job specifications,
being the other side of the coin to some of the erosion factors. The
emergence of social and political movements with language-related
ideologies is another adaptive reaction to erosion.

In addition, there are two major maintenance features which are
explored specifically. The first relates to factors of social organisation. Most Welsh-speaking areas are rural and characterised, to
use Tönnies' (1951) typology, by Gemeinschaft patterns of organisation, focusing on traditional occupations, family life and religion,
with minimal geographical mobility and limited social referents. It
seemed relevant to explore the reinforcing effect of language use
between domains in such a community and the extent to which domains
overlap. The relationship between traditional patterns of life and
modern ideological issues was also explored. While a number of

individuals whom I described as 'language consciousness-raisers' were identified it seemed important to explore the influence these people had in various domains. The identification of the language consciousness-raisers needs explaining in that it relates directly to the concept of register. The consciousness-raisers are individuals who were identified as a result of questions about awareness of different qualitative levels of spoken Welsh and occasions or situations in which people made an effort to speak their 'best' Welsh. The occasions named by respondents were nearly always linked to the presence of an individual known to feel strongly about language maintenance. These individuals would act as catalysts in such matters as avoiding the use of loan-words where a Welsh word was available and known.

3   THE RESEARCH FINDINGS

Six domains were identified as of relevance to the lives of the respondents in the community under study. These were: home and family, social life, work, education, religion and officialdom.
      Previous research with Spanish-English bilinguals in America by Edelman (1968) and Greenfield (1968) suggests the existence of a continuum between the predominant use of Spanish in the informal or intimate domains and the predominant use of English in the formal more public domains (Figure 14.1).

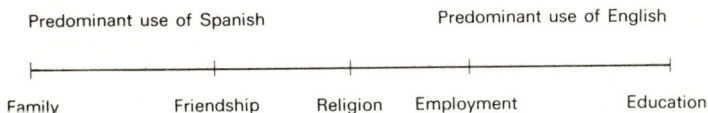

FIGURE 14.1

This continuum was kept in mind as possibly having some application to the Welsh-English situation in this study. Fishman (1972) has identified three variables associated with language shift in domains, which suggest that the language used may change in respect of the location in which the language encounter occurs, or the topic of the conversation, or the nature of the role-relationships which obtain between the speakers. The effects of these variables were also investigated.
      The data on language behaviour in domains was collected in two ways - first through an interview schedule in which respondents were asked, for each domain, which other people they communicated with, what language they spoke with them, and then which occasions, events, people or places produced a shift to another language or another register. Second, the research was involved in a range of semi-participant observation sessions covering the domain area in which the data collected by interview could be confirmed or otherwise. Whilst the self-reported behaviour on language shift was invariably confirmed by observation, since register shift was not always an activity of which respondents were particularly conscious, much

useful data on this was collected in the observation sessions. The
findings may be summarised broadly as in Table 14.1 - taking into
account both reported and observed behaviour.

Table 14.1   Language use in various domains

Domain	% Use	Dominant language
Home and family	100	Welsh
Social life	75	Welsh
Work	50	Welsh
Chapel	100	Welsh
Education	75	English
Officialdom	80	English

   In the home and family domain there were several erosion factors
present, one of the most potent being television. Most people
watched news programmes in Welsh, but 'entertainment' programmes in
English. While it is recognised that watching television is linguistically a 'consumer' activity, and therefore is not a catalyst for
language shift, nevertheless people absorb many English words and
phrases into their linguistic repertoire from television. Parents
are very conscious that while their children watch English television
this displaces participation in Welsh cultural activities.
   English neighbours and relatives also were clear catalysts for
language shift, but social distance was also an important variable
here. Where an English person had married into an all-Welsh family
there was an obligation for them to understand Welsh sufficiently for
the family members to continue speaking Welsh in their presence,
though not of course when the English member was directly involved
in the conversation. If a complete (English) stranger came into the
home, then the whole family would speak English while the stranger
was present. Thus English was always spoken in direct conversations
with English people, but the amount of Welsh spoken between Welsh
speakers in the presence of English people varied with closeness of
the role-relationship.
   Since the home is the centre of consumption and many consumer
goods are the by-products of technological advance, there are many
loan-words used in the home which are associated with consumer goods.
Thus for example any conversations about shopping, food and domestic
appliances contain a high proportion of English loan-words. It is
in the informal atmosphere of the home domain that the lag in
language modernisation seems very evident, a good example is the use
of the word "le'tric' for electricity - 'tan 'le'tric' (electric
fire) etc. in preference to 'trydan' a Welsh word neither difficult
nor unfamiliar to Welsh speakers. However, since ''le'tric' was in
widespread use before 'trydan' was coined, it would be slightly
pretentious (in this community at any rate) to use it unless one had
already established a reputation for using 'proper' Welsh.
   Similarly several maintenance factors operated in the home. In

this community the socialisation of children in a pattern which
reinforces their Welsh identity is an important value, as is language
maintenance in its own right. High value is also placed on family
life and one of the most important social activities involves interaction between members of the kinship network. The development of
strong primary group relationships through the medium of Welsh clearly
reinforces both the language and Welsh identity. Furthermore, the
family is the centre for the encouragement of Welsh cultural activities, and a supportive interest in literature, music, ideology movements, local eisteddfodau etc., serves to maintain the language.

Within the social life domain, the main erosion factors are
related to role-relationships and topic. Once again the presence of
English people is the principle catalyst for language shift and the
social distance variable already observed is even more evident in
social life since the range of differences is more observable. In a
friendly group assumptions are made that one or two English members
(usually marriage partners of Welsh group members) understand the
Welsh conversation. In a public situation such as a local pub, the
variations in social distance are clearly observable with deference
to English occurring in inverse proportion to the closeness of the
relationship. To English relatives and close friends there is a
limited concession, to local English neighbours and residents a
greater concession, for one English stranger the whole group will
turn to English.

Consistent with this was the mention by many respondents of the
fact that they were aware of speaking much more English in the
summer when the visitors are about, than in the winter.

In the field of hobbies and special interests there is a shift to
English or a strong dependence on English loan-words. Specialised
information about areas of interest tends to be obtained through the
medium of English, whether on football or motor cars, ornithology or
photography, so that an English vocabulary is more familiar whereas
a Welsh vocabulary is either not available or not known to cover
these special interests.

The maintenance factors followed a similar pattern. Many respondents claimed that their social lives were lived largely in Welsh
and these were people whose lives revolved around extended family
contacts, and Welsh cultural activities. With thriving branches of
Merched y Wawr and Plaid Cymru in the area it was possible to lead
a busy social life based on activities and involvement with these
groups. Welsh plays, concerts and Nosweithiau Llawen are also
regularly held in the area.(6)

The activities of the language consciousness-raisers is particularly evident in the social life domain. In predominantly Welsh
activities, by the use of correct Welsh in their own speech they
raise the general standard of other people's Welsh. One respondent
said; 'If you use an English word when you are talking to E..., he
will be sure to use the correct Welsh word when he replies to you.'
One cannot imagine there would be much tolerance of such 'remedial'
conversations between English speakers, but these consciousness-
raisers command much respect for their high standards and concern
for the language. In mixed Welsh-English activities they are even
more vigilant in order to ensure that the English and Welsh people
present are all aware of being in a Welsh situation.

However, since the dominant community ethos manifests against the development of an uncomfortable degree of aggression, virtually no hostility is engendered. One other feature of the situation which may not be typical of a larger community is the process of becoming a consciousness-raiser. It is difficult to become a consciousness-raiser unless one is either new to the area, in which case the initial presentation of oneself in that role serves to establish it, or one must have a history of extremism or eccentricity. People who, 10 years ago perhaps, were nationalists or language-movement supporters were regarded as both extremist and eccentric. There is now a swing, in the area under study, towards the support of both these movements, and since small communities have long memories the former eccentrics and extremists are respected for their foresight and dedication to what was formerly viewed as a lost cause. The more recent convert finds it difficult to acquire such status quickly since he must first run the gamut of accusations of bandwagon jumping, pretentiousness and not knowing his place. Such sanctions are hard to ride in a close-knit community.

The main erosion factors in the work domain were associated with role relationship and topic. Technology was a key factor instigating a register shift. For example many work conversations involving building materials, farm machinery and chemicals are conducted in a pidgin variety of Welsh, where sentence construction is in Welsh form, pronouns and conjunctions in Welsh, verbs were cymricised (e.g. by the addition of 'io' to the English root) and nouns in English.

Register is lowered in direct proportion to the amount of technology derived language used in each situation in the domain.

People in service occupations are more exposed to English residents and visitors and therefore use more English in these role-relationships. The summer-winter seasonal variation was evident in language use for this occupational group.

The possibility of locale being an important variable was explored in the work domain, but examination revealed that neither role-relationship nor topic was in fact the catalyst for language shift in different locales, e.g. the use of English in a farming livestock market was related to the presence of English farmers, not to the market situation as such.

Maintenance factors on the other hand are usually connected with the nature of employment and the size of the work group. In traditional, indigenous occupations such as farming, labouring, building, teaching, council work, etc. there is more likely to be a high level of language maintenance and much of the relevant vocabulary is available in Welsh. In more 'modern' occupations, usually involving service settings such as garages, catering, etc. there is less relevant Welsh vocabulary.

The work group, especially in traditional occupations, is often based on the family and local community and where this pattern exists, Welsh is maintained. The larger and more fragmented the work group, which is often the situation among those who worked outside the community, the more likely it is that English people, both as work mates and managers are involved in the work domain. The importance of the reinforcing effects of overlapping domains on language use is evident here.

The main erosion factors in the education domain are once again associated with topic and role-relationship but a further factor is the legacy of an educational policy which determined that English was to be the teaching medium in secondary education. The migration of English people into the area has brought more English children into the schools and while attempts are made to teach them Welsh at the primary level there is some necessity for language shift in the classroom. Where English homes are not supportive to the Welsh language this may inhibit the children's learning of it and thus manifests against Welsh-medium teaching.

Topic seemed important at both primary and secondary levels, since much of the specialised information and teaching material in some subjects was only available in English. At secondary level several subjects were associated exclusively with English and as the official school language it was also used in assemblies and in disseminating information.

It was possible in this study to look at three generations of respondents and their relationship to the education system. The oldest group, the grandparents, had generally been educated in all-age schools which gave them little exposure to English, except by way of rote learning (Gray's elegy was a popular choice with the teachers) and stock phrases such as 'My name is John', 'I walk to the window', etc. The parents' generation are those whose education had been wholly Welsh at primary level, and whose secondary education was entirely through the medium of English. For many in this group the secondary school became an isolated, alien domain. Many did not know whether or not their teachers spoke Welsh and some recalled the shock they felt when after leaving school they were greeted in the street in Welsh by teachers with whom they had only ever spoken English. Clearly, locale was a more significant variable then in this matter than it has proved to be generally in this study. The third generation, the current schoolchildren are much more language conscious. The more informal relationships in the secondary school between teachers and pupils means that the children are well aware of teachers' attitudes to Welsh and their political affiliations. Teachers seem to use Welsh with Welsh children whenever they can and either children or teachers may initiate the use of Welsh, both in and out of the classroom. The larger number of English children in the schools means that there is more English spoken in the playground, but as in the past, peer-group affiliations tend to be based on geographical considerations and the children from Welsh communities still stick together.

Seventy per cent of the respondents attend chapel weekly, the other 30 per cent attend less frequently. This is a very straightforward domain in terms of language behaviour in that Welsh is always the language of the chapel and chapel-related activities - cyfarfod bach, Sunday school trips and the singing festival (gymanfa ganu). Chapel activities overlap education and social life domains in that some community activities are held in and revolve around the school and its pupils. Thus the English parents are welcome at these occasions but few concessions are made to English in these traditionally Welsh cultural activities and the English tend to leave early. The high rate of chapel attendance probably makes this village atypical, since in general chapel attendance is on the decline in

Wales.(7)   Chapel-going is in itself an activity contributing to
language maintenance and the chapel is still the place to hear and
use high-quality Welsh.

   The officialdom domain is a rather peripheral domain which turned
out to be absorbed into other domains.   Many of the forms which
people are called upon to complete are connected with home and work
domains and contact with officials is usually associated with work.
The location of these contacts is usually at home, since occupations
like farming and building are conducted from the home.   Many official
forms, as a result of pressure group activity perhaps, are available
in both Welsh and English usually on opposite sides of the paper.
However, since bilingual forms are a relatively new development,
most respondents are accustomed to form-filling in English and moreover are more accustomed to English as the official language.   The
net result is that some people continue to fill in forms on the
English side since they do not understand the Welsh, and others said
that they fill in the Welsh version as a matter of principle, but
are unable to do so without looking at the English side in order to
be sure of exactly what was required.   It seems that this is characteristic of a number of situations in which new Welsh words are less
familiar than English loan-words in established usage and this produces general unwillingness to relearn words in the Welsh form.

4   SUMMARY AND CONCLUSIONS

The main variable which gives rise to language shift in any domain
is the presence of English people.   Role-relationships which give
rise to language shift are regulated to some extent by social
distance so that close relatives or friends will themselves be
addressed in English but will not have the language shift effect on
a group that an English stranger would provoke.   In practice English
people are not often present in most domains. The home, social life,
the chapel and work in particular were not often exposed to the
English.

   Those English families who live in this community are regarded as
a 'hippie fringe' by the native population and live rather separate
lives from the Welsh community.   Where Welsh community life is strong
it seems a realistic language maintenance strategy to create all-
Welsh cultural situations which the English will not want to attend.
The novelty of learning Welsh tends to wear off with the realisation
that learning the language does not bridge the value-system gap.

   Topic is the other catalyst both for language shift to English
and for a shift in register towards the pidgin form of Welsh.   Many
conversations, whether involving specialist interest subjects or
merely concerning everyday technology involves a lowering of register
where there is insufficient Welsh vocabulary to cover the topic.
The accustomed reduction of Welsh to a pidginised form has serious
consequences for language erosion, since it builds in erosion processes to the use of the language in various contexts.

   The extent to which domains overlap seems to be a reinforcement
feature of language maintenance.   In a gemeinschaft community several
domains overlap each other and in so far as language in these domains
is predominantly Welsh, the language is reinforced.   The integration

of domains in this way tends to be associated with the more traditional areas of life. Those people whose lives follow a more
fragmented pattern (i.e. tending towards a gesellschaft pattern of
social organisation) where work, social life and home are separated,
appear to be those who are exposed to and use more English. Taking
this into consideration, it seems that the continuum suggested by
the Edelman and Greenfield studies is not appropriate to this study.
An alternative continuum which seems more appropriate involves a
traditional - contemporary axis.

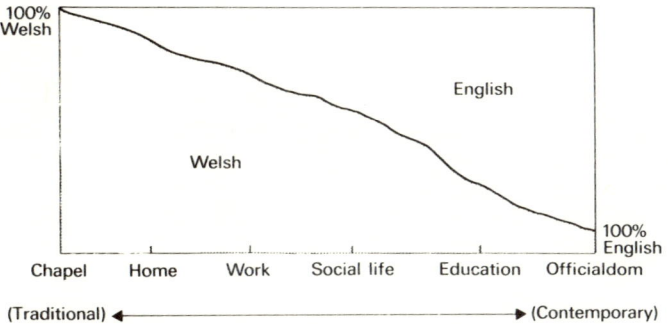

FIGURE 14.2   Traditional-contemporary continuum showing use of
              Welsh and English

   This traditional-contemporary continuum appears also to have
application within domains in that the more traditional areas of
home and social life are conducted in Welsh whereas the contemporary
areas of both these domains would involve use of a pidginised version
of the language, or shifts into English. The differential use of
language on this kind of scale would be marked by the intrusion of
erosion factors and catalysts already identified.
   So far as the relationship between register and domain was concerned, a paradigm was constructed (Figure 14.3) hypothesising a
scale of five registers in Welsh, equivalent to different levels of
language use and relating this to a range of domains. The highest,
register I, is in the chapel a formal and traditional domain;
register II refers to the very good Welsh used in the Welsh media,
though the output in this area is not very great, and the same
standards are found in the political and language ideological movements. Register III refers to the education system and the more
social of the ideology movements, where in both areas the mixture
of informal and formal interaction slightly lowers the level of
Welsh. Register IV covers areas in which there is wide variation in
the standard of Welsh, where the evidence indicates greater exposure
to erosive elements and there is a greater mixture of Welsh with
English loan-words. Register V represents the areas in which a good

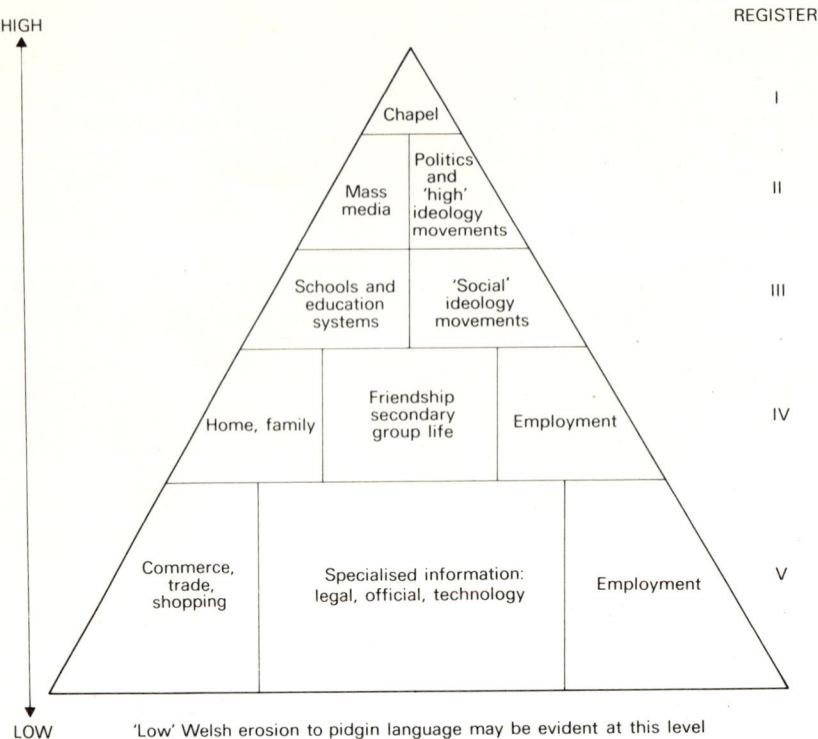

HIGH

REGISTER

I

Chapel

II

Mass media

Politics and 'high' ideology movements

III

Schools and education systems

'Social' ideology movements

IV

Home, family

Friendship secondary group life

Employment

V

Commerce, trade, shopping

Specialised information: legal, official, technology

Employment

LOW   'Low' Welsh erosion to pidgin language may be evident at this level

FIGURE 14.3 Paradigm of register-domain relationship

deal of English and English loan-words are used and a reduction to the pidgin variety is most evident.

It is at the latter two levels that the greatest amount of effort would be required, for example the intervention of consciousness-raisers, to stimulate Welsh speakers' concern with improving standards.

This study was carried out in a high-maintenance area for the Welsh language, in a county where in 1971, 73.5 per cent of the residents spoke Welsh. As already stated the issue of Welsh identity is no problem in this area, being directly correlated with speaking Welsh. Objectively, however, it is suggested that the issue of what 'Welsh speaking' actually means is problematic. There seems to be a number of Welsh speakers whose whole 'producer' command of Welsh is limited to the pidgin variety, and this is clearly recognised by other Welsh speakers who lower their register in communicating with these people. It is true of any language community that its speakers are by no means homogeneous in linguistic competence: this holds in Welsh, in English, in every language. For the Welsh-speaking community, now fighting a rearguard action against language decline, the differences in linguistic competence may be the difference between language survival and language extinction.

NOTES

1 Wonderley (1968) suggests that there are two kinds of language communication, 'producer' language – that is the range of vocabulary, speech codes and discrete languages which the individual can speak, and 'consumer' language, that range of speech and language the individual can understand, all of which he may not be participant in as a producer. The individual's producer capacity is generally more limited linguistically than his consumer capacity.
2 The concept of domain is explained fully in Fishman (1972).
3 A fuller and very useful exposition of the distinction between a speech community and a linguistic community is to be found in Hymes (1972).
4 A pidgin language is a language based on the much reduced and simplified grammar of one language, the source language, and a limited vocabulary of loan-words from another, or several other languages. Pidgins are generally spoken rather than written. A fuller exposition is to be found in Hall (1966).
5 The 'Blue Books' Report was a report of the Commission of Enquiry into Welsh Education published in 1847. It purported to demonstrate that moral turpitude, educational inferiority and lack of material and economic progress and prosperity in Wales was associated with adherence to the Welsh language.
6 Merched y Wawr, literally Women of the Dawn, began as a Welsh splinter group from the Women's Institute movement and is now a fully fledged women's organisation in its own right with branches throughout Wales and its own magazine.
    Plaid Cymru – the Welsh Nationalist Party.
    Noson Lawen – (pl. Nosweithiau Llawen) literally a merry evening, usually involving singers, comedians, poetry, sketches, etc.
7 See the paper by Day and Fitton in this volume, chapter 17.

REFERENCES

BERNSTEIN, B. (1971-4), 'Class, Codes and Control', Vols 1 to 3, Routledge & Kegan Paul, London.
EDELMAN, M., COOPER, R.L. and FISHMAN, J.A. (1968), The contextualization of school children's bilingualism, 'Irish Journal of Education', vol.2, pp.106-11.
FISHMAN, J.A. (1972), 'Language in Socio-Cultural Change', Stanford University Press, Palo Alto.
GREENFIELD, L. (1968), Situational measures of language use in relation to person, place and topic among Puerto Rican bilinguals, 'Bilingualism in The Barrio', Yeshiva University, New York.
HALL, R.A. (1966), 'Pidgin and Creole Languages', Cornell University Press, Ithaca.
HYMES, D. (1972), Models of the interaction of language and social life, in J. Gumperz and D. Hymes (eds), 'Directions in Sociolinguistics: the ethnography of communication', Holt, Rinehart & Winston, New York, pp.35-72.
TÖNNIES, F. (1951), 'Gemeinschaft and Gesellschaft', edited and translated by C.P. Loomis, Michigan University Press, Ann Arbor.

WHITELEY, W.M. (1971), 'Language Use and Social Change', Oxford University Press, London.
WONDERLEY, W. (1968), 'Bible Translations for Popular Use', The United Bible Societies, London.

Chapter 15

SOME REASONS DISPOSING YOUNG CHILDREN TO VALUE SPEAKING WELSH

Godfrey Harrison

MAINLY FINDINGS

The following points seem to summarize the better established results obtained in studies of children who have been bilingual from a very early age:

  (a) That by 20 months of age children continually addressed in more than one language are beginning to be aware that they are being presented with distinguishable systems of speech.
  (b) That by two-and-a-half years of age a child will, at least sometimes, translate.
  (c) That in their third year these children can name the languages they have and talk about them and about which one to use in given situations.
  (d) That the fluency (given comparable input to that heard by a monolingual child) in both languages of a bilingual child differs little from the fluency of a child of the same age who speaks only one of them.
  (e) That interference between languages is not great and specific examples fairly soon disappear - this holds at all levels of language, from phonetic points to those of social codes.

We may add in relation to (e) that if the two languages which a child has are culturally in contact they will, even in the speech of monolinguals, be likely to show interference. Thus in Wales Welsh-born native speakers of English will use such utterances as 'There's lovely', 'Oh! He's twp', and 'iss' (to rhyme with 'hiss') rather than 'iz' in saying 'is'. The five points are supported by studies of children having a range of bilingualisms from the earliest times that they were lingual at all, e.g. German/English (Leopold, 1939-49), French/German (Ronjat, 1913), French/English (Swain, 1972), Russian/Georgian (Imedadze, 1960) and Garo/English (Burlings, 1959). There is no reason to suppose they do not hold for Welsh/English - rather there are a variety of people in Wales who demonstrate that they do. However, as a number of children who might be expected to demonstrate an early and typical fluency in Welsh and English do not, in fact, there is some interest in considering what may influence children's emergence as fluent bilinguals or hinder that process.

   For the present it has to be accepted that quite certainly in the

more populous parts of Wales the vast majority of adults who speak
Welsh will be bilingual and almost exclusively, if they are simply
bilingual, their other language will be English. (For those who ever
have the chance to see such a person acting as interpreter for the
occasional Spanish/Welsh bilingual from Patagonia it would be of
great interest to discover if the valuation of Welsh increased in
the commoner bilingual speaker!) For children the situation is
somewhat different because Welsh-speaking parents in Wales who
intend that their children shall speak Welsh consistently use that
language with them. The strength of such an approach is apparent
when we note that indeed children born in Coventry, Liverpool and
Derby are among those who are both bilingual and happy to use Welsh.
It is then quite normal for us to find three year olds, even in
Cardiff, who speak Welsh and nothing else, and to find Welsh-speaking
parents whose children acquire English very early but who know that
Welsh is the language of the hearth even though they live in England.

   Bilingualism of itself is not the difficulty that leads a child
to drop one language of two. If it were simply a cognitive problem
we would expect at least approximately equal numbers of children who
had shown the early stage of bilingual speech to lose each of the
two languages they were mastering. Instead the dominant, and - very
often - conquering language, has been English, and Welsh has dwindled,
both in individual children and in the country. That there is no
necessity for this appears empirically in one of the results noted
by Jones and Piette (1975) in their researches into Concept and
Language Development which are supported by the Welsh Office of
Education. In their studies of children aged between three and seven
they have sought always to carry out, for example, concept tests in
their subjects' preferred language. On sixteen occasions it has
happened that the preferred language was the child's second language.
In fifteen of these instances this preferred *and* second language was
Welsh, in the remaining instance it was, of course, English. This
distribution would occur by chance once in a thousand times. Given
the linguistic history of Wales over the last century to make a comparison against chance expectation, when considering a result concerning children opting to speak Welsh, is to understate how little it
was to be looked for in terms of the whole population.

   The characteristics of the whole population manifest themselves
most interestingly in families where one parent is bilingual Welsh/
English speaking and the other is monolingual English. Dr Ceinwen
Thomas and the author had the support of the Social Science Research
Council in looking at the language development of three children who
were born into just such families. In particular they have bilingual
mothers. Recordings were made of these children in their homes and
usually at intervals of two or three weeks. The recordings were
subsequently transcribed (by Eleri Morris who was present at all of
them) and by now we have done some analysis of the children's
language development.

   A bilingual person who shows no signs at all of dominance from
either language will not have any difficulty in matching the language
used by another person speaking one of the two known languages. We
used this characteristic to get a measure of how bilingual our
subjects were.

   On some recordings it was possible to be confident that the child

was speaking in response to utterances in particular languages. On
such occasions we counted the number of matches (English/English or
Welsh/Welsh) and mismatches (English/Welsh or Welsh/English) and
found the percentage of matching. Graphs a, b, and c of Figure 15.1
present the percentage matching for each of the three children
plotted against age in months (lived through).

The measures plotted in Figure 15.1 are global and the data
presented there are limited to sessions in which it was possible to
classify 25 or more of the subject's responses as being to a specific
utterance. As a result Figure 15.1 indicates the matching performance of subjects on only 69 (or some 58 per cent) of the 118 recordings which we made of them. Fortunately this sample is well spread
out across the full recording period of 2½ years for all three
children. What very clearly emerges is that Eirian consistently
matches. The other two subjects match progressively less often as
they get older. The nature of their deficit is seen in graphs d and
f, which show the percentage of Welsh utterances taken into account
when calculating the data of graphs a and c.

Ceri and Lyn use less Welsh in later recordings: the association
between their percentage matching and their use of Welsh is statistically significant (being +0.509, which is beyond the 5 per cent
level of significance, for Lyn, and +0.896, which is beyond the 1 per
cent level for Ceri - by contrast the value for Eirian is -0.099).
Before turning to less global consideration of the data on how
bilingual our subjects were it is apt to summarise the implication
of Figure 15.1 for parents who wish their children to be balanced in
any productive bilingual ability: if the father, say, is monolingual
then the mother had best use the language that he lacks whenever it
is a feasible choice.

We have indicated that when Ceri or Lyn were not matching this
was usually because they resorted to English. Their family circumstances probably influenced their shift. Ceri's father had a long
spell off work because of an illness which kept him at home. Lyn's
mother had a second child when her first was 26 months old and
thereafter Lyn's Welsh utterance dropped significantly (p is less
than 0.02, 2-tailed). In recordings made around about that time the
mother uses more English and quite a lot of sentences with a Welsh
structure but English content words. By contrast with the other two
main subjects some of Eirian's least successful sessions from the
point of view of matching were ones in which she would not shift
from Welsh. This was true in those sessions where her mother, or
her mother and her brother, were using English with her, and her
father was not present. In such endeavours her brother was a less
than enthusiastic accomplice in the mother's attempts to lead his
sister to use English when in one sense it was pointless.

The points on graphs b and e of Figure 15.1 for the last months
of our recordings of Eirian make it quite apparent that by then
she both matched and used Welsh, or not, in a thoroughly flexible
way. In our last recording of Eirian when 4 years 1 month we
counted 242 matching responses to the mother with 111 of them being
in Welsh and 131 in English. This flexibility was realised during
the third year.

As things are presented in Figure 15.1 the prospect for there
being many bilingual children in homes where one parent is bilingual

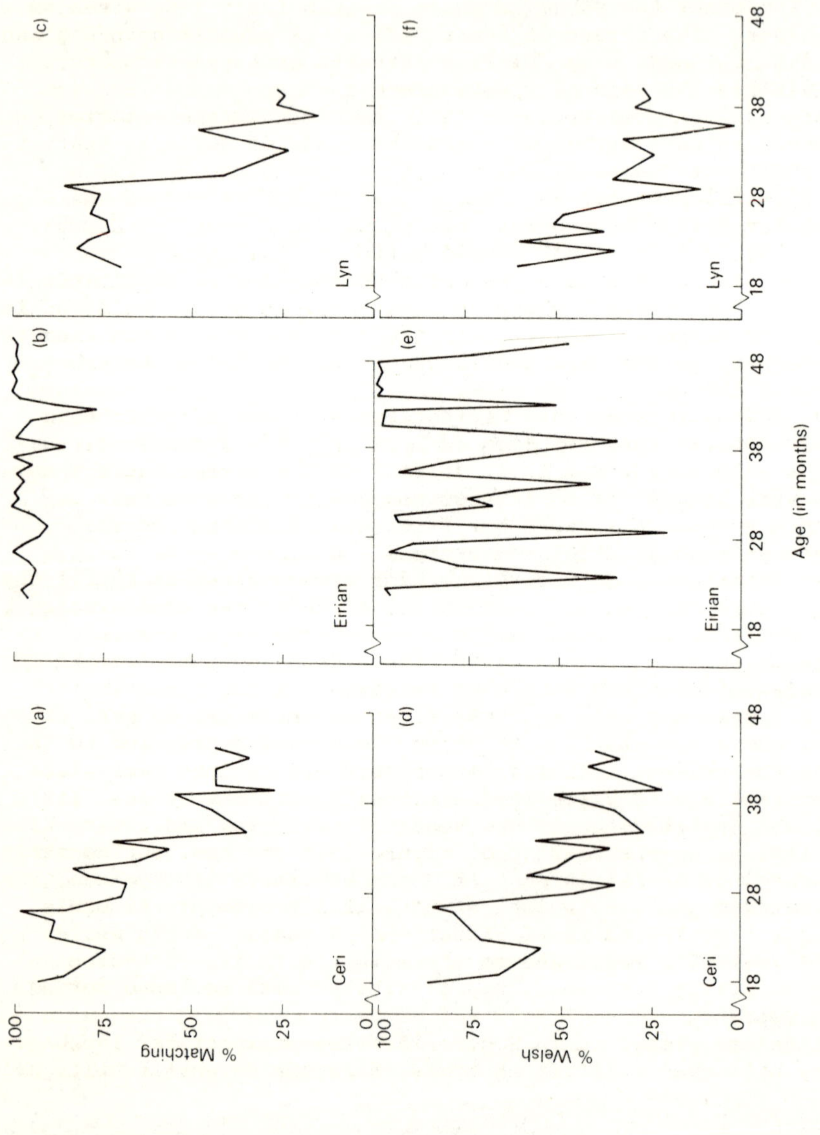

FIGURE 15.1

looks less than good. Two points in fact alter the impact of the
data of those graphs. The first centres on Lyn. In the year since
we stopped making recordings of her several things have happened.
She has got used to the idea of attending Ysgol Feithrin. Her
mother spends a morning a week in such a school helping to run it.
Her father has shown that he can manage a few words of Welsh himself.
It might be rash to claim that those things are causal. On the
other hand there is not much doubt now that Lyn not only understands
Welsh but also speaks it. The second point concerns five children
whom we recorded just once or twice but who came from homes where
only one parent was bilingual Welsh/English. They ranged in age
from 2 years and 2 months to 4 years and 10 months and every one of
those five was fluently bilingual, even the youngest, whose mastery
of his two languages had to be acknowledged as exceptional for his
age. As it happens a pair of brothers in that further five subjects
spoke French as well. These brothers had a bilingual French/English
mother and a bilingual Welsh/English father. Each parent spoke
their native language to their children and their common language
to each other, a practice in which they had been consistent from
their children's earliest days.

MAINLY ABOUT FINDINGS

The weakness of what has been presented up till now in this paper is
that it throws some light on the circumstances in which children are
more likely to speak Welsh without suggesting why they would wish to.
It is now easier to escape behaviourist or positivist injunctions
than it was a decade ago. Further, the number of people concerned
to have Welsh-speaking children is apparently increasing although
the number of Welsh speakers does not yet show the same trend.
Accordingly speculation may be in order. In these speculations about
findings which are on the topic of the paper it helps to draw on
other findings about the development of children, about their
acquisition of language, and about choice of language.(2)
    In their first year or so children are pragmatists par excellence.
They have little concern with semantics of syntax but their interest
in the relation between signs and their users is considerable.
Perhaps in their first few weeks even the notion of a sign might be
aside: there is very little that is arbitrary in the screaming or
cries of a young baby when that vocalisation falls on the ears of a
parent. Mothers especially have difficulty in not attending to the
noise. In the ensuing months a lot of differentiations take place
and we may sensibly talk about pre-linguistic communication. It is
this period that brings a child, through initiatives and interactions
that are typical both of children and those about them, to the stage
where there is something to be said. Happily there will be adequate,
if far from adult, means to say it and at least some of the basic
logical relationships of language will be available to the child.
There will even be a few features of the child's first language
around at this time. At least enough of them will be there for a
parent, usually the one who does the mothering, to help the child to
set about constructing, through successive approximations, language.
    At this time the child will not have a notion of what it will be

to have achieved that construction. The edge of speech will not be
entirely distinct from some other vocalisations. When utterances
are definitely speech they need not be, as far as the child is concerned, clearly apart from objects or people. There is no need to
separate that object, which happens to be a kind of fruit, from its
name or from its colour. Should it happen to seem involved with two
names or two colours: well everybody knows that the red and green
apple over there is a Jonathan - even if that happens to be the name
of the child eating it! It is because of the toddler's curiously
ill-defined categorisations that to be faced with two languages is
hardly different from being faced with one. Over periods of a few
seconds bilingual adults generally do not chop and change between
languages. Over much longer periods of time they tend to be reasonably consistent about the circumstances in which they use one language. Toddlers give good indications of living very much in the
present even though they develop skills, habits, and relationships
over much longer periods. If young children and adults are rather
alike in the way their actions occur within a framework of possibilities established over relatively long periods they differ in how
troubled they are by making errors. To put that another way:
children do not know what to expect because compared with adults,
they neither know well what it is to expect, nor what is expectable.
The first efforts they make to systematise the world are distant
from the ones they will eventually settle for and often they will
work not by accretion but by huge divisions: e.g. 'Me versus not
me', rather than 'nails, knuckles, fingers: HANDS'. Such crude
divisions are very apt when it comes to separating talking in one
language from talking in another. They help us to see why the
recurrent adage for having a bilingual child has been 'One parent:
one language'. Eirian shows very well that other regimes will work
well enough. For her, clarity seemed to be 'One way of talking
when Daddy is here, the other way when just Mummy is'. This rubric
at least agrees with the occasion when her mother, hoping to help
with the recording and in the absence of her husband, tried to get
Eirian to talk with just her in English. At 2 years and 6 months
Eirian only produced English in such a situation in answer to
questions like: 'Mae Mam yn dweud "Ci", beth mae Dadi yn dweud?'
To which Eirian very quietly said 'Dog'. In a similar way the two
trilingual subjects seem to have made a very simple rule about the
way to speak to adults: 'Males use Welsh, females French'. This
rubric goes along with the elder brother selecting Welsh when his
brother was born and he was 2 years and 6 months old. It also
covers that younger brother declaring 'Golau', while pointing
aptly, the first time he saw the author and before hearing him
speak. When they are more practised children with more than one
language make their language choices in more flexible ways. There
are hints that it is practice rather than just age that matters: we
may cite a 7-year-old girl whose first language is English and who
had heard a frequent visitor to her home speak to her mother, a
monolingual, in English during all her visits. The child attends a
Welsh-medium school and after two years has made sufficient progress
to ask the visitor during a conversation in Welsh 'Wyt ti'n gallu
siarad yn Saesneg?' without any suggestion that this was other than
a question to elicit information. This child, too, appears to

employ divisions in her ideas of language use that serve to impose system more than subsume all she knows.

   This kind of distinction between articulate knowledge about language use and access to the way language is used is recurrent in children who are dealing socially with people who speak in two ways. Shipley and Shipley (1969) studied the use of second person singular pronoun forms by the children of Quaker parents in 16 families in Pennsylvania. They found that very few of the children use T-forms such as 'thee' and 'thy' but that in the four families where T-forms were commonly and consistently used by children their parents employed T-forms in a number of different relationships beside parent/child and spouse/spouse. The Shipleys suggest that as young children can neither be parents nor spouses they need to be presented with examples which they can include in their own set of possible choices. For example, that T-forms can be used with friends. One child they studied was a 4-year-old boy who denied that his father used T-forms although the father consistently did so. On two separate occasions after that denial the boy made amazed comments on hearing his father use T-forms to the boy's grandfather.

   Language use inheres in social relationships. Coercion may drive it out of some relationships where it could have been used. The Welsh Not and prohibitions on telling dirty jokes to grandma demonstrate that well enough. Mere request will not avail in introducing a way of talking into a relationship and even bribery will not long sustain change: for many people in the Republic of Ireland Gaelic is worth the bounty for passing an examination in that 'subject', and that is all. Equally no schoolchild in an English grammar school unselfconsciously offered a language teacher a demonstration of his competence in say, French, when they happened to meet in a shop. In Paraguay 48 per cent of the population is reported by Rubin (1968) to be bilingual (Spanish/Guarani) and in the capital of Asuncion the figure rises to 90 per cent. Language choice is determined almost exclusively by the relationship between speakers: people without two common languages being rare. This happens to such an extent that some couples first use Guarani on signing their marriage contract and, as it were, give linguistic ratification.

   There is one last point to make before trying to bring this paper to a conclusion. It harks back to the view of very young children as pragmatists who come toward speaking through their interactions with others often around them. Such people imbue a child with their culture because they manifest it. They provide a range of possibilities that the child may begin to assimilate not passively but in a way which is monitored, sustained, and lead by the company of others. We are talking about willing partners. Beyond any genetic roots that inform a child's pattern of attention, one reason for the appeal of communication for the child is that those other people afford levers on the world. Human young are notably incapable when born. They need to be able to influence others who are near, mobile, less ignorant and far stronger. It is in their dependency that babies establish relationships which need to be close or their chance of survival will be less. In the closeness of such relationships with their pragmatic and instrumental aspects we can see why a first language is valued by a child and this holds even if they have 'Bilingualism as a first language', to quote the title of Merrill Swain's thesis.

From these points about the development of young children and about language choice it seems possible to adduce some generalities about why children will value speaking a language. These generalities should hold when the children know two languages and for any, e.g. Welsh. (It is not that children in Wales are very different from those anywhere else, rather their circumstances have peculiarities.) Children apparently value languages:

(a) that help them to influence the world they live in and the more the influence the more the value;
(b) that enable them to initiate, maintain, and pursue valued relationships;
(c) whose occasions for use are clearly discernible;
(d) and whose value to others is apparent from the child's continuing experience of their choice.

If these attempts at generalities hold implications that would seem but reasonable: for both children and language are important in any society.

NOTES

1 Some of the findings presented here were obtained with the help of SSRC Grant HR 2014/2 made to the author and Dr C. H. Thomas whose generous help is also gladly acknowledged.
2 For an extension of these themes see Newson and Newson (1975).

REFERENCES

BURLING, R. (1959), Language development of a Garo and English-speaking child, 'Word', 15, 45-68.
IMEDADZE, N. (1960), On the psychological nature of early bilingualism, 'Voprosy Psikhol', 1, 60-8 (in Russian).
JONES, R. and PIETTE, A. (1975), Report to the second meeting of the Consultative Committee of the Welsh Education Office Project on 'Concept and Language Development', June.
LEOPOLD, W. (1939-49), 'Speech Development of a Bilingual Child, A linguist's record', vols 1-4, Evanston, Illinois, North Western University Press.
NEWSON, J. and NEWSON, E. (1975), Intersubjectivity and the transmission of culture: On the social origins of symbolic functioning, 'Bulletin of the British Psychological Society', 28, 437-46.
RUBIN, J. (1968), Bilingual usage in Paraguay, in J. Fishman (ed.), 'Readings in the Sociology of Language', vol.II, The Hague, Mouton, pp.512-30.
RONJAT, J. (1913), 'Le dévelopment du language observé chez un enfant bilingué', Paris, Libraire Ancienne Champion.
SHIPLEY, E.F. and SHIPLEY, T.E., Jr (1969), Quaker children's use of thee: A relational analysis, 'Journal of Verbal Learning and Verbal Behavior', 8, 112-17.
SWAIN, M.K. (1972), 'Bilingualism as a First Language', PhD thesis, University of California, Irvine (University Microfilms reference number 72-21, 382).

Chapter 16

LINGUISTIC CONFLICT IN WALES: A PROBLEM IN THE DESIGN OF GOVERNMENT

Peter Madgwick

1 INTRODUCTION

The theme of this paper may be illustrated in the following passage:
  The pattern of religious and ethnic cleavages has not so far
  provoked a major catastrophe. The people of Wales have not been
  through the agonies of a Bangladesh, a Biafra, or a Cyprus. They
  are not trapped in the situation of a Northern Ireland, though
  there were occasions ... when such a turn of events seemed
  entirely possible. They have not fought a Boer War. But neither
  have they profited intellectually and politically from the less
  intense ethnic and religious tensions that have been a constant
  of their history. It may well be that the absence of more acute
  phases of tension has diminished the capacity of the political
  system to respond creatively to the problems of cultural diversity. In a sense Welshmen have occupied the rather colourless
  middle ground between rational problem-solving and ultimate
  disaster. It would be unreasonable to assume that so precarious
  a balance can be maintained indefinitely. (McRae, 1974:261)
  This passage was in fact written about Canada, but its transpos-
ition to Wales, if over-emphatic, is by no means absurd. The present
situation of the Welsh language, together with some other elements
of cultural difference, give Wales a peculiar source of tension and
conflict. The existing political institutions of Wales may not be
well-adapted to the management of this conflict. Current proposals
for an elected assembly in Wales give opportunity for the consideration of the institutions and procedures appropriate to the peculiar
problems of linguistic politics in Wales.

2 LINGUISTIC CONFLICT IN WALES

The present situation of the Welsh language is in outline fairly
clear. At the beginning of the nineteenth century, and perhaps well
into it, almost the whole indigenous population of Wales spoke Welsh
and a few also spoke English. By 1901 only 50 per cent spoke Welsh,
according to the census, and the number of monoglot Welsh speakers
had contracted sharply. Since 1931 there has been a steady decline

227

in the proportion of Welsh speakers in Wales, from 37 per cent in
1931 to 26 per cent in 1961, and 21 per cent in 1971. The monoglot
Welsh speaker has virtually disappeared.

The decline of the language has been uneven, and the rural areas
of the west and north west remain a stronghold of Welsh-speaking
Wales. In 1971 five of the old counties of this area all had proportions above 60 per cent of Welsh speakers; but no other county had
above 30 per cent. The causes of this transformation are to do with
economic development and movement of population, government policy
and, partly a consequence of these, popular indifference. More
recently there has been some revival of popular good will towards
the language, more specific political activity directed towards its
restoration and some government measures of maintenance and support.
Even so, the outlook of a minority language living alongside a
powerful neighbour is far from bright.

These points require substantiation and no doubt some modification; but the argument need not be elaborated here. Enough has been
said to demonstrate that the language situation in Wales is likely
to cause tension. The Welsh language is poised precariously on the
threshold of extinction, but with enough forces working for it to
make the struggle for preservation or revival seem worthwhile. As
despair gives way to hope and rising expectation, political pressures
are generated.

The resulting tensions might be easily accommodated if language
were marginal, or merely instrumental. But it is intimately bound
up with traditions, claims, states of mind, interests and pressures
which make it a powerful source of political conflict. The Gittins
Report struggled to make a case for teaching the language for the
sake of communication and culture, but gave up and conceded that the
values of the language are ultimately rooted in national values.(1)
Linguistic differences are akin to ethnic differences; they relate
to the sense of identity, to differentiation from other people,
hence to personal relations with others (Madgwick et al., 1973;
Connor, 1972:314-55; Enloe, 1973). The sense of difference may be
strong in itself, and may easily come to explain, symbolise and
reinforce tension and hostility arising from other aspects of social
relationship (religion, class, politics). Giles and Bourhis (1974)
have shown experimentally how Welsh speaking and even a Welsh accent
may serve as a badge of ethnic identity, and trigger related stereo-
types and fellings of hostility on both sides of the barrier.
'Language', writes a recent sympathetic commentator, 'has become the
plaything of an intolerant society in a disastrous game of pseudo-
issues of language and of overcharging of language alternatives with
a new and imperfectly understood symbolic content' (Evans, 1972).

Language is bound up with historical and national myth. It does
not require much, or indeed any, imagination to perceive English
exploitation and imperialism in the history of Wales and the Welsh
language since 1536. All that is in question is the degree of delib-
eration, purpose and malevolence to be read into that history, and
the extent to which it should be regarded as present and alive in
modern Wales. It may be thought unreasonable, but it can hardly be
judged irrational, for the promoters of the language to believe that
Welsh is the proper language of all people living in Wales. This
notion of the 'historic loss of language' makes for understandable

resistance to compromise solutions of language issues. The bilingualism on the Canadian pattern would be unacceptable, and what might be regarded as major concessions by monoglot English speakers, Welsh-born or immigrant, fall far short of the minimal demands of linguistic enthusiasts.

The historical myth of imperialist English has been brought up to date by new images of English cultural decay and social decline. One of the most common phrases heard in pleas for the language is 'the need for roots', along with the denunciation of the 'tastes and needs of middle-class England', the horrors of the 'concrete jungle', and the depravity of a 'mid-Atlantic norm' (Betts, 1976; Thomas, 1971:14-15; Stephens, 1973:213). A good deal of this kind of writing is lacking in precision, short of supporting evidence, and not without some absurdities. But the general tendency of the argument is not difficult to sustain for some of the way. This is hardly a golden age in the social and cultural history of England, and the only doubt (though central to the argument) is whether terms such as 'golden age' are really appropriate for serious analysis. Still, if some of the denunciation of contemporary English culture is ill-founded, far-fetched and decidedly sour, again none of it is irrational; and all of it has relevance where culture is accorded unusually high priority.

Of course the views referred to are those of writers and preachers, who, like political scientists, may inflate the significance of language problems. But such views cannot be dismissed as mere rhetoric on the literary margins of Welsh society. The claims, tensions and hostility expressed in the rhetoric cannot stop short of political conflict. There are good reasons for this. First the sentiments of the literati, however highflown, are not wanting for sympathy among Welsh people, particularly those nourished on the rhetoric of chapel and eisteddfod (for whom the literati are not all marginal) (Madgwick et al., 1973).

Second, the claims for language policy based on such a fundamental analysis of the Welsh situation are inevitably far-reaching, and apparently extreme. Saunders Lewis (no moderate of course) demanded a monoglot Welsh-speaking Wales, and valued that goal above self-government. The most recent advocate of the language, Clive Betts (with a good deal of comparative evidence on his side) has set out a substantial argument for the establishment of a Welsh-speaking heartland. Many others, including the old Glamorgan Education Committee, look to some ill-defined form of bilingualism in a relatively short time (the year 2000 is often chosen for obvious but linguistically invalid reasons). They are all in fact asking for massive shifts in language patterns within a single generation. Even the more modest of these proposals involve sharp changes in the interests of non-Welsh speakers to a degree which would be regarded as intolerable in economic matters (Simon, 1975:112-13). Yet compromise is inherently difficult, and the problems are not simply amenable to the spending of public money. It is unrealistic to believe, despite the affirmation of the Canadian Report on Bilingualism, that recognising the rights of a minority does not reduce those of the majority (Report of the Royal Commission, 1967). This is not to say that such changes are not highly desirable, but only that they are likely to meet resistance.

A third ground for accepting the inevitability of political conflict over the language lies in the nature of language movements, in
Wales as elsewhere. The leaders of language movements seem often to
be characterised by qualities of single-mindedness, devoutness, persistent and articulate anger, a certain ferocity even, and an
impressive readiness for self-sacrifice in the cause. The terms
'fanatic' and 'extremist' seem appropriate though perhaps unnecessarily pejorative. What is clear is that such people tend to ascribe
overwhelming priority to their chosen cause, and both their beliefs
and their actions make life uncomfortable for those who do not agree
with them. The Welsh language movement has had 'fanatical' leaders
of two types, devout religious and highly cultivated professional
people (often ministers of religion) and the young militant protes-
ters, also mainly college-educated. In the cause of the language
Welsh men and women (it is a cause which seems to have a special
attraction for women) have banished the English language from their
lives, deliberately and systematically offended their fellows, and
suffered the penalty of imprisonment. At its peak in 1971 over 100
members of the Welsh Language Society had spent some time in prison,
thus placing themselves among the great British prisoners of conscience in this century: the suffragists and the conscientious
objectors to military service. For such people concession and compromise soon pass the boundary of tolerance, and the non-negotiable
demand is not a tactic but a simple statement of moral principle
    Finally there is adequate evidence in the history of Wales since
the early 1960s of the occurrence of language conflict in many forms,
in Parliament, within the bureaucratic channels of central-local
relations, within local government, between parents and education
authorities, within public bodies like universities and between
language campaigners and public corporations, especially the BBC,
and some private businesses. Conflicts arise over education, broadcasting, the use of Welsh language in government and administration
and in commerce, the prescription of Welsh as a qualification for
jobs; and the use and position of Welsh on road signs, which are the
totem poles of a linguistic community, and highly vulnerable to
quick raids with a paint brush. The correspondence columns of the
'Cambrian News' (published in Aberystwyth) leap into life when someone writes to assert the virtues or the vices of the language, and
do not subside until the ritual accusations of 'extremist' and 'anti-
Welsh' have been sustained to the satisfaction of the accuser.
Language issues figure with fair frequency in the correspondence
columns of the 'Western Mail' (Cardiff). A 'phone-in' programme on
BBC Wales radio, which normally seems desperately short of communicants, had to be twice extended, to 85 minutes altogether, when it
dealt with language problems. Little of this is reflected in
Westminster-dominated party politics; but, viewed from within Wales,
language tensions are persistent and extensive, if sporadic and
uneven in intensity.
    All this is to suggest that mixed language situations run easily
to open conflict, even to violence and its contemporary obstructive
variants, usually described as non-violent.(2) The last decade may
well have been more violent than the next will be, for reasons which
are partly general and 'of the times', partly to do with Wales. But
the age of direct action has arrived, and it is no longer easy for

governments to neglect inconvenient and unusual problems. Conflict
over the language is likely to continue, and governments, both of
the UK and within Wales, must learn to deal with it, not as an
occasional nuisance but as a persisting challenge to democratic
values and good government.

3 THE GOVERNMENT OF THE LANGUAGE

If the argument so far is valid, then the language situation in
Wales requires the most skilled, perceptive and sensitive management.
In practice arrangements for the development and application of
language policy are comparatively unsystematic and diffuse. The
'arrangements' are, like much else in British government, mainly the
resultant of reactions to particular problems, and are marked by
uncertainty of objectives, privacy, the influence of selected groups
(elites), and occasional concessions to militancy. The system is
ill-designed to manage the inherent conflict in the situation, and
to develop a consistent, securely founded and widely accepted
language policy.
    It is possible to draw up a map or inventory of the government of
the language, but this could at present be no more than an outline.
Such a map would include:
  (a) The framework of law and precept, notably the Welsh Language
      Act of 1967, but also policy frameworks arising from the Gittins
      Report on Education and the Bowen Report on Road Signs.
  (b) The institutions of central Government, especially the Welsh
      Office which has a few mandatory powers (as over trunk roads)
      and some persuasive and exemplary influence.
  (c) The regional nominated advisory bodies, e.g. the Welsh Council,
      the Council for the Welsh Language (a device characteristic of
      contemporary Welsh Government).
  (d) Local governments and their associations.
  (e) Dominant groups, or elites. Many observers might argue that
      Wales has two powerful elites (Welsh and non-Welsh) but the
      evidence for this is (inevitably) difficult to assemble.
  (f) Language groups, e.g. Urdd, Adfer, some, like the Welsh Language
      Society, secretly following militant tactics.
  (g) The political parties, all of which have been a little hesitant
      in their commitment to the language.
    The major characteristics of these arrangements for the government
of the Welsh language are far from clear, and some essential detail
is lacking. The following propositions seem to be in line with
limited evidence and general impressions, but require further testing.
    (i) There is no openly avowed and clearly defined set of instit-
utions and procedures for the development of language policy and the
management of conflict. The arrangements are not fully a part of
public politics, but are rather partly private and 'under the
counter'. They tend to lack system, coherence and consistency.
    (ii) There is no consistent and avowed range of objectives, but
rather a melange of alternative aims, lying between the extremes of
Welsh and English unilingualism, and related to the imprecise and
partly self-deceptive use of the central term in the debate, 'bilingualism'.

(iii) There is no articulated agreement over the extent or limits of government power in language policy, nor a full understanding of the nature and limits of governmental power over language use.

(iv) The relationships of central and local governments are crucial but uneasy, and lacking in assurance and predictability.

(v) Policy outcomes derive more than in other fields from the pressures of elite and militant groups, modified by some concern for the limits of public tolerance.

(vi) Language disputes are targets for attention and agitation by the media, and policy-making is highly sensitive to media coverage.

(vii) The public debate is marked by passion and fervour, by a strong sense of self-righteousness (on both sides), and by the scope and sweep of its historical outlook. It is at once backward- and forward-looking to an unusual degree, and excessively so for the efficacy of immediate policy-making.

These comparatively unsystematic arrangements for the government of the language are, it has been suggested, hardly adequate to meet the political demands of a mixed-language situation. An alternative view is that they make up a flexible and pragmatic array of proced-ures, which is well-adapted to the management of the language and the avoidance of open and debilitating political conflict. This view assumes that depoliticisation of the problems exists and ought to be maintained; and offers procedures by which depoliticised management may be pursued. Depoliticisation here means removal from the major processes and institutions of government. The choice between the two views depends ultimately on tastes or values, and would be much assisted by further research in Wales. Comparative studies do, however, offer some illumination, and point towards the value of open and systematic dealing, bringing the language problem into the mainstream of public politics.

4   THE PERSPECTIVES OF CONSOCIATIONAL DEMOCRACY

The smaller countries of Western Europe are remarkable for their maintenance of what may roughly be called stable democracy in the face of formidable social and cultural cleavages. Theories of 'consociational democracy' have been developed to give an account and explanation of this historical phenomenon. The classical cases are Belgium, Switzerland and the Netherlands, with Scandinavia and Austria offering other examples. The theory is concerned with the political accommodation of cultural cleavages, rather than with specific arrangements for managing mixed-language situations.

It has been argued recently that the theory and the account on which it is based are relevant to the Canadian problem of cultural diversity:

The situation in 1972 [in Canada] is that legal and administrative accommodation of linguistic and cultural diversity is proceeding reasonably well, but accommodation of this diversity in the political process itself has lagged behind. (McRae, 1974:307, 1975:293)

The same writer has suggested elsewhere that 'accommodationist sol-utions are more civilised than forced integration, and that the inefficiencies of consociational politics are less costly than subcultural hostility and violence.' Wales lags behind Canada, markedly so in the sphere of political accommodation, and has something to learn from consociationalism, both the theory and the facts.

A starting point of consociational theory, by implication at least, is that 'majoritarian democracy' cannot deal satisfactorily with cultural cleavages, because it is inherently heavy-handed with minorities, neglecting them if they are quiescent, moved only to reluctant concession if they complain and protest. The neglect is not based on intolerance and contempt, though a lively and sensitive concern for minorities may well be lacking. Rather it is that the principles and procedures of the system do not easily provide for the accommodation of minorities. National sentiment is assumed to be strong, and the legitimacy of national institutions high. Society is not seen as deeply and persistently divided, still less fragmented. The processes of competitive representation, especially through political parties, are regarded as effective lines of com- munication and mechanisms of accommodation and incorporation for all sections of society. In Britain both the notion of alternating Governments ('the swing of the pendulum'), and of a civil service concerned for 'the public interest', encourage this view. Minorities are dealt with in the process of developing majority consent.

Now there is some truth in this account of 'majoritarian demo- cracy'. Substantial minorities may well be dealt with through the normal processes of the representative system. Some concern for portionality and for consensus modifies the sharper victories of the bare majority. Indeed the 'directionless consensus' ascribed as a characteristic to the British system implies a pursuit of consent beyond the bounds of effective government. In Britain, as in other West European democracies, parties may have become more inclusive, less ideological. Still, all this is open to argument. There is more certainly a strong tendency in majoritarian democracy, inherent in the system of party competition, to make the best electoral bargain, buying the largest fragments at the lowest price to secure the 'minimum winning coalition'. This does not encourage sensitivity to small groups, to regional or peripheral interests, or to complex cleavages which do not fit the predominant cleavage pattern of the party system. The drive of the political market is to win a majority in the soft central areas of political opinion, not on the outer fringes, where strange hard cultural attitudes persist. The assump- tion (rather than the avowed objective) is that minorities will eventually be knitted into the social fabric: they may not quite disappear, but they need not in the end be taken into separate political account.

The defects of majoritarian democracy show up more sharply once the minorities become politically aware and active.(3) This is the case in Canada, where the Federal Cabinet is no longer a sufficient instrument for dealing with cultural minorities; and it is plainly the case in Northern Ireland, where the Catholic minority is no longer willing to accept the penalties of permanent minority status. For Northern Ireland, the British Government has itself accepted the advantages of a power-sharing executive, although the Ulster Unionist majority has failed to co-operate in its establishment. Power-sharing has also been proposed for the new Welsh Assembly (though it cannot

in practice be established by legislation alone). For Britain as a
whole both coalition Government and a proportional electoral system
have recently gained academic as well as popular support and journ-
alistic interest. It is at last conceded, for a variety of reasons,
not all relevant to this paper, that majoritarian democracy may have
some defects to set beside its well-publicised virtues.

The concept of consociational democracy offers an alternative to
majoritarian democracy in culturally divided countries. It is at
once a descriptive and explanatory account and a normative prescription. To be fair, the consociational writers have stressed the
comparative more than the prescriptive aspects of the theory. It is
a theory of historical development, hence tied into a complex and
possibly unique array of political and social detail for each country
it deals with. Here, as elsewhere, this paper does not fully convey
the qualities of the consociational literature, its richness in
historical data and theoretical subtlety and enterprise. The concept has some links with the system-maintenance aspects of systems
theory, and with theories of integration, development and nation-
building mainly applicable to the Third World. But the source of
the theory and its major exemplars are the smaller European democracies.

Consociational democracy refers to a social condition, political
processes and political culture. The condition is cultural segmentation, in which cleavages are sharply and consciously defined, and
there is a minimum of interaction between groups. Stable and democratic government is then achieved by a process of agreement among
elites, or through the force of a consensual culture favourable to
accommodation (or both). The segments have been pictured as pillars
which come together for mutual support in arches; the overarching of
the pillars is the process of elite accommodation. Alternatively,
the segments are fenced-off solitudes: 'good fences make good
neighbours', or in the jargon, 'low transactions make for high
integration'. The political device appropriate to this social base
is the stable or rather stabilised coalition, through which the
interests and integrity of the segments are safeguarded. The coalition is stable because it is deliberately maintained and safeguarded from temporary shifts arising from even subdued party
competition.

The theory thus briefly summarised is novel in this particular
form, but has close connections with notions of proportionality, of
contract or concordance, and of concurrent majorities. These all
have a long history in Western politics. The special value of
consociational theory lies in its empirical foundations. It attempts
to analyse what actually happens, the processes of securing consent,
legitimacy, stability in conditions of cultural cleavage. Hence the
prime test of the theory related to the persuasiveness of its account
of the politics it claims to explain. A second and more searching
test is its power to explain, or contribute to the analysis of,
other countries with cultural cleavages. McRae (1975:290-2) has
applied the consociational analysis to Canada with some success.
Wales is a less promising subject, but the consociational perspective
throws some light on the politics of the Welsh cultural cleavage -
both what is and what might be.

There are of course difficulties in applying the analysis, some uncertainties about the theory, and about the kind of evidence required to sustain it; and even if the questions are correct, the answers for Wales are based on impression rather than hard evidence.

(i) Does Wales have the segmentation characteristic of the consociational model? (McRae, 1975:278). This implies clearly defined and observed boundaries between the sections of society; the organisation of social and cultural life (schools, media, trade unions) in separate frameworks with minimal interaction. Wales clearly falls short of the clear cut segmentation to be found in Belgium and the Netherlands. Cultural life, education and the media show some strong tendencies to segmentation; industrial and commercial activity and political life rather less. Historically, the cultural cleavage has largely coincided with religious, economic and ethnic cleavages. But economic change and secularisation have blurred the lines, and it is the recent attempts to sustain the language which have renewed more formally but perhaps less deeply the old distinctions. It may be that Wales has moved along the path of cultural cleavages from diversity towards segmentation, without approaching the formal separation found in the classic consociational countries.

This change may be deplored as a decline in the quality of life, but in consociational theory it is a move away from conflict. The organisation of 'solitudes' with clear and well-maintained boundaries is regarded as conducive to peace, in the short term at least, while the apparently more liberal pattern of an interacting and competitive admixture of groups leads to conflict.

Thus empirical questions lead on to theoretical problems. There is, in fact, a confusion of theories here. The theory of cross-cutting cleavages (a theory which itself cross-cuts the consociational) teaches that the existence of groups with several assymetrical, non-cumulative patterns of conflict much diminishes the potential for actual conflict.(4) If both cross-cutting and consociational theories are valid, then the dangerous ground, leading to instability and conflict, is the middle ground in which a complexity of cleavages is shifting towards, but has not reached, a sharp segmentation. This seems plausible, if over-subtle and beyond the possibilities of verification. In the end the relationship of segmentation to conflict is not a simple function of patterns of social division but depends on the kind of inter-action going on between the leaders of the segments: so further investigation is necessary.

(ii) To what extent do elites in Wales interact and co-operate to secure accommodation and stabilisation? At first sight the question hardly seems to apply in Wales, at least as far as present information goes. But the question is not irrelevant even though Wales does not conform to the sharp patterns of the consociational countries. It is probable that elites play some part in the semi-private system for the government of the language. A Welsh-speaking elite is more easily discerned than a non-Welsh counter-elite, perhaps because it is smaller and more cohesive; but all analysis of Welsh politics in terms of elites may exaggerate the solidarity, coherence and activity of such rather shadowy groups. It may be that the removal of the language from open politics is encouraged by the tacit agreement of the elites. This fits a significant element in the theory, its emphasis on the role of elites in achieving accommodation, which

would otherwise be upset by mass participatory politics.   Thus
Steiner found that Swiss experience confirmed two hypotheses
(Steiner, 1974).   'In a political system with strong sub-cultural
segmentation, a low level of inter sub-cultural hostility is probable
... the more frequent the interactions of the elite among the sub-
cultures; [and] the lower the political participation at the mass
level.' These hypotheses stand as empirical description and normative prescription; a system of elite accommodation and restricted
mass participation is to be preferred if stable democracy is the
objective.
    The prescription is not without some uncertainties. Elite agree-
ment to accommodate is plainly stabilising (if it works). But it
may also amount to a conspiracy to diminish participation, competition and hence representation. Thus Pulzer sees consociationalism
at least in its Austrian form as a conspiracy against the public
interest, 'a conspiratorial device arising out of the assumption by
the leaders of the main opinion groups that their followers cannot
be trusted to compete freely for power in the state. Its defects
are a diffusion of responsibility and a lack of external controls
on decision-making.'(5) Moreover the need for such a device may
well be overrated; Pulzer points out that the Austrian coalition
fell apart in 1970-1 without bringing down the system itself.
    Thus for Wales there is an empirical question about the inter-
action and co-operation of elites, and for the theory itself a more
disturbing puzzle about the advantages of the consociational solution: ought elites to behave in this way? On the one hand it may
permit a form of moderate representation in conditions which make
direct and competitive representation unsuitable (unfair or unstable);
on the other, it may sustain the power of irresponsible elites.
The consociational process may be political or apolitical, and the
difference may be a matter of fact or of evaluation of the facts.
It is assumed here that the withdrawal of major issues from politics
(depoliticisation) does not in the long term conduce to democratic
government.   Such depoliticisation is not an essential part of the
consociational prescription, but it might be an unintended consequence.(6)
    (iii) Does the political culture of Wales predispose towards
accommodation of the cultural cleavage? This third condition of
consociational democracy is alternative or additional to the role of
the elites. It requires a firmer statement about political culture
than is perhaps ever possible, especially in a country with cultural
cleavages. It is not at all clear how far there is a Welsh political
culture (one or several) and how this might relate to the British
culture. The latter is no doubt powerful in Wales, and brings with
it the integrating and stabilising forces of British nationalism,
national experience (especially war), and symbols (the monarchy,
Parliament, Downing Street). But it also brings the majoritarian and
centralist outlook which is insensitive to cultural cleavages and the
unassimilable minority.
    Welsh political culture is more enigmatic, and certainly more
fragmented. Perhaps there is a tendency to elite dominance and
single-party rule. In the non-partisan forms of rural local government this might fit the pattern of consociational democracy; in its
one-party form this is rather less certain. But Welsh political

culture is itself shot through with Welsh cultural and national
values and is thus inherently conducive to antagonism, anger and
conflict, especially when there is no external threat. Altogether
the consideration of the political culture of Wales in the light of
consociational theory does not encourage the view that Welsh
linguistic problems will find solutions naturally through the bene-
ficent influence of a peaceable political culture.

There are some obvious general weaknesses in the theory of consociational democracy. This is not surprising in a theory which
has been derived from detailed case studies, and so from the
beginning confused by the irreducible facts. Like most historical
theories the consociational analysis tends to endow transient
episodes with permanence; in this case episodes of comparative calm
in more enduring histories of conflict. It is significant, and
damaging to the theory, that all of the classical examples of consociational accommodation have recently suffered conflict and the
threat of breakdown. Thus the theory may over-value the efficacy of
the accommodative procedures for restraint, and much underrate the
potency for conflict of cultural cleavage.

If events throw doubt on the predictive power of the theory,
empirical verification is to say the least difficult. Partly this
is due to the ambivalence of the terms and the shadowy nature of the
social conditions and political processes to which they refer.
Terms central to the argument, cleavage, culture, elite, mass,
agreement, accommodation are all difficult to use with any precision
in comparative analysis. Crucial processes are neglected; for
example, in what conditions do some cleavages lead to conflict,
others not? How far is the process of accommodation affected by
particular political actors? Herein lies the familiar criticism of
social interpretations of politics, the apparent diminution of the
role of politicians compared with social forces.

Further the theory tends to overrate the desirability of consociational solutions. Pulzer points to the political irresponsib-
ility of the elites engaged in accommodation. The agreement to
accommodate limits the articulation of dissent and the emergence of
new patterns of disagreement and conflict. It preserves the power
of the parties to the agreement. It is stabilising but also immobilising. The institutionalisation of old discontents rules out
the development of new sensitivities. Innovation is not characteristic of the consociational solution. The problem for those who
would deliberately seek that solution is whether there is not a cost
in the vigour and texture of democracy.

Even so the analysis of the consociational democracies may be
instructive since they exemplify a fair if not total measure of
success in the management of cultural conflict and the maintenance
of a degree of stability. Moreover, if the consociational theory
cannot be wholly sustained, its negative implications for democracy
remain. How else, it may be asked, is a polity to develop a respon-
siveness to diverse interests and currents of opinion? Sensitivity
to new discontents, a capacity for innovation are after all not
markedly present in other forms of democracy.

Within limits then, the following 'lessons' for Wales might be
drawn from the study of consociational democracy.

(a) In the comparative perspective of the consociational

democracies Wales seems ill-prepared to cope with cultural conflict.
In particular the language issue in Wales is not recognised and
dealt with as a potential source of conflict. In the consociational
democracies, by contrast, accommodation is deliberately sought
through the political process, but without fully opening the issue
to mass participatory and competitive politics.

(b) Without some form of power-sharing or 'partnership' an
excluded minority is unlikely to have its interests sensitively
dealt with, and may reasonably lack confidence in consistent fair
dealing. Insecurity may lead to tension, anger and violence.

The British electoral and party systems have not in the past
encouraged power-sharing, and it would not be universally accepted
that this has seriously damaged British democracy. Arguably, the
pursuit of a majority of votes has offered some incentive to make
concessions on the middle ground of politics, and the major political parties have accepted an aggregative or compromising function.
This still leaves peripheral and small minorities outside the area
of conciliation or aggregation, and excluded from the package deals
which underlie the apparently ideological programmes. The lesson to
be drawn from the consociational countries is that the pursuit of a
bare majority does not in itself lead to a sensitive concern for
minorities.

Power-sharing has operated in non-partisan (mainly rural) local
government. Its record in some parts of Wales might support the
proposition at least in a negative form that non-partisan government
is likely to be more amenable to the concilation of minorities.
Since parties and party-systems cannot easily be changed by direct
government action, the implication is that electoral systems might
be changed towards a more proportional representation. This would
increase the representation of minorities and encourage the formation
of coalitions (or of majority Governments concerned for the minority
rather than the 'mandate'). The case against proportional representation is well-rehearsed. In the present context any change of
that kind involves a clear risk of the excessive politicisation of
small groups, an intensification of some kinds of conflict and a
fragmentation of the body politic. But a formal coalition is not a
necessary consequence of proportional representation, or of consociationalism.

(c) The attitudes and actions of elites, that is dominant groups,
are more significant for politics than those of the masses. National
integration may be securely founded on a bilingual elite, with a
unilingual mass. Whether or not the elite is bilingual, accommodation of the linguistic cleavage is still possible by agreement
between elites. On the other hand mass participatory democracy is
likely to agitate and irritate without leading to enduring solutions.
Similar dangers may arise from the arrival of new elites, who are
neither party to old agreements nor socialised into accommodationist
politics.

The political morality and efficacy of elite accommodation is open
to question. Much depends on the nature of the groups and of the
process. While Pulzer sees it as a conspiracy against the people,
withdrawing the cleavage from open and competitive politics, other
writers accept the legitimacy of elites and the value for the people
of understandings between them. The Pulzer interpretation amounts

to an anti-democratic manoeuvre, and this is certainly not intended
to be the characteristic virtue of the consociational solution.

(d) The separation and internal cohesion of the sub-cultures is
central to the consociational thesis. Strictly they are not sub-
cultures but cultures. The separateness is at once and paradoxically the source of conflict and the basis for accommodation.
However, this prescription hardly fits the social condition of
Wales, where segmentation is less marked. But the blurring of
cultural distinctions need not weaken, and may indeed assist, the
process of accommodation, provided that the existence of the two
cultures is recognised. In effect, leaders must play two roles,
wear two hats.

(e) For the specific problems of language management, two
linguistic 'solitudes' are conducive to the maintenance of the
weaker language, and to peaceable, because minimal, relations
between the language groups. The mixing of the languages damages
the weaker language and inflames social relations. This proposition indicates the value of territorial arrangements for mixed
language situations.

(f) Two other conditions favourable to the development of consociational democracy may not be met in Wales. The first is an external
threat, which motivates internal warring groups to settle their
differences. In the past external threats to Britain have encouraged British national integration in Wales. Now that these threats,
and the wars and military service that went with them, have receded,
the tendency towards British integration has weakened, without
encouraging the integration of Wales. Conceivably a semi-autonomous
Wales might perceive the London Government as an external threat.

The second condition, a low total load on the political system,
is even less likely to be met, given the salience of economic
problems, whether in the UK or for a semi-autonomous Wales.

(g) Generally a review of the literature on the consociational
democracies reveals by contrast the absence of extensive hard information about political aspects of the language situation in Wales.

6 THE POLITICISATION OF THE LANGUAGE ISSUE

Comparative study does not, on the whole, favour the continued
depoliticisation of the language issue. In this context politicisation means the inclusion of the issue in the central political
process, the incorporation of the forces involved in the structures
and institutions making up the political system. In a broader sense
the language issue is already political; so the refusal to learn
Welsh or the painting out of a road sign are both political acts.
What is intended here is, rather, incorporation in the processes of
the state. In the consociational democracies, cultural cleavages
are not depoliticised, in this statist sense, but are dealt with in
a carefully balanced political framework, which in theory may stab-
ilise without immobilising, and moderate without annihilating the
pressures of democracy.

Of course, there is still a case to be made for keeping the
language issue quiet. In other policy areas institutional change
has been slow, difficult and unproductive. There is a facile

attraction (though hardly for political scientists) in looking to
heroic leadership or mass regeneration for solutions; or simply
hoping the problem will find its solution by neglect, the language
dying, and/or its supporters falling silent in fatigue or despair.
Again it might be hoped that the present situation is transient, and
that in culture, as previously in religion, secularisation will
deprive language differences of significance. The evidence from
other countries suggests that these are vain, not to say inglorious,
hopes.

There are parallels in this argument with the advocacy by Patrick
Moynihan of 'benign neglect' of the race problem in the USA.
Moynihan was concerned that the expectations of the blacks should
not be continuously raised, when they were certain to be disappointed.
But there was a more general implication, not spelt out by Moynihan,
that agitation aggravates or creates but does not solve problems,
indeed makes solutions more difficult. In a sense we choose our own
problems. And why should America choose to have a Negro problem, or
Wales a language problem, when there are problems enough in other
spheres?

Now the burden of this paper in these terms is that Wales has to
choose the language as a problem. The justification for this lies
in considerations of justice (there is at present injustice) and
political stability (the problem will not go away). These were in
effect the arguments of Moynihan's critics. Of course it is still
true (and he was right about this) that in New York and Washington,
as in Caernarfon and Cardiff, political leaders exaggerate the sense
of grievance of the common people. But grievance in the end is the
motive force of political history, and to neglect it is to opt out
of politics and history.

NOTES

1 See the Gittins Report (1968:211-13). A good and neglected case
   for teaching Welsh in Wales lies in the requirement of courtesy,
   that Welsh speakers should not invariably have to shift out of
   their home language to make themselves understood by their
   fellows.
2 On the possibilities of violence in Wales see Betts (1976:214).
3 It is relevant and illuminating to consider here the future of
   white minorities in Rhodesia and South Africa under majority
   rule.
4 See inter alia Rae and Taylor (1970). Cross-cutting is there
   defined as 'the proportion of all the pairs of individuals whose
   two members are in the same group of one cleavage but in different
   groups of the other cleavage'. For discussion of the relation of
   heterogenity and homogenity to stability, see Rae and Taylor
   (1970:107-8) and A. Lijphart (1968:4), and, in terms of cross-
   cutting and segmentation, see A. Lijphart (1973).
5 In McRae (1974:177). This is in a postscript of 1973 to the
   original 1969 article.
6 Consociational systems have also failed in Nigeria, Cyprus,
   Uruguay, and, recent and spectacular, in the Lebanon.

REFERENCES

BETTS, C. (1976), 'Culture in Crisis', Ffynnon, Upton.
CONNOR, Walker (1972), Nation-building or nation-destroying, 'World Politics', XXIV, 3, pp.319-55.
ENLOE, C.H. (1972), 'Ethnic Conflict and Political Development', Little Brown, Boston.
EVANS, D. ELLIS (1972), The Welsh language, in R. Brinley Jones (ed.), 'Anatomy of Wales', Gwerin Publications, Peterston-super-Ely.
GILES, H., BOURHIS, R. and TAJFEL, R. (1974), Language as a determinant of Welsh identity, 'Eur. J. Soc. Psychol.', 3, pp.447-60.
GITTINS REPORT (1968), Report by a Committee of the Central Advisory Council on Education, HMSO, London.
LIJPHART, A. (1968), 'The Politics of Accommodation', University of California Press, Berkeley.
LIJPHART, A. (1973), Linguistic fragmentation and other dimensions of cleavage, 'International Political Science Association', mimeo.
MCRAE, K. (1974), 'Consociational Democracy', McLelland & Steward, Toronto.
MCRAE, K. (1975), The concept of consociational democracy and its application to Canada, in J.G. Savard and R. Vigneault (eds), 'Multilingual Political Systems', Les presses de l'université Laval, Quebec, pp.245-301.
MADGWICK, P.J., et al. (1973), 'The Politics of Rural Wales', Hutchinson, London.
RAE, D. and TAYLOR, M. (1970), 'The Analysis of Political Cleavages', Yale University Press, New Haven and London.
REPORT OF THE ROYAL COMMISSION ON BILINGUALISM AND BICULTURALISM (1967), Information Canada, Ottawa.
SAVARD, J.G. and VIGNEAULT, R. (eds) (1975), 'Multilingual Political Systems', Les presses de l'université Laval, Quebec.
SIMON, W.B. (1975), Occupational structure, multilingualism and social change, in J.G. Savard and R. Vigneault, 'Multilingual Political Systems', Les presses de l'université Laval, Quebec, pp.87-118.
STEINER, J. (1974), 'Amicable Agreement versus Majority Rule', University of North Carolina Press, Chapel Hill.
STEPHENS, M. (ed.) (1973), 'The Welsh Language Today', Gwasg Gomer, Llandysul.
THOMAS, N. (1971), 'The Welsh Extremist', Gollancz, London.

Chapter 17

RELIGIOUS ORGANIZATION AND COMMUNITY IN MID-WALES

Graham Day and Martin Fitton

Discussions of 'secularization' have mostly been conducted at the societal level, with a focus upon large-scale developments such as industrialization, the advance of science and technology, and their alleged consequences for the rationalization of thought. Local processes of institutional decay have attracted less attention, despite a general recognition among sociologists of religion that the relationship of religious organization to social structure and change at the level of the local community can be particularly crucial (Wilson, 1966:55). Of late, however, there has been some real interest in the relevance of this connection for the kind of commitment and involvement people have in churches, and its significance for the meaning they attach to their religious activity: enough to suggest that an important clue to understanding who it is that still goes to church in modern society may rest with their particular type of involvement in a local community.

In the past, the strength of churches often lay in their capacity to mobilize the entire wider structure of a community on their behalf. With the assistance, usually, of powerful local interests, they formed an integral part of the local social system. Perhaps the most obvious example is the alliance between Squire and Parson which once dominated large parts of rural England (Gilbert, 1976: 12 ff) but community studies carried out in small country towns comparatively recently have caught strong echoes of such a situation (Stacey, 1960:71; Birch, 1959:177).

Without necessarily presupposing the existence of a tightly knit, gemeinschaftlich 'community' surrounding them, we can refer to religious organizations as communal to the extent that they are intimately bound up with other aspects of local society, so that the administrative and organization structures of the church take their place within a larger pattern of life. Communal religion is most straightforward when a single body commands the allegiance of the whole of a local population - a foundation assumed in the traditional parish structure of the Church of England. Alternatively a religious body may practise exclusion and itself develop into a relatively closed communal group, normally described as a 'sect'.

In fact there are three points of reference for the use of the term 'communal': the characteristics of the organization and its membership seen as a whole; the orientations displayed by members toward their church; and the relationship between organization and the immediate social environment. Viewed as a congregation, a communal church is characterized by the readiness with which its members go beyond the necessities of meeting strictly 'religious' needs to form more intricate relationships with one another. Such a church provides a venue and agenda for a range of activities only loosely connected with religiosity whose functions are primarily sociable and recreational. The air of social occasion spreads over into worship itself, the time before and after service offering a chance to meet friends and exchange news. Unstated normative assumptions will rule the church as much as formal rules and duties, and the congregation will act as a major reference group for its members, its leaders holding their respect in matters other than those of the church. Over time, such relationships will solidify through intermarriage between members and their children: the congregation will come to resemble a family or set of linked families, and socialization within the family will play a major part in the continuation of membership (Moore, 1974:132; Blackwell, 1974:65-84).

Communal orientation entails a primary commitment to the local religious group, rather than any larger movement, and to fellow members as much as to doctrine and practice. From the point of view of the member, the specifically religious content of church-life and participation, and the organizational role, are an essential part of the system of social relationships he is involved in elsewhere (Clark, 1970:45-63). Being rooted in his own church, 'to join another congregation is to become a permanent visitor, but never to be at home' (Towler, 1974:167). Individuals growing up within a communal church are obviously likely to learn such attitudes.

It might be argued that all religious congregations contain within them a drive towards the communal (while perhaps every communal church has a tendency to become exclusive and sect-like) but clearly this materializes only under certain conditions, among the more important being the kinds of social relationships members encounter outside their church. Many of the features already attributed to the communal type of church require that members are able to continue their contacts beyond the perimeters of the church, carrying on their business as families and friends. Otherwise they must be able to return regularly and frequently to church-centred activities, living for example close to the building. The stimulation and maintenance of communal relations demands stability of membership, particularly if bonds between members are to extend over more than one generation. In short, communal churches are part of a wider complex of relations of the kind that has come to be referred to as 'traditional' (Stacey, 1960; Klein, 1968:101-22); that is, points (not necessarily the only, or most central ones) on which are anchored close-knit networks of people who know one another in many social contexts. While in some cases membership of a particular congregation may be a defining criterion for belonging to the network (Moore, 1974:130) it is also possible, we believe, for more than one congregation to be integrated together into such a system.

The relevance of this discussion for the Welsh context is considerable. With remarkable unanimity, historians and sociologists have depicted the centrality of religion for the Welsh way of life, and described religion, in rural Wales at least, as almost uniquely communal (Davies and Rees, 1962; Morgan, 1963:13; Verdery, 1976). According to such descriptions, active religious involvement was almost universal, while religion was by no means a sharply distinct sphere of action; the most tangible measure of this was the extent to which religious organizations, over a long period, captured the secular as well as the spiritual affairs of the people (Rees, 1950: 135). In some localities the assembling of neighbours for worship was the most visible sign of their belonging together (Hughes, 1962: 119-81). The influence flowing out from the churches is most conveniently summed up in the word 'respectability', since the various bodies put forward a set of standards of the good life, conformity with which could earn an individual considerable personal esteem and even, some would contend, cut across objective differences of wealth, occupation and class (Day and Fitton, 1975:867-92). Within this general interpenetration of religion and community, the different bodies took shape as communal churches. Commitment was chiefly to a given place of worship and a known congregation, and the presence of an individual in a particular denomination was more revealing of family background than personal religious experience. Differences of doctrine ceased to matter greatly.

It has been strongly argued that local society was fragmented by this degree of commitment, the social life of the individual and family centring so much on the particular place of worship that they had little scope for contact with members of rival bodies: co-religionists favoured one another in employment, trade, and above all in marriage, each religious group providing its own 'stream of social life' (Owen, 1962; Frankenberg, 1957; Verdery, 1976). This corresponds to the equation: one church, one community. A different possibility is, however, also indicated in the Welsh literature, that on a narrower canvas resembles the pattern of accommodation between religious movements sometimes referred to in the American context as 'civic religion'. Religion in Wales is pluralistic; although the Presbyterians have been called the 'national church of Wales', most areas contain more than one denomination, and in the small town there will usually be several. The suggestion that each church or chapel forms a really exclusive sect is implausible, and it follows from much that has already been said, concerning the devaluation of doctrine and the assimilation of other communal functions, that the churches would arrive at some modus vivendi (including the tacit agreement not to compete for members which underscores the traditional nature of commitment). The readiness with which authors can refer to 'chapel' to mean not just one chapel but a pattern of behaviour and values shared by several indicates the common ground between them - even members of the Church of England have not it seems been entirely outside this, judging by evidence of family connections between church and chapel (Jenkins, 1971). As Jenkins remarks 'the people of different chapels and societies were conscious of belonging to groups differentiated from each other, but with closer ties to one another than with "the world"' (Jenkins, 1962:1-63). Communal relations thus worked at two levels, the intimate involvement with a specific church, and the broader qualification of being 'religious', participating in a convergence between various churches and chapels in an area on a style of life, and the

mutual recognition of those who lived up to it, particularly the
religious leaders.

While later findings from survey research indicate a continuing
pattern of high involvement in formal religious activity in Wales
(Rosser and Harris, 1965:128; Madgwick, 1973:66) most of the
research on which the preceding account is based is now dated, and
much has happened since to reduce the ability of religious groups
to represent and perpetuate communal relations. The communal church
holds its members largely through inertia, aided by the mutually
supporting character of overlapping social bonds. Thus it is vulnerable to all those processes which undermine 'traditional' social
relations - in particular, patterns of social and geographical
mobility which pull individuals and families out of established
social networks, and weaken or destroy their commitment to a particular place and its institutions. Depopulation in rural Wales, which
entails considerable alteration of residence within the region, has
such repercussions. Even when people are not mobile in those
respects, they are subjected to a battery of external pressures of
unparalleled intensity, through mass media especially, which similarly challenge local attachments and attitudes which might in this
context aptly be called 'parochial'. Anglicization of Welsh culture
is a specific example. Such forces have been observed to effect a
transformation of religious organizations toward a pattern more
adapted to a situation of choice among alternatives, that of the
voluntary association. Belonging becomes a more definite, limited
commitment: the church can be viewed as 'an association providing
for the religious needs of its members' (Nelson, 1971:106) and 'going
to church' as a specialized activity set apart from others (Pickering,
1968). Members of associational type churches may resist efforts to
draw them in deeper or to extend their involvement to needs and
activities which they do not regard as falling within the sphere of
religion. Aginst the background of a broadly irreligious society,
churches are increasingly dependent on those who will enter them as
individuals; adapting to this situation imposes strains on members
and their organizations, as a result of which many potential members
are lost.

On this basis, we can make some predictions, which our research
in mid-Wales has been concerned to examine(1): that where religious
activity remains high, as apparently in rural Wales, this is because
the process of change just described has not progressed as far as
elsewhere and churches can still draw upon the reinforcements provided by a wider social framework; and consequently that those who
do attend church will be distinguished from those who do not by the
extent of their inclusion within a locally based social world, such
that their relationships, attitudes and past careers centre on the
locality, and their religious involvement is communal. As a first
measure of their plausibility some initial findings relating to the
extensiveness of religious involvement in one community are presented
here. They derive mainly from a survey of 261 respondents.

In 1851 the Machynlleth Registration District had the 'best'
supply of religious sittings in all England and Wales, with provision
for 124 per cent of population, 85 per cent of whom could be accommodated in Nonconformist chapels. Sixty years later, in the town
itself, when the population was 2,038, there was room for 3,665

worshippers (Census of 1851, Royal Commission, 1910). Today the capacity of the seven places of worship exceeds the current population of 1,768 by a thousand places.

All but 5 per cent of present residents have some contact with organized religion in their backgrounds, attending Sunday School, or church or chapel, as children. Among those interviewed, 45 per cent now regard themselves as 'belonging' to a Nonconformist denomination, 38 per cent as Anglicans. Virtually all these claim to have met the requirements for full membership of a church or chapel. However, comparison of church membership lists with the Electoral Register enabled us to identify only 42 per cent of the adult population as members. Making allowance for our failure to trace certain individuals, and for out-of-date listings, it would seem that about half those living in the town do not belong, properly speaking, to a local church - many of these keep their membership elsewhere.

If we define as active churchgoers all those who attend at least once a month, 37 per cent said they did so, 23 per cent every week. At the other extreme, 35 per cent went only for weddings and funerals. In between is a marginal group which attend irregularly, and for high spots such as Thanksgiving and Anniversary services. Since questions on attendance were put only after a long preamble covering the entire religious career of respondents and their parents, we can place some confidence in these figures. As a check, we carried out a census of attendance on two consecutive Sundays, when all adults (aged 17 or more) who attended any of the services were asked to fill in a short self-administered questionnaire. Except for one service - a Children's Harvest Festival at the Parish Church - we obtained information on 95 per cent of those present. Nearly all proved to be highly regular attenders, which justified our decision to treat the level achieved over the two weeks as a reasonable estimate of a 'typical' Sunday congregation, thus allowing for random fluctuations. Apart from 25 visitors, found exclusively in English-language services, forms were completed by 228 residents, or 16 per cent of those on the Electoral Register. Putting the refusal rate at an unnecessarily generous level of 10 per cent suggests a maximum of 250, or 18 per cent, as the consistently churchgoing population. Attendance at ordinary religious worship is therefore very much a minority affair.

What we need to examine is the representativeness of this minority, the broad outlines of which are shown in Table 17.1. Only 27 per cent of female respondents fall into the inactive category compared to 43 per cent of men, who were also twice as likely as women to say they belonged to no denomination. Consequently women account for over 60 per cent of the active churchgoers, and contribute particularly to a relatively high activity rate among Nonconformists. On the census Sundays, however, the overall proportions by sex among attenders were not too different from the population figures of the National Census. Religious involvement increased with the age of respondents. The most active were the middle generation, aged 40 to 60, where approaching half were regular attenders, contrasted with only a quarter of the under-40s and 38 per cent of those over 60. Reasons for non-attendance differed in that the elderly include many unable to go through ill-health, whereas more of the young had no interest in the churches: more than a third of

Table 17.1   Characteristics of the religious and non-religious populations of Machynlleth

	Religiously active (Attend monthly or more) *N = 97	Religiously marginal (Attend less than monthly) N = 74	Religiously inactive (weddings, funerals only) N = 90
Percent of population	37	28	35
Male	39	38	56
Born in Machynlleth	32	39	44
Fluent Welsh-speaking	73	58	47
Some Welsh	13	22	28
No Welsh	13	20	25
Aged under 40	19	30	36
40-60	43	32	28
60 +	38	38	36
Membership of clubs & organizations:			
None	38	49	58
1	18	27	22
2	19	13	12
3	11	7	5
4 +	14	4	3

* The base is normally 261 respondents, from a sample target of 300. For some measures, this varies slightly because information is missing for one or two respondents.

them gave no religious affiliation, compared with fewer than 10 per cent of the oldest group, nearly 60 per cent of whom were Nonconformists. The practical effects were clear from our census data: 43 per cent of those completing forms were over 60, including more than half the Welsh Nonconformists, but only 38 of the 228 (13 per cent) were under 40.

Individuals and families from all social levels within Machynlleth give support to religious organizations: no important element is totally unrepresented and as a body the churches do not merit Martin's description of 'clearly middle and low middle-class associations' (Martin, 1967:93). They are however skewed in that direction, for survey interviews showed non-manual respondents to be more favourable towards the churches: among them, 44 per cent could be

described as active churchgoers, as opposed to 30 per cent of manual
workers. Since the latter outnumber those in white-collar jobs by
almost two to one, they still account for just under half the active
as well as 70 per cent of the inactive population, but half those we
interviewed from manual homes said they attended church only for
weddings, funerals and christenings. A substantial majority of
those now in the non-manual category, whatever their age, had continued attending church into their teens, by which time 64 per cent
of the younger manual workers had ceased to go. With respect to
current attendance the missing groups (more than two-thirds of which
do not regularly attend church) are the under 40s, regardless of
occupational level, and the older manual workers. Middle-aged
people of both classes, and the older white-collar and professional
people, are the strongest supporters of the Machynlleth churches.
It was in line with these results for us to find marginally more non-
manual workers and members of their families in the congregations
during our census weekends than there were manual. So far as we
could judge – since a fifth of those attending did not supply the
relevant information – in most churches the balance was similar,
although one chapel lived up to its reputation for being high-class
by having less than a fifth of its attenders in manual jobs.
Farmers and retired farmers were present in strength, relative to
their position in the town. However, as no congregation was obviously
swamped by high-status individuals, each showed sufficient spread for
the members to lay claim to 'a fair cross-section' of local people.
Out of 77 manual workers about whom we had information, only 24 were
not in skilled occupations. According to the survey, about a
quarter of the townspeople were in semi-skilled and unskilled work,
but these accounted for only 13 per cent of churchgoers. The people
most estranged from church life are the young men in less skilled
trades: there was not a single person present to fit this description
while the average age of the less-skilled male workers who were in
church was 62.
    Survey evidence demonstrated that the relative stability of total
population in Machynlleth between 1921 and 1961 did not indicate a
settled population: only 38 per cent of respondents were born in the
town, and far from it being they who provide the mainstay of the
churches, as the communal enclave we thought they might be, they are
among the least committed, resembling in both present practice and
past career the other weak elements, those born and brought up outside Wales, and the most recent immigrants. Examination of census
returns revealed a striking similarity to the survey distribution –
the only category which had not found its way into the churches in
numbers roughly matching its presence in the town was that with
fewer than ten years' residence. Machynlleth churches have been able
to assimilate many newcomers, and some informants stressed their
importance in keeping things going. The chapels draw most on this
source, recruiting people who come from other parts of mid-Wales and
north Wales, rooted in a habit of churchgoing which they maintain.
This is closely related to ability to speak Welsh. Four chapels use
only Welsh, and the parish church offers separate English and Welsh
services. The Welsh speakers are 20 per cent more active than the
rest: 45 per cent against a quarter. Among Welsh speakers only 8 per
cent could give no denominational allegiance; 60 per cent were

Nonconformist. Those who could not speak Welsh were four times as
likely to have no sense of belonging to a church, and only a fifth
were Nonconformists. Almost three-quarters of regular attenders
could speak Welsh fluently.

This unexpected composition of the active minority, whereby only
a third are native to the town, results from patterns of movement in
which several factors cut across the effects of local origin. Thus,
looking at the native-born and immigrant populations in terms of the
work they do, we find immigrants concentrated at higher non-manual
levels. This corresponds to a tendency for those who do well, educ-
ationally and occupationally, to have to move away to follow a
career, with limited opportunity to return, while the few high-status
positions go to 'spiralists' from elsewhere - usually, through both
preference and suitability (speaking the language), elsewhere in
Wales. Nineteen out of twenty persons we encountered in higher
professional and managerial jobs were outsiders. In the census, a
larger proportion of manual than of non-manual churchgoers had been
born, or spent more than thirty years, in the town - 64 per cent
against 40 per cent. Local strength is greatest among routine white
collar (shop assistants) and skilled manual grades (post office,
railways) but generally greater among manual than non-manual employees. The locally born tend therefore to be in social levels which
are least religiously active. Since they also figure more promin-
ently among the younger age groups - only among the very youngest
are those born in Machynlleth in the majority - and among male
respondents, they are even less likely to appear in church.

Many of these religiously active outsiders will insist that their
real roots are elsewhere: nevertheless they are prominent in the
formal social life of Machynlleth. People active in religious
bodies provide a disproportionate share of the membership of the
large number of local clubs and associations, accounting for less
than a third of those belonging to none but over two-thirds of those
belonging to four or more, a relationship which is even more note-
worthy when we recall the age of churchgoers. The churches are
firmly bound into the intricate web of connections between the
various committees, most of which contain representatives of three
or more congregations, and local organizations provide ample scope
for members of different churches to meet. Taking the 50 individuals
who are outstandingly prominent in local societies - serving on three
or more committees - we found 40 listed as members of the churches,
twice the proportion in the population as a whole. But to say that
church members frequently hold leading positions in the town is not
to imply that leaders within churches are necessarily prominent
outside them: among 32 leaders (deacons, elders, and church wardens)
only 5 were on our list of the 50 most active persons, and half
appeared to have no commitments beyond their church. Except that
only 4 office-holders were women, and farmers were over-represented,
office-holding in the churches tallied fairly well with the characteristics of the religious population. Leaders included 11 non-
manual and 12 manual workers, of whom 3 were relatively unskilled.
As with the congregations, a third had spent their life in the town;
7 had been there less than thirty years. Only in the Church in Wales
did their average fall below sixty.

That the churches are so embedded in the pattern of voluntary

associations indicates strength, as does the number of men –
especially from working-class backgrounds – and middle-aged people
attending church. The level of involvement with religion, in
attitudes and behaviour, is greater than one would expect to find
in most parts of Britain. Yet our overwhelming impression was of
weakness, just as among churchgoers the most acute perception is of
decline. We cannot document its accuracy here, and must beware
nostalgic distortion, but it is enough to project forward from the
current situation to see the problem. Religion was not a topic of
major interest for our respondents; spontaneous reference to
churches and chapels was unusual even when they were specifically
invited to consider social differences, group formation, and
activities in the town. Many who claimed to be in some way attached
to a church treated this as a marginal fact about themselves and,
when prompted, few offered much by way of distinguishing religious
from non-religious members of the community.

A syndrome of collapse can be constructed from descriptions we
were given. As numbers fall off, it is harder for churches to
sustain the range of activities to which members were once accustomed; with fewer opportunities to meet and less to hold them
together, it is easier for some to leave, less attractive to others
to join. Congregations begin to rely heavily on a few active
members, and may have to consider ways of co-operating with each
other, rationalizing Sunday worship, and so on. In effect, there
is growing dependence on those who will seek something definite
from a church – as well as, most crucially, the young. Members
spoke of their own activism as a matter of habit. They were not
particularly conscious of pressure upon them to attend, rather the
reverse since, they contended, churchgoing elicited ridicule rather
than respect among the general population while even within the
congregation sanctions could misfire, making it difficult to begin
again after missing services. Rather than external forces, they
invoked the internal constraint of a sense of duty, the consequence
of 'having been brought up to it'. But their orientation to the
church was usually communal: their own congregation provided a
familiar environment in which they 'know their way around', most
members having 'grown old together', meeting constantly outside
when shopping, in clubs. Unconvincingly, they spoke of transferring
elsewhere if their chapel closed. There was no serious institutional
preparation for inter-denominational co-operation. Yet members of
each congregation could enter sympathetically into the affairs of
the others, and were reluctant to make distinctions, stressing that
all – Anglicans included – were similar in membership and circumstances. Characteristically, members described their social circle
as consisting mainly or entirely of people with roots in the congregations: but few drew their friends exclusively from their own
church, and they would point out that among those they had known for
many years, with whom they mixed in societies and daily life, were
members of various religious bodies. They could also point generally
to numerous occasions on which they had been inside the other places
of worship.

Given their explanation for their own behaviour, not surprisingly
much of the blame for the decline they were witnessing was put upon
failures of socialization – religion was not being taught 'on the

hearth'. A minority saw this laxness as typical of new people who
came into the town without church or chapel associations; we have
already seen that objectively newcomers provide more than their
quota of churchgoers. A much more serious perception was conveyed
by the majority, that not only were local families involved, but
good families, once closely linked to the churches. That is, there
were people outside the churches who could not be treated as
strangers, or as unrespectable, because except for their lack of
commitment to religious organization, they were just like those
inside. More than anything else, this made active churchgoers feel
marginal, aware that the inner world of church and chapel had no
support from any pattern of wider social forces. Of course, the
implication is clear: the failure in socialization has been their
own, to the extent that the active members of Machynlleth churches
have been unable to provide their own successors.

   The data cited are too crude to provide a real measure of communal
involvement in religion; they simply point towards the potential
usefulness of the framework, but also perhaps to its limitations in
that transfer of allegiance clearly happens without destroying a
broadly communal ethos. For decades, Machynlleth churches have had
to cope with the loss of those brought up within them, and their
replacement by others from a more rapidly depopulating countryside.
Rather than present members being supported by extensive networks of
kin and friends, we found their domestic and family circles small
and weak, and thinning rapidly as they aged; they were reconciled
to seeing their own children go the way their siblings had, moving
elsewhere for the work and other amenities a small country town
cannot provide. In the force of such ineluctable economic and social
forces, they appeared unable to propose means of continuation, and
regarded efforts to 'modernize' the churches as merely futile
tinkering with appearances.

NOTE

1 The research which involved the study of two localities,
   Machynlleth and Newtown in Montgomeryshire was supported by grants
   from the Social Science Research Council and the University of
   Wales Board of Celtic Studies. Details of the methods and sources
   of data can be found in the Final Report to the SSRC (British
   Library Lending Division No. HR 2235).

REFERENCES

BIRCH, A.H. (1959), 'Small-town Politics', Oxford University
Press.
BLACKWELL, T. (1974), The history of a working-class Methodist chapel,
'Working Papers in Cultural Studies 5', pp.65-84.
GENERAL REGISTER OFFICE (1863), 'Census of Great Britain, 1861:
Religious Worship in England and Wales', HMSO, London.
CLARK, D.B. (1970), Local and cosmopolitan aspects of religious
activity in a northern suburb, in D. Martin and M. Hill (eds),
'A Sociological Yearbook of Religion in Britain', no.3, SCM Press,
London, pp.45-63.

DAVIES, E. and REES, A.D. (eds), (1962), 'Welsh Rural Communities', University of Wales Press, Cardiff.

DAY, G. and FITTON, M. (1975), Religion and social status in rural Wales: 'Buchedd' and its lessons for concepts of stratification in community studies, 'Sociological Review', vol.23, no.4, pp.867-92.

FRANKENBERG, R. (1957), 'Village on the Border', Cohen & West, London.

GILBERT, A.D. (1976), 'Religion and Society in Industrial England', Longman, London.

HUGHES, T. JONES (1962), Aberdaron: the social geography of a small region in the Llyn peninsula in E. Davies and A.D. Rees, 'Welsh Rural Communities', University of Wales Press, Cardiff, pp.119-81.

JENKINS, D. (1962), Aberporth: A study of a coastal village in south Cardiganshire, in E. Davies and A.D. Rees, 'Welsh Rural Communities', University of Wales Press, Cardiff, pp.1-63.

KLEIN, J. (1968), Structural aspects of church organization, 'International Yearbook for the Sociology of Religion', pp.101-22.

MADGWICK, P. et al. (1973), 'The Politics of Rural Wales', Hutchinson, London.

MARTIN, D. (1967), 'A Sociology of English Religion', SCM Press, London.

MOORE, R.M. (1974), 'Pit-men, Preachers and Politics', Cambridge University Press.

MORGAN, K.O. (1963), 'Wales in British Politics', University of Wales Press, Cardiff.

NELSON, G.K. (1971), Communal and associational churches, 'Review of Religious Research', p.106.

OWEN, T. (1967), Chapel and community in Glan-Llyn, Merioneth, in E. Davies and A.D. Rees, 'Welsh Rural Communities', University of Wales Press, Cardiff, pp.185-248.

PICKERING, W. (1968), Religion: a leisure time pursuit?, in D. Martin (ed.), 'Sociological Yearbook of Religion in Britain', no.1, SCM Press, London.

REES, A.D. (1950), 'Life in a Welsh Countryside', University of Wales Press, Cardiff.

ROSSER, C. and HARRIS, C.C. (1965), 'The Family and Social Change', Routledge & Kegan Paul, London.

ROYAL COMMISSION ON THE CHURCH OF ENGLAND AND OTHER RELIGIOUS BODIES (1910).

STACEY, M. (1960), 'Tradition and Change', Oxford University Press.

TOWLER, R. (1974), 'Homo Religiosus: Sociological Problems in the Study of Religion', Constable, London.

VERDERY, K. (1976), Ethnicity and social system: The religious organization of Welshness, in C.A. Smith (ed.), 'Regional Systems Analysis', vol.II, 'Social Systems', Academic Press, London, pp.191-229.

WILSON, B.R. (1966), 'Religion and Secular Society', Penguin, Harmondsworth.

Chapter 18

SOCIAL RANKING IN A WELSH COMMUNITY

Glyn Williams

The conventional approach to social inequality involves the search
for the abstract dimensions of persons or units before considering
the components of these dimensions and establishing a measure for
each component. Thus, for example, the Weberian perspective employs
the three dimensions of economy, prestige and power which may be
related to one another but can also be opposed to one another. Each
dimension can be further subdivided into numerous components.
   Another facet of much writing and investigation of social inequality is apparent in the work of Parsons (1953). It is assumed
that there exists a normative framework which sets certain goals,
evaluates performances, etc. with success being measured against
this normative framework. Central to the argument is the concept of
role, with roles being grouped together into units of statuses with
status involving role performance and evaluation. In this sense
status consists of the totality of the roles enacted by a person,
Since a major ingredient of this role evaluation derives from occupation there ensues a discussion of status in terms of occupational
groups or strata. Thus it is held that the economic dimension
contributes to the items of 'life style' which symbolizes prestige
and thereby produces a congruence between economy and prestige.
Others (Runciman, 1966; Gerth and Mills, 1946) maintain that congruence of status which derives from different dimensions of status
can not be assumed.
   Studies employing this perspective relate inequality to a stratification perspective which inevitably has a macro or nationwide
connotation. Within a small community such a perspective is
problematic for at least two reasons. First within such communities
the range of occupations is relatively small and the relationship
between holders of occupations is not necessarily implicit in the
nature of the occupations. Second an analysis within a small community allows the investigator to come to terms with the personal
elements of social differentiation rather than being obliged to rely
upon the depersonalized aspects of statuses or positions enacting
roles; that is, where social distance is small, social inequality can
be understood on the level of the individual. This last point is
particularly important with reference to the subjective aspect of
status allocation and association. Members of any society are not

merely differentiated according to the roles which they perform as a result of their position in a division of labour. Furthermore even if the discussion does focus upon roles it soon becomes apparent that evaluation is based as much upon performance as upon position. If the orientation is to focus upon the individual rather than upon strata it seems more appropriate to refer to social inequality rather than social stratification. Yet such a focus does not preclude reference to the various dimensions of inequality and there is no really substantial empirical evidence for assuming a greater crystallization of status dimensions in small communities than in a nation as a whole.

It might be useful to refer to what is meant by status - a compendium of the reputational attributes of persons and the formal attributes of positions (Parkin, 1973:34-6). Davis's (1942) distinction between prestige and esteem is also relevant. Prestige derives from the social system irrespective of the qualities of the individual whereas esteem refers to the social honour an individual enjoys by virtue of his behaviour. What appears clear is that in the individual's evaluation of status there is a reference to both prestige and esteem but that within the small community esteem is given considerable prominence albeit a prominence that varies according to context. Furthermore, given a limited awareness of class, social standing will derive from prestige and esteem without any manifest reference to class.

It should be clear that it is not the purpose of this paper to discuss class boundaries but rather to focus upon the attributes of the individual that are analytically distinct from a rank in a social class or stratum hierarchy. In so doing it is essential to consider which of the relevant components of inequality are to be employed as a basis for ranking and how they are to be evaluated. Where differentiation on the basis of education or employment is minimal the most effective measure of the economic dimension is the income derived from the resources available to the individual. It might be argued that leadership as a form of power can not be conceived as a dimension distinct from economic or status attributes since both economics and status are potential forms of power. However, the attributes of leadership are far more exploitable and direct within the context of power. Given the existence of these two scales they can be compared with the ranking scale of status which, as has been suggested above, is a compendium of several attributes. In a sense the entire system of inequality can be viewed as a composite of several rank systems. Status can be assessed by administering a sociometric which can give a wealth of information, not only about ranking but also about network systems, associations, etc. It is not the objective of this paper to explore the possibilities of such analyses but merely to consider the scope for ranking within a small community as a preliminary for a more involved analysis. Such an objective is facilitated by a comparison of the different dimensions in order to ascertain the degree of consistency between the different rank systems. Any inconsistencies can then be explored in terms of our knowledge of the individual cases. A major problem associated with such an exercise is that there is a need to find some way of comparing the evaluation on the different ranking scales by referring to some generalized scale of inequality (Hartman, 1975).

The task, therefore, is to determine the exact relationship between
the separate dimensions of inequality and this general scale. This
in turn leads to the question of the relationship between the scales
in terms of importance, level of generality and context (Landecker,
1960). This is perhaps the most difficult task for as Zeldich and
Anderson (1966) imply, as yet there has been no simple way to measure
the weights of the scales found. Furthermore where possible the
dynamics of status should be ascertained so that it becomes possible
to determine whether the importance of the various dimensions varies
according to the context of the social situation. Thus, not only
should we ask whether a comparison of rank on two scales is the same
as such a comparison on a different pair of scales but are the consequences of any inconsistency limited to certain domains. I don't
pretend to have resolved these problems but I do feel that they can
be related in a more satisfactory way by referring to individual
ranking.

SETTING

The community of study is an upland village in north Wales which,
like most such villages, has been subject to considerable depopulation and a corresponding change in the occupational structure. At
the time of its demographic peak the community had a population of
854 (Census, 1861). The occupational structure at this time had a
high dependence on agriculture with 47 of the employed being farmers
who employed a total of 183 workers consisting of 29 carters, 16
shepherds, 12 cowmen, 67 labourers, 11 dairy maids and 48 housemaids.
As has been indicated in other studies (Jenkins, 1969) the farms
were differentiated according to the number of employed and these
employees held positions which were ranked in terms of prestige
accorded because of the position in the division of labour. The
remainder of the population depended upon a local woollen industry
which employed 18 workers, a nearby slate quarry employing 12
workers from the village, the estate which owned the local farms
and which employed 10 local men, while a further 6 men worked as
stone masons, and 38 residents who owned commercial establishments,
worked as commercial employees or worked as local self-employed
craftsmen. Another 3 residents were employed as schoolteachers, 2
as preachers and 1 as the parish clerk. Clearly it was easier to
talk about stratification at this time, especially since the division
of labour involved such a hierarchy of dependence.
     In a little over a hundred years the population has declined to
the order of 250. The community remains dependent upon agriculture
with 33 of the tenant farms remaining in production. However the
number of people employed in agriculture has declined substantially
with only the 33 heads of farm families together with 17 sons or
brothers and only 4 labourers being employed in such a capacity. A
further 15 residents are employed either as non-agricultural labourers, craftsmen or in their own small business. The exceptions are
the minister and the village schoolteacher. The community remains
part of the two estates owned by the same gentry families as a
century earlier. It is the policy of these owners to rent the
houses in the village to those who retire from their farm tenancy,

but their limited number means that those not employed in agriculture
are also residents in the village and a few houses are even leased
to outsiders as second homes. A few of the houses are owned privately by some of the local families.

The farmers conduct a limited form of transhumance based upon
sheep rearing. While the seasonal change of residence between upland
and lowland tracts has ceased, the annual migration of animals
between the enclosed land in the lowlands and the open mountain
grazing tracts continues. This has a marked influence on the social
organization since farmers whose sheep share adjacent sheep walks in
the upland area are obliged to interact and co-operate in certain
aspects of their economic activities. Such interaction often links
families located at different ends of the community and augments
reciprocal networks based upon spatial proximity.

RANKING

Apart from the minister and the schoolteacher the educational experience of the villagers is fairly similar, few of them having proceeded
beyond the minimum legal requirements. To differentiate the population on the basis of occupation or educational achievement is far
less meaningful than an economic differentiation on the basis of
income. Thus the income of each family has been calculated on the
basis of their available resources. For the tenant farmers these
resources include livestock and crop production, due attention being
given to production costs. Retired farmers or their widows have
been allocated the rank associated with the farm which they retired
from. Non-farmers are ranked on the basis of their incomes or the
profits that they might obtain from their activities.

In Tables 18.1a and 18.1b this ranking on the basis of income is
compared with the range of formal leadership positions in the community. Although over half of the households include an office holder,
62 per cent of the leadership positions are located in 26 per cent
of the households, suggesting that there is a concentration of
leadership positions. Of the households where the leadership
positions are concentrated 11 are farm households and 4 are non-farm
households. The correlation with the economic ranking scale appears
to be positive with 5 of the first 6 households ranked on the economic scale being among the 11 farm households with a concentration
of leadership roles. This can be expressed in another way with 44
per cent of the leadership roles held by farm households being
located in the upper quartile of the farm households on the economic
ranking scale. However 3 of the community's most prominent leaders
are to be found at the bottom of the third quartile of the economic
ranking scale.

It might be useful to consider the distribution of leadership in
the different institutional domains. Of the 7 deacons 6 were farmers
and 4 were drawn from the top third of the economically ranked
farmers. Also 65 per cent of the religious leadership roles were
assigned to 6 persons, 5 of whom were farmers. Similarly the
leadership roles associated with the young people's activities were
concentrated in a few households, with 40 per cent of such positions
being located in 4 households, the wealthier farmers again carrying a

Table 18.1a   Leadership position and economic rank, farm households

	Parish Council	Rural D Countil	Deacon	Sun. School, B.O.Hope	Singing	YFC	Urdd, Aelwyd	Eisteddfod	WI	Chwiorydd	Foxes	Sheep dog trials	Village Hall	Cemetery	Poetry, Drama	Church Warden	WEA	No
1						X			X						X			3
2									X									1
3			X	X		X	X								X			5
4						X					X		X					3
5	X		X	X	X	X						X						6
6				X			X	X							X			4
7	X											X						2
8			X															1
9						X										X		2
9a																		O
10																		O
11		X				X											X	3
12																		O
13						X							X					2
13a																		O
14																		O
14a																		O
15	X						X						X					3
16																		O
17														X				1
17a																		O
18						X		X				X	X			X		5
19														X				1
20																		O
21			X	X		X	X	X					X				X	7
22	X		X	X					X						X			5
23			X	X		X												3
24																		O
25																		O
26																		O
27																		O
28	X					X												2
29																		O
30																		O
31									X									1
32																		O
33				X		X												2
34																		O

Table 18.1b   Leadership position and economic rank, non-farm households

	Parish Council	Rural D Council	Deacon	Sun. School, B.O.Hope	Singing	YFC	Urdd, Aelwyd	Eisteddfod	WI	Chwiorydd	Foxes	Sheep dog trials	Village Hall	Cemetery	Poetry, Drama	Church Warden	WEA	No
1																		0
2	X	X											X					3
3																		0
4																		0
5																		0
6																		0
7								X					X	XX				4
8	X									X						X		3
9	X		X	X				X		X	X							6
10		X											X					2
11																		0
12			X						X									2
13																		0
14																		0
15				X									X					2
16													X			X		2
17	X											X						2
18												X						1
19																		0
20																		0
21			X															1
22																		0
23																		0
24																		0

a disproportionate influence. The elected offices of Parish councillors had a wider distribution both among the farmers and non-
farmers as did the committee which administered the village hall.

    In order to rank all of those with leadership positions it is
necessary to weight the various leadership positions in order to
differentiate those who held a similar number of positions. While
this is in many respects unsatisfactory, nonetheless it is the most
satisfactory way in which this can be done. Thus, although the
limitation of the scale should be recognized, the ranking is presented in Tables 18.2a and 18.2b.

    The assessment of status was achieved by the administration of a
sociometric index based upon responses to the request for the respondents to name any 10 people living in the community and then to rank
them in order of status. While reducing the choice universe to 10

Table 18.2a Economic, leadership and prestige rankings, farm households

Economic Rank	Leadership Rank	Prestige Rank
1	14	3
2	27	28
3	5	5
4	13	6
5	2	13
6	7	11
7	17	22
8	16	21
9	19	24
9a	X	26
10	X	49
11	9	4
12	X	27
13	10	10
13a	X	12
14	X	42
14a	X	38
15	12	33
16	X	35
17	28	14
17a	X	16
18	6	30
19	X	7
20	X	46
21	1	8
22	4	1
23	20	48
24	X	34
25	X	39
26	X	19
27	X	40
28	23	18
29	X	25
30	X	32
31	X	54
32	26	9
33	X	31
34	X	55

The cases numbered 9a, 13a, 14a and 17a are village residents who have retired from their respective farms.

Table 18.2b Economic, leadership and prestige ranking, non-farm households

Economic Rank	Leadership Rank	Prestige Rank
1	X	2
2	11	17
3	X	51
4	18	47
5	X	59
6	X	43
7	8	20
8	15	15
9	3	36
10	X	44
11	X	29
12	25	50
13	X	41
14	29	58
15	22	23
16	24	45
17	X	37
18	21	57
19	X	56
20	X	52
21	X	53
22	X	60
23	X	61
24	X	62

cases resolves several problems it also presents many methodological problems. There is a tendency for choice to be based upon locality, but with a wide range of spatial sampling this is cancelled out. It also implies that choices may be restricted by the initial naming of people on the basis of negative prestige, although this is controlled by ignoring the last 2 named in the status ranking of each respondent. Thus the final ranking is based upon an evaluation of the data in terms of the number of times a person is named and the average score received by each person. This is presented in Table 18.2 where the status ranking is compared with the economic and leadership ranking scales.

A comparison of the status rankings with the economic rankings again indicates a fairly high degree of consistency between the two ranking scales with 8 of the first 12 status ranks occurring among the first 13 of the economically ranked farmers or the highest of those ranked among the non-farmers on the same scale. A comparison of the leadership and status scales indicates a similar correlation with 9 of the highest 15 status ranks being found among the highest 15 on the leadership ranking scale.

If there exists a tendency for status groups to be determined by the sharing of economic position and a lifestyle based upon such a position we would expect associational patterns to be determined by

membership of the respective status groups. In order to investigate
such a possibility all household members were asked to indicate the
nature and extent of their formal and informal visits and telephone
calls made within the community over a period of time. It should
of course be realized that not all households have telephones. This
data is recorded from a matrix of economic rank in Table 18.3.

   Initial scrutiny of the associational data does not appear to
reveal any definite pattern. It is true that the formality of
association represented by invitations to supper etc. is not an
important feature, being restricted to only 20 cases during a six-
month period, several of these cases obviously being reciprocal. A
reciprocal relationship also appears to be in evidence with reference to the less formal aspects such as visits and phone calls,
with those who show a high incidence in terms of visiting and
'phoning also showing high scores in terms of being visited and
'phoned. This tendency of high involvement does not appear to be
related to the economic scale, nor is the nature of the visiting
determined by the economic scale with reference to the farmers.
What does appear evident is that as one would expect there is a
greater tendency for the farm population to visit the villagers than
vice versa, this being a measure of the function of the village as
a local central place. The data becomes far more meaningful when
we consider three variables, kinship, near neighbours and agricultural reciprocity. Thus among the farmers 8 per cent of all
visiting interactions and 13 per cent of all 'phoning is accounted
for by kinship relationships, 36 per cent and 32 per cent respectively by nearest neighbour and 22 per cent and 22 per cent by a
relationship between those who are neighbours in terms of open
mounting grazing tracts. These appear to be the main determinants
of the associations within the community.

   Indeed the same can be said for the status rankings with a
tendency being evident for respondents to name near neighbours or
those with whom they interact in their agricultural activities
regardless of the size of the enterprise and if relatives have been
named they will tend to be ranked highly. What one concludes from
this is that association does not appear to be related to status
groups based on lifestyle except in the context of the lifestyle
that is determined by the ecological framework, but rather that it
is based upon the familiarity that derives from being near neighbours and from the emotive context of kinship association. For
those newcomers who do not have wide kinship ties in the community
there is a greater tendency to emphasize the ties based on the
other two factors, but the isolation that emanates from being a
'dyn dwad' is apparent to such actors. An exception involves those
drawn together by leadership activities.

DISCUSSION

As should be clear from the introduction my main interest is not in
the undoubted tendency towards status consistency that has been
outlined above but rather with the cases which do not indicate such
a consistency. In view of the general tendency such lack of status
consistency requires some explanation and this is best achieved by

Table 18.3   Associational patterns

	Visits			Phone calls			Supper		
	Farm	Village	Total	Farm	Village	Total	Farm	Village	Total
Kinship	13 (8%)	19 (27%)	32 (14%)	9 (13%)	2 (33%)	11 (15%)	2 (%)	1 (%)	3 (15%)
Nearest neighbour	58 (36%)	23 (32%)	81 (35%)	22 (32%)	ſ	22 (29%)	4	2	6 (30%)
Mountain neighbour	36 (22%)	ſ	36 (15%)	15 (22%)	ſ	15 (20%)	2	ſ	2 (10%)
Other	55 (34%)	29 (41%)	84 (36%)	23 (33%)	4 (67%)	27 (36%)	5	4	9 (45%)
TOTAL	162	71	233	69	6	75	13	7	20

reference to the explanation in terms of the criteria employed by the local population in determining such a consistency. Thus the partial absence of such criteria is held to be responsible for the inconsistency. This is not to imply that models which ignore the internal view of inequality do not have some predictive value but rather that such models are improved if one discusses the relationships between the various components of inequality from the dynamic perspective of the community members. Such a discussion, usually based upon the experience of the participant observer, should serve to give greater clarity to the meaning of the relationships or lack of relationships between the various components. The predicted relationship between such components derives from the inherent logic implicit in the theoretical assumptions that they derive from. However rarely do these assumptions encompass the entire range of factors and related meanings which the actors operate from. Such an observation assumes particular emphasis with reference to the subjective nature of prestige allocation, and are obviously less relevant to the objective dimensions.

The status dimension is probably the least studied of the various social rewards associated with social inequality. Where it has been studied the tendency has been to subsume it under the study of lifestyles with the result that it is reduced to merely another element of consumption. Perhaps the reason for this lies in its intangibility with its symbolic aspect being most apparent. If we assume that status is allocated to those who best achieve the goals of the organization, the importance and significance of values becomes clear. However this seems to imply the existence of collective goals and collective values. If such collective qualities do pertain it is to be expected that they may derive from the broad sociocultural order and are related to the community's various institutions. Yet some of the goals and values are more relevant than others because of the way the community defines itself. On an individual level this raises the question of goal access and identity. If we hold that identities are denoted by particular kinds of personal attributes the place of identity in the central structure of the community is clearly based on the link between the demands of the structure and the availability of essential attributes on the part of the individual. Yet status is by no means a unitary concept but has various components, two of which might be deference which is the correlate of power, and admiration as the correlate of reward. This became clear in the administration of the questions pertaining to status with the responses relating not only to an assessment in terms of economic aspects (prestige), the qualities of leadership, but also to lifestyles and the personal qualities (esteem), which give meaning to such lifestyles as they relate to some particular standard. Thus while it is a subjective assessment it is an assessment based upon both subjective and objective criteria. Thus it became clear that the assessor in a small community such as the community studied is very much aware of the individual's income potential, source of wealth, leadership position, etc., but also employs his judgment on a variety of personal quality criteria which are not based upon such objective measures although they may serve as essential qualifications. This multi-dimensionality of prestige is what makes it such an elusive quality.

A convenient model for the understanding of local social status is that of social credit (Bennett, 1969). In this context social credit is seen as a quality that an individual achieves as a result of the various criteria that community members employ in allocating status to an individual. An individual can accumulate credit by having a high income, by being a good farmer, being respectable, by demonstrating the various social qualities that are held desirable in the community. An individual can also derive credit from the activities or attributes of his spouse, and the tendency to remind children not to 'spoil the good name of the family' by behaving badly fits into this framework, being a warning to safeguard the social credit of the household. On the other hand a person can lose credit by not conforming to the expected standards. Thus much more than a high income is required in order to achieve a consistently high status and conversely a person with a low income can acquire a relatively high status rank by conforming to the relevant standards and displaying the essential attributes.

The ability to subtract social credit implies the existence of an opportunity and a desire to act at the expense of another. This is apparent with reference to levelling with, in the words of Bailey (1971) 'people competing to remain equal'. This appears to take the form of seizing the opportunity to subtract credit and thereby to bring 'superiors' down to a common level. Much of this behaviour involves resorting to moral criteria, often within a religious context and justification. Thus qualities such as honesty, generosity, hard work and general altruism are often referred to within a religious connotation. The converse of such qualities, i.e. dishonesty, selfishness, hypocrisy and meanness are subject to criticism and the detraction of social credit from the individual who displays them. In a sense it is often reduced to a tendency to play off material and 'moral' attributes of prestige or esteem against one another. Thus in order for a person who ranks high on the economic scale to attain the high overall status of which he is capable he must also demonstrate the moral and other qualities which will allow him to amass the necessary social credit while also taking care to insure that his behaviour does not offer anyone the opportunity to detract credit through criticism.

Some of these qualities not only relate to the accumulation of status credit but also to the dimensions which generate and sustain status. Thus several qualities are necessary in order to be considered for a leadership position. The first of these is the most obvious, an interest and involvement in the affairs of the community and its institutions. This involvement includes a regular active participation and contribution. Among the families which demonstrate status inconsistency on the various ranking scales are some who are regarded as isolates having little involvement in the local community (1). This is not to imply that the members of these families do not interact with other community members nor are they regarded as deviant but rather that they do not attend and support community functions and institutions neither are they labelled as deviants. Some of these families were relative newcomers to the community (2) who had retained ties with their previous community of residence, to the extent of farming land in these areas.(3) Whether these families felt they derived their prestige from outside the community of study

or were reluctant to invest in the acquisition of social credit is
difficult to ascertain. What is clear is that these families not
only fail to appear in the list of leadership positions but also
appear as isolates on both the sociometric and associational data.

Other qualities which are required of a candidate for a leadership position include the ability to speak publicly, to make
rational decisions that will not antagonize any community members
and humility. This last quality is apparent in the way in which
leaders are nominated. An individual must not appear to desire a
leadership position but on the contrary he must put on the appear-
ance of rejecting any suggestion that he is suited for the position
for fear of implying that he is boasting the qualities associated
with leadership. This is also in accordance with the image of a
humble, deserving person which is the converse of an aggressive
'pushy' person who strives for position for reasons of self-
aggrandizement rather than community service. Furthermore it has
the advantage of appearing as if the nomination is the unanimous
agreement of the community which persuades the individual to play
his part on behalf of the community, i.e. the position is defined
in altruistic rather than egotistical terms.

Beyond these general attributes different leadership positions
carry different demands. A deacon must demonstrate a conformity
with the moral basis of community membership, the ability to speak
publicly, an involvement in religious activities. A youth leader
should have the ability to work with young people, especially with
reference to music, recitation, drama, sport, and farming activities
which form the basis of most of the young people's activities.
Similarly the Sunday School teacher must have a thorough knowledge
of the scriptures, an ability to lead, stimulate and direct discussion and an ability to argue logically the principles of religious
belief. In turn some leadership roles are extremely time consuming
and the willingness to invest time is an added deterrent to some who
do have the necessary personal qualities for such roles. One is
somewhat surprised at the ability of such a small community to generate so many leaders with such a wide range of qualifications, and
it is the absence of these qualifications which accounts for the
cases of incongruence between the economic and leadership ranking
scales.

The other consequence of the multi-dimensional nature of status
allocation is that an individual's status and the nature of the
interaction which it invokes can vary according to the context of
the interaction. Thus a person high on the income ranking scale
and who is acknowledged as a good farmer will have his status confirmed in a situation which pertains to these qualities. However
if the same person is acknowledged as a person who makes little
contribution to the community and does not have the qualities of a
leader he may well be treated as an inferior by someone of lower
economic rank within the context of a relevant situation. That is,
status does not flow automatically from one situation to another but
rather relates to the dynamics of social situation.

CONCLUSION

In the preceding discussion I have chosen to proceed from the
expectation that non-economic dimensions of inequality should conform to the economic dimension. Some workers (Marshall, 1963:216)
have claimed that a system of social status will exist given a total
knowledge of the individual and the existence of a community. This
would then give a consensus of rank in which the individual is
treated in accordance with his attributes regardless of social rank.
I argue that this is not the case in a small community where the
range of incomes is relatively small and where the occupational
spectrum involves very few interrelationships based upon the
relations of production, status inconsistency is to be understood
in terms of social constraints that are placed upon the actors in
terms of personal attributes and behaviour. While there is a general
tendency towards congruence between the income, leadership and status
rankings it is possible to explain deviations from such consistency
by referring to a knowledge of the taxonomy of inequality employed
within the community. It is suggested that a number of variables,
other than income but including kinship, proximity and reciprocity
networks contribute to an understanding of associational features.
The absence of such bases of involvement together with the absence
of certain crucial personal qualities and attributes are held to
account for the cases of status inconsistency within the community
in question. So strong is this tendency in certain cases that it
would appear that esteem receives a greater salience than does
prestige. This is the case where the individual ranks higher on
the leadership or status rank than he or she does on the economic
rank.
    In conclusion I would claim that such a situation pertains in a
small community of face-to-face interaction where the division of
labour is narrow and where people are not integrated on the basis
of relations of production. Within the area of study this is a
measure of the change in the economic structure and organization
which has taken place during the past few decades. The net result
is that the individual is disarticulated from other community members
in production terms with the result that individual evaluations of
overall status involve a greater emphasis on esteem than had
previously been the case.

NOTES

1 This would apply to numbers 20, 31, 34 and to a lesser extent
   number 2 on the economic ranking scale of the farmers and to
   number 3 on the economic ranking scale of the non-farm households.
2 Length of residence is an important ingredient of leadership.
   Newcomers do not have the kinship network which can be mobilized
   at election time and the qualities of esteem require several years
   of close scrutiny before they are accepted. This observation is
   relevant to numbers 14 and 16 on the farm economic scale.
3 This applies to numbers 10 and 12 on the farm economic scale.

REFERENCES

BAILEY, F.G. (1971), 'Gifts and Poison: The Politics of Reputation', Oxford, Basil Blackwell.
BENNETT, John W. (1969), 'Northern Plainsmen: Adaptive Strategy and Agrarian Life', Chicago, Aldine.
CENSUS RETURNS (1861), 'Population Tables I: Numbers of Inhabitants', London, 1862, II, Welsh Division.
DAVIS, K. (1942), Conceptual analysis of stratification, 'American Sociological Review', vol.7, pp.309-21.
GERTH, HANS and MILLS, C.W. (eds) (1946), 'From Max Weber: Essays in Sociology', Oxford University Press.
HARTMAN, M. (1974), On the definition of status inconsistency, 'American Journal of Sociology', vol.80, pp.706-21.
JENKINS, D. (1969), 'The Agricultural Community in South West Wales at the Turn of the Twentieth Century', Cardiff, University of Wales Press.
LANDECKER, W. (1960), Class crystallization and its urban pattern, 'Social Research', vol.27, pp.308-20.
MARSHALL, T.H. (1963), 'Sociology at the Crossroads', London, Heinemann.
PARKIN, F. (1973), 'Class, Inequality and Political Order', St Albans, Paladin.
PARSONS, T. (1953), A revised analytical approach to the theory of social stratification, in 'Class, Status and Power', edited by R. Bendix and S.M. Lipset, Chicago, Free Press.
RUNCIMAN, W.G. (1966), 'Relative Deprivation and Social Justice', London, Routledge & Kegan Paul.
ZELDICH, M. and ANDERSON, B. (1966), On the balance of a set of ranks, in 'Sociological Theories in Progress', edited by J. Berger, M. Zeldich and B. Anderson, Boston, Houghton Mifflin, pp.244-68.

Chapter 19

SOCIAL PROCESS AND ETHNIC IDENTITY: PERSONAL REFLECTIONS ON THE GREGYNOG PAPERS

Anthony Coxon

I am a marginal Englishman, having some relatives who are Scottish-Gaelic speakers and others - through my wife - who are Welsh speakers. I have made a number of attempts to master both languages, with indifferent success, and I have seen at first hand the political revitalization of Scottish and Welsh identity. But being at the margins gives a certain detachment which fosters the sociological approach and encourages me to put these movements against their social and cultural background. It was, therefore, with a good deal of personal interest that I took part in the 1976 Gregynog Conference, and it will provide a framework for my later comments if I begin by using my experience to interpret what I see of Welsh identity and ethnicity.

The link between identity and language is quite different in Scotland from in Wales. Scotland has never been truly unilingual, and since the 1745 Rebellion, topography and politics have ensured that Gaelic identity - A'Ghaidhealtachd - is contained to the north and west. Although the majority of speakers are probably located in Glasgow, Gaelic has never been an unselfconscious medium of communication in the cities. Today, the 'statistics of decline' of Gaelic are only too evident, and no areas remain where it is the only first language. The economic irruption of oil in the centre of mainland Gaelic-speaking Kishorn is only hastening the progress of the decline, and even the National Mod manifestly fails to keep Gaelic as the only language of the field. Despite the weakness of Gaelic, cultural, political and national 'Scottishness' have never been stronger, and throughout Scotland there is an almost tangible, jaunty air of self-confidence about devolution and independence, which contrasts markedly with Wales. For me this is symbolized by a ludicrous comparison: in Skye, the heartland of Gaelic, there is still political controversy about whether signposts should also be in Gaelic, whereas in Cardiff - hardly the heartland of Welsh - it is taken for granted that signposts should be bilingual.

To the incomer, Wales betrays a far greater dependence on England and upon English institutions even though its language is more widespread, and in a healthier state; this is the paradox. On virtually every count, Welsh speaking is stronger, and more entrenched than Gaelic speaking; indeed, in Scotland, there is no

equivalent for 'Cymro Cymraeg', let alone for 'Nid Cymro heb Gymraeg'.
Yet throughout the papers presented at the Conference it is a
constant theme that Welsh speaking is in crisis, that in traditional
Welsh-speaking areas there is a shift towards the ritual use of Welsh
and capitulation to English (Wenger, ch.9), that Welsh speaking is in
'decline, retreat and fragmentation' (Carter and Williams, ch.11),
and that there is increasing polarization between Welsh-speaking and
English-only-speaking Welshmen (Giles and Taylor, ch.10). To this
extent, there would seem to be strong similarities between the future
of Welsh and the present of Gaelic. But in contrast, there is a documented resurgence of Welsh learning especially in the south and
among those with strong Welsh identification, and there is a guaran-
teed role for the language in present and devolved Government.
Moreover, as Williams (Williams, Roberts and Isaac, ch.13) points
out, although the prestigious language domains are still dominated
by English in the south, the requirement of a Welsh-language qualification is leading upwardly mobile working-class parents in the
Valleys - and, it should be said, middle-class English speakers -
to ensure that their children possess enough of the Welsh language
to further their career. When it is in one's own self-interest to
learn Welsh, the tide may have turned. In these respects, Wales
resembles Eire, or even Canada. But the obvious differences still
need stating.

    In Eire, there are virtually no Erse-speakers left and the
'Gaeltacht' is confined to the north and west, rural, depopulated
areas, whilst in Canada, there is a very flourishing French-only
speaking community which includes a sizeable urban base. To this
extent at least, the significant parameters of linguistic identity
and survival are not simply numerical size or preponderance of non-
English speaking, but rather the area of life and culture from
which English is naturally excluded, together with the ability to
survive in and adapt to an urban environment. This, it seems to me,
is the critical difference between Celtic bilingualism and the
bilingualism of Canada (and, incidentally, of Creole and of Pidgin!).

    A rather pervasive and important theme in many papers is the
religious factor, and no one familiar with the scene would under-
estimate its historical importance. It is often said that the
religious independence of the Welsh (and indeed of the Highlander)
had no more natural way of asserting itself over and against
Anglican orthodoxy than in the use of Welsh. Yet, historically, this
is not entirely true, for the Church of England in Wales (as it then
was) also used Welsh in Welsh-speaking areas and the nineteenth-
century evangelicals in Wales were far more concerned to facilitate
communication of the Gospel than to impair it; Welsh speaking was
largely incidental. The relationship was probably a good deal more
subtle, and intertwined with class issues, as the 'buchedd' controversy (Williams, ch.18) indicates. Perhaps the most important point
was that, in the Highlands as in Wales, there emerged indigenous
Nonconformist religious organizations which had no equivalent in
England, by a process of fission from the (Presbyterian) established
Church in Scotland and by the growth of the Independents and the
Calvinistic Methodists in Wales. During this period of growth and
stabilization, doctrinal difference alone was enough to preclude
interaction with other denominations, but one effect of ecumenism

has been the increasing interaction with predominantly English-speaking chapels in Eisteddfodau and other meetings. Wenger rightly comments here that the ethnic markers are shifting away from language.

But the most telling information about the relation between religiosity and language identity is in Carter and Williams' paper, when they discuss the relation between 'dry' voting, Y Fro Gymraeg, and traditional Welshness. Although the authors do not draw the parallel, the relationships are virtually identical to the situation obtaining in the Western Isles of Scotland - but with one significant difference. North Wales, unlike the Hebrides, has no significant religiously contrasting community. But the Western Isles are divided, through the Uists, into the Calvinist north and the Roman Catholic south. Now whilst alcohol consumption, and the social pathology of drinking are both evident throughout the Hebrides, attitudes on Sunday opening differ almost exactly on this north/south religious divide. Yet the form and content of Gaelic identity is in no way affected. The Catholic islanders identify themselves, and are identified, in precisely the same way as their Protestant neighbours. This is hardly a clinching argument, but it shows the 'accidental' nature in general of the undoubted relation between puritanism and attitudes towards drinking to the relation between language and ethnic identity. That said, the *historical* link between religious and ethnic identity in Wales has obviously been strong to such an extent that decline in religious belonging (in general) leads to a decline in traditional Welsh identity. The important question then becomes: Is there a new form of Welsh-speaking Welsh identity emerging, which is *not* identified with religious puritanism? Several contributors think so, though on differing grounds. I am not entirely convinced. Or, rather, I do not share the tacit assumption that its emergence will be smooth and uncontested. It seems to me that this was brought out in the final session which discussed ethnic conflict, and the organized resistance and opposition to the primacy of Welsh. At present, the 'English backlash' seems to be largely confined to Gwent. But when Welsh speaking does become a widespread condition of employment in the public sector, the language moves from being a cultural symbol, tolerated and encouraged as an indication of deference and accommodation to English speaking culture, and becomes a threat to a powerful section of the populace. The nether millstones of Welsh and English primacy are then likely to grind the Anglo-Welsh grist.

The advantages of the Gregynog conference is that two diverse research traditions - broadly ethnographic and structural - were represented and each presented a fairly coherent account, within their own perspective. The misfortune was that they did not encounter each other until the final confused, but exhilarating, session when the discussion was widened to a comparative perspective and issues of power and interaction were raised. (This last point is worth stressing; we now know a good deal about the distribution of attitudes towards Welsh speaking, but almost nothing in a systematic way about the precise social relationships and interactions in which Welsh persists.) Future work will doubtless take up on these issues. In the mean time, I can think of no better tutor in the task than John Gumperz's (1972:455) comment on Fredrik Barth's transactional account

of the surprisingly relevant ethnic processes on the Pathan-Baluch
boundary in Pakistan (the reference to 'he' in the quotation is to
Barth):

> he demonstrates that ethnic boundaries frequently persist in
> spite of the regular movement of personnel across them and in
> spite of regular and institutionalized intergroup communication,
> just as language boundaries are often maintained in regions of
> almost total bilingualism. There must therefore be, he argues,
> social processes of exclusion and incorporation which lead to
> the maintenance of such boundaries. Taking an interactional
> point of view of social structure similar to that developed by
> Goffman, he views ethnic categories as categories of ascription
> by which actors identify themselves by expressing particular
> cultural values and speaking particular languages. The social
> necessity (or advantage) of maintaining such identifications is
> conditioned by a combination of underlying factors (cultural
> interactional norms, intrasocietal power relationships, ecology,
> or by factors of demography, etc.) which must be studied
> empirically for each case.

REFERENCE

GUMPERZ, J.J. and HYMES, D. (eds) (1972), 'Directions in Sociolinguistics: the ethnography of communication', New York: Holt, Rinehart & Winston, p.455.

NAME INDEX

Angle, J., 193
Arnold, M., 114

Bailey, F., 264
Barth, F., 4, 121, 270
Bell, C., 50
Bell, D., 8, 106, 107
Berry, B.J.L. and P.H. Rees, 26
Betts, C., 229
Blauner, R., 111n
Bollom, C., 7
Booth, C., 16
Bourhis, R.Y., N. Gadfield and H.
    Giles, 141; and H. Giles, 133,
    134; H. Giles and W. Lambert,
    134; H. Giles and H. Tajfel,
    134
Bowen, E.G. and H. Carter, 172,
    173, 176, 183, 190

Carter, H. and S.W. Williams, 11,
    270
Christian, J., 137
Clayton, P., 11
Corrado, R.R., 133
Coupland, R., 113

Dahrendorf, R., 6
Davidson, R.N., 30
Davies, D.J., 113
Davis, K., 254
Day, G. and M. Fitton, 12, 51
Durkheim, E., 115

Edelman, M., 209, 215
Edwards, J., 23
Eiser, R., 141
Ellis, P.B., 113
Emmett, I., 2, 10, 51
Evans, G., 98, 113

Fanon, F., 111
Fishman, J., 209
Fletcher, C., 6
Forde, D., 2
Frankenberg, R., 2

Gadfield, N., 137
Giles, H. and R.Y. Bourhis, 228;
    and D. Taylor, 9, 10
Goffman, E., 104, 271
Gonzales-Casanova, P., 112
Gorer, G., 106
Grant, G., 8
Greenfield, S., 209, 215
Gumperz, J., 270

Harrison, G., 10
Harvey, D., 17
Hechter, M., 5, 7, 112

Iwan, D., 99

Jenkins, D., 2, 51
Jones, B., 109
Jones, R. and A. Piette, 220

272

GENERAL INDEX